GARDEN PLOTS

For Dondi

Who delves in my garden
And dwells in my heart.

Garden Plots
The Politics and Poetics of Gardens

SHELLEY SAGUARO
University of Gloucestershire, UK

ASHGATE

Published by
Ashgate Publishing Limited
Gower House
Croft Road
Aldershot
Hampshire GU11 3HR
England

Ashgate Publishing Company
Suite 420
101 Cherry Street
Burlington, VT 05401-4405
USA

Ashgate website: http://www.ashgate.com

British Library Cataloguing in Publication Data
Saguaro, Shelley
  Garden plots: the politics and poetics of gardens
  1.Gardens in literature 2.English fiction–20th century–
  History and criticism 3.Plants in literature 4.Flowers in
  literature
  I.Title
  823.9'109364

Library of Congress Cataloging-in-Publication Data
Saguaro, Shelley.
  Garden plots: the politics and poetics of gardens / Shelley Saguaro.
     p. cm.
  Includes bibliographical references and index.
  ISBN 0-7546-3753-0 (alk. paper)
  1. English fiction–20th century–History and criticism. 2. Gardens in literature. 3. American fiction–20th century–History and criticism. 4. Nature in literature. I. Title.

  PR888.G33S24 2006
  823'.9109364–dc22

2006002004

ISBN-13: 978-0-7546-3753-0
ISBN-10: 0-7546-3753-0

Printed and bound in Great Britain by TJ International Ltd, Padstow, Cornwall.

Contents

Acknowledgements   *vii*

Introduction: The Politics and Poetics of Gardens   *ix*

1. Botanical Modernisms   1
   Virginia Woolf: Vision ('Kew Gardens' (1919))   6
   Katherine Mansfield: Memory ('Prelude' (1922))   21
   Elizabeth Bowen: History ('Summer Night' (1941))   35
   Eudora Welty: Myth ('A Curtain of Green' (1941))   44

2. Natural History and Postmodern Grafting   61
   John Updike: Entropy (*The Witches of Eastwick* (1984))   69
   A. S. Byatt: Evolution (*Angels and Insects* (1992))   85
   Jeanette Winterson: Gravity (*Sexing the Cherry* (1989))   98
   Carol Shields: Space (*Larry's Party* (1997))   112

3. Postcolonial Landscapes   127
   J. M. Coetzee: Belonging/Marginalisation (*Life and Times
   of Michael K* (1983))   138
   Toni Morrison: Reconciliation/War (*Paradise* (1998))   156
   V. S. Naipaul: Migration/Rootlessness (*The Enigma of Arrival* (1986))   174
   Leslie Marmon Silko: Hybridity/Homogeneity (*The Gardens in the
   Dunes* (1999))   186

4. How Does Your Cyber Garden Grow?   205
   John Wyndham: *The Day of the Triffids* (1954)
   Philip K. Dick: *Do Androids Dream of Electric Sheep?* (1968)
   Donna Haraway: 'A Cyborg Manifesto' (1985)
   Don DeLillo: *White Noise* (1984)
   William Gibson: *Virtual Light* (1993)

5. Conclusion: Coevolutionary Histories – the Poetics of a Paradox   223
   Michael Pollan: *The Botany of Desire: A Plant's-Eye View of the
   World* (2001)
   Jamaica Kincaid: *Among Flowers: A Walk in the Himalayas* (2005)

Select Bibliography   231
Index   243

Acknowledgements

My thanks, first and foremost, to those who read and commented on drafts of the manuscript, in particular, Debby Thacker and Peter Widdowson, colleagues at the University of Gloucestershire, and my daughter Jenny Saguaro, who also provided the illustrations that decorate this book. They, along with other friends and colleagues, namely Peter Childs, Simon Dentith, Penny Richards, Peter Easy and Sue Seymour, variously provided conversation, context, references, loans, gifts and inspiration during the long process of completing the project. I am also indebted to Linden Peach, formerly of the University of Gloucestershire, for arranging support for the completion of the project, including the invaluable assistance of Fleur Mortimer. I am grateful to the Paul Delvaux Foundation for permission to use Paul Delvaux's *Evening Service* (1971) as the image on the book's cover. Ann Donahue, Sarah Price and Barbara Pretty at Ashgate Publishing Limited have also been most helpful.

Introduction
The Politics and Poetics of Gardens

Our England is a garden that is full of stately views,
Of borders, beds and shrubberies and lawns and avenues,
With statues on the terraces and peacocks strutting by;
But the Glory of the Garden lies in more than meets the eye.

Rudyard Kipling, 'The Glory of the Garden' [1912], *Kipling's Verse* (1948)

There can be no mistake: gardens matter and their meaningfulness is long established. Gardens, mythical and mundane, are extremely various: Edenic, Arcadian, pastoral, paradise, natural, wild, formal, plantation, vegetable, fruit, flower, botanical, physic, orchard, arboretum, allotment, walled, country, city, park – each of these terms is familiar in relation to gardens; each gives rise to other issues, such as: myth, cultural specificity, historical context, nation, topography, class, race, religion, gender. From gardens of the most utilitarian aspect (food for survival) to those of the most decorative and ostentatious aspect, gardens are subject to, and subjects of, the discourses of history, aesthetics and ideology.

This is a book about gardens in books. To begin to consider this as a topic is to begin at 'the beginning' – at least, as the Judeo-Christian creation story has it with the Book of Genesis:

> Now the LORD God had planted a garden in the east, in Eden; and there he put the man he had formed. And the LORD God made all kinds of trees grow out of the ground – trees that were pleasing to the eye and good for food. In the middle of the garden were the tree of life and the tree of knowledge of good and evil. A river watering the garden flowed from Eden [...] The LORD God took the man and put him in the Garden of Eden to work it and take care of it. And the LORD God commanded the man, 'You are free to eat from any tree in the garden; but you must not eat from the tree of knowledge of good and evil, for when you eat of it, you will surely die.[1]

Gardens are a prevalent literary theme and trope throughout English Literature, a literature which is also informed, of course, by that of Greek and Roman and other Indo-European literatures, which have mythical gardens of their own. There are also many books of fiction, poetry and prose over the centuries which, while not always obviously or even primarily about gardens, use them as a crucial and integral part

---

1   Genesis 2:8-2:17, *Holy Bible: New International Version,* (Grand Rapids, MI: Zondervan Bible Publishers, 1978), pp. 2-3.

of the whole. The garden, then, is a familiar, diachronic and multi-determined trope used variously. On the one hand, gardens can signify a pre-lapsarian and harmonic bliss; on the other, the inevitability of a failure and Fall. These can be a testament to a place which serves as a pleasure-filled retreat from the urban world's harrying strictures of business, commerce and politics, or alternatively, as in postcolonial fiction, for example, a garden, such as a large mono-crop plantation, can serve to show the duress of toil, slave-labour and the disenfranchisement of the poor, where nothing of pastoral pleasure is realised but only inescapable hardship and meagre subsistence. Furthermore, analogies with aspects of gardening, with terms such as 'cultivation', 'nurture', 'growth', 'flowering' and 'fruition', are commonplace and are even familiarly extended to aspects of developments of selfhood. The Romantic poets, for instance, in the early nineteenth century extolled 'organicism' in terms of both the imagination and literary form. Just a few examples to indicate a long-standing literary preoccupation, from the time of Caxton's printing press to the end of the twentieth century might include: scores of passages from Chaucer, Spenser, Jonson and Shakespeare; 'The Garden' and other, 'mower poems' by Andrew Marvell; Milton's *Paradise Lost*; much of Alexander Pope's verse, in particular, 'The Epistle to Burlington' or 'Windsor Forest'; many of Tennyson's best-known poems, such as 'Maud' or 'The Princess' and Browning's 'Garden Fancies'; *Elizabeth and Her German Garden* (1898) by Elizabeth von Arnim; Frances Hodgson Burnett's *The Secret Garden* (1911); Vita Sackville West's *The Garden* (1946) and Roy Campbell's shorter piece of the same name in 1939; or more recently, included here, *Gardens in the Dunes*, by the Native American writer Leslie Marmon Silko, published in 1999.

In the late twentieth and into the twenty-first century, there is a multitude of books about gardens, ranging from comprehensive histories through practical guides to treatises on one species or another. Gardening *per se* is definitely 'in'. As we embark upon life in the twenty-first century, gardens, garden design and gardening can be seen as prevalent and ubiquitous lifestyle matters. The proliferation of garden features on television and radio, in newspapers (especially weekend editions) and specialist magazines, gardens as the focus of books, videos and websites, and the routine congestion in garden centres, all attest to the current popularity of the quest for 'better gardens'. Television, on a wide range of channels, regularly features programmes on practical gardening, garden makeovers, garden design, gardens in history (in Britain, *The Victorian Kitchen Garden*, for example, or more recently, *The Garden Through Time*), gardens at home and gardens abroad. A large number of these programmes are routinely broadcast on Friday night, which suggests that a range of gardeners, young and old, find them a successful rival to other leisure-time activities at the outset of a weekend. Gardening-show presenters are anything but rustic or crusty and many of them acquire – or are garnered from those already endowed with – celebrity status. To appear in one medium is to ensure exposure and promotion in a variety of others – and it is not simply green fingers that are presently being promoted, but something more comprehensively desirable. Having a garden, as an essential, informed (what's trendy, what's not) and eloquent (even if parroted) extension of one's home, is largely uncontested. Public spaces, too – (and perhaps public houses especially) – are compulsorily and competitively festooned. It is not surprising, then, that gardens are also a feature in a wide range of modern texts.

This volume aims to examine the multifarious aspects of the meaning of gardens in twentieth- and early twenty-first-century literary texts. The texts selected for discussion here, however, may or may not be explicitly or obviously *about* gardens or gardening as such. What they do have in common is that gardens, of one kind or another, *are* deployed within the texts for very specific and significant reasons; they are not simply incidental or facilely clichéd. The treatment of gardens, gardening and plants in many of the texts chosen has a specific and deliberate purpose within that text. In others, the incorporation of gardens is reflective, wittingly or unwittingly, of other ideological and aesthetic premises, which thus inform – and indeed, *form* – the text itself. Thus, to look at Virginia Woolf's short story, 'Kew Gardens', is to look at her deliberate choice of the Royal Botanic Gardens at Kew as a setting for a tale written between the two World Wars and in a style we now designate as 'modernist'. It is for the reader to ask simultaneously: why Kew? – and to what effect? And further: why this textual style and form, at this time, on this topic? In the course of such questioning, reference will necessarily be made to gardening history, to the contemporary historical context of the written work, aesthetic and formal premises (in garden design, in painting, in literature) and, in this instance, to Woolf's own reflections on the subject of writing and representation in 'modern fiction'. In another regard, J. M Coetzee's *Life and Times of Michael K* demands a similar mode of enquiry but with entirely different frames of reference, not least because the historical and topographical loci are very specific: set in South Africa (however fictionalised or dis-located in this text) and written from there in the early 1980s, Coetzee's novel incorporates a garden to very different effect, and in a textual mode significantly distinct, from Woolf's modernism. Coetzee's politics and poetics – almost certainly carrying the tag, 'postcolonial', and sometimes, 'postmodern' – will be explored here alongside his own polemical views on South Africa, its landscape, gardening (or farming) and colonial ideology.

Woolf and Coetzee are just two of the fifteen or so main authors that are discussed here. All of the texts included have been published in English, although the countries or regions of origin of the authors are far-flung and various: New Zealand, Canada, Ireland, America (the South, New England, Arizona), South Africa, the Caribbean. The selected texts are collected under headings which are indicative of a specific literary historical and/or literary critical category (Modernism, Postmodernism, Postcolonial, Cyberpunk). The book does not necessarily consider texts in a chronological fashion although there is a general chronological move from Modernism to Cyberpunk, or from Modernism to Postmodernism. Three of the chapters, 'Botanical Modernism', 'Natural History and Postmodern Grafting' and 'Postcolonial Landscapes', are divided into four sections with a specific text – and author – discussed in each. The penultimate chapter, 'How Does Your Cyber-Garden Grow?', takes a slightly different approach. Very topical issues, such as genetic modification and bio-technology, are discussed within an undivided chapter and with attention throughout to several science-fiction and cyber-fiction texts as well as to theoretical and polemical discussions (Donna Haraway on 'the cyborg', for instance). The aim here is not to undertake a survey of developments in literature – or in horticulture – but rather to examine the ways in which gardens, like texts, extend both the critique and the perpetuation of particular ideological premises and practices, in ways that are not always obvious.

Finally, the last chapter concludes the volume by introducing a genre that is less familiar: 'coevolutionary histories'. Here, the garden trope is projected into the twenty-first century and a new emphasis is identified. The keywords here are: paradox, co-dependence and connection. Confident anthropocentrism is further displaced, with the drive to knowledge modified by the aim of understanding. The story of Eden, for instance, with Adam and Eve as the central protagonists is familiar. The tale from the serpent's perspective is imaginable. Here, however, the apple is seen to have had a purposeful role and a point of view; the apple had an agenda too.

An anecdote to close here, paying a debt of gratitude on my part: in October, 1996, the annual Cheltenham International Festival of Literature had gardens as one of its themes and it duly invited the writer Jamaica Kincaid to be a speaker. Born in Antigua, Kincaid had already written several works of fiction and a long essay set in her Caribbean homeland. She had been living in the United States for some time and was, at that point, gardening correspondent for *The New Yorker*. The venue for Kincaid's talk was the Georgian neo-classical Cheltenham Town Hall; the time was a weekday morning. The audience was, almost certainly, entirely white, overwhelmingly middle-class, and largely female, while the few men present were probably retired. The expectations of this audience can only be surmised, other than to say that Jamaica Kincaid herself – and her point of view – was *not* what was expected. Later, Kincaid's views will be more thoroughly addressed, but in brief, she told the audience that day what it was like to be forced to learn as *correct*, the coloniser's names for plants one had grown up with – and without ever being asked what they were called commonly and indigenously. She explained what it was like to visit botanic gardens and to find collected there – with Latin and English, but never native nomenclature – plants that were often no longer available in their place of origin. It was not, she explained, that she did not appreciate or enjoy botanic collections, but rather, that there was indeed more to these 'than meets the eye'. Whilst botanic gardens may now be instrumental in preserving species from extinction (where once the quest for public and private collections was instrumental in jeopardising species, some to the point of extinction), and, while they introduce a populace to a range and variety of plant exotica brought side by side, her point was this: native and resident Caribbean islanders had been ignored and abused in a colonial drive to name and claim all that was indigenous, including flora and fauna. She went on to say that gardening, like a botanical collection, has a history – and it is not always the history that is told or remembered. That these are some of the political issues attendant on contemporary gardening came as a shock to the audience that day. Kincaid, while not aggressive, was passionate. The response she received, from one man in the audience in particular, was certainly aggressive and counter-accusatory; he was affronted not least because this line was so unexpected. He thought it nonsense that such a creative and benign recreational activity as gardening should have anything to do with guilt – especially when this pertained to events that happened 'a long time ago'. Gardening, he felt, should not be mixed up with politics.

Following Kincaid, the premise of this book is that gardens and gardening are political. Furthermore, there is ample evidence that other twentieth- and early-twenty-first-century writers think so too, and that the plots pertaining to gardens are literal, figural and, in their manifestations, of course, material. In the representation of gardens there is a complex interrelation of *all* these issues, the very complexity of which is appositely indicated in the several dictionary definitions of the word *plot*:

- (noun) a secret plan to achieve some purpose, esp. one that is illegal or underhand; (and as a verb, to plot – to plan, map, or conspire);
- (noun) the story or plan of a play, novel, etc.; (and as a verb, to construct the plot of a literary work, etc.);
- a small piece of land: as in a vegetable plot.

Certainly, imperialistic 'plots' (including the plunder and export of exotic plant species and/or the transplantation of Englishness – in garden-style as in much else – to places of conquest) and their postcolonial, multicultural aftermath have had an impact, literally, on garden plots – and on literary plots. It is by virtue of all these aspects that the present book is entitled: *Garden Plots: The Politics and Poetics of Gardens*.

Chapter 1

Botanical Modernisms

Whereas the first decorative and useful gardens had been made as redoubts against threatening nature, gardeners in the twentieth century struggle to preserve some element of natural life in their gardens to insulate themselves from increasingly hostile man-made environments.

Penelope Hobhouse, *Plants in Garden History* (1997)

How to prevent suburbia spreading over Eden (too late! it's already done) how to prevent Eden running to a great wild wilderness –

D. H. Lawrence, *Stories, Essays and Poems* (1939)

Clearly the contrast of country and city is one of the major forms in which we become conscious of a central part of our experience and of the crises of our society. But when this is so the temptation is to reduce the historical variety of the forms of interpretation to what are loosely called symbols or archetypes; to abstract even those most evidently social forms and to give them a primarily psychological or metaphysical status [...] we have to be able to explain, in related terms, both the persistence and historicity of concepts.

Raymond Williams, *The Country and the City* (1985)

The four writers included here: Virginia Woolf, Katherine Mansfield, Elizabeth Bowen and Eudora Welty, have been chosen, first and foremost, for their texts in which gardens figure prominently. Each of the writers is well known and each short story, though written in the first half of the twentieth century and not the best-known text by each of the authors, is still in print in the first years of the twenty-first. Virginia Woolf and Katherine Mansfield are today well known as 'Modernists', a term that comes into being retrospectively, to represent an aesthetic that was at its height in the early twentieth century and was the major influence in Britain and North America perhaps until as late as 1950.

At the time of writing, Woolf and Mansfield did not use the tag 'Modernist', but were, instead, developing and discussing 'modern fiction', writing which was, in line with the other arts, aiming at something new, experimental, *avant-garde*. The early twentieth century is generally typified as an era of fracture, in politics and poetics, with a breaking away from established conventions and consolidated positions. Avowedly anti-monumental, modernists were interested, rather, in pluralities of perspective and in the self-reflexive and constructed artifact; this was art aware of itself as artifice. At the same time, there was an awareness that unconscious processes would necessarily inflect any work of art, and further, that unconscious processes were themselves an aspect for exploration and representation. Modernism was 'anti-realist', in the sense of arguing, instead, for a more thorough-going representation of reality which would move beyond the surface, the material and the consolatory platitudes of positivism to an interrogation which included theories of scepticism, relativism, psychology and psychoanalysis, existentialism and chaos.

The main focus of the present chapter will be: what are gardens doing in Modernist fiction? How are they represented, and what do they mean in the light of the political, philosophical and practical revisions outlined above? While this chapter cannot aim to provide a thorough-going introduction to Modernism *per se*, the debates and experiments which constitute Modernism will be evident; the stories discussed will themselves reveal many of these facets.

Alongside Woolf and Mansfield are placed Elizabeth Bowen and Eudora Welty. Although the writing of Bowen and Welty is not often viewed as representing 'high Modernism', there is no doubt that they are deeply influenced by their Modernist precursors, and, in particular, by Woolf and Mansfield. Bowen, it is claimed, 'shares much of Virginia Woolf's perception and sensibility. She is what happened after Bloomsbury; she is the link which connects Virginia Woolf with Iris Murdoch and Muriel Spark'.[1] Welty was also, in her own estimation, profoundly influenced by Woolf: 'She was the one who opened the door'.[2] Moreover, Woolf and Mansfield were well acquainted, as were Bowen and Woolf, and Bowen and Welty also became friends, meeting, corresponding and reviewing each other's work. Welty also reviewed Woolf's work, and Bowen, variously, Woolf's, Mansfield's and Welty's. More than I was aware when I first selected their stories, these women are writing in the light of, and, often, to, one another.

Short stories written by women about gardens: this seems to be an over-determined 'female tradition' with a conventional domestic venue. Little narratives by little women on little pastimes – something floral might betoken them all. However, it is not my aim to suggest that these stories, as a literary form, constitute a gendered space or that they are *about* a gendered space, although there have been studies

---

1   Victoria Glendinning, *Elizabeth Bowen: Portrait of a Writer* (London: Weidenfeld & Nicolson, 1977), p. 1.

2   Eudora Welty, *Conversations with Eudora Welty*, ed. Peggy Whitman Prenshaw (Jackson: University Press of Mississippi, 1984), p. 75.

along these lines.[3] Rather, these stories are presented for the ways in which gardens and landscapes are used to explore complex issues of power, class, racism and war. The writers chosen here are all prodigious short story writers, but this is not their only form. Woolf, Bowen and Welty also wrote novels; Mansfield wrote poetry and they all published non-fiction. The short story form is, however, particularly suited to the Modernists and their experiments which aim to depose, as Woolf put it, prior 'tyrannies' and to defamiliarise 'the proper stuff' of art. Thus, the Modernist short story begins 'in the middle' of things and is not conclusive: it is a sketch, a slice, a glimpse, which is both disorienting (as fiction) and familiar (this is what life is really like). Joyce, Lawrence, Hemingway, and Faulkner could also have been candidates here had these aspects been the only considerations. However, gardens are, perhaps, to be found most readily in the fiction of women at this time (although Lawrence, especially, was not averse to describing a garden), but the reader is likely to be surprised at what is suggested by the gardens that follow. These women writers have chosen to incorporate their garden settings, not merely as incidental nor as a short-hand for conventional tropes about Eden or Arcadia, nor, certainly, as archetypally womb-like, romanticised feminine spheres. It is the conventional, precisely, that they aim to disrupt. (It is interesting to note, by the by, that none of these four women writers had children or led so-called conventional family lives.) Rather, the venues in the stories are significant in ways that problematise any notion that a garden is simply a garden – or that it is conveniently and familiarly symbolic. Instead, we have: a metropolitan Royal Botanical Garden and public park; a garden in New Zealand, a colony of the British Empire, now, the Commonwealth; a suburban garden in Ireland, adjacent to an Anglo-Irish demesne and its ruined castle; and a white woman and young black man in a suburban garden in Mississippi, the American South. All the stories are written and take place some time between the beginning of the First and the Second World Wars.

Gardens themselves, in early twentieth-century Britain and America at least, are rather like short fiction. The 'small plot' of the short story form could be seen as correlating with the small plot of urban and suburban gardens, of which there was such an increase in the early twentieth century. If the 'rise of the novel', in Ian Watt's well-known thesis, was engendered by the rise of economic individualism in the eighteenth and nineteenth centuries, the rise of the short story can be seen to have had a kindred genesis.[4] This 'first-stage' in the democratisation of literary forms, the novel, finds its second-stage successor in the short story. The nineteenth-century novel was still about the relation of individuals within a social order, however newly fluctuating, and however much capitalism was ultimately to revise a sense of individual autonomy and mobility. With its representation of complex communities, its narrative contiguity, its linear development in time and in tale, its resolution in

---

3   As, for example, in Louise Westling's work: in particular, *Sacred Groves and Ravaged Gardens: The Fiction of Eudora Welty, Carson McCullers and Flannery O'Connor* (1985) and *The Green Breast of the New World: Landscape, Gender and American Fiction* (1996).

4   Ian Watt, *The Rise of the Novel* (London: Hogarth Press, 1987 [1957]).

various combinations of births, death and marriages, and its general positivism, the novel continued to reflect the simultaneous integration and separation of class and power in rural communities, villages and, increasingly, urban centres.

It was the increase in suburban living that took economic individualism to another level: the economic capacity to be without individuality – to belong *en masse* by virtue of the individual economic freedom to be the same as ('keeping up with') others. One might say that, superficially, the early twentieth century, with its mobile, suburban and expanding middle class, is the era of 'economic undifferentiation' and intellectual and cultural homogenisation. For example, F. M. L. Thompson, in *The Rise of Suburbia*, notes its familiar conflating aspects:

> The suburbs appeared monotonous, featureless, without character, indistinguishable from one another, infinitely boring to behold, wastelands of housing as settings for dreary, petty, lives without social, cultural, or intellectual interests, settings which fostered a pretentious preoccupation with outward appearance, a fussy attention to the trifling details of genteel living, and absurd attempts to conjure rusticity out of *minute garden plots*. [my emphasis][5]

It was a frequent response of Modernist writers (and artists) to satirise this lemming-like rush to be indistinguishable and to be endlessly and indistinguishably purchasing the latest commodities in order to remain so – one need only think of some of the rants of D. H. Lawrence: 'How I hate the attitude of ordinary people to life. How I loathe ordinariness! How from my soul I abhor nice simple people and their eternal price-list,'[6] or the more measured disdain of E. M. Forster: 'vast armies of the benighted, who follow neither the heart nor the brain, and march to their destiny by catchwords'.[7] The short story form was one of the Modernist methods and modes used against and to resist popular mass culture. It provided a simulation and a parody of the 'small plot' that has become so prevalent, literally and metaphorically, but its sharp focus is also ideal to represent the disruptive, disturbing aspects beneath the composed (in both senses) facade. It is the effective mode for skirmishes, for 'digging deeper' to find more than the 'trifling details of genteel living' or less than the 'pretentious preoccupation with outward appearance' will admit, and exposing, with ironic brevity, a comprehensive misguidedness. As can be seen from each of the stories in this chapter, beneath the veneer of a carefully constructed public space, private dwelling or not-so-individual persona, there are some disrupting complexities. A reader should not be misled by the veneer of the story.

---

5   F. M. L. Thompson, *The Rise of Suburbia* [1982] cited in Gail Cunningham 'The Riddle of Suburbia: Suburban Fictions at the Victorian *Fin de Siècle*', in *Expanding Suburbia: Reviewing Suburban Narratives*, ed. Roger Webster (New York & Oxford: Berghahn Books, 2000), p. 52.

6   D. H. Lawrence, Letter to Aldous Huxley, *Stories, Essays and Poems* (London: Dent & Sons, 1939), p. 411.

7   E. M. Forster, *A Room with a View* (Harmondsworth: Penguin, 1983 [1908]), p. 194.

Raymond Williams, writing in 1973, discussed the implications of the intransigent distinction between the country and the city in English culture:

> It is significant [...] that the common image of the country is now an image of the past, and the common image of the city an image of the future. That leaves, if we isolate them, an undefined present. The pull of the idea of the country is toward old ways, human ways, natural ways. The pull of the idea of the city is towards progress, modernisation, development. In what is then a tension, a present experienced as tension, we use the contrast of country and city to ratify an unresolved division and conflict of impulses [...][8]

Although Williams does not explicitly suggest it, the early twentieth-century garden is, if not the bridge between the country and the city, then ideally suited to be located in this place of tension. As an integral part of this present ratification of 'unresolved division and conflict of impulses', it does not know where to turn. It is the intersection – or more aptly, the place – of a contained (in its small plot) oscillation of the two conceptual pulls. For instance, where does the modern garden find its own roots – in the country or the city? Is its aspect primarily rural, transplanted to an urban and suburban setting, or is it an urban form with gestures to a rural heritage? Was it not, in its rural location, always incorporating an aspect of the urban, or even of the international and the exotic, in all its various imports and exports? What of the long-standing relation of science and technology to gardens; what of the 'growth and alteration of consciousness' in gardeners – and scientists? How do the gardens of the present, of suburbs, negotiate the legacy of the gardens of the manor house with those, say, of the farm labourer or cottage dweller and which is more rural – or urban – than the other? Which more conservative – and of what? And finally, what of the persistence of those various, collectively pervasive and transcendent myths of gardens, of Eden and Arcadia, of paradise? As Williams cautioned, in the specific terms of the country and the city, interpretation must guard against any easy slippage to 'symbols and archetypes', and against the abstraction of 'even those most evidently social forms [...] to give them a primarily psychological or metaphysical status'. This is a slippage to which a garden, surely, is most likely to fall prey. Rather, Williams exhorts, 'we have to be able to explain, in related terms, both the persistence and the historicity of concepts'.

The garden stories that follow are not merely incidental, nor are they ponderously archetypal, although they are, variously, symbolic. They are concerned with the 'historicity of concepts', and this attention is extended through the form in which they are written – the short story – and the specifically early-twentieth-century garden venues that have been chosen. Both the form and the venues attest to 'historicity' (that is, the contingency and mutability) of the concepts of human selves within (or without) gardens. There is also, inevitably, a culturally determined conceptual persistence in the meaning of the Garden. It is in this context that each section attributed to a writer and her story has a sub-title: respectively, 'Vision', 'Memory',

---

8   Raymond Williams, *The Country and the City* (London: Hogarth Press, 1993) [1973], p. 97.

'History', 'Myth'. These are, much like the Garden, persistent premises whose foundations are about to be rocked.

Virginia Woolf: Vision

'Kew Gardens'[9] is a short story that is barely a story. More evidently an exercise in experimental fiction, now recognisably Modernist, it has a well-established and renowned metropolitan public space as its setting. *Kew Gardens* was published in May, 1919 by Woolf's own Hogarth Press, and then, hastily, by another commercial printer, due to unexpected demand generated by a glowing review. Woolf wrote in her diary on 10 June:

> [...] we came back from Asheham to find the hall table stacked, littered, with orders for *Kew Gardens* [...] All these orders – 150 about, from shops and private people – come from a review in the *Lit. Sup.* presumably by Logan, in which as much praise was allowed me as I like to claim. And 10 days ago I was stoically facing complete failure![10]

The first edition of *Kew Gardens* was illustrated with two woodcuts by Woolf's sister, the post-impressionist artist Vanessa Bell: 'a frontispiece of two women in a leafy setting and an end-piece of a caterpillar and a butterfly'.[11] In a later issue of *Kew Gardens* in 1927, Vanessa was to provide decorations for every page and she continued to work with her sister on many projects, providing illustrations and cover designs in her distinctive Omega Workshops style.[12] Of Vanessa's contributions, Hermione Lee writes:

---

9   'Kew Gardens' is now generally collected as a short story among others, as in *A Haunted House and other stories*, which was first published in January 1944 with a Foreword by Leonard Woolf. References to the short story as it appears in a collection thus use inverted commas, whereas references to the original free-standing Hogarth Press editions are made in italics.

10   Virginia Woolf, *A Writer's Diary* (London: Triad/Granada, 1978 [1953]), p. 24.

11   Ibid., p. 366.

12   The Omega Workshops were started by Roger Fry in London in 1913. In December 1912 he explained in a letter to Bernard Shaw: 'I am intending to start a workshop for decorative and applied art [...] I propose to begin with those crafts in which painters can most easily and readily engage – the design of wall decorations in tempera and mosaic; of printed cotonnades; of silks painted in Gobelin dyes for curtains and dresses; painted screens; painted furniture. I hope to develop gradually the application of our designs to weaving, pottery and furniture construction', Roger Fry cited in Frances Spalding, *Roger Fry; Art and Life*

What she provided was a kind of 'visual underscoring' which gave the books a sympathetic atmosphere – feminine, imaginative, delicate, modern but domestic [...] As Virginia Woolf's writing developed, the decorativeness of the covers became, to an extent, misleading: the heavy dark rose lying over the interlocking circles on the cover of *The Years*, the pretty swagged floral curtain design for *Between the Acts*, make these novels look less powerful and angry than they are.[13]

Vanessa Bell's decorations contributed to the positive 1919 reviewer's sense of the collaborative integrity of *Kew Gardens* as 'a thing of original and therefore strange beauty, with its own "atmosphere", its own vital force'.[14] With or without Vanessa's visual enhancement – and most readers in the early-twenty-first-century will read 'Kew Gardens' without accompanying decorations – the story itself has these attributes including, in its own terms, the quality of a sketch. It has no particular causative or consequential narrative – thus, no plot as such – and is devoid of any conventional beginning, middle and end. Something ad hoc or adventitious is its mode and theme: some perceptions are caught haphazardly or inadvertently by the eye and ear of the otherwise disembodied and unidentified narrator. There is no development in character, motive or moral. Highly descriptive, acute observation seems to be its purpose so that the prevailing effect is, indeed, its evocation of an atmosphere. This narrative is more like eavesdropping or the random sweep of the cine-camera. Crude or domestic cinematography is, perhaps, a more apt analogy than sketch. The 'eye' of the story sweeps over the Gardens, catching, from one perspective and distance, 'the oval-shaped flower-bed' with its 'heart-shaped or tongue-shaped leaves' and its variety of bright flowers, and then from another, to come in close as the light falls, zooming in upon 'the grey back of a pebble, or, the shell of a snail with its brown circular veins, or falling into a raindrop'. The scope moves out again, with the stirring of the breeze, to the 'figures of men and women [who] straggled past the flower bed'. Human subjects are presented (present themselves as they wander, conversing, in the park) in a sequence: a family; two men; two elderly women; two young lovers, a man and a woman, punctuated by the return to the snail, 'between the acts'[15] of human observation. Magnified detail suggests, first, a snail's own view of the gardens:

(London; Granada, 1980), pp. 176-7. Hermione Lee describes the Workshops as: 'Roger Fry's original, unorthodox and hugely influential design centre at 33 Fitzroy Square, committed to inventiveness, spontaneity and playfulness, vibrant Italianate colours and bold new shapes, in every area of domestic decoration – textiles, ceramics, pottery, woodwork, silkscreening'. H. Lee, *Virginia Woolf: A Biography* (London: Chatto & Windus, 1996), pp. 369-70.

    13 Ibid., p. 369.
    14 Ibid.
    15 It seems unavoidable not to call upon Woolf's own terms and phrases, or titles of her other work: 'moments of being', sketch (as in 'the memoir 'A Sketch of the Past') and in *A Writer's Diary*: on *Mrs Dalloway* : 'suppose one can keep the quality of a sketch in a finished and composed work'; *Between the Acts* , Woolf's last novel, was published in 1941 after her death.

Brown cliffs with deep green lakes in the hollow, flat, blade-like trees that waved from root to tip, round boulders of grey stone, vast crumpled surfaces of a thin crackling texture – all these objects lay across the snail's progress between one stalk and another [...][16]

and later, the snail's 'consciousness':

The snail had now considered every possible method of reaching his goal without going round the dead leaf or climbing over it. Let alone the effort needed for climbing a leaf, he was doubtful whether the thin texture which vibrated with such an alarming crackle when touched even by the tip of his horns would bear his weight; and this determined him finally to creep beneath it, for there was a point where the leaf curved high enough from the ground to admit him. He had just inserted his head into the opening and was taking stock of the high brown roof and was getting used to the cool brown light when two other people came past outside on the turf. (pp. 37-8.)

This sharp focus is combined with descriptions elsewhere in the story of evanescence and haziness. The description of the ambling of couples who 'passed the flower-bed and were enveloped in layer after layer of green blue vapour' is highly poetic. This evocation of an atmosphere, the colour, heat, movement and hum in a London public park on a day in July is further combined with the sense of a narrative which suggests or simulates the complexity and simultaneity of perception, consciousness and representation. .

The story concludes with a view that is at once close-up and far-away, with an inclusive, aerial prospect of the Gardens and the city beyond: it pans over the glass roofs of the palm houses, including the drone of an aeroplane, noting shapes and colours, human and floral, on the ground. The concluding description, metaphoric and mesmeric, presents an ambiguity of chaos and order, dissolution and resilience, silence and sound, garden and city and, finally, metal and petal:

Yellow and black, pink and snow white, shapes of these colours, men, women and children were spotted for a second on the horizon, and then, seeing the breadth of yellow that lay upon the grass, they wavered and sought shade beneath the trees, dissolving like drops of water in the yellow and green atmosphere, staining it faintly with red and blue. It seemed as if all gross and heavy bodies had sunk down in the heat motionless and lay huddled upon the ground, but their voices went wavering from them as if they were flames lolling from the thick waxen bodies of candles. Voices. Yes, voices. Wordless voices, breaking the silence suddenly with such depth of contentment, such passion or desire, or, in the voices of children, such freshness of surprise; breaking the silence? But there was no silence; all the time the motor omnibuses were turning their wheels and changing their gear; like a vast nest of Chinese boxes all of wrought steel turning ceaselessly one within another the city murmured; on top of which the voices cried aloud and the petals of myriads of flowers flashed their colours into the air. (p. 40)

---

16   V. Woolf, 'Kew Gardens', *A Haunted House and Other Short Stories* (London: Granada,1982 [1944]), p. 35.

This vivid passage is reminiscent of another well-known passage by Woolf that is frequently cited. The essay 'Modern Novels', published in 1919, the same year as 'Kew Gardens' and later reworked into the better known 'Modern Fiction' of 1925, explains the theory behind the fictive exercise of this period:

> Is it not possible that the accent falls a little differently, that the moment of importance came before or after, that, if one were free and could set down what one chose, there would be no plot, little probability, and a vague general confusion in which the clear-cut features of the tragic, the comic, the passionate and the lyrical were dissolved beyond the possibility of separate recognition? The mind, exposed to the ordinary course of life, receives upon its surface myriad impressions – trivial, fantastic, evanescent, or engraved with the sharpness of steel. From all sides they come, an incessant shower of innumerable atoms, composing in their sum what we might venture to call life itself; and to figure further as the semi-transparent envelope or luminous halo, surrounding us from the beginning of consciousness to the end. Is it not perhaps the chief task of the novelist to convey this incessantly varying spirit with whatever stress or sudden deviation it may display, and as little admixture of the alien and external as possible? [...] the proper stuff of fiction is a little other than custom would have us believe it.[17]

Looked at in the context of this polemical piece written at the same time, the story is obviously a vehicle for the deployment of the techniques and accentual difference that Woolf was advocating at the time, and which she continued to develop throughout her work. The story is, in its form and content, a challenge to the customary in fiction and an attempt at recording the mind's 'myriad impressions'.

That Virginia Woolf should choose Kew Gardens as the setting for one of her experiments in writing fiction is not immediately surprising or particularly significant; a metropolitan park on a summer's day is a fine 'canvas' (as many paintings of the period attest) and as good a place as any to observe and depict 'life itself'. London was familiar to Woolf both as a long-time inhabitant, with related childhood memories, and as a writer. As she extolled in *Mrs Dalloway* ('"I love walking in London", said Mrs Dalloway. "Really, it's better than walking in the country!"'), there was much to celebrate about city life, including its great public parks and gardens. As a 'painterly' writer, all Woolf's texts include vivid and atmospheric descriptions of outdoor settings, whether urban or rural. In texts set outside the metropolis, *To the Lighthouse*, *The Waves* or *Between the Acts*, gardens figure significantly, in her exploration of memory, time and representation. Both Lily Briscoe's painting and Miss La Trobe's play-pageant are accomplished out of doors, and Woolf's own *raison d'être* for *The Waves* (originally to be called *The Moths*) is described in *A Writer's Diary* with a garden-orientation: 'I shall have two different currents – the moths flying along; the flower upright in the centre; a perpetual crumbling and renewal of the plant';[18] 'I hope to have kept the sound of the sea and the birds, dawn and garden subconsciously present, doing their work

---

17 V. Woolf, 'Modern Novels' (1919) in *The Esaays of Virginia Woolf, Volume 3: 1919-1924*, A. McNeillie , ed. (London: Hogarth, 1988), p. 33.

18 V. Woolf, *A Writer's Diary*, p. 142.

under ground.'[19] In her writing, gardens are frequently incorporated, not least, for their resonance in childhood memory: '[...] that garden (which now appeared to her the place where she had spent her whole childhood, and it was always starlit, and always summer [...]'.[20] Or, at times, gardens afford the sense of something secret and malign beneath the beauty: '[...] speaking circumlocuitously of spring and summer and winter frost and flowers in a fair garden he reveals obliquely his illicit passion for the girl [...]. There is something gross behind the flowers.'[21] In her memoir 'A Sketch of the Past', Woolf notes three momentous memories, significant 'moments of being' in a backdrop of the 'cotton wool of non-being'. All three take place in the garden; 'two of these moments ended in a state of despair',[22] the other, in a vision of integrity and a 'state of satisfaction'.[23] This image will be considered in depth at the end of this section in a discussion that finds a further element to Woolf's vision of integrity and 'satisfaction'.

Woolf also depicts the harshness of the natural world; as Hermione Lee states, the early entries in her diary, which she starts in August 1917, include 'brief exact nature notes' made at Asheham:

> These country notes are unflinching, not idyllic – a chicken is found with its head wrung off, a hawk has dropped a dead pigeon, butterflies feed on dung – but they also communicate an almost trance-like state of mind which is part of her recovery, and feeds her writing.[24]

In *Between the Acts*, written in the context of the Second World War, a grotesque event in the garden is a parody of idylls, whether Edenic, pastoral or heroic:

> There crouched in the grass, curled in an olive green ring, was a snake. Dead? No, choked with a toad in its mouth. The snake was unable to swallow; the toad was unable to die. A spasm made the ribs contract; blood oozed. It was birth the wrong way round – a monstrous inversion. So, raising his foot, he stamped on them. The mass crushed and slithered. The white canvas on his tennis shoes was bloodstained and sticky. But it was action. Action relieved him. He strode to the Barn, with blood on his shoes.[25]

---

19   Ibid., p. 166.

20   V. Woolf, 'The Ancestors', *The Complete Shorter Fiction*, ed. Susan Dick (London: Triad Grafton Books, 1991), p. 183.

21   V. Woolf, draft manuscript version of 'Anon', cited in Silver, B. R., ed., '"Anon" and "The Reader": Virginia Woolf's Last Essays', *Twentieth Century Literature*, Vol. 25, No. 3/4 (1979), pp. 394-5, ll. 515-36. Silver notes that in the manuscript, above the line 'reveals obliquely his illicit passion [...]', Woolf had written 'Some horror is concealed [beneath] the flowers.' Silver notes it is 'an idea which is repeated, and I have inserted, at l. 536'.

22   V. Woolf, 'A Sketch of the Past', *Moments of Being: Unpublished Autobiographical Writings*, Jeanne Schulkind, ed. (Triad /Granada, 1982 [begun April, 1939]), pp. 82 -3.

23   Ibid., p. 82.

24   H. Lee, op. cit., p. 379.

25   V. Woolf, *Betweeen the Acts* (St Albans & London: Granada, 1978), p. 75.

Thus, the manner in which Woolf incorporates her many references to gardens is not, at any stage in her career, identifiably formulaic. Kew Gardens seems an apparently innocuous backdrop, providing a palette of colours more than any symbolic resonance, but the choice of Kew Gardens as a setting for this early story represents more than simply an opportune out-of-doors venue in which the pulse and flow of life, mechanical and organic, public and private, can be depicted at once in a new and plotless literary form. In many respects, Kew is less a garden and more a national monument and institution. Woolf's overriding preoccupation is with institutions and conventions, and her choice of Kew is, I suggest, made on this basis.

For an author so conscious of a time of transition and hiatus, literary and otherwise, the choice of Kew Gardens, *at this time*, is in itself highly significant. Kew needs to be considered in the context of British political history, particularly in the nineteenth century and in its early-twentieth-century upheaval. It is a context in which Woolf's own radical aesthetic must also be situated. In the history of British botanical imperialism and its effects, from developments in medicine and science, manufacturing, commerce, economics, agriculture, domestic horticulture, cuisine, and indeed, the landscape, Kew is, literally, a monument. At the time the story was written, Kew Gardens represents, on the one hand, all that was integral to British colonialism, particularly in its Victorian heyday, and equally, on the other, the Empire's probable dissolution, and certainly its severe modification. The story is both written at and set during the time of the First World War (explicitly referred to by the confused and 'eccentric' elderly man: 'and now, with this war, the spirit matter is rolling between the hills like thunder'), but also to be inferred from the drone of the aeroplane overhead and its 'fierce soul', or the white butterflies who make, with their fluttering activity, 'the outline of a shattered marble column'. Kew Gardens functions here as a metonymy for complex ideological and historical determinants. These determinants Woolf was to call elsewhere, in shorthand 'nonsense' terms, Nin, Crot and Pulley:[26]

> [...] a stream of influences. Some we can name – education; class; the pressure of society. But they are so many and so interwoven and so obscure that it is simpler to invent for them nonsense names – say Nin Crot and Pully. Nin Crot [sic] and Pully are always at their work, tugging, obscuring, distorting. Some are visible only to the writer. Others only to the reader. More and more complex do they become as time passes. The song beneath is only to be discovered in a flash of recognition.[27]

It is these aspects, 'always at their work', integral to the National Botanical Gardens at Kew as to so many other cultural manifestations, that are crucial to a full understanding of Woolf's own Modernist project. Just as 'the Angel in the House'[28]

---

26 See 'Anon' and 'The Reader' respectively, in Silver, B. R., ed., '"Anon" and "The Reader", op. cit..

27 V. Woolf, draft manuscript version of 'Anon', ibid., pp. 403-04.

28 The title of a Coventry Patmore poem but used more generally to signify the ideology of middle-class Victorian womanhood with its 'separate spheres' for men and women. See V.

8

figure is a metonymy for middle-class Victorian womanhood and an ideology of
separate spheres, so also is Kew Gardens such a trope. In Woolf's essay, 'Professions
for Women', 'The Angel in the House' is discussed as an unavoidable legacy for
the post-Edwardian, woman writer of modern fiction. She is revealed as thoroughly
familiar and, in many respects, deeply appealing to both sexes, (if not to all classes
and ethnicities), and therefore, all the more dangerous since she is able to be both
romanticised and normalised. For Woolf, the figure is, in fact, spectral and inhibiting.
(Kurtz's 'The Intended' in Conrad's *Heart of Darkness* is a figure along these lines).
As Woolf reiterated in so much of her work, customs, institutions and cultural
discourses, including those that seem most 'natural' and intransigent – or, indeed,
most pleasant to behold – are historically determined and contingent. In 'Professions
for Women', this angel figure must be killed so that the woman writer can flourish,
more free to explore other modes of being. In *A Room of One's Own*, the female
narrator visits a fictional but familiar Oxbridge college and, along with interrogating
her own exclusion as a woman, ponders the seeming permanence and inevitability
of the institution which is so appealing and yet so exclusive. It is, in more than one
sense, a construction:

> The outside of the chapel remained. As you know, its high domes and pinnacles can be
> seen [...] visible for miles, far way across the hills. Once, presumably, this quadrangle
> with its smooth lawns, its massive buildings and the chapel itself was marsh too, where
> the grasses waved and the swine rooted. Teams of horses and oxen, I thought, must have
> hauled the stone in wagons from far countries, and then with infinite labour the grey
> blocks in whose shade I was now standing were poised in order one on top of another
> [...] An unending stream of gold and silver, I thought, must have flowed into this court
> perpetually to keep the stones coming and the masons working; to level, to ditch, to dig
> and to drain. But it was then the age of faith, and money was poured liberally to set
> these stones on a deep foundation, and when the stones were raised, still more money
> was poured in [...] Hence the libraries and laboratories; the observatories; the splendid
> equipment of costly and delicate instruments which now stands on glass shelves, where
> centuries ago the grasses waved and the swine rooted. Certainly, as I strolled round the
> court, the foundation of gold and silver seemed deep enough; the pavement laid solidly
> over the wild grasses.[29]

Kew Gardens, similarly, was an institution built upon money from 'the coffers of
kings and queens and great nobles'.[30] As the Royal Botanic Gardens, first established

---

Woolf, 'Professions for Women' [1931], *Women and Writing*, ed. Michèle Barrett (London:
Women's Press, 1979), pp. 57ff.

29   V. Woolf, *A Room of One's Own* (St Albans & London: Grafton, 1983 [1929]), pp.
10-11.

30   The quotation is Woolf's, from *A Room of One's Own*, p. 11. Richard Drayton
chronicles some fitting examples: 'Frederick Louis, the Prince of Wales, his wife Augusta,
and their son George III, came to plant a botanic garden at Kew in opposition to Caroline's
[his mother] Richmond. The Prince, hating his parents, flirted with their political opponents.
Frederick leased the White House at Kew with its fine collection of exotic plants, from the

formally as such in the 1750s and further consolidated with the accession of George III, Kew was designed, increasingly, to signify:

> some of the most popular and enduring symbols of Kew, were exotic follies, typical playthings of a royal pleasure ground in the age of Enlightenment – a Mosque, an Alhambra, a House of Confucius, and a Pagoda [...] several structures were direct allegorical references to the advance of British power internationally under the Hanoverian dynasty: temples to Arethusa (1758), Victory (commemorating the Battle of Minden, 1761), and the Peace (1763). Kew became fully a theatre in which George III attempted to project the glory of his reign. Botany was at the centre of this endeavour.[31]

Re-designated as The National Botanic Gardens in the 1840s, Kew was a botanical testament to the inter-relation of science, economics and colonialism that characterised the nineteenth century. Joseph Dalton Hooker, who succeeded his father, William Jackson Hooker, as Director of Kew in 1865, noted that Kew's role was to serve no less than as 'the official referee and servant of the British Government at home and abroad'.[32] Kew was to be the metropolitan 'hub' in an enterprise which would oversee a world-wide colonial network of satellite gardens and institutions in the search for plants. The project was both epistemological –devoted to the expansion of knowledge through collection, categorisation and scientific method – and utilitarian: gathering 'everything that is useful in the vegetable kingdom [...] Medicine, commerce, agriculture, horticulture, and many valuable branches of manufacture would benefit from the adoption of such a system.'[33] The expansion of Kew in the nineteenth century was, without doubt, directly linked to the expansion of the British Empire and its interests, as this précis of the activities of Kew's 'eminent Victorians' reveals:

> The first official Director, appointed in 1842, was Sir William Jackson Hooker, previously Professor of Botany at Edinburgh University and father of William Dawson Hooker, author of a doctoral thesis on cinchona, and Joseph Dalton Hooker, who plant hunted in the Himalayas [...] Sir William revivified the gardens and expanded Kew's extent from 15 to over 250 acres [...] within five years. In 1848 both the Museum of Economic Botany and the Palm House, designed by Decimus Burton, were opened [...] In 1865 Sir Joseph Dalton Hooker became Director [...] and by the turn of the century 7000 Kew-trained botanists and gardeners were working around the world. Joseph further improved Kew's efficient infrastructure for the gathering, processing and redistribution of plant material

---

Capel family – a convenient act of identification with a great aristocratic family which had stood loyal to Charles I [...] For a long and detailed history see Richard Drayton, *Nature's Government: Science, Imperial Britain, and the Improvement of the World* (New Haven, CT & London: Yale University Press, 2000), pp. 40ff.

31   Drayton, p. 43.

32   Cited in Drayton, p. 239.

33   Treasury Committee Report of 1838 cited in T. Musgrave and W. Musgrave, *An Empire of Plants: People and Plants that Changed the World* (London: Cassell, 2000), p. 149.

and knowledge that proved essential in the development of many plantations in the colonies.[34]

Woolf's 'Kew Gardens', therefore, with its references in passing to 'the forests of Uruguay' or 'the first red water-lilies I'd ever seen' (not an indigenous species), and orchids, 'a Chinese pagoda and a crimson crested bird' or the 'glass roofs of the palm house', need, for their fullest resonance, to be considered in the context of Kew as an axis and instrument of Empire.

Kew as a Botanic Garden in the Victorian era also needs to be placed in the context of domestic policies, 'the great age of the public garden':[35]

> [...] Hyde, Green, St. James, Vauxhall, and Battersea Parks, like their equivalents at the centre of New York and at the eastern and western flanks of Paris, all found their modern form in the middle decades of the nineteenth century. This urban gardening clearly reflected a response to the consequences of rapid growth. Between 1821 and 1851 the population of London had doubled to almost seven million [...] In dense cities, flooded with cinders and smoke, poorly drained of garbage and sewage, and afflicted with cholera epidemics and endemic tuberculosis, parks had a sanitary importance. But moral and political health were equally desirable to urban planners. Serpentine lakes and avenues of trees might divert the crowd away from many kinds of evil [...] The energy which the Victorian English spent on greening cities should be seen as connected to their mania for the building of churches: both revealed piety mixed with anxieties about the impact of industry and democracy. Public gardens similarly attracted the support of those who feared revolution more than vice.[36]

Of course, the British botanic and public garden designs were also to be found abroad in colonial replicas. Richard Drayton, whose work on the role of Kew in British economic and scientific expansion enhances a reading of the inflections present in Woolf's story, was born in Guyana 'at the fall of the British Empire'. He proposes that 'it would be wrong to see any conspiracy here: the British simply took their horticultural passions, and the flowers and fruit they loved, wherever they took up residence, founding horticultural societies in Bengal, the Punjab, Sydney and elsewhere',[37] but he also explains the effects of these horti- (and other) cultural transplantations:

> I jouneyed as a child through the botanic gardens of the city, never thinking of the king after which it was named. After Georgetown's wooden cathedral, high gates opened on a road which led to a pool crowned with vast saucers of water lilies. These were *Victoria regia* – the lilies which came in the 1840s from the Guyanese jungles to inspire Joseph Paxton's plan for a Crystal Palace. Everything green wore a mysterious Latin name [...] Somewhat older, I found the place strangely ennobled by the fact that, like the British Governors before him, our erudite tyrant of a Prime Minister lived here. I was more

---

34 Drayton, op. cit., p. 149.
35 Ibid., p. 180.
36 Ibid., p. 181.
37 Ibid., p. 182.

surprised to learn that the Victorian proconsul who founded the gardens had given them in part to agricultural experiments.[38]

Later, Drayton adds, in a vein apposite to Woolf's story: 'It is likely that few promenaders in any botanic garden recognise the many faces of what they simply see as a beautiful space. Nor indeed, perhaps, in general, do those who live in the ruins of empire yet understand what this means'.[39] Botanic public gardens, at home and abroad were, 'theatres in which exotic nature was, literally, put in its place in a European system'.[40] By the twentieth century, the apparent democracy, utility and healthful ease of a metropolitan botanic garden open to the public as a pleasure ground masked the diligence with which so much – flora and human beings alike, at home and abroad – had been put in its place in a European system. Woolf's promenaders are unwitting, in this 'theatre' which she adopts for her story, as indeed her readers may also be, but Woolf is certainly aware of these aspects of her chosen venue. This 'beautiful space', like the beautiful Angel of the House, requires some discomposition.

It is in her essay, 'Mr Bennett and Mrs Brown', that Woolf makes the enigmatic assertion: 'in or about December, 1910, human character changed [...] All human relations have shifted'.[41] Edward VII died in May, 1910 and, while the death of Edward and the succession of George V signalled very explicitly the end of the Edwardian era and the beginning of the Georgian, the catalyst event or events, had, in Woolf's view, already occurred. Pre-war Britain was, it is true, subject to the challenges of numerous political and social upheavals, from the campaign for female suffrage at home to increasing tensions abroad, in colonies such as India, and in its relations with Germany. However, Woolf, placing 'the emphasis differently', recognises instead the significance of an event not otherwise recorded in the conventional chronicles of British and European history. It was an occurrence both reflective and generative of a change and a break: 'in or about December 1910' coincides with the date (8 November 1910 to 15 January 1911) of the first exhibition of post-Impressionist art, 'Manet and the Post-Impressionists', held in London at the Grafton Galleries. A second followed in October 1912.

The exhibitions were coordinated by the English painter and critic, Roger Fry, and displayed work by Cézanne, Van Gogh, Matisse and others. Roger Fry was an intimate friend of Vanessa Bell, Woolf's sister, and one of the circle known now as the Bloomsbury Group. In a lecture on Fry in 1964, Quentin Bell (son of Vanessa and art critic, Clive Bell) asserted that 'the post-impressionist exhibitions in London had destroyed the whole tissue of comfortable falsehoods on which that age based its views of beauty, propriety and decorum',[42] (in which cataclysm gardens and

---

38   Ibid., pp. xii-xiii.

39   Ibid., p. xiii.

40   Ibid., p. 183.

41   Virginia Woolf, 'Mr. Bennett and Mrs. Brown', [1924], *Collected Essays: Volume 1* (London: Hogarth, 1966), pp. 320-21.

42   Quentin Bell, cited in Frances Spalding, *Roger Fry: Art and Life*, op. cit., p. 140.

gardening would surely be implicated). Roger Fry's essay and defence of 1912, 'The French Post-Impressionists', also emphasises a new and modern *zeitgeist*, to which Woolf similarly referred with a literary perspective in numerous essays, articles and reviews. Fry's claims for new methods of representation and a radical aesthetic are highly evocative of Woolf's later ones for the medium of writing fiction:

> Now these artists do not seek to give what can, after all, be but a pale reflex of actual appearance, but to arouse the conviction of a new and definite reality. They do not seek to imitate form, but to create form; not to imitate life but find an equivalent for life. [...] In fact, they aim not at illusion but at reality.[43]

Woolf's views on history, event and time were complex. In general, she was dedicated to what she called a 'tunnelling process', to exploring the 'dark places of psychology' and, in her writing, 'to sink deeper and deeper, away from the surface, with its hard separate facts', all processes in which temporality was necessarily reconfigured. 'Kew Gardens', which we can surmise is set, specifically, on a Friday afternoon in July at some stage in the First World War (circa 1917, when Woolf first began drafting it) is, in most other respects, very imprecise. What period of time is represented by the various 'characters' who walk by the flower bed and what by the progress of a snail? Is the time it takes to represent someone's thoughts or speech equivalent to its representation in written, and reading, time? How does a linear, contiguous mode (Western European writing) record and denote the spatial and temporal simultaneities of apprehension and of event. What events take priority in the telling and why? This attention to varieties and priorities of temporal experience makes 'Kew Gardens' similar to the central section of the three which make up *To the Lighthouse*. 'Time Passes', set in war-time and in the family's absence, parenthetically notes events such as the deaths of key characters, Andrew, Prue, Mrs Ramsay, and yet, in other respects, events such as a dinner party or a domestic quarrel are represented as triumphs and battles with far more significance than those recorded in the annals of History and Biography. These views are crucial to an understanding of all Woolf's work from 'Kew Gardens' to *Between the Acts*, and they are playfully deployed in *Orlando*, her fanciful exploration of history, biography and gender, with a central character who lives through four centuries and a transformation from male to female. It is in a well-known passage from *Orlando* that she announces her view on 'Time', referring to the cycles of the natural world, landscape, season or garden, and to the conventions used to mark them:

> But Time, unfortunately, though it makes animals and vegetables bloom and fade with amazing punctuality, has no such simple effect upon the mind of man. The mind of man, moreover, works with equal strangeness upon the body of time. An hour, once it lodges in the queer element of the human spirit, may be stretched to fifty or a hundred times its clock length; on the other hand, an hour may be accurately represented on the timepiece

---

43   Roger Fry, 'The French Post-Impressionists', *Vision and Design* (London & New York: Oxford University Press, 1990 [1920]), p. 167.

of the mind by one second. This extraordinary discrepancy between time on the clock and time in the mind is less known than it should be and deserves fuller investigation.[44]

Woolf does not mean that chronological time is an irrelevance; the simple statement 'time passed' belies the importance Woolf gave to the effects of passing time, particularly on a landscape or in the accretion of conventions and habits which become so familiar as to seem 'natural'. The writings of Henri Bergson[45] and his theories of Time and Duration (duration being expansive, differing from the conventional spatio-temporal logic) and of *élan vitale*, a creative spirit that is 'fluid, mobile and intuitive' were influences on Woolf and her contemporaries, artists and writers alike.[46] The garden is a locus germane to such preoccupations; with its cycles and seasons, its constantly changing aspects and atmosphere – colours, scent, foliage or flowers – it is always in flux. But it is also a place of enduring features: seminal, underground and unseen, or surface structures of bare branch or flower bed. With such presence and absence, which include the presence or absence of human figures, the garden is a rich exemplar of, and theatre for, theories of time and duration.

Artists, Impressionist and post-Impressionist, not only painted flowers and gardens as subjects; they also gardened. Monet at Giverny and Pissaro at Eragny, or Duncan Grant and Vanessa Bell at Charleston, gardened *and* painted their gardens, flowers and other produce. Modernist garden design was also affected by the turn-of-the century attention to new accents and innovative combinations, with gardens as a medium in their own right. Nonetheless, garden design was controversial and subject to factionalism, both radical and conservative. The factions are typified on the one hand by William Robinson's innovative 'multi-cultural' combinations of indigenous species and naturalised hardy exotics: 'many different types of plants and hardy climbers from countries as cold and colder than our own',[47] and, on the other, by Sir Reginald Blomfield, the champion of formality in the garden.[48] By the time of the staging of the first post-Impressionist exhibition, the key figure in garden design was undoubtedly Gertrude Jekyll and had been since the turn of the century. Significantly, had it not been for her myopia, painting would have been her chosen medium. This enforced change in direction, notwithstanding, Gertrude Jekyll saw herself as an artist: 'For planting ground is painting a landscape with living things and I hold that good gardening takes rank within the bounds of the fine arts, so

---

44   V. Woolf, *Orlando* (London: Grafton, 1977, [1928]), p. 61.

45   Henri Bergson, *Time and Free Will: An Essay on the Immediate Data of Consciousness* (London: San Sonnenschein, 1910 [1889]) and *Creative Evolution* (London: Swan Sonnenschein, 1910 [1907]).

46   See *Modernism*, eds M. Bradbury and J. McFarlane (Harmondsworth: Penguin, 1983 [1976]), p, 82 and p. 614.

47   William Robinson cited in G. van Zuylan, *The Garden: Visions of Paradise* (London: Thames and Hudson, 1995), p. 153.

48   William Robinson, *The Wild Garden* (1870) and Sir Reginald Blomfield, *The Formal Garden in England* (1890).

that I hold that to plant well needs an artist of no mean capacity.'[49] And, like artists working in other media, she was developing a new aesthetic. The famous partnership of Gertrude Jekyll and the architect Edwin Lutyens was one in which the former 'warring factions are reconciled',[50] by virtue of Jekyll's informality of planting and Lutyens' linear or geometric architectural designs. This kind of integration was also deeply important to Virginia Woolf.

Woolf's own method relies on just such a combination. Perhaps Modernism across the arts is best typified by a combination of novelty and informality with function and technological advance. Indeed, the description in *To the Lighthouse* of Lily Briscoe painting, which is also so reminiscent of the descriptions in 'Kew Gardens', demonstrates Woolf's belief in a generative artistic mode, that absolutely relies on combination:

> Beautiful and bright it should be on the surface, feathery and evanescent, one colour melting into another like the colours on a butterfly's wing; but beneath the fabric must be clamped together with bolts of iron. it was to be a thing you could ruffle with your breath; and a thing you could not dislodge with a team of horses.[51]

In fact, this combination is alluded to throughout the book in a variety of contexts: Mrs Ramsay's meditations on 'masculine intelligence [...] like iron girders spanning the swaying fabric, upholding the world',[52] (with which the Botanic Gardens, that 'central institution of both Victorian science and the British Empire',[53] could be aligned); the boar's skull, mounted on the wall of the nursery, remaining there on the insistence of James Ramsay, but swathed in a loose shawl to appease his sister, Cam; Lily's painting described as ' colour burning on a framework of steel; the light of a butterfly's wing lying upon the arches of a cathedral',[54] in terms reminiscent of Monet's series of paintings of Rouen Cathedral.

By the end of the novel, it is Roger Fry's post-impressionist aesthetic that Lily accomplishes. Fry's view, in 'An Essay in Aesthetics', collected in *Vision and Design*: 'one chief aspect of order in a work is unity; unity of some kind is necessary [...] In a picture this unity is due to a balancing of the attractions of the eye about the central line of the picture',[55] is unmistakably put to work in the closing lines of *To the Lighthouse*: 'With a sudden intensity, as if she saw it clear for a second, she drew a line there, in the centre. It was done; it was finished. Yes, she thought, laying down her brush in extreme fatigue, I have had my vision.'[56] And if Lily Briscoe's

---

49   G. Jekyll, *Wood and Garden* (1899), cited in D. Kellaway, ed., *The Virago Book of Women Gardeners* (London: Virago, 1995).
50   G. van Zuylen, op. cit., p. 117.
51   V. Woolf, *To the Lighthouse* (Harmondsworth: Penguin, 1974 [1927]), p. 194.
52   Ibid., p. 114.
53   Drayton, op. cit., p. xiii.
54   Op. cit., p. 56-7.
55   Fry, op. cit., p. 22.
56   Ibid., p. 237.

aesthetic is Fry's, it is also Woolf's. To Roger Fry, she wrote: 'I meant <u>nothing</u> by *The Lighthouse*. One has to have a central line down the middle of the book to hold the design together. I saw that all sorts of feelings would accrue to this [...]'.[57]

If 'Kew Gardens' is like Lily Briscoe's painting, a canvas for Woolf's developing aesthetic of combination, unity and vision, there is also a profound sense of dissolution in this vivid short story. What will become Woolf's trademark attention to conjunction and unity is also set alongside her life-long preoccupation with dissolution and nothingness, which, some speculate, has to do with her recurring bouts of madness and her suicide. The garden is, in her work, an apt venue for her speculations on death, resilience and regeneration, but it is equally appropriate for those theories of combination or 'cross-fertilisation'.

One of Woolf's, often controversial, views is certainly about creativity and union: the androgynous mind. In *A Room of One's Own*, she explained:

> Perhaps to think [...] of one sex as distinct from the other is an effort. It interferes with the unity of the mind [...]But there may be some state of mind in which one could continue without effort because nothing is required to be held back [...] And I went on amateurishly to sketch a plan of the soul so that in each of us two powers preside, one male, one female; and in the man's brain the man predominates over the woman, and in the woman's brain the woman predominates over the man. [...] If one is a man, still the woman part of his brain must have intercourse with the man in her. Coleridge perhaps meant this when he said that a great mind is androgynous. It is when this fusion takes place that the mind is fully fertilized and uses all its faculties [...] Some collaboration has to take place in the mind between the woman and the man before the art of creation can be accomplished. Some marriage of opposites has to be consummated. The whole of the mind must lie wide open [...] The writer, I thought, once his experience is over, must lie back and let his mind celebrate its nuptials in darkness.[58]

It is clear by this, that Lily's exhaustion after she has had 'her vision' is precisely her mind's post-'nuptial' celebration and release. Mrs Ramsay's artistry is also represented by her experience of 'the rapture of successful creation' and the 'pure joy of two notes sounding together'. At the end of 'Kew Gardens', the 'vision' of the unnamed narrator, represents a similar culmination. The increasing tempo and the sensual synaesthesia of the final paragraph signifies the movement to the visionary and creative climax. What has been a pan-optic sequence of descriptions changes at this point to what might be seen, in the context of Woolf's theorising, a representation of the 'mind's nuptials'. The words 'dissolved' and 'dissolving' are less about the intense heat and its effects, or the consequences of war, or Woolf's own nihilistic propensities, but more about the concentric sense of the dissolution of orgasmic tension. In this regard, 'dissolution' is not simply about negation – or even, using Woolf's own term, 'non-being' – but rather about creative rapture, which is one of the artist's most profound 'moments of being'. Many of Woolf's characters

---

57 Cited in Quentin Bell, *Virginia Woolf, 1912-1941* (St Albans: Triad/Paladin, 1971), p. 129.

58 V. Woolf, *A Room of One's Own*, pp. 93-99.

undergo these moments of vision and revelation. For instance, Mrs Dalloway's experience is recognisably akin to that described six years previously at the end of 'Kew Gardens':

> It was a sudden revelation, a tinge like a blush which one tried to check and then, as it spread, one yielded to its expansion, and rushed to the farthest verge and there quivered and felt the world come closer, swollen with some astonishing significance, some pressure of rapture, which split its thin skin and gushed and poured with an extraordinary alleviation over the cracks and sores. Then, for that moment, she had seen an illumination; a match burning in a crocus; an inner meaning almost expressed. But the close withdrew; the hard softened. It was over – the moment.[59]

The concluding description of 'Kew Gardens' – 'the petals of myriad flowers flashed their colours into the air' – is an exemplum of this 'fountain of creative energy' and of the benefits of a hybridity in the service of her theory of 'vision' and 'rapture'. On the completion of 'Kew Gardens', Virginia wrote to Vanessa: 'my vision comes out much as I had it'[60] – a precursor to Lily Briscoe's 'post-nuptial': 'I have had my vision'.

While Kew Gardens represents the bastions of Victorian Britain, it affords Woolf the scope for her Modernist vision to be brought to bear in her story, both in juxtaposition *and* in combination. She is also acutely attuned to historical contingency and aware that beneath a Victorian Kew there must be those traces of prior landscapes that she identified in *Between the Acts* as: 'rhododendron forests in Picadilly', 'the scars made by the Britons; by the Romans; by the Elizabethan manor house; by the plough [...] in the Napoleonic wars',[61] just as there is another 'song beneath' and 'landscape behind' the customs established by Caxton's press or the vested interests of patriarchal and imperial power. Gardens are palimpsests; gardens are contingent, subject to and reflective of 'the historicity of concepts'. The garden, very familiarly, is also a place of combination and cross-fertilisation; it is a place of efflorescence and fecundity and these are the tropes Woolf uses to convey the necessary aspects of fruitful artistic creativity 'in the mind': 'I was on the right path; [...] what fruit hangs in my soul is to be reached there [...] I now invent theories that fertility and fluency are the things.'[62] In other respects, Woolf uses gardens but there is no static or straightforward symbolism, while metaphors are used variously to represent multiple and shifting states of consciousness or the fruition of the creative act. There is, however, one reference which should, perhaps, stand as a symbol for the integrity of Woolf's 'vision'; it is the image she refers to in the memoir, 'A Sketch of the Past', a childhood memory recalling a time when she was:

---

59   V. Woolf, *Mrs Dalloway* (St Albans: Granada, 1981 [1925]), p. 30.
60   H. Lee, op. cit., p. 369.
61   V. Woolf, *Between the Acts*, pp. 10; 7.
62   V. Woolf, *A Writer's Diary*, p. 89.

[...] in the garden at St. Ives. I was looking at the flower bed by the front door; 'That is the whole', I said. I was looking at a plant with a spread of leaves; and it seemed suddenly plain that the flower itself was a part of the earth; that a ring enclosed what was the flower; and that was the real flower; part earth; part flower. It was a thought I put away as being likely to be very useful to me later.[63]

Looking back as a well-established writer, Woolf found in this emblematic flower something akin to Lily Briscoe's 'line in the centre', the sign of a new mode of inclusiveness and a writer's commitment to her own '<u>conception</u>' and vision:

When I said about the flower 'That is the whole' I felt that I had made a discovery. This intuition of mine [...] has certainly given its scale to my life ever since I saw the flower in the bed by the front door at St Ives. If I were painting myself I should have to find some – rod, shall I say – something that would stand for the conception [...] one is living all the time in relation to certain background rods or conceptions. Mine is that there is a pattern hid behind the cotton wool. And this conception affects me every day. [...] I feel that by writing I am doing what is far more necessary than anything else. All artists I suppose feel something like this.[64]

Katherine Mansfield: Memory

Katherine Mansfield was Woolf's contemporary and, despite some difficulties and differences, they were friends. The difficulties were largely to do with a sense of rivalry but they also recognised the aspects they had in common, and both women valued their exchanges on writing and other topics. In the summer of 1917, Mansfield's

---

63 V. Woolf, 'A Sketch of the Past', *Moments of Being*, p. 82.

64 Ibid., pp. 83-4.

Prelude was accepted for publication by the Woolfs' Hogarth Press, which later, in May 1919, was also to publish *Kew Gardens*. In a letter dated simply August 1917, Mansfield thanks Virginia Woolf for a visit to Asheham, her Sussex home. According to an earlier letter, the visit was proposed for 17 August. The concern here with specific dates arises because of the following: in her letter of thanks, Mansfield expresses a writer's solidarity and remarks particularly on Woolf's 'Flower Bed' piece, very obviously a pre-publication *Kew Gardens:*

> It was good to have time to talk to you; we have got the same job, Virginia, and it is really very curious and thrilling that we should both, quite apart from each other, be after so very nearly the same thing. We are you know; there's no denying it [....] Yes, your Flower Bed is *very* good. There's a still, quivering, changing light over it all and a sense of couples dissolving in the bright air which fascinates me –[65]

Intriguingly, however (and this is where the dates and sequence seem puzzling), Mansfield wrote to her friend Lady Ottoline Morrell, whom she had also visited in August, prior to her visit to Virginia at Asheham. In that thank-you letter to Ottoline, Mansfield praises the Morrells' garden at Garsington Manor, and projects a garden story inspired by it; it bears an uncanny resemblance to Virginia Woolf's 'Flower Bed', which she was to see in a few days' time:

> Your glimpse of the garden, all flying green and gold, made me wonder again who is going to write about that flower garden. It might be so wonderful, do you know how I mean? There would be people walking in the garden – several pairs of people – their conversation – their slow pacing – their glances as they pass one another – the pauses as the flowers 'come in' as it were – as a bright dazzle, an exquisite haunting scent, a shape so formal and fine, so much a 'flower of the mind' that he who looks at it is really tempted for one bewildering moment to stoop and touch and make sure. The 'pairs' of people must be very different and there must be a slight touch of enchantment – some of them seeming so extraordinarily 'odd' and separate from the flowers, but the others quite related and at ease. A kind of, musically speaking, conversation set to flowers.[66]

Despite this seeming coincidence and overlap, with Mansfield describing a garden-piece so very like the one Woolf had yet to publish but had already written (albeit set in the public space of Kew Gardens rather than the private one at Garsington Manor), the 'flower-bed' manifestations of each were quite distinctive. Although there is a similarity in their projects and their method, with both women committed to new modes of representation in writing, Mansfield's gardens are used to different effect, as we shall see.

At times, each was extremely critical of the other's work. In a review of Woolf's *Night and Day*, published in *The Athenaeum* in 1919, Mansfield described it as: 'Miss Austen up-to-date', 'extremely cultivated, distinguished and brilliant',

---

65 K. Mansfield to Virginia Woolf, August 1917, *The Letters of Katherine Mansfield*, ed. J. Middleton Murry (Hamburg: Albatross, 1934), pp. 61-2.

66 letter to Lady Ottoline Morrell, August 15, 1917, ibid., p. 60-61.

'deliberate', but claimed that: 'in the midst of our admiration it makes us feel old and chill'.[67] Woolf, for her part, wrote in her diary in 1918 after reading Mansfield's story 'Bliss':

> Indeed I don't see how much faith in her as woman or writer can survive that sort of story. I shall have to accept the fact, I'm afraid, that her mind is a very thin soil, laid an inch or two upon very barren rock. For 'Bliss' is long enough to give her a chance of going deeper. Instead she is content with superficial smartness; and the whole conception is poor, cheap, not the vision, however imperfect, of an interesting mind. She writes badly too. And the effect was as I say, to give me an impression of her callousness and hardness as a human being.[68]

It is interesting to note the horticultural analogies and metaphors in their criticisms of each other: the one, 'cultivated' and 'chill'; the other of 'thin soil'. Nevertheless, it was Mansfield's *Prelude* that the Hogarth Press chose to publish in 1917 as one of its earliest publications, and for which Virginia expressed a jealous admiration.[69]

Hermione Lee's biography of Virginia Woolf has a chapter, 'Katherine', which presents an interesting portrait of the friendship, peer supportiveness and rivalry between these two women writers, whose short relationship was terminated by Mansfield's death from tuberculosis in 1923. Lee's summary comparison of the relationship between the two writers finds a major difference in Mansfield's 'colonialism', which Woolf never entirely approved of or understood:

> Katherine Mansfield was six years younger than Virginia Woolf, utterly different from her in looks and temperament and experiences, but with some strong affinities, like her fierce dedication to work, her childless marriage, her dangerousness as a friend, and her battle with illness and bereavement (she too lost a loved brother, in the war in October 1915). But her colonialism and her itinerant uprootedness were the opposite of Virginia's ancestral network.[70]

Colonialism and exile, and certainly, once her illness was established, 'itinerant uprootedness' in search of benign climates, are powerful factors which affected her relationships and her writing. Angela Smith, in a biography of Mansfield, cites Elizabeth Bowen's estimation, along these lines, of Mansfield's literary skill:

> Elizabeth Bowen sees the power of Mansfield's writing as lying in the homelessness that wearied her in personal life, but made her alert: 'Katherine Mansfield was saved [...] by two things – her inveterate watchfulness as an artist, and a certain sturdiness in her nature which the English at their least friendly might call "colonial"'.[71]

---

67   Cited in C. Tomalin, *Katherine Mansfield: A Secret Life* (London: Viking, 1987), p. 198.

68   *A Writer's Diary*, p. 12.

69   See discussion of the relationship in Lee, op. cit. pp. 386-401.

70   Ibid., p. 387.

71   Cited in A. Smith, *Katherine Mansfield: A Literary Life* (Basingstoke: Palgrave, 2000), p. 149.

In many of Mansfield's stories, she does look back, as an outcast and an exile, to the colonial locus of her childhood, but these personal memories are transposed into stories in which memory itself, as a psychological process and aspect of consciousness, is the topic. In other stories, she writes as an outsider, to the European (and cosmopolitan) world which she had adopted, but once again, her overwhelming interest is in 'secret selves' more than in specific places.

Prelude, which was a reworking of the earlier *The Aloe*, has, as the original title suggests, plants and gardens integral to it. In a letter to her friend Dorothy Brett in October, 1917, Mansfield rejoices at the story's acceptance for publication and explains her method, 'more or less my own invention':

> I threw my darling to the Wolves and they ate it and served me up so much praise in such a golden bowl that I couldn't help feeling gratified. I did not think they would like it at all and I am still astounded that they do. 'What form is it?' you ask. Ah, Brett, it's so difficult to say. As far as I know, it's more or less my own invention. And 'How have I shaped it?' This is about as much as I can say about it. You know, if the truth were known I have a perfect passion for the island where I was born. Well, in the early morning there I always remember feeling that this little island has dipped back into the dark blue sea during the night only to rise again at gleam of day, all hung with bright spangles and glittering drops. When you run over the dewy grass you positively felt that your feet tasted salt. I tried to catch that moment – with something of its sparkle and its flavour. And just as on those mornings white milky mists rise and uncover some beauty, then smother it again and then again disclose it, I tried to lift that mist from my people and let them be seen and then to hide them again ...[72]

The 'little island' of her birth is New Zealand, which she left permanently in 1908 when she was just twenty. In 1915, she and her brother, Leslie, who had come to Europe in that year in order to enlist, had spent precious time together reminiscing about their childhood and discussing its future depiction in *The Aloe*. After her brother's death at the front in France in 1915, she wrote in her journal:

> [...] now I want to write recollections of my own country [...] because my brother and I were born there, but also because in my thoughts I range with him over all the remembered places. I am never far away from them. I long to renew them in writing [...] I want for one moment to make our undiscovered country leap into the eyes of the Old World [...] all must be told with a sense of mystery, a radiance, an afterglow, because you, my little sun of it, are set. [...] Now I must play my part.
>
> Then I want to write poetry. I feel always trembling on the brink of poetry. The almond tree, the birds, the little wood where you are, the flowers you do not see [...] But especially I want to write a kind of long elegy to you ... perhaps not in poetry. Nor perhaps in prose. Almost certainly in a kind of <u>special prose</u>.[73]

---

72 Ibid., p. 63.

73 K. Mansfield, January 22, 1916, *Letters and Journals*, ed. C. K. Stead (Harmondsworth: Penguin, 1977), pp. 65-6.

And then, another entry attests to *The Aloe*, not just as a memorial to, but as an ongoing collaboration with, her dead brother:

The Aloe is right. *The Aloe* is lovely. It simply fascinates me, and I know that it is what you would wish me to write. And now I know what the last chapter is. It is your birth – your coming in the autumn. You in Grandmother's arms under the tree, your solemnity, your wonderful beauty [...] The next book will be yours and mine [...] My little brother, it is good, and it is what we really meant.[74]

Whereas 'vision' is the term which might best typify Woolf's writing, 'memory' may be the term to encapsulate Mansfield's. It is not that Woolf's writing is without memory or memories – memory is integral to her work, as, indeed, is elegy. Of *To the Lighthouse*, Woolf explained that her father, mother, St Ives (where she vacationed with her family as a child) and childhood would be 'done complete in it',[75] and pondered: ' I have an idea that I will invent a new name for my books to supplant "novel" [...] But what? Elegy?'[76] Like Woolf, Mansfield believed her business was 'invention', to challenge and modify the ossified categorisation of literary forms by 'a kind of special prose'. Mansfield's journal entry on her aims for *The Aloe* – 'A story – no, it would be a sketch, hardly that, more a psychological study'[77] – is reminiscent of Woolf's interest in 'the dark places of psychology', for instance, or her own aim to 'keep the quality of a sketch in a finished and composed work'.[78]

Interestingly, one of her earliest publications, written when she was nineteen and 'at home' in New Zealand, was a vignette entitled: 'In the Botanical Gardens';[79] ('the form that Mansfield devised for what she called vignettes enabled her to avoid the conclusiveness of a conventional narrative line'[80]). It was published in 1907, under the pseudonym Julian Mark, in the *Native Companion*, a new monthly magazine in Melbourne. In the view of Angela Smith, the piece shows a politicised engagement with colonialism, although the extract she cites is evidence more of a romanticised primitivism, which many writers and artists of the time were also appropriating in order to regenerate an effete, bourgeois, cultural sensibility:

'In the Botanical Gardens', however, engages obliquely with the nature of colonialism, its repressions and its guilt; the subject itself suggests veneration of that Mecca of colonial travel, the Royal Botanic Gardens at Kew. As early as this [...] she identifies Impressionism with surface realism: within 'the orthodox banality of carpet bedding' in the Central Walk of the Botanical Gardens, people 'seem as meaningless, as lacking in individuality, as the little figures in an impressionist landscape'. Unexpectedly, the Decadents are not entirely

---

74 Ibid., p. 66.

75 V. Woolf, *A Writer's Diary*, p. 81.

76 Ibid., p. 84.

77 K. Mansfield, cited in 'Introduction', *The Aloe*, ed. V. O'Sullivan (London: Virago, 1985), p. xii.

78 V. Woolf, *A Writer's Diary*, p. 72.

79 A. Smith, op. cit., p. 25.

80 Ibid.

absent from the evocation of the scene in the gardens; anemones 'always appear to me a
trifle dangerous, sinister, seductive but poisonous'. This seduction is one of the alternatives
offered by the 'artificial' part of the gardens; it is all contained within the Enclosure,
within the boundaries that form a crucial part of colonial life, and are reproduced within
the gardens. When the speaker turns from the 'smooth swept paths' to a steep track, she
becomes dimly aware of another history and a different way of living with the land [...]
'And, suddenly it disappears, all the pretty, carefully-tended surface of gravel and sward
and blossom, and there is bush, silent and splendid [...] As I breathe it, it seems to absorb,
to become part of me – and I am old with the age of centuries, strong with the strength of
savagery'.[81]

Rather than positing any particular view on aboriginal wilderness, however, this
is the wild of Oscar Wilde, whose writings and precepts, particularly on art and
sexual adventurousness, were much admired by the young Mansfield.[82] Moreover,
whereas Woolf's gardens and landscapes can have a 'political' force, in that they do
attend to cultural determinants, material manifestations and the vestiges of historical
contingency, Mansfield's gardens, with this early exception are almost exclusively
bound up in consciousness and subjectivity. The wild, disorderly places are emblems
of the mind and spirit rather than a cultural critique, as when Jonathan in 'At the
Bay' expresses a longing to escape from his imprisoning, work-a-day existence
and imagines 'there's this vast dangerous garden, waiting out there, undiscovered,
unexplored',[83] or when Mansfield, in her Notebooks, writes:

[T]he mind I love must still have wild places – a tangled orchard where dark damsons
drop in the heavy grass, an overgrown little wood, the chance of a snake or two (real
snakes), a pool that nobody's fathomed the depth of, and paths threaded with those little
flowers planted by the wind.
    It must also have *real* hiding places, not artificial ones – not gazebos and mazes. And
I have never yet met the cultivated mind that has not had its shrubbery. I loathe & detest
shrubberies.[84]

Thus, 'wild places' and 'dangerous gardens' constitute landscapes of the mind and
a habit of being rather than, say, simply Mansfield's testament to a remembered
'real' New Zealand. This attention to the particularity of 'sublime' (or suburban)
landscapes of individual consciousness is, paradoxically, a universalising one. It
matters little whether Mansfield's gardens (inner and outer) are situated in a colonial
outpost or European metropolis; what they focus on, predominantly, are women and
children, food and flowers, comings and goings, and in relation to these, perceptions

---

81   Ibid. pp. 25-6.

82   See C. Tomalin, op. cit. and Angela Smith, *Katherine Mansfield and Virginia Woolf:
A Public of Two* (Oxford: Clarendon Press, 1999) for discussion of Wilde's influence on
Mansfield.

83   K. Mansfield, 'At the Bay', *Collected Stories of Katherine Mansfield* (London:
Constable & Co., 1953 [1945]) (hereafter *CS*), p. 237.

84   Cited in A. Smith, *Katherine Mansfield: A Literary Life*, op. cit., p. 125.

and processes which are deeply interior, the conscious and unconscious aspects of 'secret selves'.[85] For example, the manuka tree in 'At the Bay', like the aloe in 'Prelude' or the pear tree in 'Bliss', stands at the centre of a narrative, but with little ostensible significance. That 'manuka'[86] is the Maori name for a tender species and medicinal plant indigenous to New Zealand, with a particular meaning for, and relation to, the island's human indigents, is not, here, the issue. Rather, the tree in this tale takes on a private significance in the eye and consciousness of its beholder, Linda Burnell, languorously musing on the futility of fertility:

> In a steamer chair, under a manuka tree that grew in the middle of the front grass patch, Linda Burnell dreamed the morning away. She did nothing. She looked up at the dark, close, dry leaves of the manuka, at the chinks of blue between, and now and again a tiny yellowish flower dropped on her. Pretty – yes, if you held one of those flowers on the palm of your hand and looked at it closely, it was an exquisite small thing. Each pale yellow petal shone as if each was the careful work of a loving hand. The tiny tongue in the centre gave it the shape of a bell. And when you turned it over the outside was a deep bronze colour. But as soon as they flowered, they fell and were scattered. You brushed them off your frock as you talked; the horrid little things got caught in one's hair. Why, then, flower at all? Who takes the trouble – or the joy – to make all these things that are wasted, wasted ...[87]

'At the Bay', in part Mansfield's testament to her native New Zealand, her family and, in particular, her beloved, late brother – here, the infant asleep in the garden at the feet of his mother – is, first and foremost, a testament to theories, aesthetic, psychological and philosophical, which are firmly rooted in a European *zeitgeist*, of and on which Freud, for instance, is both a product and major influence. As she wrote to her friend, Dorothy Brett, in September 1921, after finishing 'At the Bay' ('a continuation of *Prelude*'), the writing had a double aspect: to bring a particular past to life again and to acknowledge a general psychological trope:

> It is so strange to bring the dead to life again [...] All is remembered [...] And one feels possessed. And then the place where it all happens. I have tried to make it as familiar to 'you' as it is to me. You know the marigolds? You know those pools in the rocks [...] And, too, one tries to go deep – to speak to the secret self we all have – to acknowledge that.[88]

Similarly, Linda Burnell, finding that 'she had the garden to herself; she was alone', moves from the 'pale yellow flowers' of the manuka and the garden of the restrictive, vivid present – 'dazzling white the picotees shone; the golden-eyed marigolds glittered; the nasturtiums wreathed the veranda poles in green and gold flame' – to another time and place, a veranda located in the dreamy past and a past of dreams:

---

85   See also, for example, Mansfield's short story, 'Psychology', of the same period: 'Their secret selves whispered'. *CS*, op. cit., p. 111.

86   A tree otherwise known by its Latin name *Leptospermum scoparium*.

87   *CS*, op. cit., pp. 220-21.

88   The Letters of Katherine Mansfield, p. 332.

... Now she sat on the veranda of their Tasmanian home, leaning against her father's knee. And he promised, 'As soon as you and I are old enough, Linny, we'll cut off somewhere, we'll escape. Two boys together. I have a fancy I'd like to sail up a river in China.' Linda saw that river, very wide, covered with little rafts and boats. She saw the yellow hats of the boatmen and she heard their high, thin voices as they called ... 'Yes, papa'. But just then a very broad young man with bright ginger hair walked slowly past their house and slowly, solemnly even, uncovered. Linda's father pulled her ear teasingly, in the way he had. 'Linny's beau,' he whispered. 'Oh, papa, fancy being married to Stanley Burnell!' Well, she was married to him.[89]

Memory, here, is multiple in its aspects, and what is 'remembered' is for Mansfield a fiction. While Mansfield is remembering the 'little island' of her home, she is imagining her mother's consciousness, and particularly, her thoughts and feelings about marriage and motherhood. Linda's reveries include memories of her own past, but these memories also include remembering the imagined, possible futures she projected in the past ('a river in China', 'the yellow hats'), that were curtailed by other past events, such as her marriage, and are linked to the present, motherhood. Here, the colour yellow takes on an obscure signifying chain, meaningful to Linda's consciousness alone.

Linda's garden reveries are less about the flowers in their particularity; musings on her present ('why, then, flower at all?') and her past may be instigated by present garden flowers and betokened by those of the past, but they represent condensations or nodal points of larger issues and deeper events. The yellow manuka flowers of the present lead to the remembered imagining of yellow hats on an imagined Chinese expedition with a loved parent; the vivid nasturtiums and marigolds to a recollection of her then husband-to-be's ginger hair. In *Prelude*, Linda dreams a dream, again in relation to her father, for which a Freudian analysis would be hard to avoid:

She was walking with her father through a green paddock sprinkled with daisies. Suddenly he bent down and parted the grasses and showed her a tiny ball of fluff just at her feet. 'Oh, papa, the darling'. She made a cup of her hands and caught the tiny bird and stroked its head with her finger. It was quite tame. But a funny thing happened. As she stroked it began to swell, it ruffled and pouched, it grew bigger and bigger [....] It had become a baby with a big naked head [...][90]

The distillations in signifying colours or symbolic plants, for which there is private rather than consensual meaning, betoken complexities of memory, fantasy and desire. In the language of dreams or the process of repression, there is much that is both revealed and concealed, and much that remains unconscious, and therefore secret, to the individual subject. Any reading method must also take these inevitably partial (in both senses) disclosures into account.

As with the green and white of the pear tree in 'Bliss' – 'a tall, slender pear in fullest, richest bloom; it stood perfect as though becalmed against a jade-green

---

89   *CS*, op. cit., pp. 221-2.
90   Ibid., p. 24.

sky' – the colours and particulars of the plants themselves are far less significant than the memories and emotions they come, through no straightforward or common symbolism, to betoken. Again, there is little 'meaning' ascribed to the pear tree apart from Bertha Young's blissful apprehension of its perfection, and then, her realisation that all the perfections in her own life for which she adopts it as a symbol are a sham. When she realises that Pearl Fulton, with whom she has felt such communion looking at the tree, is her husband's lover, the final image of the tree is unchanged, perfect and perfectly dispassionate: 'But the pear tree was as lovely as ever and as full of flower and as still.' In her delight, Bertha projects all her inner satisfactions and musings of her 'secret self' onto the pear tree; she has identified herself with the perceived symbolic perfection of the tree (dressed for a dinner party she appears in: 'a white dress, a string of jade beads, green shoes and stockings'), whereas Pearl is fantasised as the silver moon in which her, and the tree's, beauty will be offset: 'And still in the back of her mind, there was the pear tree. It would be silver now [...] silver as Miss Fulton':

> And the two women stood side by side looking at the slender, flowering tree. Although it was so still it seemed, like the flame of a candle, to stretch up, to point, to quiver in the bright air, to grow taller and taller as they gazed – almost to touch the rim of the round, silver moon.
>
> How long did they stand there? Both, as it were, caught in that circle of unearthly light, understanding each other perfectly, creatures of another world, and wondering what they were to do in this one with all this blissful treasure that burned in their bosoms and dropped, in silver flowers, from their hair and hands?[91]

Although related in the third-person, the story is at once objective and intensely subjective, given from Bertha's perspective alone; no other character's consciousness or thoughts are given. The objective third-person narration is suffused with Bertha's own patterns of speech and thought, a commonly used modernist technique known as free indirect speech, at which Mansfield was adept.[92] At times, Bertha's uncertainly about what she has heard, overheard or inferred in relation to others, and her own faltering search for words to express her emergent views, are represented with ellipses, dashes and questioning: all the perceptions and misperceptions, the solipsistic bliss, the imagined communion and ensuing disillusionment and dismay is Bertha's alone; the apprehension of irony is the writer's and readers'.

There is no doubt that the pear tree *has* symbolic status (indeed Bertha explicitly gives it that: 'a symbol of her own life'), and critics have interpreted it variously. In a recent book on Modernism, Peter Childs discusses the central motif of the pear tree in 'Bliss':

> [...] the story's central image is of a treasured 'pear tree' in Bertha's garden, which seems to symbolise her innocence (it is her 'lovely pear tree'), leading the reader to infer a

---

91   op. cit., p. 102.

92   Peter Childs, *Modernism* (London: Routledge, 2000), p. 88.

reference to the Tree of Knowledge and to construe pears in terms of the female body as well as the forbidden fruit of Eden.[93]

An inference of the Tree of Knowledge may be ubiquitous in all Western texts containing fruit-bearing trees, and certainly desire and a 'fall' are common to the story of Eden and to 'Bliss'. In the context of Mansfield's work, however, the pear tree has more in common with the manuka tree in 'At the Bay' or the aloe in 'Prelude', and, thereby, disrupts more conventional correlations, as we shall see. Another critic, Gillian Hanscombe, provides a reading which attends to what she finds as the covert or coded lesbianism of the story: 'The story was about the surge of feelings between women who did not know "what to do with" them'. [94] Hanscombe also includes an exploration of a personal pear-mythology that Mansfield shared with her brother; in this respect, she finds and makes a case for the cryptic incorporation of incestuous, as well as lesbian, desire. Pears connote then, a counter-signification to the more conventional forbidden fruit of the heterosexual mythology of desire and outcast in Eden. Moreover, as Hanscombe discusses, the pear tree is both phallic and flowering, thus, in its symbolic attributes, both male and female.[95] There are symbolic correlations suggested by the emphasis on: silver, white, green, moonlight, upright, flowering, the potential of womb-shaped fruit and there is the linguistic coincidence of the nearly identical 'pear' and 'Pearl', (or that 'pear' is an anagram for 'rape'). There are the various triangular desiring relations in the story, most obviously in the adulterous affair of Pearl and Bertha's husband, but Bertha finds her husband sexually desirable for the first time by virtue of the bliss of her own infatuation with Pearl. Thus, Oedipal triangles in childhood are also suggested. Further, critical consideration could also include Mansfield's relationship with her brother and others, her own barrenness and her complicated sexual history. However, these could all be brought to bear on the pear-tree image without being thoroughly or finally fruitful.

The aloe in 'Prelude' (as formerly in *The Aloe*), like the pear tree in 'Bliss', stands at the centre of the story, and just as enigmatically but unlike the pear-tree in 'Bliss', the aloe is seen and described from several perspectives. The child, Kezia, sees it from her small-child perspective as she explores the garden ('red-hot pokers were taller than she; the japanese sunflowers grew in a tiny jungle') of the family's new home:

> [...] she came to that island that lay in the middle of the drive [...] The island was made of grass banked up high. Nothing grew on the top except one huge plant with thick, grey-green, thorny leaves, and out of the middle there sprang up a tall stout stem. Some of the leaves of the plant were so old that they curled up in the air no longer; they turned back, they were split and broken; some of them lay flat and withered on the ground.

---

93   Ibid., p. 91.

94   G. Hanscombe, 'Katherine Mansfield's Pear Tree', *What Lesbians do in Texts*, eds E. Hobby and C. White (London: The Women's Press, 1991), p. 113.

95   Ibid., pp 128-9.

Whatever could it be? She had never seen anything like it before. She stood and stared. And then she saw her mother coming down the path.

'Mother, what is it?" asked Kezia.

Linda looked up at the fat swelling plant with its cruel leaves and fleshy stem. High above them, as though becalmed in the air, and yet holding so fast to the earth it grew from, it might have had claws instead of roots. The curving leaves seemed to be hiding something; the blind stem cut into the air as if no wind could ever shake it.

'That is an aloe, Kezia', said her mother.

'Does it ever have any flowers?'

'Yes, Kezia,' and Linda smiled down at her, and half shut her eyes. 'Once every hundred years'.[96]

The aloe is primal and mysterious, more totemic than a plant of decoration or even of utility. It is the females of the Burrell family who notice and acknowledge together its strange, under-cultivated beauty and power. 'Prelude' is comprised of twelve sections; Kezia's view of the aloe and the moment shared with her mother takes place in section VI. In section XI, Linda and her mother, in yet another female communion before a significant plant, stand on the verandah looking out at the aloe in the 'dazzling light' of the moon, which has revealed what look like flower buds. In this passage, the consciousness represented is primarily Linda's and the metaphors presented in the third-person narration are those to which Linda's imagination has given rise:

As they stood on the steps, the high grassy bank on which the aloe rested rose up like a wave, and the aloe seemed to ride upon it like a ship with the oars lifted. Bright moonlight hung upon the lifted oars like water, and on the green wave glittered the dew.

'Do you feel it, too,' said Linda, and she spoke to her mother with the special voice that women use at night to each other as though they spoke in their sleep or from some hollow cave – 'Don't you feel that it is coming towards us?'

She dreamed that she was caught up out of the cold water into the ship with the lifted oars and the budding mast. Now the oars fell, striking quickly, quickly. They rowed far away over the top of the garden trees. the paddocks and the dark bush beyond. Ah, she heard herself cry: 'Faster! Faster!' to those who were rowing.[97]

As Linda and her mother approach the aloe, her fantasy of escape, protection and solitude continues:

Looking at it from below she could see the long sharp thorns that edged the aloe leaves, and at the sight of them her heart grew hard ... She particularly liked the long sharp thorns ... Nobody would dare to come near the ship or to follow after.

'Not even my Newfoundland dog,' thought she, 'that I'm so fond of in the daytime.'[98]

---

96   *CS*, op. cit., pp. 33-4.

97   Ibid., pp. 52-3.

98   Ibid., p. 53.

The 'Newfoundland dog', whose night-time antics so appall her, is her husband Stanley. The seemingly sexualised aspects of oars beating, 'quickly, quickly', evolve into an image of frigidity, 'her heart grew hard' and chastity, 'nobody would dare come near'. Like the pear tree, the aloe is both phallic and flowering, and like the pear tree, it is at once a symbol apart from and identical with the subject who views it and claims its symbolic value. That is to say, the pear tree symbolises Bertha's life in its presumed perfection, but it is clear, too, since Bertha dresses in green and white, that the pear tree represents her. The aloe is the vehicle for escape, the ship with a budding mast, but the aloe also stands for Linda. There is a famous passage, with which all students of Mansfield, or of Modernism, in general, must be familiar, but it is worth citing again in this context for the centrality of the plant imagery and the correlation with selfhood:

> True to oneself! which self? Which of my many – well, really, that's what it looks like coming to – hundreds of selves? For what with complexes and repressions and reactions and vibrations and reflections, there are moments when I feel I am nothing but the clerk of some hotel without a proprietor [...] Nevertheless, there are signs that we are intent as never before on trying to puzzle out, to live by, our own particular self [...] Is it not possible that the rage for confession, autobiography, especially for memories of earliest childhood, is explained by our persistent yet mysterious belief in a self which is continuous and permanent; which, untouched by all we acquire and all we shed, pushed a green spear through the dead leaves and through the mould, thrusts a scaled bud through years of darkness until, one day, the light discovers it and shakes the flower free and – we are alive – we are flowering for our moment upon earth? This is the moment which, after all, we live for – the moment of direct feeling when we are most ourselves and least personal.[99]

Of course, Bertha's or Linda's epiphanic projections of the integrity of their flowering beings onto emblematic plants are necessarily flawed and unable to be sustained. (Mansfield also writes in 1919 to her friend, Ottoline Morrell: 'Why are human beings the only ones who do not put forth fresh buds – exquisite flowers and leaves?') The symbolic stature of these plants both represents and hides the full range of the determinants of meaning, including those determinants which are unavailable to the individual subject's conscious mind and memory. Mansfield's representation must include the levels of the representable and unrepresentable; as her story 'Psychology' makes clear, there is the social 'conscious', the hidden 'conscious' (of 'secret selves'), and the repressed unconscious. It is Mansfield's task to indicate psychological complexities, and for the reader, like the psychoanalyst, to attend to the given and the ungiven. The symbolic plants, 'standing in the middle', are thus, in anticipation of a Freudian framework, standing between the super-ego and the id.[100]

---

99 C.K. Stead, ed., op. cit., p. 173.

100 Freud's revised account of the mind's structure according to the tri-partite model of the super-ego, ego and id was published in *The Ego and the Id* in 1923. Editor of the Pelican Freud Library, James Strachey, explains: 'Quite late in his life, indeed, influenced by the ambiguity of the term "unconscious" and its many conflicting uses, he proposed a new structural account of the mind in which the uncoordinated instinctual trends were called

Standing in the place of ego, they represent the individual's complex negotiations between societal requirements and unconscious instincts and repressions.

Mansfield's overriding interest in memory (and desire) is certainly informed by Freud's early work on psychoanalysis. Particularly relevant are Freud's *The Interpretation of Dreams*, the English translation of which appeared in 1913, and *The Psychopathology of Everyday Life*, translated into English in 1914 and, incidentally, reviewed by Leonard Woolf the same year.[101] After reading both, in preparation for this review,[102] Leonard Woolf wrote:

> It is [Freud's] aim to show that it is the 'dark half' of the mind which in the perfectly normal waking man produces all kinds of trivial errors and slips and forgettings and rememberings, and which under other conditions will, following the same laws, produce the absurd fantasies of sleep or the terrible fantasies of madness.[103]

Indeed, the Woolfs' Hogarth Press later published Freud, 'instigated by Leonard's decision in the early 1920s to publish translations of the International Psychoanalytical Library Series founded by Ernest Jones',[104] although Virginia Woolf does not appear to have read the primary texts herself until the 1930s.[105] It is just as difficult to be certain of the extent of Mansfield's specific engagement with psychoanalysis, but it is nonetheless a pervasive aspect in the journalism, literature and discussion of the period. Angela Smith's biography discusses at length the influence on Mansfield of the Fauvists, in particular, the artist J. D. Fergusson, himself much influenced by Bergson,[106] and of the writers and artists involved with and contributing to the *avant-garde* arts journals, *New Age* and *Rhythm*.[107] Clare Tomalin describes the typical contents of *New Age*, a magazine founded circa 1908:

> [...] crammed with eugenics, marriage reform, socialism, free love, protests against sweated labour and capital punishment, women's questions from abortion to the vote, psychoanalysis, foreign affairs, philosophy and theatre criticism, together with drawings by Augustus John and Walter Sickert, sometimes candid studies of nudes.[108]

Rhythm, founded in 1911 by John Middleton Murry (later to become Mansfield's lover and husband), J. D. Fergusson and Michael Sadler, was designed 'to cover the French and English avant-garde in literature and art, with forays into other languages,

---

the "id", the organised realistic part the "ego", and the critical and moralising function, the "super-ego" – *On Psychopathology*, Pelican Freud Library (PFL), Vol. 10 (Harmondsworth: Penguin, 1987), p. 23.

101 A. Smith, *Katherine Mansfield: A Literary Life*, op. cit., p. 117.

102 H. Lee, op. cit., p. 197.

103 Ibid.

104 Ibid. p. 372.

105 Ibid. p. 191.

106 A. Smith, Katherine Mansfield: A Literary Life, op. cit., pp. 69ff.

107 Ibid., pp. 57-96.

108 C. Tomalin, p. 48.

and to sell as far afield as Munich, New York and Glasgow.[109] Mansfield, as an 'inner circle' contributor to both *New Age* and *Rhythm*, and a friend of the Woolfs, D. H. and Frieda Lawrence, and the American painter, Anne Estelle Rice, was surely, as Angela Smith acknowledges, 'aware of Freudian theory before the war'[110] despite the difficulty of pin-pointing her explicit engagement with it.

There are many instances in Mansfield's stories which are suggestive of the processes outlined in *The Interpretation of Dreams* and *The Psychopathology of Everyday Life*. *The Psychopathology of Everday Life*, with its attention to the complex psychological causes alongside 'everday life' manifestations of slips of the tongue and pen, forgetting, misreading and other parapraxes, has much of relevance. It is, however, the chapter 'Childhood Memories and Screen Memories' which is most pertinent to Mansfield's preoccupations with both childhood and memory, and most revealing in relation to her method of representing these. Freud explained:

> The indifferent memories of childhood owe their existence to a process of displacement: they are substitutes, in [mnemic] reproduction, for other impressions which are really significant. The memory of these significant impressions can be developed out of indifferent ones by means of psychical analysis, but a resistance prevents them from being directly reproduced. As the indifferent memories owe their preservation not to their own content but to an associative relation between their content and another which is repressed, they have some claim to be called 'screen memories' [...] One is thus forced by various considerations to suspect that in the so-called earliest childhood memories we possess not the genuine memory trace but a later revision of it, a revision which may have been subjected to the influences of a variety of later psychical forces.[111]

Further clarification of the Freudian concept of Screen Memories is provided by J. Laplanche and J. B. Pontalis, who explain why something as apparently innocuous, benign or straightforward as a flower or garden is the veiling intermediary 'between repressed elements and defence':

> A childhood memory characterised both by its unusual sharpness and by the apparent insignificance of its content. The analysis of such memories leads back to indelible childhood experiences and to unconscious phantasies. Like the symptom, the screen memory is a formation produced by a compromise between repressed elements and defence.[112]

This helps to reveal the ways in which, according to Freudian theories of memory, dream and displacement, mundane but vivid images function in genesis and effect. The full story of Bertha's sexuality, Linda's relations with her father, or even of Mansfield's with her brother, is material which is condensed and displaced onto

---

109 Ibid., pp. 98-9.

110 A. Smith, *Katherine Mansfield: A Literary Life*, op. cit., p. 117.

111 S. Freud, Vol. 5,. *PFL*, pp. 83, 88.

112 J. Laplanche and J. B. Pontalis, *The Language of Psychoanalysis* (London: Karnac, 1988 [1973]), pp. 410-11.

token plants. In her stories, Mansfield represents (and screens) her own childhood; in these she imagines and represents this process for a variety of characters. 'That is the satisfaction of writing – one can impersonate so many people',[113] wrote Mansfield, and in the impersonation of people, all their complex psychology can also be represented by deploying Freudian theories of the 'everyday'. Thus, the daisies in Linda's dream of her father, or the pear tree in 'Bliss', are the vernacular symbols laden with psycho-sexual meanings which the reader can only guess at and which the characters, at any rate, would never consciously recall. Approaching the aloe in the moonlight, Linda says to her mother: 'I like that aloe. I like it more than anything here. And I am sure I shall remember it long after I've forgotten all the other things.' This is the significance of Mansfield's garden plants; they constitute a memorial to memory, including all the forgotten, the repressed and the unrealised dreams and desires.

Elizabeth Bowen: History

Elizabeth Bowen's short story, 'Summer Night', written in 1941 and first published in her collection of that year, *Look at All Those Roses*, is set in Ireland in the early years of the Second World War. It incorporates, within its various garden topographies, codes for the complex history and contemporary backdrop of Irish politics. A member of the Protestant Anglo-Irish ascendancy, with a large family home in County Cork, Bowen's Court, Elizabeth Bowen was thoughtful (and often ambivalent) about her allegiances in the turbulent affairs of British and Irish politics. Born in 1899, her early childhood was spent in Dublin and at Bowen's Court. She

113 Cited in A. Smith, p. 46.

moved with her mother to England in 1907, where she continued her schooling and married, settling eventually in Oxfordshire. However, she maintained a vital connection with her ancestral home, visiting Bowen's Court throughout most of her life, inheriting it in 1930, often inviting friends to stay, and devoting a book, in 1942, to its history. Nevertheless, she was as at home in and familiar with Kent, London and Oxfordshire as she was with Ireland, and she believed she was able to see, and thus to represent, 'both sides', a facility she extended in her writing. In terms of her writing mode, she was equally non-partisan: 'Elizabeth Bowen came in on the tail-end of Bloomsbury, of which she'd been conscious throughout the twenties, but she was never interested in allying herself exclusively with any group, either social or literary'.[114] She was, however, somewhat defensive on behalf of her own Anglo-Irish heritage and class: 'she thought that, however dubiously her ancestors and others had obtained their Irish holdings, they'd sufficiently enriched the life of the country to mitigate the initial injustice'.[115] Her allegiance to the British war-effort was unequivocal, as was made clear by her approach to the Ministry of Information in 1939, with a proposal that she compile a series of 'undercover reports' on the 'mood of the Irish, with regard to the war, also touching on more specific issues',[116] but she also thought of herself as Irish enough to act as an intermediary, for instance, on the issue of Ireland's neutrality and refusal to allow Britain to requisition Irish ports. As her critical biographer, Patricia Craig, summarises, Bowen felt herself to be in a position to discuss both sides in relation to that issue, as to so many others:

> 'The childishness and obtuseness of this country [Ireland] cannot fail to be irritating to the English mind,' Elizabeth announced in one of her undercover reports to Lord Cranborne at the Ministry of Information. The enormity of the current situation, she felt, ought to have prompted the Irish nation to jettison its long-standing grievances; however, 'there seems ... only one basis on which Eire would consider treating for the ports. That is, on some suggestion from the British side that the Partition question was at least likely to be reconsidered ...' Support for Britain, and sympathy for the British cause was a fluctuating ethic in neutral Ireland: one minute in the ascendant, the next on the wane. It was apt to evaporate at any suggestion that Britain might try to requisition the ports. Eire, Elizabeth said, had invested its self-respect in its neutrality. The republic was making a stand, and meant to stick to it. It was also unwilling to expose itself to the threat of German bombing. Elizabeth didn't have very much sympathy with this attitude, which smacked to her of the unheroic; but neither did she admit the charge of 'disloyalty' when it was levelled against the Irish: 'given the plain facts of history', she says, the word simply isn't applicable. 'I could wish that the English kept history in mind more, that the Irish kept it in mind less'.[117]

Power, land and its produce have been key elements in precisely this history, which the English were prone to forget, and the Irish never could. Gardens and plants have

---

114 Patricia Craig, *Elizabeth Bowen* (Harmondsworth: Penguin, 1986), p. 62.

115 Ibid., p. 51.

116 Ibid., p. 96.

117 Ibid., p. 97.

a very particular resonance in Ireland's past. After centuries of conflict and troubles, a defining nadir was that of the Great Famine, of which this is Elizabeth Bowen's own description:

> The Great Famine reached is height in 1847: that is the date given it, but actually it lasted for great portions of four years – '46, '47, '48, '49. It had been seen coming: in the autumn of '45 a potato blight spread all over the north of Europe; its effects in Ireland, where three-fourths of the people were wholly dependent for subsistence on the potato crop, were at once to be dreaded. Great efforts [...] were made to stop the export of Irish wheat. But these failed: food that could have fed the people continued 'in the interests of commerce,' to be shipped abroad. Had the grain and meat stayed in the country, it may be said that the people had not the money to pay for it; agricultural wages, over the south of Ireland, averaged eightpence a day. And thousands were not in work at all [...] Party strife and the untouchability of ruling interests in Ireland had, together, made 'measures' planless and incomplete [...] In 1846, in Ireland, no potatoes were saved [...] By 1847 the horror had reached its height. The people tried to eat the diseased potatoes and a bowel fever followed starvation's work. Two millions died; of those who fled to America, thousands died, thousands died at the ports, or died in the coffin-ships.[118]

The Great Famine, generated by the repeated failure of the subsistence potato crops, thus resulted in the radical depletion of the rural, largely indigenous, Irish population by starvation, eviction, displacement to the workhouses or emigration, particularly to America. The great houses of the Anglo-Irish, then, with their history of land appropriation and their walled demesnes ('English people ... say "park" where we say "demesne"'[119]) are in stark juxtaposition to the victims of the Great Famine, with its communal famine burial pits, mass homelessness, poverty and disease.

Bowen's Court begins by describing in detail the location and then the features of this ancestral home; it is an account both particular and general:

> Gentlemen's houses round here are all a little alike. Some stone, some plastered and painted, they stand in crescents, or broken crescents, of trees, their front steps rising from gravel sweeps. Where possible, they face south. Few are modern, still fewer are very old; most of them were built throughout the eighteenth or in the early nineteenth century. Few demesnes are quite flat, so that the lawns round houses run either up or down. Ornamental planting of trees makes a pleasant pattern; the demesnes are outlined by 'screens' (or narrow ribbons of wood). The walled gardens are often some way away; sun and shelter are always objects in this country [...] Handsome stables are seldom quite out of view; the home farm buildings are generally planted out. Rich soil, clement softness and Anglo-Irish genius in this direction have produced some great gardens [...] Each of these family homes, with its stable and farm and gardens deep in trees at the end of long avenues, is an island – and, like an island, a world.[120]

---

118 E. Bowen, *Bowen's Court and Seven Winters* (London: Vintage, 1999 [1942]), p. 309.

119 Ibid., p. 21.

120 Ibid., pp. 18-19

Nuala O'Faolain, in a recent, fictionalised account which remembers the Famine and incorporates official source material verbatim, also catalogues the aspects of just such 'a moderate sized' Anglo-Irish estate :

> – of largely boggy and hilly land – perhaps 80,000 acres would typically consist of a 25-30-room mansion, a village at the gates and dependent houses and cottages in the vicinity in considerable number. The following features of a comparable estate would have been present within the demesne itself:
>
> Walled gardens and orchards, lawns and gatehouses and at least one fishpond, a kennels, a deer park, a bull-paddock, a piggery, a harness-room, a vegetable garden, calf sheds, various stables, including one for hunters, duckponds, lofts for the storage of grain, etc., beehives, a heated brick wall behind green houses for the cultivation of exotic fruits such as peaches, and flowers such as camellias for the house. A fernery. An inner walled garden for vegetables and soft fruit [...] A dairy. A varying but very large number of pedigree cattle and sheep. Breeding sows and their bonhams. A lumber mill and one or two cornmills. A mock hermitage or ruined castle. An icehouse. Staff comprising at the least, cooks, housemaids, kitchenmaids, parlourmaids, gardeners, stewards, yardmen, farmhands.[121]

The contrast between settler opulence, with their 'island' mentality, and the impoverished plight of the rural Irish indigent is but a single example – and symbol, perhaps – of this country's wrongs. As Bowen's own summary of the Great Famine mildly suggests, and many others have stressed more vehemently, the English did not intervene (adequately) to avert the disaster for the Irish (and this is central, of course, to the resistance to the 1939 war-time request from the English that the Irish now act to intervene on Britain's behalf). Such apparent passivity was frequently combined, however, with a more active spate of evictions and dispossessions by some Anglo-Irish landowners, many of them absentee. Ensuing hatred and resentment resulted in concerted attacks and counter-attacks between republican guerillas and British forces, particularly virulent in 1919. Ancestral homes, such as Bowen's Court, were frequently the targets for destruction. The ruined castle, and its now overgrown demesne in 'Summer Night', is likely to have been a casualty of one of these skirmishes. It is these aspects of landscape, landownership and history that are crucial to an understanding of Bowen's story with its otherwise benign references to gardens, orchards and derelict demesnes.

'Summer Night' opens with a lyrical description of a landscape at sunset, otherwordly and transcendent, an incandescent *tabula rasa*:

> As the sun set its light slowly melted the landscape, till everything was made of fire and glass [...] In the not far distant hills with woods up their flanks lay in light like hills in another world – it would be a pleasure of heaven to stand up there, where no foot ever

---

121 Nuala O'Faolain, *My Dream of You* (Harmondsworth: Penguin, 2001), p. 87.

seemed to have trodden, on the spaces between the woods soft as powder dusted over with gold.[122]

What follows is immediately bathetic, realistic and tangible, with a specific locus, inevitably suggesting a history at odds with the immaculate glow of the opening: 'Against those hills, the burning red rambler roses in cottage gardens along the roadside looked earthly – they were too near the eye. The road was in Ireland' (p. 61). To look immediately at the ending is to find another telling reference to time, landscape and, indeed, to the resilience of the myth and fantasy of pleasure in gardens so at odds with historical eventuality. The story concludes with an image of 'the rusted gates of the castle', ruined and its demesne overgrown – although, we are told earlier, it remains a place to be frequented by furtive lovers. Queenie, the deaf, middle-aged and whimsical sister in the story, finds herself stimulated to recall a time, twenty years previous, when she had herself visited with a lover, the 'then fresh aghast ruin'. This, then, is one of the Anglo-Irish great houses, ruined in the spate of attacks in the name of republicanism, occurrences which were particularly severe in 1919 and 1921, and to which Bowen's Court was vulnerable. Bowen's Court, however, withstood what many of its neighbours did not, as Bowen records:

Meanwhile, in Dublin and in the country, Ireland's bitter struggle for Ireland entered on a new phase. Between the armed Irish and the British troops in the country, reprisal and counter-reprisals – tragic policy – raged. Fire followed shootings, then fires fires. In the same spring night in 1921, three Anglos-Irish houses in our immediate neighbourhood – Rockmills, Ballywater. Convamore – were burnt by the Irish. The British riposted by burning, still nearer Bowen's Court, the farms of putative Sinn Feiners – some of whom had been our family's friends.[123]

This period is also the setting and subject matter of Bowen's 1925 novel, *The Last September*, with its Bowen's-Court-like household in these times of trouble. However, without the specific reference in 'Summer Night' to the cause of ruination, 'they burnt down the castle', its ruins might otherwise have been supposed to be one of those earlier, whimsical accoutrements to the demesnes: the picturesque ruin, cherished for its Romantic sublimity, which Bowen also discusses:

I know few demesnes, however, that do not contain *some* ruin – chapel, watch tower or massive keep. Set on lawns, these frowning derelict 'castles' overtop the facades of Georgian homes. Strictly, they are antiques rather than ruins; their structures and stairs are sound; to them have often been added leaded roofs from which one looks at the view [...] Sometimes the castles stand some way from the houses, in which case they [...] make romantic objectives for strolls ....[124]

---

122 Elizabeth Bowen, *Elizabeth Bowen's Irish Stories* (Dublin: Poolbeg Press, 1978), p. 61.

123 E. Bowen, *Bowen's Court*, op. cit. p. 439.

124 Ibid., p. 17.

As Bowen goes on to explain, wealthier, eighteenth-century English landowners, for instance, could afford to build the requisite atmospheric and aesthetic 'expensive fancies – perspectives, obelisks, grottos, constructed waterfalls, temples' that the 'settlers' in Ireland could not: 'We planted trees effectively, but beyond that have had to rely on nature and on antiquity [...] and the monuments of greater Ireland stand in place of the follies we did not need to build'.[125] It is in *Bowen's Court* that she explains the over-determination of 'ruin' in Ireland: 'this is a country of ruins [...] some ruins show gashes of violence, others simply the dull slant of decline'[126], adding: 'only major or recent ruins keep their human stories; from others the story quickly evaporates.'[127] However, writing both 'Summer Night' and *Bowen's Court* in the early years of another European World War, there is an added sense of impending, and potentially, major, ruination.

Living alone in her dead father's house, Queenie's reverie of love among the ruins seems immaturely romantic and anachronistic on a number of fronts. The war which is such a preoccupation of others seems not to affect her, and as she substitutes a surrogate fantasy of love with the barely known Robinson for the brief and singular romantic moment of her youth, she is depicted as a girlish dreamer where the signifiers of love's young dream are: 'heart-shaped', summer night, secret, out-of-this-world ('under a film of time'):

> Contemplative, wishless, almost without an 'I', she unhooked her muslin dress at the wrists and waist, stepped from the dress and began to take down her hair. Still in the dark, with a dreaming sureness of habit, she dropped hairpins into the heart-shaped tray. This was the night she knew she would find again. It had stayed living under a film of time. On just such a summer, once only, she had walked with a lover in the demesne [...] They had gone down walks already deadened with moss, under the weight of July trees; they had felt the then fresh aghast ruin totter above them; there was a moonless sky. (pp. 93-4)

Critics have noted that the *bois dormant*, the fairy-tale-like sleepers' wood, once actually a feature of the demesne, is a recurring Bowen image.[128] This dream, however, has overtones of nightmare and horror; there is something profoundly elegiac in these images, further reinforced by the final description of the recumbent, dreaming woman who is reminiscent of the statues of royals adorning a tomb. This is a parodic 'Sleeping Beauty' invoking Yeats's refrain: 'Romantic Ireland's dead and gone'. Queenie's name, royal but childish and diminutive, takes on a particular significance. Whether representative of the royal lineage of the usurper settler British or of the romantic Queens of Gaelic Ireland, Queenie's anachronistic dreaming trespasses – unrealistic and politically unwitting – in a foreign domain. It is worth noting that Queenie's dream-state, described as 'almost without an 'I', is indicative of Ireland, linguistically losing its own 'I'; Ireland too is 'almost without

---

125 Ibid., p. 18.
126 Ibid., p. 15.
127 Ibid.
128 P. Craig, op. cit., p. 48.

an I' in its recent incarnation as a new, albeit transitional, republic, Eire, from 1937-49. Queenie is visited by her awkward, nervy, and effete brother, Justin, the 'neutral Irishman' who 'disliked the chaotic scenery of his own land'. (Here it is interesting to refer to the sentiments expressed in Bowen's Ministry of Information report and her own views on Irish neutrality.) Justin is in Ireland this summer because the war has interrupted his usual holiday excursions to France, Germany or Italy. He is linked to his sister in this story, not simply as a blood relation, but by virtue of immaturity. While Queenie's is manifest in inappropriate romantic dreams, Justin's is revealed in his unresolved oedipal anxieties, his petulant, even tearful outbursts, all triggered by an overweening sensitivity and avowed unfamiliarity with love. His incongruous theorising on 'new forms', to stalwart, commercial, ego-driven Robinson, brings him to a point of I-lessness, too, which, on the one hand, appears more familiar as a modernist aesthetic, perhaps, than a representation of the politics of war-time Ireland:

> 'Now that there's enough death to challenge being alive we're facing it that, anyhow, we don't live. We're confronted by the impossibility *of* living – unless we can break through to something else. There's been a stop in our senses and in our faculties that's made everything around us so much dead matter – and dead matter we couldn't even displace. We can no longer express ourselves: what we say doesn't even approximate to reality; it only approximates to what's been said. I say, this war's an awful illumination; it's destroyed our dark; we have to see where we are. Immobilised, God help us, and each so far apart that we can't even try to signal each other. And our currency's worthless – our 'ideas', so on, so on. We've got to mint a new one. We've got to break through to the new from […] On the far side of nothing – my new form. Scrap 'me'; scrap my wretched identity and you'll bring to the open some bud of life. I not 'I' – I'd be the world ... You're right: what you would call thinking does get me rattled [...] Take myself away, and I'd think. I might see; I might feel purely; I might even love –' (pp. 70-71)

Queenie and Justin are the offspring of contemporary Ireland, land-less and sense-less, the one fantasising tales of love in by-gone ruins, and the other, an urban-living bachelor, a 'neutral' cosmopolitan wanderer in Europe. There is a sterility in their existence, a cul-de-sac mode of being epitomised by Queenie's inward-looking small-town square and Justin's 'monkish life in the city'.

This lack of vitality finds a compensatory depiction in the child, Vivvie. She and her sister, Di, are the daughters of the Major and his wife, Emma, who dwell, with the Major's elderly Aunt Fran in an 'obscure country house' with adjacent orchards. For all its connotations of order and middle-class stability – the father's rank, the established orchards, the chintz drawing-room with its piano and harp, a governess – these aspects are soon to be qualified: 'this was not a good apple year'; the Major is 'an unmilitary-looking man' with a stoop; the harp has two broken strings; and Emma is, as a focal aspect of the story, driving to an adulterous rendezvous to spend one night with Robinson at his 'uphill house' in the small town sixty miles from her home.

Vivvie, however, is as lively and as vivid as her name suggests. Having been put to bed, her sister drops immediately asleep (not for nothing is she called Di) but Vivvie lies alert, imagining, listening, turning:

> One arbitrary line only divided this child from the animal: all her senses stood up, wanting to run the night [...] She got right up and stepped out of her nightdress and set out to walk the house in her skin [...] She returned to the schoolroom, drawing her brows together, and straddled the rocking-horse they had not ridden for years. The furious bumping of the rockers woke the canaries [...] She dismounted, got out the box of chalks and began to tattoo her chest, belly and thighs with stars and snakes, red, yellow and blue. Then, taking the box of chalks with her, she went to her mother's room for a look in the long glass – in front of this she attempted to tattoo her behind [...] The anarchy she felt all through the house tonight made her, when she had danced in front of the long glass, climb up to dance on the big bed [...] chalk dust flew from her body [...] Vivvie paused on the bed, transfixed, breathless, her legs apart. Her heart thumped, her ears drummed; her cheeks burned. To break up the canny and comprehensive silence she said loudly: 'I am all over snakes'. (pp. 78-80)

For Aunt Fran, who discovers Vivvie thus, 'There are no more children: the children are born knowing'. Shadow, evil, 'the infected zone'; Aunt Fran laments the war, Ireland's troubles, her own shortcomings, her sense of Emma's transgression, her alienation from the primal vigour of her great-niece. Here in Ireland, where no snakes dwell, a paradoxically serpentless Eden, the stars and snakes on the 'knowing' child's body (and her orchard-locus) have a complex significance. Innocent rather than corrupt, primal rather than evil, lively rather than confined, alert and vigorous rather than self-conscious; the portrait of Vivvie is a hopeful one. There is the lack of heart, 'the stranger in her ribs', in her Aunt Fran, the lack of fidelity in her mother, the lack of meaningful connection in the coupling of 'the maid lumped mute in a man's arms' or in Emma's affair with the 'efficient' Robinson – and there is the war. But Vivvie is full of life; with her dancing body painted with stars and snakes, she is her own garden and potential. Interestingly, it is the daughter of the successful, modern, masculine Robinson whose daughter is without life: 'the third child, the girl, was dead.'

Robinson, the factory owner ('he worked at very high pressure in his factory office, and in his off times his high powered car was to be seen streaking too gaily out of the town'), has a house and garden with its own connotations. He lives alone and separate from his wife in an 'uphill house' which, significantly, overlooks, across the road, the woods of the ruined castle and its demesne. Queenie calls this 'the china house' because it looked 'like china up on a mantlepiece – it was a compact, stucco house with mouldings, recently painted a light blue'. With its glass porch and, again, significantly, empty conservatory it has an 'almost sensuous cleanness [...] reproduced in the person of Robinson'. This parvenu house has a parvenu name: Bellevue. Its kitchen 'shone with tiling and chromium and there seemed to be switches in every place'. Its manicured lawn, maintained with the help of a 'motor mower', is 'set with pampas and crescent shaped flower beds'. Like his house and garden, Robinson is practical, efficient and thoroughly up-to-date – as are his relationships. Nervous and compromised, Emma realises that Robinson's view of desire or romance is as practical and conformist as all the other features of his existence. Once again, there is the reference to the derelict demesne as a haunt for lovers – but atmospheric ruins are not part of Robinson's experience or aesthetic. While Queenie dreams of Robinson as her companion in the ruined demesne, Emma abandons any such 'fairy tale'; she grows up and she wakes up. The prosaic, prototypical and derivative suburban garden – and all it represents in her lover and bodes for her love affair – brings her to a dark but liminal reality:

> Her shyness of further words between them became extreme; she was becoming frightened of Robinson's stern, experienced delicacy on the subject of love. Her adventure became the quiet practice with him. The adventure (even, the pilgrimage) died at its root, in the childish part of her mind. When he had headed her off the cytherean train – the leaf-drowned castle ruin, the lake – she thought for a minute he had broken her heart, and she knew now he had broken her fairytale. He seemed content – having lit a new cigarette – to wait about in his garden for a few minutes longer: not poetry but a sort of tactile wisdom came from the firmness, lawn, under their feet. [...] There was no moon, but dry, tense, translucent darkness: no dew fell. (p. 90)

The description of the incandescent, other-worldly sunset scene which opened the story, and momentarily belied complex historical determinants and scars, has changed here, at nightfall, to a darker and more realistic blank screen. The 'dry, tense, translucent darkness', devoid of romantic moonlight and dew, is the wide-awake, dreamless, grown-up view of the setting for the next installment in Ireland's history and upon its landscape.

Bowen, in a letter to Virginia Woolf, with whom she became acquainted in the 1930s, wrote: 'Places are so exciting, the only proper experiences one has. I believe I may only write novels for the pleasure of saying where people are'.[129] Later, in the posthumously published *Pictures and Conversations*, she asks: 'Am I not manifestly a writer for whom places loom large?' In 'Summer Night', the place, obviously and specifically, is Ireland. Set during the Second World War and written before its resolution, the story posits aspects of Ireland's past, present and potential. In most respects, and in contrast to Mansfield's, for instance, here Bowen's characters are primarily typological, rather than psychological, and are typical of the varied inheritors of a particular place and its historical legacy. Reviewing *The Collected Stories of Elizabeth Bowen* in 1981, eight years after Bowen's death, Eudora Welty wrote: 'Of all the stories it is "Summer Night" that I return to';[130] she commends Bowen's imagination, her 'highly conscious' artistry, and her profound awareness of place and time: 'of *where she was* [...] equalled only by her close touch by the passage, the pulse, of time' (adding 'there was a clock in every story and novel

---

129 Cited in Ibid., p. 72.
130 E. Welty, *A Writer's Eye: Collected Book Reviews*, P. A. McHaney, ed. (Jackson: University of Mississippi Press, 1994), p. 235.

she ever wrote').[131] Although Welty does not mention it, it is surely Bowen's use of landscape and of gardens (orchard, demesne or suburban plot) which is so instrumental in the exploration of 'private energies' in a particular 'part of the world in wartime', all informed by the specificities of the past.

Eudora Welty: Myth

Eudora Welty is another writer whose work is dedicated to the importance of place; in her case, the location is Mississippi. She was a visitor at Bowen's Court on several occasions, introducing herself to Elizabeth Bowen on a trip to Dublin in 1949. Bowen, who was already an admirer of her work, wrote of Welty's first visit in a letter to a friend:

> You know my passion for her works. She had apparently drifted over to Dublin on her own […] and I asked her to come down and stay … I take to her immensely [...] A Southern girl from the State of Mississippi; quiet, self-contained, easy, outwardly old-fashioned, very funny indeed when she starts talking ... She's reserved [...] so although we have chatted away a good deal, I really know little about her life, nor she about mine. I think she's like me in preferring places to people, and any unexpected sight or view while we are driving about the country makes her start up in the car with a smothered cry as though she had been stung by a wasp ... [...] I think she's a genius rather than an interesting woman, which I am glad of as I prefer the former.[132]

Eudora Welty was born in 1909 in Jackson, Mississippi and lived there, in her father's house, for most of her long life. She died in 2001 at the age of ninety-two, having received myriad awards and honours including the Pulitzer Prize, the American Book Award for Fiction and the Gold Medal for the novel. With a few early exceptions, all Welty's writing takes place in the South and is about its traditions and inhabitants: 'We in the South have grown up being narrators. We have lived in a

---

131 Ibid., p. 232.

132 Elizabeth Bowen to Charles Ritchie cited in Elizabeth Evans, *Eudora Welty* (New York: Frederick Ungar, 1981), pp. 4-5 and in V. Glendinning, *Elizabeth Bowen: Portrait of a Writer*, op. cit., pp. 209-10.

place – that's the word. Place – where storytelling is a way of life.'[133] Although Welty situates herself firmly in a Southern tradition, she was also influenced by her wide reading of classical and contemporary writing. One of the most startling authors she encountered was Virginia Woolf, whom she described in the following terms:

> She was the one who opened the door. When I read *To the Lighthouse*, I felt, Heavens, *what is this?* I was so excited by the experience I couldn't sleep or eat [...] That beautiful mind! That was the thing. Lucid, passionate, acute, proudly and incessantly nourished, eccentric for honorable reasons, sensitive for every reason, it has marked us forever.[134]

A deeply private person, as Elizabeth Bowen was to perceive, Welty did nevertheless write an autobiographical piece, *One Writer's Beginnings*. It was first published in 1984, and comprised three lectures that had been delivered at Harvard University in April, 1983. The title of each lecture marks what she sees as significant aspects of her development as a writer: 'Listening', 'Learning to See' and 'Finding a Voice'. In these lectures, Welty discusses her childhood and young adulthood, and recollects her parents and grandparents, memories of her education and her early, tentative commitment as a writer. She studied for a BA degree at the University of Wisconsin and then, 'to prepare for a job', went to study advertising in New York City at the Columbia University Graduate School of Business. A year later, in 1931, after the death of her father, she returned to Jackson. For a time, Welty worked on newspapers and for radio but, in 1933 she began to work as a publicity agent for Franklin Roosevelt's Works Progress Administration (WPA) and 'was sent about over eighty-two counties of Mississippi [...] writing the Projects up for the county weeklies'.[135] In *One Writer's Beginnings*, Welty explained how this work, which took her throughout rural Mississippi in the Depression years, ('the Depression, in fact, was not a noticeable phenomenon in the poorest state in the Union'[136]), informed her skills as a writer and a writer of Place:

> My first full-time job was rewarding to me in a way I could never have foreseen in those early days of my writing. [...] Traveling over the whole of Mississippi, writing news stories for country papers, taking pictures, I saw my home state at close hand, really for the first time.
>
> With the accretion of years, the hundreds of photographs – life as I found it, all unposed – constitute a record of that desolate period; but most of what I learned for myself came right at the time and directly out of the taking of the picture. The camera was a hand held auxiliary of wanting-to-know.

---

133 Cited by Candace Waid, 'Eudora Welty', in *Modern American Women Writers: Profiles of Their Lives and Works – from the 1870s to the Present*, eds E. Showalter, L. Beacher and A. Walton Litz (New York: Collier, 1993 [1991]), p. 367.

134 E. Welty, 'Interview with Linda Keuhl' (1972) in *Conversations with Eudora Welty*, ed. P. Whitman Prenshaw (Jackson: University of Mississippi Press, 1984), p. 95.

135 Eudora Welty, 'Preface', *One Time, One Place* (Jackson: University of Mississippi Press, 1996 [1971]) (hereafter *OTOP*), p. 7.

136 Ibid.

It had more than information and accuracy to teach me. I leaned in the doing how <u>ready</u> I had to be. Life doesn't hold still [...] Photography taught me that to be able to capture transience, by being ready to click the shutter at the crucial moment, was the greatest need I had. Making pictures of people in all sorts of situations, I learned that every feeling waits upon its gesture; and I had to be prepared to recognize this moment when I saw it. These were things a story writer needed to know. And I felt the need to hold transient life in <u>words</u> – there's so much more of life that only words can convey [...] The direction my mind took was a writer's direction from the start, not a photographer's, or a recorder's.[137]

Welty finished working for the WPA in 1936, but taking the photographs, which was a project of her own volition, had afforded her invaluable acquaintance with and insight about her fellow Mississippians, many of whom, she would not otherwise have seen:

In snapping these pictures I was acting completely on my own, though I'm afraid it was on their time; they have nothing to do with the WPA. But the WPA gave me the chance to travel, to see widely and at close hand and really for the first time the nature of the place I'd been born into. And it gave me the blessing of showing me the real State of Mississippi, not the abstract state of the Depression.[138]

The year that saw a one-person show of her photographs in New York City coincided with the first publication of her stories, 'Death of a Traveling Salesman' and 'Magic'. In 1941 Welty published her first collection of stories, *A Curtain of Green*. She was developing these first published stories in the years during her WPA work, and certainly the link she herself indicates between her training as a photographer and her development as a writer is manifest in these early stories. The locations are also those of her experience during the period: 'Death of a Traveling Salesman' takes place in 'desolate hill country' with 'people [who] never knew where the very roads they lived on went to,' living in 'a shotgun house, two rooms and an open passage between, perched on the hill [...] slanted a little'. 'A Worn Path' is set 'far out in the country', and the protagonist is 'an old Negro woman with her hair tied in a red rag', carrying 'a thin, small cane made from an umbrella' and wearing 'a dark striped dress reaching down to her shoe tops, and an equally long apron of bleached sugar sacks' and 'unlaced shoes'. These are the subjects and settings recorded in the photographs, and are short stories which, like Welty's snapshots, 'capture transience'.

A Curtain of Green was published with a preface by Katherine Anne Porter, the very well-known Texas writer, also associated with the Southern Renaissance writers. Porter introduced and endorsed this fledgling writer from Mississippi, emphasising not just Welty's Southern, but also her wide-ranging literary, background which included 'the ancient Greek and Roman poetry, history and fable, Shakespeare, Milton, Dante, the eighteenth-century English and the nineteenth-century French

137 Eudora Welty, *One Writer's Beginnings* (London: Faber & Faber, 1985 [1984]) (hereafter *OWB*), pp. 84-5.
138 Eudora Welty, 'Preface', *OTOP*, op. cit., p. 7.

novelists, with a dash of Tolstoy and Dostoievsky'.[139] Also, wrote Porter, Welty was a writer who 'loved folk tales, fairy tales, old legends, and [...] the songs and stories of people who live in old communities whose culture is recollected and bequeathed orally'.[140] In Welty's later work, the inclusion of classical mythology or of fairy tale and legend, albeit continually combined with the local and folkloric, is even more apparent than in this first collection. *The Robber Bridegroom*, published in 1942, a year later than *A Curtain of Green*, alludes to the Grimm story of the same name in a tale of the Deep South in the eighteenth century, whereas the 1949 collection, *The Golden Apples*, which focuses on the fictional town of Morgana, Mississippi, relies on myriad classical allusions, not least in the title's reference to the golden apples of the tales of Perseus and of Atlas, who 'had a tree on which shining leaves of glittering gold covered golden boughs and golden fruit'.[141] *The Golden Bough: A Study in Magic and Religion*, James Frazer's influential work, abridged into one volume in 1922, was a rich source for Welty who read it in the 1930s. Symbolic trees, sacred groves and rites of fertility and sacrifice are features of classical mythology and central to Frazer's study. They are evident in Welty's own fiction, not least in the title story of her 1941 collection, 'A Curtain of Green' with its verdant, suburban glade and its central, albeit fallen, tree. Welty has acknowledged the pervasive, but not formulaic incorporation of mythology in her work, cautioning that 'anyone who attributes my stories to myths very specifically and thoroughly is overshooting it' (she prefers 'to suggest things'),[142] and explaining that myth is as familiar to her as those other aspects that she brings into her fiction: 'I've lived with mythology all my life. It is just as close to me as the landscape. It *naturally* occurs to me when I am writing fiction.'[143]

'A Curtain of Green' is entirely set in a garden with a nemesis tree at the story's core. The garden is located in the American South, in a suburb of the state of Mississippi, in the twentieth century, presumably in a year contemporaneous with its time of writing in the late 1930s. The story is told in the third-person by an omniscient narrator who is able to relate the thoughts and feelings of a number of characters, including the peripheral neighbourhood women who observe, from their own homes only, the garden at the centre of the story. The central figure is a widow, Mrs Larkin. The other main character is the young 'Negro' boy, Jamey, who occasionally helps her in 'the extreme fertility' of her overgrown garden, the object of Mrs Larkin's obsession. Since her husband's death, she has worked daily in this garden, from morning until after dark: 'Since the accident in which her husband was killed, she had never once been seen anywhere else.' Enclosed 'within its border of hedge, high

---

139 Katherine Anne Porter, 'Introduction', Eudora Welty, *A Curtain of Green and Other Stories* (1941) in *The Selected Stories of Eudora Welty* (New York: Random House, 1943), pp. xiv-xix.

140 Ibid., p. xiv.

141 Ovid, *Metapmorphoses*, trans. Mary Innes (Harmondsworth: Penguin, 1955), p. 111.

142 *Conversations*, op. cit., p. 224

143 Ibid.

like a wall', the garden is an exemplary *hortus conclusis*, symbolic of impenetrability and inviolability (conventionally, purity) and seclusion. To her neighbours, who view it from their upstairs windows, the garden is anathema, having neither purpose nor beauty: 'she would never send a flower [...] if she thought of beauty at all [...] she did not strive for it in her garden'. To these onlookers, Mrs Larkin's garden 'had the appearance of a sort of jungle'. It is planted with:

> every kind of flower that she could find or order from a catalogue – planted thickly and hastily, without stopping to think, without any regard for the ideas that her neighbors might elect in their club as to what constituted an appropriate vista, or an effect of restfulness, or even harmony of color.[144]

At the centre of this garden, affording Mrs Larkin shelter if it rains, is a vigorous, leafy pear-tree.

Thus, there is in this jungle, a suggestion of Eden (apple-less and Adam-less, for Jamey in this role would be taboo). Medieval *hortus conclusis*, Eden, jungle; each of these paradigms is both presented and undercut, made ironic. Ironically, it is a Southern, white widow's suburban garden, the 'extreme fertility' of which has rendered it 'a sort of jungle'. Jamey, the other figure in this garden, is 'only the colored boy who worked in the neighborhood by the day', and thus, the trope 'jungle' is used to dramatic effect by introducing the jungles of Africa, a metonymy for the 'dark continent' that was Jamie's ancestors' home and which constitutes his *roots* (roots – or their lack – are very significant in this story). Jungle; colored boy; white woman; American South – all bring us to another garden trope, that of the Southern plantation in the pre-Civil War period of slavery. Of course, there is further irony in that, once the plantations had been dismantled in the post-bellum period known as Reconstruction, the Southern landscape had reverted to its own, inherent jungle-state. In an occasional piece, 'Some Notes on River Country', written in 1944, Welty described this reversion to 'a cloak of vegetation' over Rodney's Landing, Natchez County, a 'small section of old Mississippi River country', now that 'the river has gone away and left the landings' of the slave-trading ports; 'old deeds are done, old evil and old good [...], there are no mansions, no celebrations':[145] Mrs Larkin's garden, then, has reverted to the autochthonous jungle of the American South, released from the order (or disorder) that had been imposed by plantation culture.

The plantation culture of the 'old South' is, in and of itself, the stuff of legend, as one Southern notable historian, W. J. Cash, describes, writing in the same year that 'A Curtain of Green' was published:

> What the Old South of the legend in its classical form was like is more or less familiar to everyone. It was a sort of stage piece out of the eighteenth century, wherein gesturing gentlemen move soft-spokenly against a background of rose gardens and duelling grounds,

---

144 *Selected Stories*, op. cit., pp. 211-12.

145 Eudora Welty, 'Some Notes on River Country', in *The Eye of the Story: Selected Essays and Reviews* (London: Virago, 1987), p. 286.

through always gallant deeds, and lovely ladies, in farthingales, never for a moment lost that exquisite remoteness which has been the dream of all men and the possession of none [...] They dwelt in large and stately mansions, preferably white and with columns and Greek entablature. Their estates were feudal baronies, their slaves quite too numerous ever to be counted, and their social life a thing of Old World splendour and delicacy.[146]

Certainly, vestiges of this legend are incorporated into the short story in unobtrusive but unmistakable ways. Although the setting is suburban rather than mansion and plantation, and while Mrs Larkin's garden, though large, has a house that is small in which she lives alone, the house is repeatedly described as 'white', which, with its front porch, is reminiscent of Southern plantation architecture. Mrs Larkin 'lives alone', but she is not without company; she has a servant, a cook (very likely to be black), who daily 'would call her at dinnertime', and she has, from time to time, the help of Jamey in the garden. In a narrative voice inflected with the views of the neighbouring women and Mrs Larkin alike, Jamey is 'only the colored boy' and thus fails to count as a companion, although he is the only other presence in the garden that Mrs Larkin allows. Mrs Larkin's home is in Larkin's Hill, a town named after her husband's father, revealing him to be prestigious, patriarchal and land-owning. There is no doubt that this story is set in the post-bellum *New* South, about which, Cash continues, yet another legend has been established:

> [...] in the legend of the New South the Old South is supposed to have been destroyed by the Civil War and the thirty years that followed it, to have been swept both socially and mentally into the limbo of things that were and are not, to give place to a society which has been rapidly and increasingly industrialized and modernized both in body and in mind – which now, indeed, save for a few quaint survivals and gentle sentimentalities and a few shocking and inexplicable brutalities such as lynching, is almost as industrialized and modernized in its outlook as the North.[147]

I have found no other evidence to suggest that Eudora Welty knew W. J. Cash's work (although I cannot imagine that she did not, for it was immediately a prominent and controversial book), nor that she purposefully deployed some of his own metaphors and analogies. Nevertheless, they are there, synchronous and apt. For instance, there is the persistence of 'quaint survivals' in Mrs Larkin's demeanour and in Jamey's 'docility', and 'the limbo of things that were and are not' is aptly emblematised in the short story. The weather indicates a sultry, static interregnum before the rain and contributes to Mrs Larkin's frozen moment of violence and swoon into unconsciousness. More strikingly coincidental to the progress and setting of this story, however, is Cash's description of Southern weather and the 'influence of the Southern physical world – itself a sort of cosmic conspiracy against reality in favour of romance':[148]

---

146 W. J. Cash, *The Mind of the South* (Harmondsworth: Penguin, 1973, [1941]), pp. 20-21.

147 Ibid., pp. 21-2.

148 Ibid., p. 66.

The country is one of extravagant color, of proliferating foliage and bloom, of flooding yellow sunlight, and, above all, perhaps, of haze [...] through the long slow afternoon cloudstacks tower from the horizon and the earth-heat quivers upward through the iridescent air, blurring every outline and rendering every object vague and problematical [...] The dominant mood [...] is one [...] of a hush [...] It is a mood, in sum, in which directed thinking is all but impossible [...]

But I must tell you also that the sequel to this mood is invariably a thunderstorm. For days – for weeks, it may be – the land lies in reverie, and then ...

The pattern is profoundly significant – was to enter deeply into the blood and bone of the South – had already entered deeply therein, we may believe, by the time of the coming of the plantation.[149]

In Welty's story, this deeply inherent 'pattern' is precisely dramatised using terms that are strikingly similar to those used by Cash. Mrs Larkin 's trance-like threat of violence to Jamey is averted only by the breaking storm:

There was no wind at all now. The cries of the birds had hushed. The sun seemed clamped to the side of the sky. Everything had stopped once again, the stillness had mesmerized the stems of the plants, and all the leaves went suddenly into thickness. The shadow of the pear tree in the center of the garden lay callous on the ground. Across the yard, Jamey knelt, motionless.

'Jamey!', she called angrily.

But her voice hardly carried in the dense garden.

[...]

In that moment, the rain came. The first drop touched her upraised arm.[150]

However, the interruption by the weather does not bring Mrs Larkin to her senses, but rather, tellingly, renders her into a state of unconsciousness. Violence and tragedy is averted by accident rather than by choice.

In Cash's view, both legends, that of the Old South and of the New, need the modification of reality, but so too does the prevailing exaggeration, circa 1941, concerning 'the extent of the change and of the break between the Old South that was and the South of our time'.[151] In the course of his argument, Cash then uses a botanical analogy for the persistence of the past in the South's present: 'The South, one might say, is a tree with many age rings, with its limbs and trunk bent and twisted by all the winds of the years, but with its tap root in the Old South'.[152] In yet another correlation, a tree, very like the one Cash uses to symbolise the South, has been the cause of Mr Larkin's death and Mrs Larkin's widowhood. As Mrs Larkin gardens compulsively alongside Jamey, she recollects, 'as if a curtain had been jerked unceremoniously away from a little scene', the details of her husband's death by a falling tree:

---

149 Ibid., p. 66-7.
150 *Selected Stories*, op. cit., pp. 214-17.
151 W. J. Cash, op. cit., p. 22.
152 Ibid.

[...] the front porch of the white house, the shady street in front, and the blue automobile in which her husband approached, driving home from work. It was a summer day, a day from the summer before. In the freedom of gaily turning her head [...] she could see [...] the tree that was going to fall. There had been no warning. But there was the enormous tree, the fragrant chinaberry tree, suddenly tilting, dark and slow like a cloud, leaning down to her husband[...] the tree had fallen, had struck the car exactly so as to crush him to death.[153]

Cash's symbolic tree, an unnamed species, has its persistent tap-root inextricably in the 'Old South'; Welty's tree, the Larkins' chinaberry, is, in a significant revision, uprooted. The white male is struck down by an introduced exotic species, the chinaberry tree, leaving his wife and a young black man alone in a garden that is becoming a jungle.

Melia azederachi, the Chinaberry or Chinese bead tree, 'often in early documentation confusingly referred to as a Persian lilac because of its lilac-coloured sweetly fragrant flowers',[154] is a member of the mahogany family. Indigenous to Asia, it is a short-lived, tender exotic, introduced to America by eighteenth-century plant-hunters such as the American-born Quaker, John Bartram, or the Frenchman, André Michaux.[155] George Washington at Mount Vernon and Thomas Jefferson at Monticello incorporated on their respective Virginian plantation estates a wide range of new and tender exotic imports, including the Chinaberry, easily grown as an ornamental tree in the climate of the American South. In Welty's story, the imported exotic and plantation specimen-plant, weakened and ailing, falls and kills Mr Larkin. It is the indigenous and hardy pear tree that remains standing in the centre of Mrs Larkin's garden.

These two trees provide a parodic reference to the two most significant trees standing in the garden of Eden, a tree of life (blighted) and a tree of death. According to the Bible, God planted a garden in Eden and within it he placed 'all kinds of trees [...] trees that were pleasing to the eye and good for food. In the middle of the garden were the tree of life and the tree of knowledge of good and evil',[156] or in Milton's rendition:

---

153 *Selected Stories*, op. cit., pp. 213-14.

154 Penelope Hobhouse, *Plants in Garden History: An Illustrated History of Plants and Their Influence of Garden Styles – from Ancient Egypt to the Present Day* (London: Pavilion Books, 1997 [1992]), p. 148.

155 Ibid., pp. 276-9.

156 Genesis 2:9, *The Holy Bible* (New International Version) (Grand Rapids, MI: Zondervan, 1978), p. 3.

Out of the fertile ground he caused to grow
All trees of noblest kind for sight, smell, taste;
And all amid them stood the Tree of Life,
High eminent, blooming ambrosial fruit

Of vegetable gold; and next to life
Our death, the Tree of Knowledge, grew fast by
Knowledge of good brought dear by knowing ill.[157]

The chinaberry – in Welty's story, correlating to the 'Tree of Knowledge' – consitutes a play on 'the Fall'; the tree itself falls, and it fells the Southern white male. In this parable, transposed to the post-Reconstruction South, the forbidden fruits are those forms and functions bound up with the slave-holding plantation culture of the past. The correlative 'Tree of Life' in Welty's tale is the pear. However, it is described here without flower or promise of any fruit, let alone 'ambrosial fruit'. It has, instead, a dense, protective canopy of foliage, its own thick 'curtain of green', 'which in mid-April hung heavily almost to the ground in brilliant full leaf'. Like the rest of the garden, it seems vigorous and densely verdant, but to no fruitful purpose. Once again, as in Mansfield's story, 'Bliss', it is a central pear-tree that appears to stand for the female protagonist, but if this is, at first glance, a female appropriation and revision of a patriarchal myth, it is simultaneously undercut by the figure of the widow, childless and alone.

There is yet another tree suggested by the South, which pertains to a particularity of time and place that cannot, here, be ignored. Southern trees, in the words of the 1939 song made famous by Billie Holliday, 'bear a strange fruit'.

Southern trees bear a strange fruit,
Blood on the leaves and blood at the root,
Black body swinging in the Southern breeze,
Strange fruit hanging from the poplar trees.

Pastoral scene of the gallant South,
The bulging eyes and the twisted mouth,
Scent of magnolia sweet and fresh,
And the sudden smell of burning flesh!

---

157 John Milton, 'Paradise Lost', Book IV, ll. 216-22, *Poetical Works* (Oxford University Press, 1979), p. 280.

Here is a fruit for the crows to pluck,
For the rain to gather, for the wind to suck
For the sun to rot, for the tree to drop,
Here is a strange and bitter crop.[158]

'Strange Fruit' was written by a white Jewish teacher, Abel Meeropol, and it became a prominent feature in anti-lynching campaigns. The song itself depicts lynching in a grotesque parody of both classical pastoral and various fertility rites centring on human sacrifice and the blood scattering on crops, such as those described by Frazer in *The Golden Bough*. It is worth noting that in terms of recorded lynchings state by state, in the years between 1882 and 1930, Mississippi had the highest number.[159]

That the false premises manifested in slavery and the class-ridden, feudal inequities of England and Europe – which the new Republic was established to abolish – should have taken root in the verdant, agrarian South was often depicted as a Fall in a garden, ravaged with ensuing disgrace. In 'A Curtain of Green', the Edenic aspect is ironic and shocking, particularly in the 1940s, when lynchings were common and the rape of white women by black men was the most frequently attributed cause. Set in a segregated, Jim Crow [160] Mississippi, this story of a lone white woman in a garden (alone – and most vulnerably, fainting) with a young black man is a story of mythical resonance but shocking topicality. Mrs Larkin is an ironic Eve and something more akin to a classical Diana-figure, or a pagan Green Man, with her men's overalls, stained 'almost of a color with the leaves'. At first she appears antithetical to the stereotypical version of the Southern belle. In W. J. Cash's description, this figure was ' the South's Palladium, this Southern woman – the shield bearing Athena gleaming whitely in the clouds [...] the lily-pure maid of Astolat and the hunting goddess of the Boetian hill'. [161] As Mrs Larkin raises her hoe above her head, warrior-like, 'the clumsy sleeves both fell back, exposing the thin, unsunburned whiteness of her arms, the shocking fact of their youth', and in this, there is a resonance of the legendary Southern woman. Mrs Larkin aims to strike at the head of Jamey, but there is no real foe other than impotence and lonely grief: 'the workings of accident, of life and death, of unaccountability'. Mrs Larkin's fury and near violence against Jamey, whose back is turned and who, she notices, 'closely for

---

158 Abel Meeropol (Lewis Allan), 'Strange Fruit', cited in David Margolick, *Strange Fruit: Billie Holliday, Café Society and an Early Cry for Civil Rights* (Edinburgh: Canongate, 2002 [2000]).

159 *Major Problems in the History of the American South, Volume II*, eds Paul D. Escott and others (Boston, MA: Houghton Mifflin 1999), p. 158-9.

160 Jim Crow is the term used for the policy and/or practice of segregating blacks. It derives, in part, from the 19th century song of the same name used by the American entertainer Thomas Rice (1808-60). *Collins Concise Dictionary* (Glasgow: HarperCollins, 1999), p. 775.

161 W. J. Cash cited in L. Westling, *Sacred Groves and Ravaged Gardens; The Fiction of Eudora Welty, Carson McCullers, and Flannery O'Connor* (Athens: University of Georgia Press, 1985), pp. 9-10.

the first time [...] looked like a child', melts with the raindrops which at last begin to fall, and she swoons, now a Sleeping Beauty figure amidst the flowers:

> Then Mrs Larkin sank in one motion down into the flowers and lay there, fainting and streaked with rain. Her face was upturned, down among the plants, with the hair beaten away from her forehead and her open eyes closing at once when the rain touched them. Slowly her lips began to part. She seemed to move slightly, in the sad adjustment of a sleeper.[162]

Jamey, of course, is in no position to be a hero or a prince in this tale:

> Jamey ran jumping and crouching about her, drawing in his breath alternately at the flowers breaking under his feet and at the shapeless, passive figure on the ground. Them he became quiet, and stood back at a little distance and looked in awe at the unknowing face, white and rested under its bombardment. He remembered how something had filled him with stillness when he felt her standing there behind him looking down at him, and he would not have turned around at that moment for anything in the world [...] He bent down and in a horrified, piteous, beseeching voice he began to call her name until she stirred.
>   'Miss Lark'! Miss Lark'!'
> Then he jumped nimbly to his feet and ran out of the garden.[163]

This is the end of the story. In this garden of confusion and profusion, the white husband is struck down, the wife collapses, and the hired black flees; this is a legend of the South. A 'curtain of green', emblematic of the verdant American South, is drawn back to expose a drama in mythical, yet vernacular or local vein.

Critics have had very little to say about the story. Katherine Anne Porter, in her introduction to the first edition of the collection, *A Curtain of Green*, mentions, albeit briefly, most of the seventeen stories in the collection but she does not refer to this title-story. More recent critics, such as Elizabeth Evans or Louise Westling writing in the 1980s, also fail to discuss the story. Louise Westling's [164] more recent critical biography of Welty does discuss the story very briefly. She introduces it thus: 'One of the strangest stories in the collection is the title story, "A Curtain of Green", in which the feminine setting of a flower garden is used to explore the interrelation of fertility and death.'[165] Fertility and death are, of course, the stuff of legend (and of gardens). Mrs Larkin is impotent to save her husband, as many white Southern women had been impotent before her, in an ante-bellum slaveholding context.[166]

---

162 Ibid., p. 219.

163 Ibid., p. 219.

164 Elizabeth Evans, op. cit. and Louise Westling, *Eudora Welty* (Basingstoke: Macmillan, 1989).

165 Ibid.

166 L. Westling explains: 'The position of the Southern lady is in many ways an especially long-lived version of the Victorian situation of women in England and Europe, with all its attendant ironies. Unique complications existed in the Southern situation, however, because of the South's peculiar racial institution. As the region grew defensive in response to national pressures, the white female representative of Christian virtues was lauded in public to divert

Here, it is love and the potency of magical thought, her protective words, 'you can't be hurt', that have proved ineffectual against accident and fall. (There is also an autobiographical element to this failure which Welty discusses in *One Writer's Beginnings:* her mother's longstanding sense of grief and failure at not being able to save her husband's life, by a blood transfusion and the magical power of ardent thought.)[167] Welty takes mythical aspects of magical potency and of transformation, such as those elaborated in Frazer's *The Golden Bough* or Ovid's *Metamorphoses*, and transposes them to the story of a garden in the twentieth-century American South.

Eudora Welty has often been criticised for her lack of engagement with those very issues of race which have perplexed the American South for so long. In the estimation of one critic reviewing *The Collected Short Stories of Eudora Welty* in 1980, her fiction is a 'family-centred, somewhat laundered version of life in Mississippi', and it fails: 'to reflect the larger social and racial issues. Bilbo, Vardaman, the Klan – we hear nothing of them'.[168] Welty was not unaware of the charges. Writing in 1965, as the Civil Rights movement was at its peak (with a Civil Rights Act passed in 1964 and, after violent demonstrations in Mississippi and Alabama, the Voting Rights Act of 1965), Welty responded to such challenges and calls for more direct action such as: 'All right, Eudora Welty, what are you going to do about it? Sit down there with your mouth shut?' [169] Her essay, 'Must the Novelist Crusade?', asks, 'Are fiction writers called upon to be crusaders? For us in the South who are fiction writers, is

---

attention from problems of slavery and racism. She was forced to represent a racial purity which was required by her men for the maintenance of their caste but which many of them regularly transgressed in their own sexual adventures with black women. In the context of the problems of slavery and miscegenation for which the Southern patriarchy was responsible, the Southern lady held a position of moral superiority. She was painfully aware of the hypocrisy of her father, brothers and husband; they knew it and guiltily acceded influence to her', ibid., pp. 8-9.

See also Elizabeth Fox-Genovese, *Within the Plantation Household: Black and White Women of the Old South* (1988) cited in *Major Problems of the American South, Volume I*, op. cit., p. 311: 'For slaveholding women, gender relations merged seamlessly with the sense of their own social roles and personal identities. Modern sensibilities may view them as the oppressed victims of male dominance, but few of them would have agreed, notwithstanding some bad moments. Their men's abuse of prerogatives, notably sexual philandering [with slave women] [...] caused them untold distress. But their resentment of these abuses rarely passed into rejection of the system that established their sense of personal identity within a solid community.'

A black woman's view of this situation is addressed to white women in the following: 'He purchased you. He raped me. I fought. But you fought neither for yourselves or me. Sat trapped in your superiority and spoke no reproach'. Beulah Richardson [source presently unknown].

167 *OWB*, pp. 92-3.

168 Robert Tower, *New York Review of Books*, 4 December 1980, cited in H. McNeil, 'Introduction', *The Ponder Heart* [1955] (London: Virago, 1980), p. 7.

169 E. Welty, *The Eye of the Story*, op. cit., p. 147.

writing a novel <u>something we can do about it</u>?[170] However, in Welty's considered views 'there is absolutely everything in fiction but a clear answer': [171]

> What must the Southern writer of fiction do today? [...] There have already been giant events, some of them wrenchingly painful and humiliating. And now there is added the atmosphere of hate. We in the South are a hated people these days; we were hated first for actual and particular reasons, and now we may be hated still more in some vast unparticularized way. [...] Our people hate back. The hate seems in part shame for self, in part self justification, in part panic that life is really changing. Fury at ourselves and hurt pride, anger aroused too often, outrage at being hated need not obscure forever the sore spots we Southerners know better than our detractors.[172]

However, these are views which Alice Walker, for instance, interviewing Welty in 1973 (before *The Color Purple* in 1983 would establish her own fame), seems to have found less than satisfactory. The interview is an interesting vignette of a meeting between two writers of the American South, one young, black and angry and the other white, in her 60s, established in her art, and determined to be serene about fiction's scope. In Walker's introduction to the interview, she notes its (for her) inevitable complexity:

> When we face each other, talking at first in starts, I think how odd it is that I feel entirely relaxed, entirely comfortable. Considering how different we are – in age, color, in the directions we have had to take in this life, I wonder if my relaxation means something terrible. For this is Mississippi, U.S.A., and black, white, old, young, Southern black and Southern white – all these labels have meaning for a very good reason: they have effectively kept us apart, sometimes brutally. So that, although we live in the same town, we inhabit different worlds. [...] Though we are both writers, writing in some cases from similar experiences, and certainly from the same territory, we are more strangers, because the past will always separate us; and because she is white and not young, and I am black and not old. Still, I am undaunted, unafraid of discovering what I can. She is modest, shy, quiet and strong as the oak tree out in the yard.[173]

The reader of the interview is unlikely to feel 'entirely comfortable'. Pressed repeatedly by Walker to be more specific about race, and indeed black writers, Welty persists in her benign (and rather evasive) view: 'I see all my characters as individuals, not as colors, but as people, alive – unique'.[174]

A few years before this interview, in 1971, Welty wrote a Preface to the publication of a selection of her photographs, the subjects in this collection, predominantly black, taken in the late 1930s. She writes through a lens not then available to her as a young,

---

170 Ibid., p. 148.

171 Ibid., p. 149.

172 Ibid., p. 155.

173 Alice Walker, 'Eudora Welty: An Interview', in *Conversations with Eudora Welty*, op. cit., pp. 131-32. The oak tree, which Walker notes as, the tallest oak tree I have ever seen' was planted by Eudora Welty's father when she was a child.

174 Ibid., p. 137.

white, female photographer, 'equipped with a good liberal arts education': the lens of the Civil Rights movement and all that it exposed and decried, in yet another wave of humiliation for the South:

> In particular, the photographs of black persons by a white person may not testify soon again to such intimacy. [...] And had I no shame as a white person for what message might lie in my pictures of black persons? No. I was too busy imagining myself into their lives to be open to any generalities. I wished no more to indict anybody, to prove or disprove anything by my pictures, than I would have wished to do harm to the people in them, or have expected any harm from them to come to me. [...] When a heroic face like that of the woman in the buttoned sweater [...] looks back at me from her picture, what I respond to now, just as I did the first time, is not the Depression, not the Black, not the South, not even the perennially sorry state of the whole world, but the story of her life in her face. [...] Her face to me is full of meaning more truthful and more terrible and, I think, more noble than any generalization about people could have prepared me for or could describe for me now. [...] I knew this, anyway: that my wish, indeed my continuing passion, would be not to point the finger in judgment but to part *a curtain* [my emphasis], that invisible shadow that falls between people, the veil of indifference to each other's presence, each other's wonder, each other's human plight.[175]

Written at the time that these photographs were taken, 'A Curtain of Green', is the exemplary curtain-parting on an allegorical garden-setting in a deep-South drama of which this story is simply one scene. Rather than pointing a finger in judgment or writing polemic in order 'to indict' or 'to prove or disprove', Welty extends the facility of her early snapshots 'to capture transience' to a Modernist short story form. In this she is able to combine the universalising aspect of myth to convey 'human plight' whilst locating her subjects in a very specific place and time. In both of these endeavours, the Garden serves her well.

* * * *

Each of these four Modernist short stories have features in common; their garden settings are: a metropolitan park in London; a 'town' garden in the colonial outpost of New Zealand; a suburban garden in Ireland and a ruined demesne; a suburban garden in Mississippi. There is – however much we are able to identify diversity in cultural, historical and social contexts – something about gardens that appears unchanging. Fundamentally, most gardens involve plants and plants are seen as natural, organic, age-old, neutral and transcendent.

Modernism, on the other hand, is a challenge precisely to each of these categories. Affected by the growth of industry, technology, cities and migration, the twentieth century is propelled into an engagement with the synthetic, the mechanical, and the new. Modernism's commitment to experimentation is both an effect of and an engagement with modernisation rather than a reaction against it. The stuffiness of Victorian and Edwardian bourgeois values and the pomposity of its customs – already

---

175 Eudora Welty, 'Preface', *OTOP*, op. cit., pp. 10-12.

beginning to lose their credence – are the targets of Modernism as it embraces critiques that are experimental, *avant-garde* or bohemian. Thus, experiments with new media such as film, or the growth of cities and suburbia, contribute to Modernism's own theories and analogies. Those qualities of the garden, then, have an unexpected role to play in the service of an aesthetic that was committed to the defamiliarisation of so many cultural aspects that had been assimilated or construed as natural – sexual, racial and class distinctions, gender roles, progress, 'survival of the fittest'. Thus, 'tree' can no longer signify in a straightforward reference to cultural certainties based on the Bible, just as 'woman' or 'race' or imperial rights and wrongs were also being redefined. In the garden stories here, therefore, there is nothing of the utopian and blandly progressive. There is no hint of the utopian vision of, say, Ebenezer Howard's *Garden Cities of Tomorrow*, first published in 1902, with its synthesis of the best aspects of town and country: 'Beauty of nature/ social opportunity; fields and parks of easy access; low rents/high wages; low rates/plenty to do; low prices/ no sweating; field for enterprise/flow of capital; pure air and water/good drainage; bright homes and gardens/no smoke, no slums; freedom/cooperation'.[176] Rather, the gardens in this chapter are used, upon the small canvas of the short story form, to reflect a range of political and personal complexities, many of them disruptive of what had been previously established as norms and certainties.

Modernist politics have often been accused of lack of engagement, being eclipsed by a preoccupation with aesthetics and psychological self-reflexivity. There is little doubt that the writers' experiments represented a measure of subversiveness, but any radical agenda also seemed to be appeased by a (false) democratisation of new art forms – the short story, photography, film and post-impressionist painting included. Gardens, too – although incorporating the consolations of the intransigently 'natural' and of a nostalgic 'rural' – were implicated in this seeming democratisation:

> The small garden was thus established across a wide spectrum of society and amongst the higher echelons of artistic taste when the First World War started. When the men came home in 1918 there was little doubt about what they wanted, and 'a garden' summed up the space, air and privacy for living that they felt they had earned [...] The three-bedroomed 'semi' of the inter-war years is now regarded as a triumph of housing design, and it certainly gave the most enormous boost to the small garden; indeed it was the beginning of popular gardening as one of the great marketing success stories of this century [...] From the long front gardens of the countryside to the street-bound façades of town houses, the suburbs had settled on a happy medium: the small front garden and long rectangle at the rear.[177]

---

176 Ebenezer Howard, *The Garden Cities of Tomorrow* (1902) cited in Jane Brown, *The Pursuit of Paradise: A Social History of Gardens and Gardening* (London: HarperCollins, 1999), p. 155. This list of the attributes of the hybrid 'Town-Country', an integral aspect of the Garden City, is taken from his The Three Magnets diagram, also included in Brown, p. 155.

177 J. Brown, ibid., pp. 159-60.

If the small front garden stands as a metaphor for the individual display of acceptable social facets, then the long rectangle at the rear represents something more private and uneven, perhaps. In the terms of a Modernist aesthetic, the rear garden is much worthier of interest. It constitutes a place redolent of dreams and desires as well as being the space where the constraints of the familial, mundane and workaday are more evident. Here, too, psychological dramas may be played out, just as, behind the innocuous veneer of a short story, something darker and deeper is given free rein. The 'rear garden', however, is not merely a domestic or private space; each of the stories in this chapter explores the impact of the politics of the wider world upon the politics of a personal one.

All the stories were written at a time of Western crisis: Woolf's and Mansfield's during the First World War, and Bowen's and Welty's during the Second. 'Modernity', writes Peter Childs, 'is both the culmination of the past and the harbinger of the future, pinpointing a moment of potential breakdown in socio-cultural relations and aesthetic representation'.[178] In Modernism, the hiatus of modernity still seems to offer more in terms of potential than of dissolution, particularly in relation to aesthetics. The fragmentation characteristic of a Modernist aesthetic aims for revision and reconstruction rather than the reflection of 'breakdown'. In socio-cultural terms, however, there is indeed a prevailing sense of the prospect of breakdown, including collapses that are mental, marital, political and social. As each of the writers selects the garden that befits their story and its location, it is interesting to see the ways in which the gardens themselves are imbued with contingency and transition rather than represented as simple paradigms of paradise or retreat. Not one of the gardens presented here has impermeable boundaries or a static symbolism – both highly significant features. Where there is a gesture to the past, it is not with nostalgia but with a view to interrogating its processes. This is the project that postmodernism will further advance.

---

178 P. Childs, op. cit., pp. 15-16.

Chapter 2

Natural History and Postmodern Grafting

7 April 1852

Went to the Zoo.
I said to him –
Something about that Chimpanzee over there
reminds me of you

Carol Ann Duffy, 'Mrs Darwin' (1999)

Suppose you live in a world where you have to be bigger and more beautiful than your neighbour to attract a mate, where rivals offer free parking and fast food to their lovers and disreputable opportunists offer nothing at all, but lure partners with false promises and murder them. Imagine that your paramour lives across the street but you cannot get together, so you pay an intermediary. What if you wanted desperately to have children but possible partners had been killed or lived too far away? As a last resort you fertilize yourself. Imagine being male or female for a while and then switching to the other sex? This may all sound like supermarket tabloid sensationalism but it happens every day. It is the sex in your garden.

Angela Overy, *Sex in Your Garden* (1997)

Political gardening versus gardening for fun: The very act of taking someone else's land and using it to your own end is in itself a political act. Whether or not you want your guerrilla gardening to act as a political message, with publicity and its own public impact is entirely up to you and the way your horticultural deeds are constructed. Planting pretty tulips on old industrial sites is one message, growing marijuana outside government offices is quite another.

buffcorePhil, 'Guerrilla Gardening' (2004)

Most texts or treatises on postmodernism, across the range of disciplines where it is a familiar term, highlight the difficulty of defining precisely what it is. Most often the answer seems to be: everything and nothing, yet something distinct. So – what would a postmodern garden be like? It would be eclectic, taking the best of everything available to it but privileging nothing. Notions of taste and taste's class-ridden hierarchies would have been dismantled and the 'high' and low' would be brought together, with playful knowingness, with irony. Garden gnomes could sit alongside the classical features, the kitsch alongside the canonical. Any medium or material might be included; this garden space is ultra-democratic and inclusive – and yet it will be costly. Other eras, other climes, various traditions, can be casually re-enacted (parody) or brought together like a collage (pastiche). However, the postmodern garden, while showing an awareness of the past, will never aim for exact replication or verisimilitude – heritage-sites are not its forté. The gardener who creates this postmodern plot will not be free of the dictates of fashion, but they will show their awareness of this with frank self-reflexivity. The postmodern gardener will use all that technology and commodity can offer but nothing of this will be hidden; the garden's artifice and the gardener's techniques will be on the surface. Above all, the postmodern gardener will be aware – as far as it is possible to be aware, for awareness is elusive and illusory – that terms such as 'Nature' or 'natural' are not to be used without scare-quotes. For the postmodern gardener would understand that 'like the Victorians, we have – although in very different ways – lost our sense of what is "natural" while our sense of what it is to write history is similarly under threat.'[1]

The postmodern writer (who may include attention to gardens and natural history) takes an approach very much like the postmodern gardener described. The terms most frequently associated with postmodern writing are those used above: irony, parody, pastiche, self-reflexivity, but in order to deconstruct Western orthodoxies (what Linda Hutcheon calls 'cultural "de-doxification"'.[2]) At the core of these narrative strategies is the 'awareness of the discursive and signifying nature of cultural knowledge' and the questioning 'of the supposed transparency of representation'[3] in a genre once 'firmly rooted in realist representation'.[4] Postmodern fiction thus moves to 'an exploration of the way in which narratives and images structure how we see ourselves and how we construct our notions of self, in the present and in the past'.[5]

In previous eras, certainly in Europe since the sixteenth century, an optimism of discovery and the positivism of development had been promulgated, up to and including the Modernists, who identified a European culture in crisis but still hoped to contribute the elements needed to 'make it new'. The aftermath of the Second World War, however, heralded an attitude, in the arts, in particular, that was at once

1   Sally Shuttleworth, 'Writing Natural History: "Morpho Eugenia"', in *Essays on the Fiction of A. S. Byatt*, eds A. Alfer and M. J. Noble (Westport, CT & London: Greenwood Press, 2001), p. 151.
2   Linda Hutcheon, *The Politics of Postmodernism* (London: Routledge, 1989), p. 4.
3   Ibid.
4   Ibid.
5   Ibid.

more sceptical and more careless (though not carefree): there could be nothing new – utopianism it seemed had been predicated on false and arrogant premises. Knowledge – in the pursuit of which so many things had been trampled – had progressed to the point where it could put a person on the moon – or annihilate the planet in a second. The facts of History were seen to be the subjective renditions of vested interests, stories which had credence on the basis of power, but which could be variously contested by other 'subjects' with perspectives at odds with or not the same as the dominant one (on the basis of nationality, ethnicity, class, wealth, race, gender, sex). For example, the great individualistic quests to name countries, mountains, rivers, plants and to place them in systems of classification in the light of Knowledge, Truth and Order (Grand Narratives) is, in postmodern fiction, inflected by individual subjectivities that are 'split' or fluid or the multiple perspectives ('petit histoires') of the Other. Thus, notions of historicity and historiography are frequent lines of enquiry in postmodern texts, which return to former periods – and their ideological premises – not to reproduce them, as such, but to revision them by virtue of what might be called a 'dislocated' self-reflexivity.

Postmodern fictions about gardens and garden-related matters – as evidenced by the four texts under consideration here – will certainly contain these deconstructive aspects. The texts included are – in the order that they are discussed: John Updike's *The Witches of Eastwick*, A. S. Byatt's novella, 'Morpho Eugenia', Jeanette Winterson's *Sexing the* Cherry and Carol Shields's *Larry's Party*. In this chapter, A. S. Byatt's William Adamson with his 'double consciousness' or Jeanette Winterson's Jordan, John Trandescant's protégé, are pertinent examples of subjectivities that are not confidently coherent models of monumental 'I-ness'. The Modernists had already identified consolidated and self-evident identities as fictions; that sense of the subject was: 'Bourgeois perhaps, patriarchal certainly – it is the phallocentric order of subjectivity.'[6] Thus, the texts analysed here will explore those subjectivities still in the grip of their deluded self-aggrandisement alongside those conventionally posited as Other in order to reveal some of the fabrications of identity and progress. These authors will also expose how the text itself (as any text) is authored by a split-subjectivity, with its 'unconscious' aspects, both personal and cultural. Just as history will be seen to have a less straightforward teleological projection than is commonly supposed so will the text take multiple routes, keeping the 'madeness' of the text to the fore. It will also not be easy to be passive as a reader, innocuously guided along by a lulling, familiar meta-narrative. You, the reader, are in this too, they say – and you will have choices to make and may well be led up the wrong garden path.

Sometimes a work will offer texts within texts such as fictive poems, diaries, other narratives or stories – or 'real' and recognisable ones: well-known poems, extracts from the Bible or familiar fairy-tales. Different typefaces alert us to different 'authors' – some real, some parodied – in Byatt's work as in Winterson's. Visual incorporations are also common paratextual features. Byatt's 'Acknowledgments' at the end of *Angels and Insects* cites sources for her Victoriana-decorations, which

---

6   Hal Foster, ed. *Postmodern Culture* (London & Sydney: Pluto Press, 1985).

include, for 'The Conjugial Angel', reprints of two engravings by John Martin from *Paradise Lost* and of drawings by the Pre-Raphaelites, Edward Burne-Jones and Dante Gabriel Rossetti. The period-looking prints of butterflies, caterpillars and moths, however, are Victorian masquerades by the twentieth-century natural-history guide-book illustrator, Brian Hargreaves.[7] Winterson's text similarly includes decorations, primarily of fruit, presented in a variety of unexpected ways so that facile symbolic correlations are disrupted but she also refers to a real seventeenth-century work of art, the painting *Charles II and His Gardener*. Shields, on the other hand, incorporates many maze designs from verifiable though mostly unacknowledged sources (apart from some embedded clues). To complicate matters, she includes as an epigraph to the text a 'real' baby's photograph of the fictional character. She also includes a shopping list and dinner-party seating plan. Updike's novel alone does not include visual images (though many works of Pop Art are mentioned) but he does include historical epigraphs at each of the three section headings. All the texts, however, make detailed references to art or artists, events and phenomena, some of these being identifiable in the public domain and others belonging solely to the realm of the fiction. Ascertaining the difference is 'the point', simultaneously unimportant and futile. These paratextual features are both extraneous and integral, serious and playful, accurate or fictive – from the period, or a parody of it. Intertextuality replaces allusion; these are not narratives that simply direct us to precursor texts or artefacts but, rather, demonstrate an awareness of being enmeshed by the web of cultural discourse so that categories such as original, real, authentic, fact or fiction are all problematised. What is created then is a text that cannot be and does not aim to be thoroughly 'original' but, rather, reconfigures these elements in a ways that are unsettling and ironic. These texts thus present themselves as unreliable, just as the stories called History may be unreliable and yet history is still its touchstone. The term used to describe this paradoxical literary 'de-doxifying' is 'historiographic metafiction':

> For the most part historiographic metafiction, like much contemporary theory or history, does not fall into either 'presentism' or nostalgia in relation to the past it represents. What it does is de-naturalize that temporal relationship. In both historiographic theory and postmodern fiction, there is an intense self-consciousness (both theroretical and textual) about the act of narrating in the present the events of the past [...] In both historical and literary postmodern representation, the doubleness remains; there is no sense of either historian or novelist reducing the past to a verisimilar present[...]This is deliberately double coded narrative, just as postmodern architecture is a doubly coded form: they are historical and contemporary.[8]

Each of the texts included here has this double-coded aspect. On the one hand they have in common the notion that Natural History – and thus the garden – has been

---

    7   Prolific illustrator of books on insects, e.g. in Michael Chinery, *Butterflies and Moths* (London: Collins, 1981).

    8   L. Hutcheon, op. cit., p. 71.

a key player in the construction of cultural doxa and thus rely on it for historical reference. On the other, Natural History – and the garden – must therefore be present in texts which 'de-doxify'. This is not to say that Natural History has no credence but rather that the way it has been posited is anything but natural.

John Updike's *The Witches of Eastwick*, published in 1984, is set in the 1970s, but it is heavily inflected by the history of Puritan New England and the nineteenth-century rendition of it by Nathaniel Hawthorne, in particular. Updike is a prolific writer of the collective and individual 'stream of angst' (his best-known character from the *Rabbit* series, Harry Angstrom, is 'a representative Kierkergaardian man'[9]) of middle America and typical of the fiction of the post-atomic, Cold-War-dominated Western world of the 1950s and 1960s. Updike is a Christian and a regular church-goer ('in three Protestant denominations – Lutheran, Congregational, Episcopal')[10] a reader of Karl Barth and Søren Kierkegaard and a writer who begs to 'be absolved from any duty to provide orthodox morals and consolations.'[11] These aspects might seem at first to suggest a writer *on* the postmodern rather than a postmodern writer. However, in *The Witches of Eastwick*, there are features which are decidedly postmodern. For instance, combined with his attention to detail is the fundamental premise that all is not as it seems – and here rumours and 'evidence' of witchcraft generating hysteria and prosecution sets a compelling historical precedent. 'Legend' is a repeated word throughout, for this is a text taking a knowing – and playful – look at its own status in perpetuating the various 'legends' upon which it draws. Further, the novel mocks realist conventions by inscribing a consumerist 'ultra realism' in the 1960s and 1970s and combining it with 'magic' or 'alchemy' in a techno-world, where in games played on a state-of-the-art domed Asphlex composition court, tennis-balls turned into snakes and bats or where selenium, the 'magical element' that dissolves gold is 'the secret of those doors in airports that open automatically'. However, Updike represents in meticulous detail the 'commercialized and somewhat trashy world of middle America' with its 'bottle caps, commercial containers and pop imagery'.[12] Updike has explained that this 'realism' is along the lines of Andy Warhol's Heinz soup tin, for instance, a textual Pop Art artefact[13] where the simulacra of the real become more real than real – hyper-real. Above all, Updike is interested in cultural reflexes, the post-Enlightenment mass responses to those '"Three Great Secret Things" (sex, religion, and art).'[14] A fourth term to be added is Nature, which Updike

---

9   John Updike, 'Remarks upon Receiving the Campion Medal', in *John Updike and Religion: The Sense of the Sacred and Motions of Grace*, ed. James Yerkes (Grand Rapids, MI & Cambridge, UK: Wm. B. Eerdmans, 1999), p. 5.

10   Ibid., p. 4.

11   Ibid., p. 5.

12   John Updike with Mark Lawson, *Front Row*, BBC Radio 4, 18 March 2002.

13   Ibid.

14   James Plath, 'Introduction', *Conversations with John Updike*, ed. James Plath (Jackson: University of Mississippi Press, 1994), p. xv. (citing Updike, 'The Dogwood Tree: A Boyhood', *Assorted Prose* (New York: Alfred A. Knopf, 1965), pp. 151-87.

explores with a wry attention to witches and an application of the second law of thermodynamics, hence the subtitle of this section: 'Entropy'.

A. S. Byatt sets her novella 'Morpho Eugenia', one half of *Angels and Insects*, in the 1860s, but she is similarly interested in Updike's 'Three Great Secret Things' although she might also substitute 'Three Great Thinkers': Freud, Marx, and Darwin, who in their own period had the 'double aspect' of radically challenging established post-enlightenment doxologies, and yet, furthering them too. She ventriloquises a range of voices in the light of the dramatic challenges posited by these figures in the mid-nineteenth century. Byatt's own work, which is now firmly installed in the category of 'distinctly postmodern', is also well-known for its convincing evocation of the Victorian period and her mimicry of its writers and other voices. Her unstinting research into the intellectual and aesthetic foundations of the era that she parodies tends to complicate the categorisation of a 'playful postmodernist', however. It has been suggested that she slips too readily into the very genre she mimes and ironises. J. M. Coetzee is one such, and in his comments on her work he notes this slippage:

> Her more recent fiction shows a great deal of textual variety (embedded stories and documents and so forth) and plays with some of the devices of postmodernism. Nevertheless, it continually falls back on the close social observation and moral attentiveness of the great English realists.[15]

Sally Shuttleworth would agree, finding that Byatt's texts do reveal 'an absolute, non-ironic fascination with the details of the period and with our relations to it'.[16] (Shuttleworth also speculates on the renewed interest in Darwin by writers of fiction in the early 1990s, after the publication of the biography by Adrian Desmond and James Moore in 1991.) 'Morpho Eugenia', claims Shuttleworth, by being so singular in its historical location, 'foregoes the emancipatory potential of a twentieth-century frame, setting natural history, science, and loss of religious faith at the very heart of the text'.[17] What Byatt does provide is a range of contesting voices and their texts: Sir Harald Alabaster's treatise on Darwin and the Bible; William Adamson's journals; William's book *The Swarming City: A Natural History of A Woodland Society, its polity, its economy, its aims and defences, its origins, expansion and decline;* and Matty Compton's fable, set in Lewis Carroll-like enigmatic gardens: 'Things Are Not What They Seem'. Byatt also includes in the novella, not just references to, but fragments of, a range of myths and fables including the tale of Psyche and Cupid, Victorian verse, biblical Proverbs, Milton (a favourite of Charles Darwin himself) Browning, Clare and Tennyson. The novella itself is a deliberate masquerade of many Victorian narratives and Victorian consciousnesses. It is an imaginative reconstruction of what it might have been like to write, think and act 'in relation to evolutionary

---

15   J. M. Coetzee, *Stranger Shores: Essays 1986–1999* (London: Vintage, 2002), p. 185.

16   S. Shuttleworth, 'Writing Natural History: "Morpho Eugenia"', in Alfer and Noble, op. cit., p. 148.

17   Ibid., p. 152.

theory, in the phase when "a fact is not quite a scientific fact at all" and when "the remnant of the mythical" is at its most manifest',[18] while being written and addressed to an audience in the inevitable context of post-Freudianism ('it is impossible, in our culture, to live a life which is not charged with Freudian assumptions, patterns for apprehending experience, ways of perceiving relationships, even if we have not read a word of Freud').[19] Scientific endeavours, too, such as the Human Genome Project, which began formally in 1990 or, in England, the Eden Project, which also commenced in the 1990s, necessarily inform the reader's approach to the debates outlined in the ostensibly nineteenth-century narrative.

Jeanette Winterson, however, harks back to the seventeenth century and the English Civil War, with some historical characters to the fore, for example, Charles II and the famed botanist, collector and plantsman, John Tradescant. Her tale has the double focus of small sections of contemporary narrative, too. Like Byatt, she includes a range of narratives within the main text, most notably with a series of revised fairy tales, which are more familiar as nineteenth- rather than seventeenth-century renditions. This tale, for all it historical reference is obviously fantastic and fanciful and yet her topics are extremely serious; they are, again: Sex, Religion, Art and Nature.

Certainly, *Sexing the Cherry*, like 'Morpho Eugenia' is a mix of historical figures (the plant collector and Royal Gardener John Tradescant, the Younger, Charles I and Charles II), and fictional characters namely, a most 'unfeminine' giantess, known as the Dog-Woman and the foundling, cross-dressing traveller, Jordan. Historical events such as the Civil War and the Great Fire of London are discussed alongside fabulous tales in strange, unknown places. The narrative begins with two epigraphs, immediately alerting the reader first to post-structuralist questions about language and temporality and then, to those about matter, space and light raised by post-Einstein quantum physics ('Empty space and points of light. What does this say about the reality of the world?') This novella-length text has numerous sections rather than chapters, some headed with rather crude line-drawings of fruit, (which, one learns are markers for who is speaking in each section) whereas other sections have headings such as: 'THE FLAT EARTH THEORY'; 'HALLUCINATIONS AND DISEASES OF THE MIND'; 'FORTUNATA'S STORY', or alternatively, both an emblem and a title: a pineapple and 'THE NATURE OF TIME'. These small sections are sometimes collected within Parts, namely 'THE STORY OF THE TWELVE DANCING PRINCESSES' (preceded by a full-page line drawing of twelve figures floating upwards and into the distance from a casement window); '1649' (crudely drawn images of sword, hook and axe) and 'SOME YEARS LATER' (drawing of enormous waves; sailboat atop one of these; dark, starlit sky with crescent moon).

Such playful, experimental narrative strategies are the 'fruits' of postmodernity – and indeed, appear to be emblematised by fruit. Jeanette Winterson's best known

---

18 Gillian Beer, *Darwin's Plots: Evolutionary Narrative in Darwin, George Eliot and Nineteenth-Century Fiction* (London: Routledge & Kegan Paul, 1983), p. 4.

19 Ibid., p. 5.

68 _Garden Plots_

novel, the loosely autobiographical _Oranges are Not the Only Fruit_ written when she was just twenty-four and published in 1985, used the trope to explore issues of forbidden fruit (as found in the Garden of Eden) and fruits that flourish to tempt or taint, sanctify or signify – in the 'fallen' world. Jeanette's dourly religious mother believes 'oranges are the only fruit', renouncing still the 'rotten' fruit that led Eve astray, whereas Jeanette learns that, for her, there must be more fruit, more choices: 'What about grapes and bananas?' In _Sexing the Cherry_, the reader is also asked to compare pineapples and apples. Here we witness another Fall, this time in the context of Newtonian physics. The apple, it appears, is bad news yet again.

Another deliberately anti-linear narrative is Carol Shields's _Larry's Party_. While the maze in this novel is an obvious model for the narrative style, the maze and its history is also a topic. However, the genre Canadian Literature has itself been deemed paradigmatically postmodern. Linda Hutcheon, a Canadian academic whose extensive writing on the politics and poetics of postmodernism is well known, has also discussed postmodernism in a particular national context: _The Canadian Postmodern_.[20] Canada, it is claimed, is ideally suited to manifestations of the postmodern because of its complex relation to the European – and American – dominance in the construction of discourses of power and progress. Hutcheon cites 'the expatriate Canadian filmmaker and critic Laura Mulvey', whose metaphor for Canada itself is a literary one:

> Canadian culture is not yet a closed book. The historical anomalies that Canada has grown from make contradictions visible. Uniform national identity is challenged by a pride in heterogeneity and difference.[21]

Carol Shields uses the maze as the model for just such a combination of the prescription of uniformity and open-endedness. The maze, then, is a model of a model that is itself maze-like – not just for the representation of story generally but of the cultural specificity of an 'outpost' country. The Canadian postmodern makes visible some general principles:

> In their self-reflexivity, Canadian postmodern novels offer yet another example of the self-conscious or 'meta-' sensibility of our times, that is, of the awareness that all our systems of understanding are deliberate and historically specific human constructs (not natural and eternal givens), with all the limitations and strengths which that definition entails. These are novels that admit openly they are fiction, but suggest that fiction is just another means by which we make sense of our world (past and present) and that, as such, it is comparable to historiography, philosophy, physics, sociology, and so on.[22]

20   Linda Hutcheon, _The Canadian Postmodern: A Study of Contemporary English-Canadian Fiction_ (Oxford, Toronto and New York: OUP, 1988).
21   Ibid., p. ix.
22   Ibid., p. x-xi.

In reading Shield's maze-like novel, the *Canadian* postmodern is as significant for what it might represent about Canada, but more particularly, what Canada represents for/of postmodernism.

Each of the texts included here explores the impact of science on the modern world. Every one of those persistent features – Sex, Religion, Nature, Art – has been profoundly affected by science and scientific discourse. The authors considered here are in a position to review the far-reaching impact of Newton or Darwin in the light of the subsequent one made by Einstein: the scientific double- coding in postmodern texts. Science is, for the postmodern novel, the Master Builder of Grand Narratives and also their deconstructor. Further, there is a reversal, albeit circuitous, taking place. Whereas science looked to metaphor and myth as it endeavoured to describe and classify the world, now postmodern fiction looks to science for its own de-classifying analogies. It is for this reason that each of the following section headings bears a scientific sub-title: 'Entropy', 'Evolution', 'Gravity', 'Space'.

John Updike: Entropy

In John Updike's *The Witches of Eastwick* no one gardens very well; where gardens are made, matters quickly get out of control. It is at first difficult to see what Alexandra's rampant crop of rotting tomatoes, for instance, might signify. The garden to be identified or signified in this novel, however, is America itself. The setting is New England where Puritans once established a hopeful utopia in a New World, although the specific location, Rhode Island, was for religious dissenters such as Roger Williams (c. 1603-38) and Anne Hutchinson (1591-1643), 'an accustomed refuge for the exiles of Massachusetts, in all seasons of persecution'.[23] The optimism of the seventeenth century soon took on turbulent features with Indian wars, theological dissension and the witchcraft trials, all emblematised as battles between civilising Christian Fathers and 'the devil' (anyone or thing who did not comply with the Puritan theocracy), who had plenty of space to spring from in the

---

23 Nathaniel Hawthorne, 'Mrs Hutchinson', *Selected Tales and Sketches* (Harmondsworth: Penguin, 1987), p. 20.

untamed wilderness. In the eighteenth and early nineteenth century, America was publicly shamed by the institution of slavery, in which Rhode Island played its part. Suffragism, abolitionism and feminism had overlapping but distinctive agendas in the nineteenth-century, aspects of which were to re-emerge in the twentieth, with the Civil Rights and Women's Liberation movements. The historical present of the novel reflects much of the social and political utopianism of the 1960s as it confronts the war in Vietnam, a war whose consequences Updike knows thoroughly from writing later, in the period of the 1980s. It is not just politics that run amok (like the tomatoes), but bodies, too. Cancer is a frequent point of reference in the novel; like the devil lurking in the dark forests of New England, it is a surreptitious attacker. In 1981 the first cases of a sexually transmitted immune deficiency disorder had been described (the 'gay syndrome', as it was described then), and by 1983 bore the name of AIDS (Acquired Immune Deficiency Disorder). The garden of 1960s sexual liberation was stricken by a cruelly ironic blight in much the same way as the best principles of a new nation had repeatedly failed in its own project. The other feature that brings this novel into the frame of gardens is its attention to Nature: is it inherently friend or foe, and what have humans made of the relationship? What is to be done now? However, at the very moment that national environmental campaigns were being launched at home, toxic chemicals were being liberally (as it were) administered: DDT on domestic fields and napalm in foreign jungles. Further, the radical scientific advances of the period had afforded a vision at once to advance mankind beyond imagining and to annihilate it in a flash. The title of the scientific bestseller of the period, Rachel Carson's *Silent Spring*, was no punning oxymoron but an all-too-easily realisable threat. Even if the end of the earth in an atomic bang could be averted, then it would surely go riddled with untreatable diseases or unmanageable pollution. John Updike manages to depict the angst but nevertheless remains optimistic, despite all the evidence he himself sets out that he should relinquish hopefulness now.

In the Updike oeuvre, *The Witches of Eastwick* is certainly not his best known work, nor his most highly regarded. It has had relatively sparse critical attention,[24] and was too quickly eclipsed, perhaps, by the film that followed a mere three years after publication, with Jack Nicholson and Cher in the lead roles, in a lively but loosely related rendition of the text. In a review written at the time of the novel's publication, Margaret Atwood noted that *The Witches of Eastwick* was, for Updike, 'a departure from baroque realism' and she granted that its storyline (famously tagged in the film promotion as a tale of 'three beautiful women; one lucky devil') sounded an

---

24   Harold Bloom is one critic who views *The Witches of Eastwick* as one of Updike's 'most remarkable', *John Updike: Modern Critical Views*, ed. Harold Bloom (London: Chelsea House, 1999), while James Plath has discussed it approvingly on several occasions, including in conversation with Updike, *Conversations with John Updike*, op. cit. and in J. Plath, 'Giving the Devil His Due: Leeching and Edification of Spirit in *The Scarlet Letter* and *The Witches of Eastwick*', in *John Updike and Religion: The Sense of the Sacred and Motions of Grace*, ed. James Yerkes (Grand Rapids, MI & Cambridge, UK: Wm. B. Eerdmans, 1999).

'unpromising framework for a serious novelist'.[25] Atwood finds the title, however, to be 'literal': 'It's indeed about witches, real ones, who can fly through the air, levitate, hex people and make love charms that work [...].'[26] (This view is, however, quickly debatable; many a witchy act is undercut or contested by another view, sometimes the witches' own: 'We're not hurting Jenny. DNA is hurting Jenny.') What is real and what is fantastic is open to question throughout the novel even extending to who is and is not a witch; more women than the three main characters are called witches by someone or other. Witchcraft hysteria, of course, with its contagion of accusation and counter-accusation, is embedded in New England's history and its legends. These include literary engagements, from Nathaniel Hawthorne's Puritan tales in the nineteenth century to Arthur Miller's drama, *The Crucible*, in the mid-twentieth.

This novel is set in Rhode Island, which in fact has little history of witch-hunts and trials, compared to, and outdone by, neighbouring Massachusetts. In a 1984 interview, Updike claimed that he chose Rhode Island for the setting of the novel because few books have their setting in this, America's smallest state, and because it was a 'no man's land between Connecticut and Massachusetts' in which, in the seventeenth century, outlaws, dissenters, Quakers and Jews had found a place of refuge. As a passage from the novel, delivered by an intermittent but unidentified narrator makes clear, stories related to these twentieth-century suburban witches have joined their precursor witches in the collective consciousness of a particular place (in this fictional case, Rhode Island) with its history already 'stained' by 'the rumor of witchcraft':

> Insofar as they were witches, they were phantoms in the communal mind [...] Certainly, the fact of witchcraft hung in the consciousness of Eastwick; a lump, a cloudy density generated by a thousand translucent overlays, a sort of heavenly body [...] for years after the events gropingly and even reluctantly related here, the rumour of witchcraft stained this corner of Rhode Island, so that a prickliness of embarrassment and unease entered the atmosphere with the most innocent mention of Eastwick. (pp. 216-17)

The narrative voice that punctuates the novel on several occasions, usually at or near the end of each of the three sections, does so not to clarify but to complicate. The voice is, first, deliberately collective: 'Our town of Eastwick' (p. 121) or 'We all knew there was something about them' (p. 216) and then, transcendent and sententious: 'We all dream, and we all stand aghast at the mouth of the caves of our deaths'(p. 216). Finally, in the last paragraph of the novel, a similar pattern is repeated, and its effects are subversive and unsettling – of the status of story, of suburbia, of historical truth:

---

25   M. Atwood, 'Wondering What It's like to be a Woman', *New York Times Review of Books* (13 May 1984).

26   Ibid.

The witches are gone, vanished; we were just an interval in their lives, and they in ours. But as Sukie's blue-green ghost continues to haunt the sunstruck pavement, and Jane's black shape to flit against the moon, so the rumors of the days when they were solid among us, gorgeous and doing evil, have flavored the name of the town in the mouths of others, and for those of us who live here have left something oblong and invisible and exciting we do not understand. We meet it turning the corner where Hemlock meets Oak; it is there when we walk the beach in off-season and the Atlantic in its blackness mirrors the dense packed gray of the clouds: a scandal, life like smoke rising twisted into legend. (p. 316)

After some three hundred pages, the novel dissolves, ephemeral like life itself, unless legend remains to keep its 'rumors' present. This is a sceptical – and self-mocking – view for a novelist so often deemed to be a realist but the estimation is extended not just within a fictional contexts, but also to 'factual' historical events.

The story that has been told is both familiar and unfamiliar, realistic and fantastic, popular and political. Its historical markers, past and present, appear to be real and verifiable enough; although published in 1984, the novel is set more than a decade earlier, and there are frequent references to the Vietnam War and to political figures and situations of the late 1960s and early 1970s. Even these references to verifiable historical events, however, serve also to alert us to unreliability: 'Our town of Eastwick was to gossip that winter – for here as in Washington and Saigon there were leaks' (p. 121). Rumour and gossip were also attendant on other major historical reference points with which the book engages, in particular, the New England witchcraft trials of the seventeenth century, but also the years of McCarthyism and the communist 'witch-hunts' of the 1950s which set the contemporary context for Arthur Miller's exploration of the seventeenth-century version of hysterical naming and shaming in *The Crucible*.

History, then, however unreliable, is certainly not negligible even if some of its effects are intangible: 'phantoms in the communal mind'. The landscape is described throughout in terms that show the legacies of particular generations through the centuries: the Narraganesett tribe, the Puritans, the slave-holding landowners, the Congregationalists and Unitarians, the asphalted shopping malls and windowless plants of companies 'with names like Dataprobe and Computech'. At the novel's end, more time has passed and more changes have been wrought:

Dock Street has been repaved and widened to accept more traffic, and from the old horse trough to Landing Square, as it tends to be called, all the slight zigzags in the line of the curb have been straightened. New people move to town; some of them live in the old Lenox mansion, which has indeed been turned into condominiums [...] An area has been dredged and a dock and small marina built, as tenant inducement. The egrets nest elsewhere. The causeway has been elevated, with culverts every fifty yards, so it never floods – or has only once so far, in the great February blizzard of '78. The weather seems generally tamer in these times [...] (pp. 315-16)

This combination of omniscience and vagueness is not just to another of Updike's narratorial provisos and ironies (from 'never' to 'only once so far') but to another of the novel's themes: Nature. Whereas there is the intimation that the weather is now more settled because the witches have gone, the instability of the weather, and of the entire natural world, is, perhaps, the only certainty.

Environment and ecology are always mentioned in terms of disequilibrium, chaos, entropy. Cancer, too, is a frequent reference, as are dirt, waste, excrement, cracks, decay, parasites, overabundance, death; are these related to the natural principle of 'divestment' or the consequence of human neglect and abuse? These combine in a novel that suggests, on the one hand, that the witches and their devilish consort do have power, and on the other, that there is no power, by magic or scientific intervention, that can or could entirely control Nature and 'decomposition's deep-woven plaid' (p. 74). As the cavalier Devil of the tale, Darryl Van Horne says when he's asked to protect the snowy egret's wetland habitat: 'Once they're filled [...] they're not wet.' Either 'the whole damn world was going up in napalm' (p. 239) or another cycle of historical contingency and Nature's adaptations would ensue. As Updike puts it in his memoir, *Self Consciousness*, published five years after *The Witches of Eastwick*, a sense of certain doom and finiteness now prevails (or at least, it did in the late 1980s):

> The universe itself we now know to be, like our individual lives, singular in its career, beginning in the Big Bang and ending in entropy. Our species, too, arose but once, through a set of unreproducible contingencies. And the planet Earth, once endowed, pole to pole, with all sorts of imagined abysses and wonderlands, now is seen as the extensive but finite thing it is [...] The Amazonian jungle, the very symbol of impenetrability, is displayed in the high perspective as fragile, diminishing, and unique, as vulnerable to the human animal as the buffalo, the whale, and the rhinoceros have been, and the ozone over Antarctica. Things in general take on a tragic once-and-doneness, displacing the ancient comedy, bred of ignorance, of infinite possibility and endless cycle.[27]

Similarly, Michael Pollan, writing in the early 1990s, concedes that 'entropy is the great faith of our time'.[28] Although this is not Pollan's credo – nor, indeed, Updike's, as will be explored later – there is no doubt that entropy is also a dominant theme in postmodern fiction (as in science and environmentalism), and a readily identifiable feature of writers such as Thomas Pynchon, John Barth or Don DeLillo. Tony Tanner, for instance, finds Updike unexpectedly aligned with Pynchon and others of his postmodern ilk, albeit in an estimation written in 1971, before the appearance of *The Witches of Eastwick*:

> Updike's prose does give the impression of being a somewhat rococo version of fairly conventional naturalism, but at its best it is edged with dread. This dread stems from related sources: the terror at the sense of the infinite spaces in which the world tumbles, and the horror which attaches to what he thinks of the Darwinian demonstration that 'the

---

27   John Updike, *Self-Consciousness: Memoirs* (Harmondsworth: Penguin, 1990 [1989]), p. 240.

28   Michael Pollan, *Second Nature: A Gardener's Education* (London: Bloomsbury, 2002 [1991]), p. 157.

organic world, for all its seemingly engineered complexity, might be a self-winnowing chaos.

These feelings of cosmic vertigo seem to feed the basic dread in Updike's work – the fear of death, the fact of decay and the inevitable collapse into nothingness [...] The universal fact of continuous erosion falls like a shadow across Updike's mid-century American suburbia. 'Waste' is a crucial word and obsession in his work, and his sense of the pathos and horror of a wasting world brings him into unexpected relationship with writers like Pynchon. Updike has also had his vision of an entropic world [...][29]

There is much in *Witches of Eastwick* to support the view that he continues to be preoccupied by waste, dirt, decay and dissolution. However, another view would be to suggest that while there is no doubt that Updike depicts a world dominated by these doom-laden aspects, his own ethic may not be under their sway. His characters represent a range of views. For instance, Clyde, whose own 'ecology' of mind is so disturbed as to kill his wife and commit suicide, at one stage tellingly recalls an 'innocent' time, (similar to Updike's own phrase in the extract from *Self-Consciousness:* 'bred of ignorance'). Then, he had hoped for something more certain in the world than science-endorsed chaos, and wrote a paper called 'The Supposed Conflict Between Science and Religion', 'concluding that there was none'. However, thirty-five years later, he recants the view: 'The conflict was open and implacable and science was winning' (p. 130). Darryl Van Horne, at the other extreme, is an exuberant inventor intending to bring Science and Nature together in order to find 'a loophole in the second law of thermodynamics', a 'combination [...] to generate electricity without further input' (p. 139) and 'a selenium-based solution to the problem of energy' (p. 213). His cutting-edge work is on 'the Big Interface' between solar and electrical energy. Nature is still in the picture, harnessed to (some would say exploited by) science in the creation of the new, as with 'the brave new world' of durable protective synthetic polymers: 'you can *grow* the raw materials, and when you run out of land you can grow 'em in the ocean' (p. 47). 'Move over Mother Nature, we've got you beat' is this particular devil's motto and challenge to the defeatism of accepting entropy.

His acolytes, the witches, however, are divorced women whose quests for sustainability extend primarily to their careers, homes, children, pets, lovers and each other. The witches, Alexandra Spofford, Sukie Rougemont and Jane Smart, thus all have unkempt, chaotic gardens. Sukie, a writer for the Eastwick newspaper, *Word*, has a tiny house on Hemlock Lane and a yard that bears only one tree, 'a slender young pear tree overburdened with pears' (p. 35). Jane Smart, the musician of the trio, 'was no gardener' and the surrounds of her suburban house in Cove Homes (so nearly 'Coven Homes'), contain only 'the neglected tangle of rhododendrons, hydrangea, arborvitae, barberry and box around her foundations [which] helped muffle the outpour from her windows' (p. 21). Alexandra, the 'head witch', the artist who models little female figurines, her 'bubbies', has the largest garden and a strong

---

29   Tony Tanner, *City of Words: A Study of American Fiction in the Mid-Twentieth Century* (London: Jonathan Cape, 1976 [1971]), pp. 275-6.

affinity with the natural world – for its ruthlessness as much as its beauty ('Nature requires sacrifice'). Her garden on Orchard Road, is prolific and out of control: 'Every year it does feel [...] more of an effort. For gardeners anyway.' (p. 85) Her crop of tomatoes 'came on like a plague', a 'preposterous fecundity' and eventually, after making as much spaghetti sauce as she – and her Italian-American lover, Joe Marino – can manage, she simply lets them rot on the vine: 'Of plants tomatoes seemed the most human, eager and fragile and prone to rot' (p. 6). This is the harvest that, in Michael Pollan's words, is 'nature's gothic'.[30] The rest of her garden also has a sinister, or gothic, aspect:

> Fungi – blobs of brown loaded by nature with simples and banes and palliatives – had materialized in the low damp spots of this neglected lawn during this moist summer [...] The wild area beyond the tumbled stone wall was itself a wall of weeds and wild raspberry canes [...] this little wilderness where a hundred species of plants were competing for sunlight and water, carbon dioxide and nitrogen [...] an implacable festering of protein chains as nature sought not only to thrust itself outward with root and runner and shoot but to attract insects to its pollen and seeds. (pp. 290-91)

These witches are somewhat at odds with the conventional view of witches. They rarely tend or utilise their gardens to enhance their powers or to establish a familiarity with the 'simples and banes and palliatives' that their gardens could render. However, in the legendary history of their seventeenth-century forbears, witches' gardens were potent – as a resource but also as an emblem according to the *story* 'still being retold, in full or in part, by women who are academics, but also by poets, novelists, popular historians, theologians, dramatists':[31]

> Once upon a time, there was a woman who lived on the edge of a village. She lived alone, in her own house surrounded by her garden, in which she grew all manner of herbs and other healing plants. Though she was alone, she was never lonely; she had her garden and her animals for company, she took lovers when she wished, and she was always busy. The woman was a healer and midwife; she had practical knowledge taught her by her mother, and mystical knowledge derived from her closeness to nature, or from a half-submerged pagan religion. She helped women give birth, and she had healing hands; she used her knowledge of herbs and her common sense to help the sick. However, her peaceful existence was disrupted. Even though this woman was harmless, she posed a threat to the fearful. Her medical knowledge threatened the doctor. Her simple, true spiritual values threatened the superstitious nonsense of the Catholic church, as did her affirmation of the sensuous body. Her independence and freedom threatened men. So the Inquisition descended on her, and cruelly tortured her into confessing to lies about the devil. She was burned alive by men who hated women, along with millions of others just like her.[32]

---

30 Pollan, op. cit., p. 155.

31 Diane Purkiss, *The Witch in History: Early Modern and Twentieth-century Representation* (London & New York: Routledge, 1996), p. 7.

32 Ibid., p. 7.

The fictional witches of Eastwick in the 1960s and early 1970s had different powers and means. 'In the right mood and into their third drinks they could erect a cone of power above them like a tent to the zenith' (p. 35) and, having become witches by virtue of their status as divorcees (power comes from being left or 'doing the leaving;' it doesn't make any difference'), their healing powers now reside in sex; the 'gardens' used in this healing are in their bodies, 'being for any man a garden stocked with antidotes and palliatives' (p. 78):

> Healing belonged to their natures, and if the world accused them of coming between men and wives, of tying the disruptive ligature, of knotting the *aiguillette* that places the kink of impotence or emotional coldness in the entrails of a marriage seemingly secure in its snugly roofed and darkened house, and if the world not merely accused but burned them alive in the tongues of indignant opinion, that was the price they must pay. It was fundamental and instinctive, it was womanly, to want to heal – to apply the poultice of acquiescent flesh to the wound of a man's desire, to give his closeted spirit the exaltation of seeing a witch slip out of her clothes and go skyclad in a room of tawdry motel furniture. (p. 69)

The witches, who now devote themselves to 'healing' various 'odd husbands let stray by the women who owned them', still have material vestiges of their own former spouses present in their homes – souvenirs. Alexandra's ex, Ozzie, is mere dust collected in a tightly sealed jar kept on a high kitchen, whereas Sukie's former husband Monty, has been 'permanized in plastic' as a placemat and Jane's Sam hangs with the dried herbs in the cellar. Furthermore, they compete for the attention and patronage of the philandering 'horny devil', Darryl Van Horne. As Margaret Atwood puts it:

> These are not 1980s Womanpower witches. They aren't at all interested in healing the earth, communing with the Great Goddess, or gaining Power-within (as opposed to Power-over). [...] They are spiritual descendents of the 17th-century New England strain and go in for sabbats, sticking pins in wax images, kissing the devil's backside and phallus worship [...][33]

However, these fictional witches of the 1960s and 1970s are reminiscent of a literary precursor, the adulterous – and artistic – Hester Prynne of *The Scarlet Letter* (1986 [1850]). Nathaniel Hawthorne based a good measure of his depiction of Hester Prynne on Anne Hutchinson, having earlier, in 1830, written the sketch 'Mrs Hutchinson'. Anne Hutchinson, like the fictional Hester is also made an outcast by the Puritans' patriarchs for her independent views. Indeed, Anne Hutchinson is mentioned several times in *The Witches of Eastwick*, for it was to remote Rhode Island that she was exiled, and where she died. Updike's own interest in Hawthorne is well documented, and he cites *The Scarlet Letter* as 'not only a piece of fiction, it is a myth by now,'[34]

33   M. Atwood, op. cit.
34   Ibid., p. 129.

America's 'first masterpiece'.[35] Updike's engagement with Hawthorne's ubiquitously influential work is evidenced in *'The Scarlet Letter' Trilogy*, which comprises *A Month of Sundays*, published in 1975, and *Roger's Version* and *S*, both published after the *Witches of Eastwick*, in 1985 and 1986 respectively. Despite being outside the trilogy itself, in the view of one critic at least, *The Witches of Eastwick* is Updike's 'most Hawthornesque work'.[36]

Prior to writing the novel, Updike had also been reading widely about witchcraft and about the witchcraft trials, calling upon, in particular, Margaret Murray's work,[37] *The Witch-Cult in Western Europe* (1921) and *The God of the Witches* (1931), and having formerly read Jules Michelet's nineteenth-century classic treatise, *Satanism and Witchcraft in the Middle Ages*. However, although Updike clearly draws upon these significant literary and historical precursors, it is not at the expense of contemporary reference – that is, reference to the late 1960s and early 1970s. The witches of Eastwick are clearly witches of their time, a time when second-wave feminism was beginning to celebrate 'witchiness'. Updike, writing from the perspective of the mid-1980s, is able to imbue what was incipient at the time of the novel's setting with elements of what was to burgeon throughout the 1970s and early 1980s. The list is long but perhaps most relevant to this novel would be the writings of American radical feminist historians such as Barbara Ehrenreich and Dierdre English (also reliant on Murray and Michelet) with their 1973 volume, *Witches, Midwives and Nurses: A History of Women Healers*, or eco-feminist writers such as Mary Daly with her highly influential *Gyn/Ecology*, first published in 1978, and Susan Griffin's *Woman and Nature: The Roaring Inside Her* in 1979. Adrienne Rich published *Of Woman Born: Motherhood as Experience and Institution* in 1976; in a chapter entitled 'Hands of Flesh, Hands of Iron', Rich discusses amongst other issues, the 'classic pamphlet' *Witches, Midwives and Nurses* in which Anne Hutchinson, who also so 'present' in *The Witches of Eastwick*, is seen as a model *:*

> Barbara Ehrenreich and Deirdre English trace the rise of this elitist medical profession, which emerged out of the suppression of women healers during the centuries of witch-hunting, persecution, and murder [...] wisewomen, healers and midwives were especially singled out by the witch-hunters. [...] The case of Anne Hutchinson is instructive because it illuminates the many levels on which the American Puritan midwife was seen as threatening and subversive [...] She became a witch. Anne Hutchinson as not alone [...], a colleague of Hutchinson's [...] was charged with 'familiarity with the devill'.[38]

---

35 Updike in Schiff, *Updike's Version*, cited in Plath, *Conversations with John Updike*, p. 209.

36 Schiff cited in Plath, *Conversations with John Updike*, p. 212.

37 John Updike, *Audio Interview with John Updike*, interview with Don Swaim (1984), http://wiredforbooks.org/johnupdike/.

38 Adrienne Rich, *Of Woman Born: Motherhood as Experience and Institution* (London: Virago, 1984 [1976]), pp. 135–7, and also citing Ben Barker-Benfield, 'Anne Hutchinson and the Puritan Attitude Towards Women', *Feminist Studies*, Vol. 1, No. 2 (Fall, 1972).

Updike's witches of the 1970s are certainly familiar, and vying to be ever more so, with the devil in the guise of Darryl Van Horne, whose last name resonates with both intimations of the phallic Horned God and a hint of the Transylvanian count. It is Van Horne who gives voice to the 'classic' feminist stance of the time (rather gallingly for a feminist audience, no doubt, although Brenda Parsley also reiterates these views[39]), when he proclaims to his own 'Triple-Goddess' accolytes:

> the whole witchcraft scare was an attempt – successful, as it turned out – on the part of the newly arising male-dominated medical profession, beginning in the fourteenth century, to get the childbirth business out of the hands of midwives. That's what a lot of the women burned were – midwives. They had the ergot, and atropine, and probably a lot of right instincts even without germ theory. When the male doctors took over they worked blind, with a sheet round their necks, and brought all the diseases from the rest of their practice with them. The poor cunts died in droves. (pp. 112-13)

There is an irony in that these witches in Eastwick find their sisterly solidarity and their 'cone of power' so fragile and uncertain. They compete frantically for Van Horne's attentions and readily acquiesce to his 'help' in furthering their self-confidence and their careers: 'think big'. Of course, Darryl eventually opts for the younger model, frail X-ray technician, Jenny, who herself contracts the dreaded cancer. (Cancer, noted Susan Sontag in 1978, 'is often experienced as a form of demonic possession – tumors are "malignant" or "benign", like forces – '[40]). When Darryl disappears with her brother Chris, rumour has it that he was gay all along (from the shadow of cancer to that of AIDS). The knowing witches have diminished their own powers by competing for the attentions of a man who 'won't commit', colluding again with 'the death-dealing sexual, economic and spiritual oppression of the Imperialist Phallic Society'.[41] Eastwick's witches, then, are not the signed up, radical and separatist witches such as those who, in New York in 1968, formed WITCH: Women's International Conspiracy from Hell, whose members hexed the Chase Manhattan Bank, and invaded the Bride Fair at Madison Square Gardens dressed as witches.[42] Rather, these witches were generically suburban women, living in a part of America steeped in witchcraft history and folklore. They are also affected by a contemporary range of cultural discourses and events, including 'second-wave

---

39   Brenda Parsley, replacing at the pulpit her errant and now deceased husband, the Reverend Ed Parsley, discusses Anne Hutchinson and the Puritan patriarchs: 'Our own dear valiant Anne Hutchinson believed in a covenant of grace, as opposed to a covenant of works, and defied – this mother of fifteen and gentle midwife to sisters uncounted and uncountable – the sexist world-hating clergy of Boston in behalf of her belief, a belief for which she was eventually to die' (pp. 277-8).

40   Susan Sontag, *Illness as a Metaphor/Aids and its Metaphors* (Harmondsworth: Penguin, 1991[1978/1989]), p. 70.

41   WITCH, 'Spooking the Pariarchy', in *The Politics of Women's Spirituality: Essays on the Rise of Spiritual Power Within the Feminist Movement*, ed. Charlene Spretnak (New York: Doubleday, 1982), p. 76, cited in D. Purkiss, op. cit., p. 9.

42   D. Purkiss, ibid., p. 9.

feminism' and the women's liberation movement, a new environmental movement in the United States, first given impetus, perhaps, by Rachel Carson's ground-breaking *Silent Spring* in 1962, and increasing anti-pollution lobbies. ('The Crying Indian' public service announcement, part of the 'Keep America Beautiful' campaign, was launched on Earth Day in 1971, the same year that saw the National Cancer Act established and *The Female Eunuch* published).

Whereas eco-feminist writers or promoters of the Ancient Goddess religion, such as Starhawk or Judith Ochshorn, believed that women's stewardship of the Earth would be intrinsically healing and regenerative, there have been others who questioned whether such an essentialist and utopian view was tenable. Updike was engaging with this debate about women and power – and with the utopian notion that a Pagan rather than a Judeo-Christian tradition might afford a new version of a Paradise-Garden: 'there have been feminist interpretations of all branches of Paganism, and of alchemy, astrology and the tarot [...] Covens are usually given a name, like Darkmoon, or Tree [...or] Compost'.[43] The post-pill sexual revolution also had its utopian hopes; 'erotic utopianism', notes David Lodge, while being 'at odds with conventional Christian morality', is 'at the same time [...] basically religious in its values', abjuring 'worldly and materialistic standards of achievement and success.'[44] Significantly, the only time the witches in this novel refer to paradise ('this is paradise') is when they are all together with Jenny in the hot tub they have shared so often with Darryl, but on this occasion, have uninhibitedly all to themselves. Updike is parodying this and other utopian notions; the hot tub orgies might have represented a communal space of polymorphous play and sexual 'seethe', but it is not untainted by competition, duplicity or murderous intent:

> I never saw Eastwick as a paradise, exactly – certainly not for these divorcées. The book was somewhat about the predicament of divorced women. Now that divorce has become common, what do women do with their freedom from male or patriarchal authority, and how do women handle power? It was a convention of feminist thought, at least in the sixties and seventies, that men were murderous in their use of power, and that women, were they allowed power, would of course *not* be – even though Indira Gandhi and Golda Meir and other female leaders throughout history had not proven to be conspicuously more clever at avoiding war than men had. So I was trying to explore, on the realistic level, the whole question of power in women. Would it become less murderous in female hands? And, of course, my thought was, it wouldn't. Witness their own murder of their fellow witch, the ingénue witch, Jenny.[45]

Writing the book was, Updike has claimed, 'an attempt to write about women and nature and power, all somewhat from the standpoint of opinion and belief, 'rather

43   Ibid., p. 39.
44   David Lodge, 'Post-Pill Paradise Lost: John Updike's *Couples*', in *John Updike*, Harold Bloom, ed. (New York; New Haven; Philadelphia: Chelsea House, 1987), p. 30.
45   John Updike in an interview with James Plath, *Conversations with John Updike*, op. cit., p 264.

than "this is my material"'.[46] Further, he was exploring 'what it's like to be a free woman, the loneliness of divorcées and the financial pressures they almost all live under. And the consolation they find in each other'.[47] In *Hugging the Shore*, Updike noted: 'Witchcraft is a venture, one could generally say, of woman into the realm of power.'[48] However, these witches are not able to establish the new paradigm for an American Paradise. They re-marry, leave Eastwick and their sisterhood, and move on; Alexandra, for instance, goes 'back west [...] where all the witchcraft belonged to the Hopi and Navajo shamans' (p. 312). This ending sits uneasily with many feminists, no doubt, but in the novel's own terms there is equality: the witches fail no more or less than anyone else. This is simply another instance of composition and decomposition – another cycle, another season, including the literary narrative ones of pastiche and parody.

What Updike proffers in the novel about the events of the late 1960s and early 1970s is inflected with the irony that hindsight affords. *Self-Consciousness* contains a revealing chapter on Updike's own somewhat angst-ridden and not unequivocal political stance during the Vietnam War: 'On Not Being a Dove'. The story told is of Updike's 'coming out' as a Democrat-but-not-a-Dove, who found dove protests in relation to the Vietnam War to be 'too reflexive, too Pop'.[49] Reflecting from a vantage point in 1989 on the position he felt compelled to adopt, despite the minor 'witch-hunts' that ensued in that 'polluted and fractious time',[50] Updike provides an added dimension in which to consider the novel:

> [It was] a darkly happy in-between time after the Pill and IUD had freed sex from fear of pregnancy and before AIDS hobbled it with the fear of death [...] a time luxurious in the many directions of its craziness, since the war and the counterculture and the moon shots were all fuelled by an overflowing prosperity no longer with us [...] What with Woodstock and *Barbarella* and *The Joy of Sex* and the choral nudity in *Hair*, there was a consciously retrieved Edenic innocence, a Blakean triumph of the youthful human animal, along with napalm and defoliation.[51]

Woodstock Music and Art Fair, a massive open-air festival, an anti-establishment, anti-war 'love-in' and music extravaganza, billed as 'an Aquarian Exposition', was held over three days in August 1969 at Max Yasgur's dairy farm in Bethel, New York, some fifty miles from the town of Woodstock. Estimates of attendance vary because the festival was free but figures of 400,000–500,000 ('half a million strong')[52] were regular at an event that hosted over thirty top names, including Jimi Hendrix, Joan

---

46   John Updike in an interview with George Christian in 1985, ibid., p. 169.

47   Ibid., p. 171.

48   John Updike, *Hugging the Shore: Essays and Criticism* (Harmondsworth: Penguin, 1985 [1983]), p. 855.

49   Op. cit., p. 109.

50   Ibid., p. 110.

51   Updike, *Self-Consciousness*, pp. 140-41.

52   Joni Mitchell, 'Woodstock', *The Complete Poems and Lyrics* (London: Chatto & Windus, 1997), p. 59.

Baez and the Grateful Dead. Joni Mitchell was not there, but she wrote the lyrics that became not just an ode to the festival but to a generation, with its refrain and invocation: 'We are stardust, we are golden/ And we got to get ourselves back to the garden'. Several verses, in particular, are familiar in relation to *The Witches of Eastwick*:

And I dreamed I saw the bombers
Riding shotgun in the sky
And they were turning into butterflies
Above our nation.
We are stardust [A billion year old carbon]
We are golden, [We just got caught up in the devil's bargain]
And we've got to get ourselves
Back to the garden. [To some semblance of a garden][53]

This is the theme song of the 'Blakean triumph of the youthful human animal', as Updike put it, protesting against the wrongs perpetrated by the Establishment, and invoking instead a 'consciously retrieved Eden', ' back to the garden' where peace and love would prevail: 'Make Love Not War', as the slogan said.

There are several such idealistic anti-war protesters in *The Witches of Eastwick*, and here, they are not to be congratulated for their idealism, which is depicted as facile and formulaic; these are the kind of protests that Updike himself found 'too reflexive, too Pop'. They include the Reverend Ed Parsley (with a name indicative of a 'getting-back-to-the-garden' wholesome herb, or a mere, often redundant, garnish), who abandons both his wife and his church community. Taking his girlfriend Dawn Polanski with him, he eventually blows himself up making home-made bombs in the service of the revolution. Like Felicia's, Ed's views are a kind of reflex, espousing ideology without commitment or thorough thought, as when he rounds on Van Horne: 'You're a man of sophistication and know as well as I do that the connection between the present atrocities in Southeast Asia and that new little drive-in branch Old Stone Bank has next to the Superette is direct and immediate'(p. 43). Having immediately surmised that Van Horne was 'a banker type', and thus 'an implementer of the System', Ed is described as wanting to be 'the agent of another System, equally fierce and far-flung'. Ed's commitment to the church is also vague and superficial and he is defensive and self-conscious; his aura exudes 'sickly chartreuse waves of anxiety and narcissism'. Even his adulterous guilt seems to have no depth, but is, rather, just another automatic reflex. Felicia Gabriel is another character devoted to causes by default rather than devotion, someone who 'was in this day and age outraged by everything' (p. 76). As she rants, self-righteous and intransigent in her mimic-views on one thing or another, feathers begin to emerge from her mouth, which increasingly reeks of a chicken coop or birdcage. Eventually, she is bludgeoned to death with a poker at the hands of her husband, who had 'lost

---

53 Ibid. Lines in square brackets are variously available/recorded but are not included in the collection *The Complete Poems and Lyrics*.

the habit' of happiness or hopefulness. Brenda Parsley is another pontificator-by-rote, as she fills her husband's vacancy in the church. Her inconsistent diatribes have familiar themes (from 'evil wrought in Southeast Asia by fascist politicians and an oppressive capitalism seeking to secure and enlarge its markets for anti–ecological luxuries' to 'evil brewing in these very homes of Eastwick'). Her pronouncements are delivered under the auspices of a new, inclusive symbolism: 'Above her head hung not the tarnished brass cross that had been suspended there for years in irrelevant symbolism but a solid new brass circle, symbol of perfect unity and peace'. From *her* mouth, however, come insects: bumblebees, moths, butterflies:

> As from the bell of a hollyhock a bumblebee sleepily emerged from between Brenda's plum painted lips and dipped on its questing course over the heads of the congregation [...]She took a shallow breath and tried to speak out through the something else gathering in her mouth [...] a pale blue moth, and then its little tan sister, emerged [...] and her mouth gave birth to an especially vivid, furry, foul-tasting monarch butterfly, its orange wings rimmed thickly in black[...] 'Pray!', Brenda shouted [...] Something was pouring over her lower lip, making her chin shine. 'Pray!' she shouted in a hollow man's voice, as if she were a ventriloquist's dummy. (pp. 280-82)

Like the other anti-System protestors, Brenda speaks words and thoughts that are not her own, a puppet of some other discourse to which she has 'signed up' and by which she is manipulated to spout, albeit beautiful, rubbish.

Darryl Van Horne also has a lot to say and he does plenty of pontificating in a crude manner and is usually offensive on a wide range of topics. For instance, at an early stage in the novel, he outlines to the witches his views on the vernal season:

> Spring [...] All that growth, you can feel Nature groaning, the old bitch; she doesn't want to do it, not again, no, anything but *that*, but she *has* to. It's a fucking torture rack, all that budding and pushing, the sap up the tree trunks, the weeds and the insects getting set to fight it out once again, the seeds trying to remember how the hell the DNA is supposed to go; all that competition for a little bit of nitrogen; Christ, it's cruel. Maybe I'm too sensitive. I bet you revel in it. Women aren't that sensitive to things like that. (pp. 84-5)

Indeed, he takes an opportunity to deliver a sermon of his own making at the little Unitarian church. The title of his talk is: 'This is a Terrible Creation'. His 'good book' is *Webster's Collegiate Dictionary* and it prompts him to musings on centipedes, tarantulas, tapeworms and other parasites such a fluke or roundworm ('as real a creature as you or me. He's as noble a creature, designwise – really *lovingly* designed'). His sermon is rambling and wide-ranging: evolution, human nature, human history (including the torture of witches in Germany) and, throughout, terror – 'this mess of torture'. However, claims Van Horne, no amount of human cruelty can compare with that which 'natural organic friendly Creation has inflicted on its creatures since the first poor befuddled set of amino acids struggled up out of the galvanized slime' (p. 297). Darryl's graphic and grisly sermon ends in outrageous blasphemy (but then, he is the devil – and a designer):

'You got to picture that Big Visage leaning down and smiling through Its beard while those fabulous Fingers with Their angelic manicure fiddled with the last fine-tuning of old *Schistosoma's* [blood fluke] ventral sucker: that's Creation. Now I ask you, isn't that pretty terrible? Couldn't you have done better, given the resources? I sure as hell could have. So vote for me next time. O.K? Amen.' (p. 302)

There is no proselytising 'peace, love and happiness' here.

Unlike Milton who, Blake claimed, was of the 'Devil's party without knowing it', Updike knows where his own allegiance lies. His devil, Darryl, does have his vote – largely. Updike's own religious commitment is well documented and has been widely discussed – by Updike himself. That this devil is a hero, however, presents no real contradiction in terms of Updike's stance. What Darryl Van Horne ultimately represents is a dynamic, and thus, hopeful, view of the world. Darryl is a designer, inventor, Pop Art collector; he's also ludicrous, evasive, exuberant, flawed, protean (none of his monograms are ever the same) priapic (horny) – and sexually ambiguous. In classical and pagan terms he is Dionysian. His view of the creation is not anthropocentric, sanitised and romantic. Like Updike himself, Darryl is prepared to discuss war, sex, religion and science without resorting to politically correct platitudes or becoming some ventriloquist's dummy; rather, he is earthy, inconsistent, crude and speaks 'live' – not evil, its anagrammatic obverse. Darryl is not 'establishment' nor anti-establishment or anti-anti-establishment – and he is no saint. He has an interest in things of the future, such as finding a solution to the conundrum of entropy. In reply to an interviewer's question, 'Why do you bring the devil back to earth?', Updike responded:

He was never away. *My* devil, Darryl Van Horne, is a weaker figure – no monster. I had an idea to create him as a kind of experimenter, where it would be possible for him through some short-cut in the physical theory of thermodynamics, to forever solve the energy problems on earth. He's definitely not a Mephisto – but I'm also not an expert of devils.[54]

Like his hero, Updike seems to be opposed to stasis, to the platitudes and certainties of the sanctimonious. In another case, the narrator delivers this meditation:

Before plumbing, in the old outhouses, in winter, the accreted shit of the family would mount up in a spiky frozen stalagmite and such phenomena help us to believe that there is more to life than the airbrushed ads at the front of magazines, the Platonic forms of perfume bottles and nylon nightgowns and Rolls-Royce fenders. (p. 216)

The frozen excrement will thaw and will be transformed; in its own way it will be matter changed again into energy rather than simply 'waste'. Included in Platonic forms might also be included The Garden, the kind that is 'bowdlerised', 'sacrificed to a cult of plant prettiness that obscures more dubious truths about nature, our

---

54 Willi Winkler, 'A Conversation with John Updike', in Plath, *Conversations with John Updike*, op. cit,. p. 175.

own included'.[55] If the 'natural' is what is to be restored to sustain the Earth, this anthropocentric fixation on the garden that is beautiful and benign only will not do anything but lead to despondency. A lighter touch and a harsher sense of reality are what seem to be needed, according to writers like Updike and Pollan. Just as the close of the novel allows for transition and change, so entropy is overcome – but death, disease and the sacrifice nature requires and simply takes, is not. In Michael Pollan's view, contemporary views on entropy are fundamentally misguided:

> We take it as an article of faith today that the Earth is running down, that we are using up its finite supplies of energy, fertility, and resources of all kinds. We've come to think of the Earth as a closed system; one of the age's presiding metaphors is 'spaceship Earth'. Conceived as such, it's easy to imagine the ship's provisions gradually being exhausted; as more and more matter is converted to energy, we must eventually run out [...] But the second law of thermodynamics, under which entropy increases as matter converts to energy, applies only to close systems, and [...] the global ecosystem is not a closed system. The Earth in fact is nothing like a spaceship, because new energy is continually pouring down on it, in the form of sunlight – free, boundless, virtually infinite sunlight. And sunlight come down to Earth is used by the process of photosynthesis to create new plant matter. Plants, in other words, are energy returned to matter – entropy undone, at least here on Earth.[56]

In a collection of poems entitled *Facing Nature*, published a year after *The Witches of Eastwick*, John Updike included 'Seven Odes to Seven Natural Processes', beginning with an 'Ode to Rot'. The seven processes are in sequence: Rot; Evaporation; Growth; Fragmentation; Entropy; Crystallization; Healing. The conclusion of 'Ode To Entropy' concurs with Pollan's view that it is by acknowledging Nature's paradigms rather than asserting our own that the conviction of an entropic demise is overthrown:

> Death exists nowhere in nature, not
> in the minds of birds or the consciousness of flowers,
> not even in the numb brain of the wildebeest calf
> gone under to the grinning crocodile, nowhere
> in the mesh of the woods or the tons of sea, only
> in our forebodings, our formulae.
> There is still enough energy in one overlooked star
> to power all the heavens madmen have ever proposed.[57]

It is the hypotheses or 'articles of faith' used by the doves, hippies, environmentalists and eco-feminist witches that Updike (and his hero Van Horne) aim to refute in this novel. To put Van Horne's sermon, 'This is a Terrible Creation' or Updike's

---

55   Michael Pollan, *The Botany of Desire: A Plant's-Eye View of the World* (London: Bloomsbury, 2002 [2001]), p. 129.

56   M. Pollan, *Second Nature*, op. cit., pp. 157-8.

57   John Updike, *Facing Nature: Poems* (New York: Alfred A. Knopf, 1985), p. 87.

'Ode to Rot', alongside Brenda Parsley's 'sound-bytes', or, say, that anthem of the moment, Joni Mitchell's 'Woodstock', is to find the crux of Updike's resistance. His objection is to a facile utopianism and ventriloquism in the face of extraordinarily complex questions: war, religion, science, sex and death – death which is both rot and 'reprocessing':

> All process is reprocessing;
> give thanks for gradual ceaseless rot
> gnawing gross Creation fine while we sleep,
> the lightening-forged organic conspiracy's
> merciful counterplot. [58]

The Witches of Eastwick, itself an example of postmodern 'reprocessing', is an ode-in-prose and a 'counterplot' to the various arrogant, anthropocentric and apollonian 'lightening forged' discourses of the time: we are not golden, but gross – and to Updike, that is both terrible and terrific.

A. S. Byatt: Evolution

A. S Byatt's novella 'Morpho Eugenia' was published in 1992 with its companion novella, 'The Conjugial Angel', together comprising the volume entitled *Angels and Insects*. 'Morpho Eugenia' is the first of the duo. Its title alludes to the Latin nomenclature for a species of insect, a tropical butterfly, brought back to England in the story, as part of a collecting expedition to the Amazon. Eugenia is also the name of one of the main characters. The tale is set in the early 1860s, and central to it is the impact of advancements in science and natural history. The text specifically alludes to the work of Alfred Wallace and his publication several years earlier, in 1852, of *Narratives of Travels in the Amazon and Rio Negro*. Wallace's own work on 'the survival of the fittest', 'On the Tendency of Varieties to Depart from the Original Type', published in 1858, precipitated the most notable publication of the period, Darwin's *On The Origin of Species by Means of Natural Selection, or the Preservation of Favoured Races in the Struggle for Life* in 1859.

---

58 Ibid., p. 78.

In the novel, a young collector, William Adamson, has recently returned from a ten-year expedition to the Amazon. In the manner typical of postmodern texts, real and fictive aspects combine. Both Alfred Wallace and Henry Walter Bates are referred to as colleagues and acquaintances of the fictional character, Adamson. 'The social insects' become the focus of Adamson's scientific observations, and it is as an entomologist that he sets forth to the jungle with the hope of claiming and naming new species as his own discovery: 'There were millions of miles of unexplored forest [...] There would be new species of ants, to be named perhaps *adamsonii*. There would be space for a butcher's son to achieve greatness.'[59] Ant colonies are also the focus of the lay scientific-study on the habits of social insects, which William oversees once back in England and as the guest of wealthy patron and collector, the Reverend Harald Alabaster of Bredely Hall. It is soon clear, despite various warnings within the novel itself against this tendency ('analogy is a slippery tool', 'men are not ants') that the ant-heap and the Victorian household tend to function as metaphors for each other. Just as there are obvious analogies between the butterfly of the title, Morpho Eugenia, and the beautiful eldest Alabaster daughter, Eugenia, so the corpulent brood-Queen of the ant colony and the matron of an upper-class Victorian household have an equivalence, as do the scurrying, much less visible workers – ants and human – that support these systems. The butterflies of the story are also emblematic: the collectors' trophy of the pair of mounted Morpho Eugenia, destined to 'dance together forever, in their white satin and lavender silk' in 'a special glass case' are aligned with the visually splendid, high-born museum-piece-on-display, Eugenia Alabaster. The strong-winged, vigorous flight and long-distanced migrations of the Monarch butterfly, which appears at the end of the novella refers, finally, to the independent, intelligent, classless or unclassifiable 'worker', Matilda Compton.

In the aristocratic Victorian household, flora and fauna are memorialised not just in glass display-cases but also in women's attire – 'bedecked with respective flowers: white rosebuds, blush-tipped daisies, violets' – or in their homes with such opulent décor as: 'a stained glass roundel depicting two white lilies'; 'a mahogany bed intricately carved with ivy leaves and holly berries'; 'a snowy bedspread embroidered with Tudor roses'; dark pomegranate-red wallpaper, sprinkled with sprigs of honeysuckle' and 'a nest of cushions, all embroidered with flowers and fruit and blue butterflies and scarlet birds'. The glass-house, too, which contains living material, nonetheless is more about opulence and show than of anything natural:

> – a series of wrought iron grilles, in the form of ivy leaves and twining branches, supported a mixture of creeping and climbing plants, making a series of half-hidden bowers, inside which hung huge wire baskets, always full of flowering plants, brilliantly coloured, delicately scented. Palm trees stood here and there in gold-gleaming brass tubs, and the floor was tiled in shiny black marble, giving the impression, from certain angles in certain lights, of a deep dark lake with a reflecting surface. (p. 50)

---

59   A. S. Byatt, *Angels and Insects* (London: Vintage, 1992), p. 11.

For the Alabaster family – and others like them – the *appearance* of life, including pedigree, fecundity, prosperity and power, is more important than its actual sustenance. As the novella will show, in the context of its Victorian themes of natural selection and sexual selection, 'good breeding' and the survival of the fittest can be at odds. At first, William accepts the appearances that confront him; he finds Eugenia desirable, beautiful and chaste; he finds in the artifice of the glass house 'a palace where his two worlds met': 'English primroses and bluebells, daffodils and crocus shone amongst evergreen luxuriant tropical creepers, their soft perfumes mingling with exotic stephanotis and sweet jasmine'. Matty Compton, however, he views as somewhat irrelevant: dark and sexless. The ironies that will be revealed later make a mockery of the Alabasters' façade of good breeding and of their moral superiority. Despite Eugenia's fecundity once she has married the lowly William and her breeding 'true to stock', what is revealed is the lack of vigorous blood (as the name Alabaster signifies, and, conversely represented by Matty's more sanguine aspect – and her study of *sanguinea*, Blood Red Ants). Eugenia's fate is one of insularity, stasis and replication; Matty – or Matilda as she later insists on being called – has a chrysalis aspect – transfigured in William's eyes when she writes the fable 'Things are Not What They Seem' and when she finds her own self-assured voice: 'It is what I will do'; 'My name is Matilda'; 'Look at me'; 'I should like you to stay'. This particular unveiling, however, is after Matty has opened William's eyes to the truth about his aristocratic wife and her long-term incestuous relations with her half-brother, Edgar.

The story takes on another sexually allegorical dimension when the study of insects leads to the exposure of incest, and when Matty's knowledge of the secret is represented in a game of anagrams by the close linguistic equivalence of INSECT and INCEST. Another closely related word, instinct, is also being evoked here, and not surprisingly, since Darwin and others were contributing to a debate on instinct as it relates to animal, including human, behaviour. Also, circa 1860, Sigmund Freud was coining the term 'psychoanalysis' and, thereafter, developing further and publishing his theories of human sexual instinct and cultural taboos, including incest. From anthropological studies to entomological ones, such as William's treatise on the 'marriage flight' and the 'nuptials' of ants, comparisons between the customs of a variety of social and sexual arrangements in the animal kingdom were giving rise to a thorough-going review of what constituted 'natural behaviour' and what differentiated the higher and lower orders: from angels to insects.

It would seem at first glance that, in the volume's title, 'Insects' refers to the first novella and 'Angels' strictly to the second, 'The Conjugial Angel', with its specific allusions to Swedenborgian views on celestial beings and its incorporation of illustrations of angels by John Martin, Dante Gabriel Rossetti and Edward Burne Jones. However, the Victorian double-preoccupation with religion and with science is integral to both novellas. As the narrative unfolds, the concept of 'Angels' inflects 'Morpho Eugenia' too. Eugenia Alabaster is a beautiful 'social butterfly' and a

Victorian 'angel'. The perfection in moral and aesthetic terms that 'Angel' denotes is subtly nuanced by a name that combines the scientific with the religious: eugenia, with its connotations of selective breeding and alabaster, resonant of lily-whiteness, in an albeit sepulchral medium. It is undercut by her sexual sin, or stain, a 'smutch', to borrow from the Ben Jonson poem, which, for William, even before he realises its aptness, Eugenia's beauty evokes:

> Have you seen but a bright lily grow,
> Before rude hands have touched it?
> Have you marked but the fall o' the snow,
> Before the soil hath smutched it? (p. 12)

Her sexual transgressions are decidedly un-angelic, un-Christian, un-English, amoral and taboo; the cultural superiority which was extended to the study and conquest of 'Others' is let down badly here. It must be remembered that the Alabaster fortune rests upon the cotton trade, and thus slavery also, in plantations abroad. Harald Alabaster, confirmed in his own moral superiority, is as curious about and concerned for 'the religious beliefs of the Natives' as any other objects of study in foreign climes, such as 'the hummingbird hawk-moth and the Saüba ant'. The Alabaster notion of 'good-breeding' is also undercut by Eugenia's secretive actions. Edgar's estimation of William's inferiority – 'You are underbred, Sir. You are no match for my sister. There is bad blood in you, vulgar blood [...] You are a miserable creature with out breeding or courage' – is countered by Robin Swinnerton as 'an anachronism'. Edgar's blood-quantum views are also refuted by William himself, but on the basis of a different measure of quality: merit, endurance and survival:

> As for breeding, I count my father as a good man, and an honest man, and a kind man, and I know no other *good* reasons for respect except his high achievement. As for courage, I think I may claim to have lived ten years in great hardship on the Amazon, to have survived murder plots and poisonous snakes, and shipwreck and fifteen days in a lifeboat in the mid-Atlantic [...] (p. 62)

Edgar's hypocrisy, of course, is clear in the full knowledge of his decadent behaviour: a 'centaur or satyr', he is a parasite on his father's fortune and good grace, a predator of young female servants such as Amy, who ends up pregnant and abandoned in the workhouse, and the despoiler of his sister. His rhetoric to her has been on a different tack to that proclaimed publicly to humiliate William. Eugenia, exposed, reports: '*he* thought it wasn't [bad] – he said – people like making rules and others like breaking them – he made me believe it was all perfectly *natural* and so it was, it was *natural*, nothing in us rose up and said – it was- *un*-natural.' (p. 159) However, this socially taboo but 'natural' act is also 'transgressive ' in scientific and genetic terms. As William remarks contemptuously, once he has discovered his wife's long-term incestuous relations with her half-brother, even 'breeders know [...] that even first-cousin marriages produce inherited defects'. (There is an irony here in that Darwin himself married his own cousin Emma Wedgewood in 1839). As Gillian

Beer outlines, Darwin's emergent views on evolutionary 'breeding' nonetheless emphasised the importance of diversity:

> Sex and sexual congress is central to Darwinian evolutionary theory. The pairing of *unlike* in the couple produces diversity of offspring – and that diversity increases exponentially. Other forms of reproduction – hermaphroditism, parthenogenesis, division, for example – produce offspring that replicate the previous generation. Sexual reproduction inclines *away* from any such standard identity. So unlikeness and empathy were as important to him theoretically as emotionally.[60]

What has been, in Victorian terms, ostensibly angelic, asexual (though maternal), monogamous and well-bred (like the paradigmatic '*Angel* in the House' of the Victorian poem of that name), is revealed in Eugenia as having an active sexuality, albeit one that selects its mate in an ill-conceived mode that will lead to weakness, deformity and extinction. The Alabaster instinct is not healthy and the aristocratic focus on good breeding has more to do with power and rhetoric than with robustness – a corollary known to plant and animal breeders for some time, and a taboo acknowledged instinctually even among 'primitives' and insects. In the context of Darwin's recently espoused theories of survival and extinction, Eugenia and Edgar's incestuous liaison signifies a multiply-determined and far-reaching degeneracy, as alien to Angels as to Insects, and everything in-between.

This story of the refined Alabasters, at home at the fittingly named Bredely Hall, and their guest, the collector William Adamson, who, after nine years of jungle expeditions then survived shipwreck, is obviously presented in the context of the Victorian obsession with extending scientific knowledge and collecting specimens worldwide in its service. However, the developing system of classification, particularly plant classification, was curiously bound up with and represented by analogies of sexual congress and fidelity with a frankness of attitude that was at odds with published sexual mores. While eighteenth- and nineteenth-century discourses of human sexuality were discreetly coy, those pertaining to the scientific classification of plant families depended on a 'sexualised version of nature [that] verged on the pornographic'[61] and included terms such as 'clandestine marriage', 'libertine', and 'nuptials' – thereby rendering botany an unsuitable study for Victorian young women.[62] The tale of incest at Bredely Hall must be inflected not just by the contributions made by Darwin, Wallace or Freud in the nineteenth century, but also by earlier discourses that arose from the collection of new scientific data at home and abroad and led to the establishment of new knowledge and methods of classification. The fascination with plants and their own 'families' and 'behaviours',

---

60   Gillian Beer, *Open Fields: Science in Cultural Encounter* (Oxford University Press, 1996), p. 29.

61   Patricia Fara, *Sex, Botany & Empire: The Story of Carl Linnaeus and Joseph Banks* (Cambridge: Icon, 2003), p. 12.

62   Ibid.

and their methods of sexual reproduction, was of long-standing by the time Charles Darwin published *The Origin of Species.*

Carl Linnaeus (1707-78) developed a radically new method for the scientific classification of plants that depended on numbering and categorising the sexual organs, dividing them by 'counting the numbers of male and female reproductive organs inside flowers'.[63] Linnaeus and his colleagues in the eighteenth century were looking to nature, botany and the world not just to gain new knowledge but to find their own bias in ordering the world confirmed. The enterprise that was turning to the natural world for models that would reinforce societal conventions as universal, 'natural, even God-given',[64] was certainly not unproblematic. Plants, however, would not comply with the nice distinctions imposed on and expected of them; plants, it became evident, were promiscuous, or hermaphroditic and these Linnaeus dealt with by construing them in pejorative human sexual terms such as 'concubine' and 'clandestine'.[65] His description of botanical relationships was based on a model of explicit and erotic sexuality, transposing the innocent femininity of flora to something altogether more risqué. A century later, Freud was found to be shocking for his use of graphic terms and his explicit attention to the human female genitals and to female sexuality. Linnaeus's descriptions, however, prefigure Freud, but *his* ideas and human sexual analogies are in the service of plants and plant classification:

> When he organized plants into class, order, genus, species and varieties he chose sexuality as the key, classifying flowering plants by the stamens, the male 'genitals'. He grouped them into twenty-three classes, which were then divided into orders by the structure of the stigmas, the female 'genitals', while the supporting structure, the *calyx*, became the nuptial bed. This meant, of course, that some flowers had far more than a single male sharing a bed with the female – and the sexual naming went further, with some structures compared to *labia minora* and *majora*, let alone a whole class called *Clitoria*. Even fungi, mosses and ferns, which have no flowering parts, were labelled the *Cryptogamia*, plants that marry secretly.[66]

The writings of the Swedish Linnaeus were translated into English by Erasmus Darwin, who was developing an evolutionary theory of his own in advance of his grandson's, and writing such epic poems incorporating Linnaean and other advancements in botanical knowledge as *The Loves of the Plants* (1789) and *The Botanic Garden* (1792).[67] He includes in his versifying on plants and botany, anthropomorphic metaphors similar to those used by Linnaeus, who also extended

---

63   Ibid., p. 22.

64   Ibid., p. 22.

65   Ibid., p. 24.

66   Jenny Uglow, *The Lunar Men: The Friends Who Made the Future, 1730-1810* (London: Faber& Faber, 2003 [2002]), p. 271.

67   *The Botanic Garden* included 'The Economy of Vegetation' and 'The Loves of the Plants'.

these in his own invocation to keep blood-lines clear in the maintenance of political and social order:

> Observe too what irregularity passes
> From the want of distinction of Sexes & Classes ...
> Can marriage made public & Marriage clandestine
> The same common bed with strict decency rest in
> Shall a Couple as constant as Darby and Joan
> In a basket with libertine flaunters be thrown ...
> No no my gay empire will soon dissever
> And my Colonists claim independence for ever[68]

So-called objective scientific treatises based on the observation of empirical evidence were thoroughly inflected by early-modern Western ideologies and interpretive frames. Patricia Fara explains some of the ways in which preconceptions rather than observation determined the scientific 'proofs':

> Even though many plants are hermaphrodites, which carry both male and female parts, Linnaeus settled on this sexual dichotomy for organising the plant world.

> As his model for this supposedly objective system, Linnaeus turned to human relationships. The prejudices of Enlightenment Christian moralists are built right into the heart of this scientific plan for plants, which Linnaeus outlined by using romantic words such as 'bride' and 'marriage'. In his anthropomorphic scheme, the most basic division is between male and female – exactly the same distinction as in the highly chauvinistic society of late 18th-century Europe. Linnaeus gave priority to male characteristics; in other words he imposed the sexual discrimination that prevailed in the human world onto the plant kingdom. His first level of ordering depends on the number of male stamens, but only the sub-groups are determined by the number of female pistils.[69]

It is not surprising, then, that 'Linnaeus called plants in the first class *monandria*, from the Greek for "one man"', 'or that, betraying the ideology of the time and his own confidence as a Christian husband and a pastor, he should nickname his wife "a monandrian lily" – a virgin with a single husband'.[70] Eugenia Alabaster, with her 'pale-gold' hair and 'ivory' complexion, dressed in her white tarlatan, 'at once so milky-wholesome and so airily untouchable' should also be – or is perceived to be – 'a monandrian lily', when in reality she is of an entirely other order. That convention and taboo – or the social necessity of maintaining appearances and the imperatives of 'good breeding' and a thoroughbred blood-line – should be unable to constrain such behaviour was worrying indeed. In truth, the expanded opportunities for observation and increased knowledge of the natural world was doing nothing to

---

68   Carl Linnaeus, *A System of Vegetables*, translated by Erasmus Darwin in 1783, cited in P. Fara, op. cit., p. 19.

69   Ibid., p. 21.

70   P. Fara, op cit., p. 24.

confirm class prejudices or assuage socio-sexual fears, but was, rather, increasing them.

By the time Charles Darwin was publishing his theories, the consoling or self-congratulating analogies were losing credence:

> It was inevitable that these new versions of nature would complicate traditional moralities. Conflict, chance, survival, reproduction, the family, sexual satisfaction and death were newly minted words in these stories, quickly shedding some of their more familiar associations. Darwin and Freud had produced scientific and quasi-scientific redescriptions of nature as continual flux. [...] History, natural history, had become the most transgressive of disciplines.[...][71]

> For Darwin, and his contemporaries, there was a stark question of analogy: What was nature like? And this brought with it – by implication, as it were – one of Darwin's abiding preoccupations: What, if anything, about nature newly conceived (newly analogized) should we now celebrate, or admire, or even, indeed, emulate?[72]

The 'new versions of nature' observed included more than just plants, rocks and animals that afforded new data. Humans were there, too. William Adamson, as he dances in turn with the Alabaster sisters in the ballroom of their fine country house, recalls his experiences abroad, noting some similarities to his own culture and some perturbing (and stimulating) differences:

> The waltz was danced in certain kinds of society in Pará and Manáos; he had whirled around with olive-skinned and velvet-brown ladies of doubtful virtue and no virtue [...] these dances were designed to arouse his desire in exactly this way, however demure the gloves, however sweetly innocent the daily life of the young woman in his arms. He remembered the palm-wine dance, a swaying circle which at a change in rhythm broke up into hugging couples who then set upon and danced round the one partnerless scapegoat dancer. He remembered being grabbed and nuzzled and rubbed and cuddled with great vigour by women with brown breasts glistening with sweat and oil, and with shameless fingers. (pp. 5-7)

Of course, William's somewhat ashamed sense of himself as sexually experienced and his future wife as innocent and inexperienced is thoroughly misguided, and he misses the import of Eugenia and Edgar dancing together so expertly, or the irony of Eugenia's apparently innocuous and endearing claim: 'I love my family [...] We love each other very much.' Equally ironic is Sir Harald's pious sermonising on 'God's Parental love and the family of all creation' as a model for the 'natural ties between the members of the family group, the warmth of the mother, the protection of the father, the closeness of brothers and sisters'. The dichotomy that Adamson perceives between his culture and those he encounters in the Amazon jungle leaves

---

71   Adam Phillips, *Darwin's Worms* (London: Faber & Faber, 1999), p. 20.
72   Ibid., pp. 35-6.

him with a sense of 'double consciousness' as he tries to negotiate his way between two different orders:

> He felt he was doomed to a kind of double consciousness. Everything he experienced brought up its contrary image from *out there*, which had the effect of making not only the Amazon ceremonies, but the English sermon, seem strange, unreal, of an uncertain nature. (p. 24)

Even before he is in a position to realise the full and personal irony of Sir Harald's claims that 'we are fearfully and wonderfully made, in His image, father and son, son and father, from generation to generation, in mystery and ordained order' (p. 89), William replies:

> '"*Homo homini deus est*", our God is ourselves, we worship ourselves. We have made God by a specious analogy [...] we make perfect images of ourselves, of our lives and fates, as the painters do of the Man of Sorrows, or the scene in the Stable [...] of a grave-faced winged Creature speaking to a young girl. And we worship these, as primitive peoples worship masks of terror, the alligator, the eagle, the anaconda. You may argue anything at all by analogy, Sir, and so consequently nothing [...] We need loving kindness in *reality;* and often do not find it – so we invent a divine Parent [...] We desire things to be so, and so we create a tale, or a picture, that says, we are so and so. You might as well say, we are like ants, as that ants may develop to be like us.' (p. 89)

William has, in effect, summed up the myth-making pitfalls of scientific as well as religious discourse.

At first, his desire for Eugenia has the quality of something culturally pre-scripted, mimed and prompted by his memory of a romantic line in a childhood fairy-tale: 'I shall die if I cannot have her.' Matty Compton, on the other hand, is virtually invisible to him at the beginning of their acquaintance. Like William, she has a role that is hard to define or categorise in the Bredely household. She is neither a governess nor a domestic servant and she is not a relative or a friend of the family. It is not until they embark on the study of the ant colony that he begins to see her, to perceive her qualities and skills and appreciate her keen interest in the world around her. He professes himself to be 'amazed at [her] accomplishments'. Latin, Greek, draughtsmanship of a high quality, a thorough knowledge of English Literature, which, she explains, come largely from being educated with her 'betters', 'in the schoolroom of a Bishop' where her father was a tutor. It is Matty who encourages William to write up the ant study for publication and she who assists him with it. The treatise, ostensibly about ant colonies, gives rise to a wide range of digressions and reflections, in which analogies between the insect and human societies are sought, with reference to history, myth, religion, philosophy, natural history and to William's own experiences in the Amazon:

> We find parables wherever we look in Nature, and we make them more or less wisely [...]
> I have mentioned the role of Instinct as Predestination, and of Intelligence as residing in

communities rather than individuals. To ask, what are the ants in their busy world, is to ask, what are we, however we may answer … (p. 116)

This project gives rise to her own writing of the 'illustratory fable' set in strange gardens, 'Things Are Not What They Seem', in which she exploits her own interest in the powerful combination of entomology and etymology, and in the Classical names bestowed by Linnaeus and others, such as the Sphinx Atropos: 'how much of mystery, of fairy *glamour* – is added to the creatures by the names bestowed upon them'. William acknowledges:

> I used to think of Linnaeus, in the forest, constantly. He bound the New World so tightly to the imagination of the Old when he named the swallowtails for the Greek and Trojan heroes, and the Helliconiae of the Muses. There I was, in lands never before entered by Englishmen, and round me fluttered Helen and Menelaus, Apollo and the Nine, Hector and Hecuba and Priam. The imagination of the scientist had colonised the untrodden jungle before I got there. There is something wonderful about *naming* a species. To bring a thing that is wild, and rare, and hitherto unobserved under the net of human observation and human language – and in the case of Linnaeus, with such wit, such order, such lively use for our inherited myths, tales and characters. (p. 118)

Curiously, there is no mention, it seems, of the inherited myths of brother-sister incest, 'customary in ancient ruling families' and 'everywhere the practice of the elder gods and goddesses', so that Edgar and Eugenia might be seen to join the tradition of 'Isis and Osiris, Artemis and Apollo, Fauna and Faunus, Diana and Dianus, Zeus and Hera, Yama and Yami, Freya and Frey'.[73] However, in the mundane world of natural and sexual selection, such couplings are bound for extinction.

Matty's own narrative about natural history, a riddling story within a story that is itself riddled with stories, is aptly and deliberately named: 'Things Are Not What They Seem'. She explains to William that she had simply wanted to explore the Latin etymology of the Hawk Moth caterpillars and thus writes an '*instructive fable* around those strange beasts'. Her protagonist, however, is an explorer, Seth (the biblical Seth is, of course, Adam's son, a clue to William Adamson that he should pay particular attention to the tale's coded message). Seth finds himself in the Garden of a powerful fairy named Dame Cottitoe Pan Demos (meaning 'for all the people'), a pastoral place that is a world reminiscent both of china ornaments and a pig-sty – the Alabasters are perhaps her target here. Outside this Garden is the domain of another more powerful Fairy to which Mistress Mouffet, the Recorder of the Garden, escorts him. Seth is able to ascertain that the name of the veiled Sphynx-like fairy is Dame Kind. Kind signifies both the adjective ('we need loving kindness *in reality*') and the noun (identifying the kind). By her story Matty is exhorting William to look behind appearances and identify her as one of his kind. They are kindred spirits (not kin) and thus strong and 'ready to grow'.

---

73   Barbara Walker, *The Woman's Encyclopedia of Myths and Secrets* (San Francisco, CA: Harper & Row, 1983), p. 122.

The classical fable of Cupid and Psyche introduced early in the story has a moral pertaining to matters of seeing and sorting. Psyche, the Greek name for butterfly, is the same as the word for soul, and conventionally the Classical story posits a time of trial and tribulation from which transformation and joy eventually emerge. In that tale 'the butterfly' is assisted by lowly ants; in this, the ant comes into its own. The obvious butterfly of the piece is, at first, Eugenia, whereas Matty, with her thin brown wrists and sharp, angular body cocooned in its dark colours and her worker status, is more akin to the ants of the fable. However, Adam Phillips notes Darwin's jotted marginalia-credo: 'Never say higher or lower',[74] and his long fascination with the Earth's seemingly lowliest of creatures: the earth worm. From his 1837 paper 'on the Formation of Mould' to his last book in 1881, *Formation of Vegetable Mould Through the Action of Worms* – he outlined their significance; 'traditionally associated with death and corruption and lowliness' he saw them as 'maintaining the earth'[75] and a sign of vitality, rather than decay. Myth is thus overturned and the conventional hierarchies, from angels to earthworms (and insects), disrupted.

Matty is also the one who understands early in the novella that William needs to undertake some task of sorting – and therefore new seeing – of his own :'I hope your *sorting* may be completed to everyone's satisfaction'. Later, as they work with analogies and fables as they pertain to their nature studies, Matty, through her own story-telling, confirms her understanding of the propensity for myth-making and its persistent appearance in scientific developments; she has Mistress Mouffet explain to Seth: 'Names, you know, are a way of weaving the world together, by relating the creatures to other creatures and a kind of *metamorphosis*, you might say, out of a *metaphor*, which is a figure of speech for carrying one idea into another' (p. 132). What Mattie is trying to suggest to William, however, is that their interpretative models need to go beyond familiar cultural bounds. Matilda, as we shall see, is not of the same kind as Eugenia. If Eugenia is Morpho, 'the opposite of amorphous', Matty is her opposite, the one who will metamorphose, but what she is asking of William is that he look beyond the surface character he has been trained to see, and to recognise her potential: things are not what they seem. Eugenia is weak, Matty is strong; Matilda will survive, Eugenia will become a fossil.

Byatt has explained the process she herself undertook in the genesis of the novella, including the significant naming of character in her own 'parable' combining the scientific and the literary. She selected the names of her characters with this same deliberation shown by Matty, but encountered coincidence and some unexpected contradictions to her original aims:

> I decided quite early to make my hero an Amazon explorer from the lower middle classes like Wallace and Bates and Spruce. I called him William and the old collector Harald out of a blatant reference to Scott's historical vision of old and new rulers, Saxon and Norman. I called the eldest daughter Eugenia, because she was well-born and because the

74 '"Never say higher or lower," Darwin jotted in the margins of a book', A. Phillips, op. cit., p. 42

75 Ibid., p. 42

story was something to do with Sexual Selection as well as Natural Selection. Much later in my thinking I saw that I needed another woman, not confined to her biological identity, and invented Matilda – who masquerades through the early part of the story as Matty Crompton, a kind of governessy poor relation, making herself useful in the schoolroom. […]

I read. Ants, bees, Amazon travels, Darwin, books about Victorian servant life, butterflies and moths – resisting, rather than searching out useful metaphors, but nevertheless finding certain recurring patterns. For instance the Amazonian explorers' use of the imagery of Paradise, which to Wallace in South America was an English field and hedgerow, but in England became the openness of the native people and the fecundity of the virgin forest. Knowledge of both places unsettled the images of both, in terms of the Other. I had called William 'Adamson', as a kind of ironic reference to the first man in the first Garden.

I discovered […] the full beauties of the Linnaean system of naming the lepidoptera.[…] I thought this a strange and innocent form of colonialism – the Englishman wandering through the Virgin Forest in pursuit of creatures called Menelaus and Helen, Apollo and the Heliconiae, and all the Danaides. I was particularly pleased when I discovered in Bates – long after the name of my character was settled – a passage about the Morphos – the large blue butterflies – and discovered there was one called Morpho Eugenia […] I was even more pleased when I discovered elsewhere that Morpho is one of the ways of naming Aphrodite Pandemos, the earthly Venus. I was pleased in the way one is when one *discovers* a myth still alive and working, despite the fact that part of my intention was to undo anthropomorphic imaginings and closures –[76]

Despite Byatt's avowed intention to 'undo' the densely woven fabric of myth-making, she has herself been caught in its warp finding it is impossible not to be implicated in the design and woof. She has also identified the way in which one discipline does not stand out, distinctive and discrete from another, but is over-determined and similar by virtue of persistent 'recurring patterns'. A literary writer reading scientific treatises but 'resisting useful metaphors' is a very circular route by which to encounter the literary models that science had already appropriated in it own construction; Gillian Beer has noted the ways in which:

scientists themselves in their texts drew openly upon literary, historical and philosophical material as part of their arguments: Lyell, for example, uses extensively the fifteenth book of Ovid's *Metamorphoses* in his account of proto-geology, Bernard cites Goethe repeatedly, and – as has often been remarked – Darwin's crucial insights into the mechanism of evolutionary change derived directly from his reading of Malthus's essay *On Population*. What has gone unremarked is that it is derived also from his reading of the one book he never left behind during his expeditions from the *Beagle: The Poetical Works of John Milton*. The traffic, then, was two-way. Because of the shared discourse not only *ideas* but metaphors, myths, and narrative patterns could move rapidly and freely

76 A. S. Byatt, 'True Stories and the Facts in Fiction', *Essays on the Fiction of A. S. Byatt*, eds A. Alfer and M. J. Noble (Westport, CT & London: Greenwood Press, 2001), pp. 193-4.

to and fro between scientists and non-scientists: though not without frequent creative misprision.[77]

Byatt's postmodern narrative presents just how difficult it was for Victorians to think of themselves and others in new ways when the old myths and analogies were – and are – so reflexive and persistently embedded. To find one's way between Milton's Paradise and Malthus's populace, between the old myths and the new speculations, was also to risk losing confidence in the dignity and priority accrued to anthropocentric and racial hierarchies. The earthworm and the ape, for instance, had hitherto had little elevated mythical resonance. It was one thing to name a butterfly after a goddess – and an aristocratic English 'angel' after a butterfly – but entirely another to think that an earthworm or insect could be a king or queen.

Matilda emerges from her insect-like shell to command William's attention. By this William changes and is able to resolve those internal conflicts that have kept him prisoner in the Alabaster 'Garden'. He is also able to recognise Matilda as his equal and his partner, a healthy and vigorous alternative to Eugenia. His task of sorting has been accomplished. Matilda and William are thus able to adapt to new requirements and to relinquish anachronistic myths in ways that none of the Alabasters and their effete ilk are likely to achieve. They represent the possibilities of new orders and revised – taxonomical and cultural – analogies, as Adam Phillips explains:

> Darwin and Freud had produced scientific and quasi-scientific redecorations of nature as continual flux. There was no longer such a thing as a relatively fixed and consistent person – a person with a recognizable identity – confronting a potentially predictable world, but rather two turbulences enmeshed with each other. If through increasingly sophisticated scientific experiments a new nature was emerging, this new nature was revealing that lives themselves were more like experiments than anything else.[78]

Matilda and William leave the mausoleum of the Alabaster household, with its museum pieces and lifeless artifice, to encounter together their unpredictable, vital experiment in countries where 'few of the population were racially pure, either white, black or Indian'(p. 80).

The final image in the novella is of Matilda and William, standing side by side. 'William's brown hand grips her brown wrist' on the deck of 'the strong little ship', (albeit with the mythical name, *Calypso*), rushing through the mid-Atlantic night, 'as far from land as she will be at any point on this voyage'. This is liminal and uncertain in many respects ('on the crest of a wave, between the ordered green hedgerows, and the coiling, striving mass of forest along the Amazon shore'), but in its *potential* it is a triumph of escape and survival. As William once noted: 'It requires great force to break out of the pupa. The insects are all at their most vulnerable at the moment of metamorphosis'(p. 53). Captain Papagay affirms this, too, when together from the ship's deck they consider a strong-flying Monarch butterfly (royally named, in

---

77 G. Beer, *Open Fields*, p. 7.

78 A. Phillips, op. cit., p. 20.

transit and not gender specific), on its migratory way to somewhere indeterminate: the 'main thing' is 'to be alive'. 'As long as you are alive, everything is surprising, rightly seen'.

Jeanette Winterson: Gravity

Winterson's *Sexing the Cherry* was in published 1989, four years after her highly acclaimed *Oranges Are Not the Only Fruit*. It extends the attention to 'tropical fruit' (that is, fruit tropes), and this time includes a veritable forbidden-fruit salad – exotic tropicals and hothouse cultivars never before seen at the time in which the fiction, primarily, is set: the seventeenth-century world of Commonwealth and Restoration London. There are peaches (grown by John Tradescant from the King's own tree), oranges and, of course, the cherry – but again, no apples appear, although at one stage Dog Woman promises one to Jordan – but Tradescant's three sumptuous peaches intervene. Drawings of fruits represent the narrative sections: the pineapple is used to head the passages where the foundling, Jordan, speaks and the banana, for his adoptive mother, the Dog-Woman. Yet these fruits are rarities, discovered abroad and brought to England as treasures. The banana, for instance, causes great consternation when it is introduced to the London populace, for nothing like it has been encountered in temperate London, as Dog Woman recounts:

> When Jordan was three I took him to see a great rarity [...] There was news that one Thomas Johnson had got himself an edible fruit of the like never seen in England [...] I [...] whipped off the cover myself, and I swear that what he had resembled nothing more than the private parts of an Oriental. It was yellow and livid and long.
> 'It is a banana, madam,' said the rogue.
> A banana? What on God's good earth was a banana?
> 'Such a thing never grew in Paradise,' I said.
> 'Indeed it did, madam,' says he, all puffed up like a poison adder.
> 'This fruit is from the island of Bermuda, which is closer to Paradise than you will ever be.' [...]
> 'It's either painted or infected,' said I, 'for there's none such a colour that I know.'
> Johnson shouted above the din as best he could ...

'THIS IS NOT SOME UNFORTUNATE'S RAKE. IT IS THE FRUIT OF A TREE. IT IS TO BE PEELED AND EATEN.'

At this there was a unanimous retching. There was no good woman could put that to her mouth, and for a man it was the practice of cannibals. We had not gone to church all these years and been washed in the blood of Jesus only to eat ourselves up the way the Heathen do.[79]

However shocking the banana is to the Dog Woman, a banana emblem, whole, half peeled and, it would seem incongruously, phallic, is used to announce the Dog-Woman's narrative passages throughout the book. A variation of this motif is also used in the section entitled 'Some Years Later' to represent the first-person narrative of the young environmentalist, camping by the polluted river, but this is a peeled banana, with the tip sliced off and set apart. Jordan's sections are represented in turn by a whole pineapple resting on a solidly flat surface. Jordan, when he was ten, met the botanist, collector and gardener, John Tradescant, and joined him first as a gardener's boy at Queen Henrietta's garden at Wimbledon and then on his travels collecting rare specimens, of which the pineapple is one prize. The pineapple is brought by Jordan to be presented to the King, an event that has been chronicled in a painting of 1675 *Charles II and His Gardener*, a work alluded to in the twentieth-century part of the narrative as by an unknown artist, but it is generally attributed to Hendrick Danckerts.[80] The Dog-Woman also observes the presentation:

The pineapple arrived today. Jordan carried it in his arms as though it were a yellow baby; with the wisdom of Solomon he prepared to slice it in two. He had not sharpened the knife before Mr Rose, the royal gardener, flung himself across the table and begged to be sawn into bits instead. Those at the feast contorted themselves with laughter, and the King himself, in his new wig, came down from the dais and urged Mr Rose to delay his sacrifice. It was, after all, only a fruit. At this Mr Rose [...] reminded the company that this was an historic occasion. Indeed it was. It was 1661, and from Jordan's voyage to Barbados the first pineapple had come to England. (p. 104)

Such slicing may have had a particular resonance for King Charles II, son of a beheaded father, whose respective reigns had been separated by the Civil War and Commonwealth Protectorate. However, in terms of the fiction's signifying emblems, the pineapple, like the banana, becomes bisected in those passages set in the twentieth century. The other twentieth-century narrative, that of Nicolas Jordan, a young sailor in the Navy, has a pineapple motif that is severed from top to bottom. These sliced and separated emblems signify the postmodern 'split subjectivities' as opposed to those representing the early-modern belief in the coherence or 'undividedness' of the individual and the solidity of the flat surface of the earth. The gendered mis-alignments, however, with the phallic banana representing the passages by women

---

79 J. Winterson, *Sexing The Cherry* (London: Vintage, 1989), pp. 11-13.

80 Charles Quest-Ritson, *The English Garden: A Social History* (London: Penguin, 2003), p. 74.

and the solid, soft-fleshed and juicy pineapple standing for those by the men, return the reader to the conundrum of 'sexing' that is to be found in the book's title.

An image of a single dark cherry adorns the very first page. Perhaps the most resonant fruit-analogy in the book is that of the cherry tree and the horticultural technique of grafting. Garden historian Charles Quest-Ritson notes that 'the pleasures of growing fruit and the desire for variety', leading to a search for new and better cultivars, were the most pronounced horticultural aspects of the sixteenth and early-seventeenth centuries.[81] The Tradescants, father and son, had a long involvement in just such enterprises. John Tradescant, the Elder, born in the 1570s, introduced a phenomenal range of specimens to the gardens of Hatfield House, where he was head gardener to Robert Cecil, the Earl of Salisbury. It was Salisbury who sent him to France and the Low Countries for fruit trees ('cherries, quince and medlars'),[82] and here that Tradescant had made a series of 'coloured drawings of all the fruits he grew for the Earl of Salisbury at Hatfield House',[83] a collection now known as 'Tradescant's Orchard'. 'The Tradescant Cherry', artist unknown, is one of these, presently held at the Ashmolean Museum in Oxford.[84] Indeed, Tradescant filled his own house and garden at Lambeth 'with oddities and rarities from the far ends of the earth' (as is accurately outlined in *Sexing the Cherry)* and his 'Closett of Rarities', also known as 'The Ark', was to become the nucleus of the Asmolean collection.[85] After his father's death in 1638, John Tradescant the Younger (1608-62) succeeded as Keeper of the Royal Gardens at Oatlands Palace for Queen Henrietta Maria (at a time when André Mollet was also laying out the gardens at St James's Place for the Queen).[86] This is the André Mollet who is discussed by the Dog-Woman as mentor to Tradescant on the 'French ways with water fountains and parterres' and who was persistently amorous to every woman but herself and whose 'tirelessness' was to be memorialised by 'a stream shooting nine feet high with a silver ball balanced on the top'(p. 41). Prior to, during and after the period of the Civil War, Tradescant made several trips to Virginia ('in 1637, 1642 and 1654 – while Britain was immersed in Civil War and the Commonwealth experiment – he was still exploring')[87] – and avoiding the danger he was in as a Royal appointee, as dramatised in *Sexing the Cherry*.

Incidentally, the Puritans, upon whose representatives the Dog-Woman wreaks her vengeance for their sexual hypocrisy and pleasure-denying prohibitions, had their own views about profligacy and corruption in gardens, too. It is not so much that Tradescant or the Kings he serves are meant to represent a defence of the

---

81   Ibid., p. 37.

82   P. Hobhouse, *Plants in Garden History*, p. 126.

83   Quest-Ritson, op. cit., p. 58.

84   Tradescant's   Orchard,   Ashmolean   Museum,   http://www.bodley.ox.ac.uk/dept/
scwmss/wmss/1500-1900/mss/ashmole/1461a.htm (MS. Ashmole1461, fol. 25r).

85   Jane Fearnley-Whittingstall, *The Garden: An English Love Affair* (London: Weidenfeld
& Nicolson, 2002), p. 94.; C. Quest-Ritson, op. cit., p. 60.

86   P. Hobhouse, op. cit., p. 111.

87   J. Brown, *The Pursuit of Paradise*, p. 174.

monarchy, divine Right of Kings, aristocratic privilege and patronage, colonialism or any other particularly conservative view; rather, they are there to represent freedom, intellectual curiosity and novelty. Interestingly, Charles Quest-Ritson, in his history of the English Garden has a section entitled: 'Civil War, Commonwealth – & the Apple'. As Quest-Ritson explains, Samuel Hartlib, an influential Puritan educationalist, social reformer and horticulturalist, 'proposed a new law to make the planting of fruit trees compulsory – an obligation on every landowner […] set out in his *Design for Plentie by a Universall Planting of Fruit Trees*[88] with apples, pears, quinces and walnuts deemed the most appropriate for the temperate climate. The number would be specified, and the planting of such would be enforced by law and fines levied on those who did not comply; 'Even wastelands and commons should be planted with these fruit trees so that all England became the "Garden of God"'.[89] Another Puritan, 'the preacher and cleric Michael Jermin […] maintained that the one purpose of the garden should be to use it as a place to contemplate the mystery which Christ suffered for mankind. A garden full of flowers was a garden full of vanities.'[90] This is the obverse of the orangery, such as the one at Queen Henrietta Maria's Wimbledon Manor House,[91] the glasshouse (or conservatory, a term first used for a glasshouse by John Evelyn), or greenhouses such as Tradescant's with its tender 'palergoniums, jasmines, plumbago and hibiscus'.[92] Pomegranates, too, began to be grown in these heated glasshouses. The hot-house pomegranate presents an interesting conundrum. It is frequently noted – including by Winterson herself – that the fruiting tree in the Garden of Eden would not have been the apple, 'that part of the world is generally too hot for apples, but at least since the Middle Ages northern Europeans have assumed that the forbidden fruit was the apple'.[93] Rather, it is likely to have been the pomegranate. The pomegranate has its own mythical resonance, being the fruit associated with both Kore and Euridice's journey to the Underworld and in the Bible, was a symbol of uterine fertility.[94] To return to the Tradescants: John Tradescant later became head gardener to the restored monarch, Charles II. The churchyard of St-Mary-at-Lambeth where both John Tradescants are buried is now the Museum of Garden History.[95]

Jordan explains the manner in which new techniques as much as new specimens were to be introduced to the Royal and aristocratic gardens of England:

> It was Tradescant's plan to stock up with seeds and pods and any exotic thing that might take the fancy of the English and so be natural in our gardens. It was our hope to make

---

88   C. Quest-Ritson, op. cit., p. 67.

89   Ibid.

90   Ibid., p. 69.

91   Ibid., p. 73.

92   Ibid., p. 75.

93   M. Pollan, *The Botany of Desire*, p. 22.

94   B. Walker, op. cit., pp. 805-06.

95   The Tradescant Garden, Museum of Garden History, http://www.cix.co.uk/~museumgh/garden.htm.

more of a success of the new fashion of grafting, which we had understood from France, and had already been done to some satisfaction on certain fruit trees.

Grafting is the means whereby a plant, perhaps tender or uncertain, is fused into a hardier member of its strain, and so the two take advantage of each other and produce a third kind, without seed or parent. In this way fruits have been made resistant to disease and certain plants have learned to grow where previously they could not.

There are many in the Church who condemn this practice as unnatural, holding that the Lord who made the world made its flora as he wished and in no other way.

Tradescant has been praised in England for his work with the cherry, and it was on the cherry that I first learned the art of grafting and wondered whether it was an art I might apply to myself.

My mother, when she saw me patiently trying to make a yield between a Polstead Black and a Morello, cried two things: 'Thou mayest as well try to make a union between thyself and me by sewing us at the hip,' and then, 'Of what sex is that monster you are making?'

I tried to explain to her that the tree would still be female although it had not been born from seed, but she said such things had no gender and were a confusion to themselves.

'Let the world mate of its own accord,' she said, 'or not at all.'

But the cherry grew, and we have sexed it and it is female. (pp. 78-9)

Dog-Woman's views are here evocative of the Mower's in perhaps the best-known garden poem of the period, 'The Mower Against Gardens' by Andrew Marvell (1621-78). In it, the mower inveighs against artifice in the garden, the decadent strategies of 'luxurious man' who, 'to bring his vice in use/ Did after him the world seduce', transgressively meddling 'where nature was most plain and pure'. More specifically, Marvell's grafted cherry in this poem is a specific allusion in Winterson's book:

> No plant now knew the stock from which it came;
> He grafts upon the wild the tame:
> That th'uncertain and adulterate fruit
> Might put the palate in dispute.
> His green seraglio has its eunuchs too,
> Lest any tyrant him outdo.
> And in the cherry, he does nature vex,
> To procreate without a sex.[96]

It is not grafting *per se* that intrigues Jordan most, but the appeal of the *analogy* of grafting. Jordan wants to be 'grafted onto something better and stronger', since his own identity, particularly in gender terms, is not secure. Jordan's wish is to be a hero in the manner of Tradescant: 'For Tradescant being a hero comes naturally. His father was a hero before him [...] He wants to bring back rarities and he does' (p. 101). On the one hand, Jordan longs 'to be like other men, one of the boys, a back-slapper', but he is quiet and sensitive, smaller and weaker than his adoptive mother:

96	Andrew Marvell, 'The Mower Against Gardens', *The Complete English Poems* (London: Allen Lane, 1974), p. 105.

'and that's not how it's supposed to be with sons'. On the other hand, his mother has masculine qualities that Jordan envies: 'I want to be like my rip-roaring mother who cares nothing for how she looks [...] She is silent the way men are supposed to be. [...].' A further complication is that he cross-dresses willingly, continuing as a woman for some time in the city of words, searching for the dancer, Fortunata: 'In my petticoats I was a traveller in a foreign country. I did not speak the language.' Jordan finds that 'women have a private language. A language not dependent on the constructions of men but structured by signs and expressions' (p. 31). Although he claims to like women, he knows little about them and is shocked at 'the conspiracy of women' and their hatred of and pity for men.

Neither Jordan nor the Dog-Woman are in accord with gender stereotypes of masculinity and femininity, but they love and respect each other hugely, despite their difficulties communicating this. The Dog-Woman's size and her violent rages when confronted with sanctimonious hypocrisy render her 'masculine', and yet, although she has never borne a child, she is nonetheless 'maternal' and adopts Jordan as her own. In this sense, the banana signifies her as 'phallic,' but as the 'phallic mother', the 'mother who has everything'[97] rather than the Freudian, Oedipal being who is perceived, by an anxious son especially, as castrated and passive. The cultivated pineapple, a specimen of which Jordan holds like 'a baby' in his presentation to the King, is produced parthenocarpically – that is, it forms fruit without pollination and fertilisation, but does not develop seeds. In this sense, the pineapple emblematises Jordan's own 'birth' as a foundling discovered in the mud of the Thames with his own sex obscured by layers of grime. Jordan's search for the elusive dancer Fortunata, too, is not implicated in the propagations of heterosexual coupling but, rather, in seeking something of his own self that is lost. Furthermore, Fortunata, who both 'is and is not', is in the service of Artemis, who 'didn't want to get married, [...] didn't want to have children. She wanted to hunt' (p. 130). Fortunata, like Artemis and like Jordan, is looking 'for something different' and 'not just the old things in different disguises' (p. 130). They are also looking for their lost and separate selves; as Artemis puts it: 'In the end [...] she would have to confront herself' (p. 130). Jordan begins the 'novel' with a description of just such a confrontation, in the night-time fog: 'I began to walk with my hands stretched out in front of me [...] and in this way, for the first time, I traced the lineaments of my own face' (p. 9). At the novel's conclusion as they sail from London in the great fire of 1666, the Dog Woman perceives 'someone standing beside him, a woman, slight and strong [...] Then she vanished and there was nothing next to Jordan but empty space' (p. 144). Artemis, Jordan and the Dog Woman have enacted the 'third that is not given', a transformation that moves beyond logic, reason, cause and effect, common sense and gravity. Fortunata, too, in her dancing school 'teaches her pupils to become points of light' and 'empty space' rather than creatures fallen into mere matter, into compulsory scripts for sexed bodies, into binary oppositions. She and her sisters,

---

97 Juliet Mitchell, 'The Question of Femininity and the Theory of Psychoanalysis', in *Psychoanalysis and Woman: A Reader*, ed. S. Saguaro (London: Macmillan, 2000), p. 138.

beings of light, reside in the weightless city, freed from gravity. These are the reasons why the apple, despite the pentacle-star at its centre, it is not a desired fruit. The apple has severally fallen into matter and masculine myths of matter.

The apple belongs to Eden, of course, with its tale of forbidden fruit and temptation, of the Fall into a consciousness of two distinct and opposing sexes, of labour (toil and childbirth), estrangement and decay. The apple is also integral to the scientific theory of gravity, developed in the seventeenth century by Isaac Newton. Newton's apple-tree scenario has also taken on the status of myth, a myth, says John Gribbin, that Newton himself 'cultivated so assiduously'.[98] Newtonian or classical physics has in large part been displaced by Einstein's theories of relativity, which continue to be augmented by quantum physics. One of the best-known exponents of these theories is the physicist, Stephen Hawking, whose popular work *A Brief History of Time: From Big Bang to Black Holes* was published in 1988 and has now been translated into at least thirty-three languages. Winterson has long been fascinated with, and has consistently incorporated into her writing, topics both scientific and religious, exploring the ideas and their relation to her writing experiments with narrative form: 'Until now religion has described it better than science, but now physics and metaphysics appear to be saying the same thing' (p. 90) interjects a polemical unnamed narrator in 'THE NATURE OF TIME' section of *Sexing the Cherry*. Time travel, the overthrow of gravity, and the exploration of matter as empty space and light are fundamental to *Sexing the Cherry* and, though less fantastically deployed with regard to princesses, sub-atomic dancers and other-worldly cities, fundamental to the revision of classical physics. 'Inside books there is a perfect space and it is that space which allows the reader to escape from the problems of gravity' explains Winterson in her essay, 'Art and Life',[99] and it is this space that allows *her* the opportunity to dramatise and display those two profound and contesting forces: 'The expansion of the universe spreads everything out, but gravity tries to pull it all back together again. Our destiny depends on which force will win.'[100] This and other passages from a Stephen Hawking website appear thoroughly familiar to readers of Winterson's work, and in particular *Sexing the Cherry*:

> Not surprisingly time travel has always been considered impossible. After all, Newton believed that time was like an arrow; once fired, it soared in a straight undeviating line. One second on earth was one second on Mars. Clocks scattered throughout the universe beat at the same rate.
>
> Einstein gave us a much more radical picture. According to Einstein, time was more like a river, which meandered around starts and galaxies, speeding up and slowing down as it passed around massive bodies. One second on earth was NOT one second on Mars.[101]

98   John Gribbin, *Science: A History (1543-2001)* (London: Penguin, 2003), p. 182.

99   J. Winterson, 'Art and Life', *Art Objects: Essays on Ecstasy and Effrontery* (London: Vintage, 1996), p. 157.

100 Stephen Hawking, http://www.pbs.org/wnet/hawking/universehtml/univ/html.

101 S. Hawking, http://www.pbs.org/wnet/hawking/mysteries/html/uns_kakul-2html.

In her collection *The World and Other Places*, 'Newton' is of interest in this regard; into the little town of Newton and its population of 'Classical Physicists' whose actions are all determined by a 'clockwork universe' comes Tom, a 'quantum child' (and dedicated reader of works of genius and imagination), who must make his escape. In the view of the explicator of 'THE NATURE OF TIME' in *Sexing the Cherry* , Tom would be one those who fights against the force of gravity, weight, matter and one-dimensional time-by-the-clock:

> Artists and gurus are, in the language of science, superconductors. [...] It is certainly true that a criterion for true art, as opposed to its cunning counterfeit, is its ability to take us where the artist has been, to this other different place where we are free from the problems of gravity. When we are drawn into the art we are drawn out of ourselves. We are no longer bound by matter, matter has become what it is: empty space and light. (p. 91)

There is another compulsory and constraining element in Newton (the town) and this, to borrow from Adrienne Rich's well-known essay, is 'compulsory heterosexuality'.[102] Newton is 'jammed with married couples', with 'battered baby buggys' and 'DIY stores crammed with HIM and shopping malls heaving with HER'. 'Complacent', 'normal' and 'nice' are the adjectives used to describe the men and women marching 'two by two', playing their pre-scripted roles ('Don't they know too much role playing is bad for the health? [...] They do it the way they do everything else in Newton. Tick-tock says the clock.'[103]) Winterson's first novel *Oranges Are Not the Only Fruit* had as its context the combination of 'Classical Physicists' with 'Religious Fundamentalists', Newton's apple combined with Eve's, two Falls in one: Gravity and Sin. In her 1991 introduction to the novel, Winterson wrote reflectively: 'Oranges is a threatening novel. It exposes the sanctity of family life as something of a sham; it illustrates that what makes life difficult for homosexuals is not their perversity but other people's.'[104]

The Dog-Woman and Jordan, albeit from another time and place, do not comply with gendered roles, as has already been discussed. On occasion, both of them wish they were better able to but ultimately they are too much themselves, too 'quantum' to fit easily into such constraining stereotypes. Early in the novel, Dog Woman muses on the experience of childbirth, which will not be hers, although, as an adoptive mother, motherhood will: 'I would have liked to pour out a child from my body but you have to have a man for that and there's no man who's a match for me' (p. 11). Dog-Woman does eventually mate with a man, but like any of her other sexual exploits, it is disastrous; first, her vagina swallows the man whole and then, when he is retrieved and offers to pleasure her orally instead, unused as he

---

102 A. Rich, 'Compulsory Heterosexuality and Lesbian Existence', *Blood, Bread and Poetry* (London: Virago, 1987).

103 J. Winterson, *The World and Other Places* (London: Vintage, 1999 [1998]), pp. 170-71.

104 J. Winterson, *Oranges Are Not the Only Fruit* (London: Vintage, 2001 [1985]), p. xiii.

is to failure, he is again overwhelmed: 'I cannot take that orange in my mouth. It will not fit. Neither can I run my tongue over it. You are too big, madam' (p. 107). This playful and humorous extension of Dog Woman's sexual misadventures (once when invited to fellate a man, she bit off his member, and although surprised, believed it would grow again) has its serious points. Winterson engages here with those sexual theories and stereotypes that delimit women and aggrandise men; in *Sexing the Cherry* these impact negatively on both Jordan and his mother. Freudian and post-Freudian versions of castration complexes and penis envy are signified here and, here again, is the equation of fruit: Dog Woman's clitoris is described as an orange, and further, it is 'too big'. More commonly, of course, the clitoris, so long seen either as non-existent or negligible, a protean but failed penis. In Freud's terms, for instance, the clitoris is the 'leading genital zone' for the female infant, but as she becomes aware of the superiority of the penis, she is forced to give up her 'phallic activity' and to turn instead to the passivity of the vagina. Passivity equates with femininity; to resist is to fail to accede that the clitoris is not the envied penis and never will be. If the penis is a banana, then the clitoris is, as slang often has it, a mere cherry. This aspect of an anatomical analogy, first suggested with the banana emblem signifying the Dog Woman's narrative, brings a further resonance to the task of 'sexing the cherry'. Indeed, since Freud posited his theories (the précis above is taken from his 1931 essay 'Female Sexuality'), a great deal of scientific research has been done on 'the cherry'.

In a book published just two years before the publication of *Sexing the Cherry*, medical sexologist Josephine Lowndes Sevely presented some startling findings that refuted the theory that the clitoris and the penis were counterparts or 'homologues', and that 'the tip of the clitoris corresponds to the tip of the penis', both 'called the glans, a Greek word meaning "acorn"'.[105] However, the penis is an acorn that grows, while not into a mighty oak, then into a robust trunk, whereas the clitoris is *relatively* dormant; the penis is an organ of reproduction whereas the clitoris is redundant in this regard. Further, its only purpose is pleasure, and such superfluous (and female) pleasure was therefore especially repudiated. As Catherine Blackledge explains: 'defining the clitoris as a non-reproductive organ justified its deletion from medical diagrams and discussion [...] [so] the organ itself began to disappear from common, as well as medical knowledge'.[106] The inaccuracies, ignorance or prejudice surrounding the clitoris were long-standing, and of course influenced the ways in which it was discussed: 'Button, cherry, bell, spot, small, pearl. They reduced my idea of what the clitoris was to a confined and finite spot' writes Catherine Blackledge in her 2003 study of the vagina, *The Story of V: Opening Pandora's Box*. 'It took the words and pictures of an Australian research team to make me view [it] [...] not as a button, bell or pearl [...] [but] an incredible expanding, highly sensitive structure

    105 J. Lowndes Sevely, *Eve's Secrets: A New Perspective on Human Sexuality* (London: Bloomsbury, 1987), p. 3.
    106 Catherine Blackledge, *The Story of V: Opening Pandora's Box* (London: Weidenfeld & Nicolson, 2003), p. 131.

sunk deep, and tethered well, inside [...]'.[107] The announcement, made by a team of Australian surgeons and urologists in August 1998, was that the clitoris is 'at least twice as large as anatomy textbooks depict, and tens of times larger than most people realise'.[108] However, as Blackledge acknowledges, the headlines generated in 1998 were not the first to discuss the giant proportions of the clitoris, 'composed of crown, corpus and cura' (legs); it was also a finding published in Lowndes Sevely's *Eve's Secrets* in 1987.

> This book made very similar observations on clitoral structure to those of the Australian anatomists. However, Lowndes Sevely, in turn, also revealed how her observations about the design of the clitoris were not strictly a discovery. Instead, she illustrated how they were a reappraisal of an earlier work, by the seventeenth-century Dutch anatomist, Reinier de Graaf. [...] it seems that in the seventeenth century, knowledge of the clitoris was profound. Its existence had been written about and discussed for centuries, its role in sexual pleasure was rejoiced in, and the dimensions of its deep internal and tripartite structure were realised. Yet, over the next three hundred years, each of these three areas of clitoral knowledge would be dismissed, overlooked or forgotten, instead of becoming common knowledge.[109]

This provides another interpretative frame for *Sexing the Cherry;* it is as much about anatomical voyages of discovery as it is about botanical ones. Freud famously called female sexuality a 'dark continent', resonant as this was with the double aspects of mystery (discovery) and colonisation. However, the female body had already had its discoverers and colonisers; indeed, it had its very own Columbus in the Italian anatomist Mateo Realdo Columbo, who, in 1559, published *De Re Anatomica* with the claim: 'if it is permissible to give names to things discovered by me, it [the clitoris] should be called "the love or sweetness of Venus" [dulcedo amoris]'.[110] Columbo's colleague, Gabriel Fallopius, who named the Fallopian tubes, also 'staked his claim to be the first to uncover the clitoris' in his *Observationes Anatomicae* of 1561, whereas Kaspar Bartholin, whose grandson Kasper was to name the female's Bartholin glands, wrote extensively on the clitoris but rebuked Columbo and Fallopius for claiming 'discovery' rather than description; 'he noted that the clitoris had been known to everyone since the second century'.[111] Winterson largely sets her tale in the seventeenth century when scientific knowledge and world-wide travel were bringing many things into view, while at the same time, the Christian church and colonisation was censuring and secreting others. Further, Winterson sets the novel in a century where Kings can lose their 'divine rights' and their heads, and where Civil War can result in a Puritanical 'democracy' that purges and prescribes. This displaced setting is used by Winterson to extend her earlier engagement in

---

107 Ibid., pp. 124-5.
108 Ibid. p. 124.
109 Ibid., pp. 128-30.
110 Ibid., p. 125.
111 Ibid., p. 127.

Oranges Are Not the Only Fruit with the consequences of religious fundamentalism and self-righteously intolerant ideologies.

Sexing the Cherry combines with this historical attention a fascination with myth, fables and storytelling . The gigantic Dog Woman is indeed Rabelaisian in her size – and her rage – but most obvious in this regard are the twelve dancing princesses. Each of the stories is a new version of the tales that are familiar through the Brothers Grimm but each also contains within it the vestiges of other nineteenth-century narratives, such as Browning's 'that's my last husband [duchess] painted on the wall' or Byron's: 'He [she] walked in beauty', or obvious allusions to Snow White or Prometheus. As one book-cover summary says: '*Sexing the Cherry* celebrates the power of the imagination as it playfully juggles with our perceptions of history and reality; love and sex; lies and truths; and twelve dancing princesses who lived happily ever after, but not with their husbands.' Juggling perception in relation to sexuality and sexual relationships is indeed one of Winterson's most pressing agendas. In her fiction, including the short piece 'The Poetics of Sex' or the novel, *Written on the Body*, where the sex/gender of the narrator is never identified in the terms 'man' or 'woman', and in her polemical essays, such as 'The Semiotics of Sex',[112] Winterson diligently disrupts conventionally gender-ascribed modes of being.

Jeanette Winterson is a lesbian who objects to the literary-critical and arts-media obsession with her 'sex life': 'Every interviewer I meet asks me about mine and what they do not ask they invent. I am a writer who happens to love women. I am not a lesbian who happens to write', she claims in 'The Semiotics of Sex'.[113] She notes, too, that 'literature is not a lecture delivered to a special interest group'[114] and that it is reductive to assume that she would want to write books only for women or solely for lesbians just as she does not want 'to read only books by women, only books by Queers'.[115] However, what is nonetheless apparent in her writing is the sustained attempt to destabilise those conventions that see heterosexuality as 'natural' and 'normal' and 'right'. In the same way that the clitoris was excised from science, art and common knowledge on the basis that it was superfluous to the reproductive continuum and the patriarchal order of things, so the lesbian has had a similar status; either they were deemed an irrelevance, and, consciously or unconsciously, excluded or they were deliberately censored and excised. This is perhaps what the pineapple signifies most; whereas Linnaeus developed a botanical classification system that depended on allegories of heterosexual and monogamous conjunction and reproduction, Tradescant in this tale returns from 'exotic places' and 'voyaging in Virginia' with a Pineapple. *Ananas **cosmosos***; its name more evocative of 'empty space and points of light' than can accrue to the other familiar apple myths and with the ability, like the grafted cherry, to grow (to be) without being born from

---

112 J. Winterson, 'The Semiotics of Sex', *Art Objects*, op. cit.
113 Ibid., p. 104.
114 Ibid., p. 106.
115 Ibid., p. 110.

or bearing seed, it breaks representatively the continuum of allegories of compulsory heterosexuality. Here is 'a third kind, without seed or parent'.

The compulsion to package everything according to gendered norms, keeping prescribed sexual difference to the fore, is what Winterson seeks to disrupt: 'X and Y have different values on different days'.[116] It is the compulsion to count, categorise and script X and Y chromosomes that causes the extreme preoccupation with genitals from the day a human is born and that cannot abide any deviation from prescribed binary norms:

> At birth, the extreme similarity of female and male genitalia is more pronounced, and often causes confusion and consternation. A lack of understanding of this, coupled with a somewhat rigid adherence to what constitutes the 'norm' in the western world in the twenty-first century, leads to many baby girls undergoing clitoridectomies in the first few days of their lives. [...] At present, medical standards allow clitorises up to 0.9 cm at birth to represent femaleness, and penises as short as 2.5 cm to mark maleness. Infant genitalia which is between 0.9cm and 2.5 cm is deemed too variant and is up for the chop or the snip. It's estimated that 'normalising' surgery is performed on one or two children out of every thousand births. This means that, in the UK, between 700 and 1,400 babies a year have their genitalia branded as abnormal and in need of surgery. In the US, it's estimated that about 2,000 babies a year undergo some form of clitoral mutilation, or genital reassignment, as it is sometimes known.[117]

Whereas sex is often seen as the natural base on which gendered norms are cultivated, recognising that sex itself is subject to wide variations which gender identities aim to categorise and control leads to a recognition that so called 'naturally' sexed beings have been forced to conform to myths and 'regulatory fictions'.[118] This is related to what Judith Butler identifies and theorises as 'performativity', 'the stylised repetition of acts', that appear to constitute 'naturally' sexed bodies and a normative heterosexuality; that is: 'the very notions of an essential sex and a true or abiding masculinity or femininity are also constituted as a part of the strategy that conceals gender's performative character'.[119] It is by such familiar repetition and 'the sedimentation' of norms that other 'performative possibilities for proliferating gender configurations outside the restricting frames of masculinist domination and compulsory heterosexuality',[120] are occluded. Butler attempts to explain the difficult concept that what we 'see' is actually determined by the 'sedimentation' of what we have enacted culturally:

> Consider that a sedimentation of gender norms produces that peculiar phenomenon of a 'natural sex' or a 'real woman' or any number of prevalent and compelling social fictions,

---

116 J. Winterson, 'Introduction', *Oranges Are Not the Only Fruit*, op. cit., p. xiii.

117 C. Blackledge, op. cit., pp. 151-8.

118 Judith Butler, *Gender Trouble: Feminism and the Subversion of Identity* (London & New York: Routledge, 1990), p. 141.

119 Ibid.

120 Ibid.

and that this is a sedimentation that over time has produced a set of corporeal styles which, in reified form, appear as the natural configuration of bodies into sexes existing in a binary relation to one another [...] Gender ought not to be construed as a stable identity or locus of agency from which various acts follow; rather, gender is an identity tenuously constituted in time, instituted in an exterior space through a *stylised repetition of acts*.[121]

Both Jordan and the Dog-Woman are at the mercy of such regulatory fictions, but as characters they also disrupt these. Although there is no ostensible defence of homosexuality or of lesbian existence there are nonetheless the signs of an advocacy of a way of being beyond 'man' and 'woman': a third term (or beyond) that is no longer bound by what we perceive as matter (remember Fortunata's 'the third is not given'). *Sexing the Cherry* is not about lesbianism but, nevertheless, lesbianism provides a useful way of shifting the compulsory paradigm of two opposites. Judith Butler refers to Monique Wittig's controversial assertion in 'One Is Not Born a Woman' that a lesbian is not a woman: 'a lesbian *has* to be something else, a not-woman, a not-man'[122]:

> Lesbian is the only concept I know of which is beyond the categories of sex (woman and man) because the designated subject (lesbian) is *not* a woman, either economically, or politically, or ideologically. For what makes a woman is a specific social relation to man, [...] a relation which implies personal and physical obligation as well as economic obligation ('forced residence', domestic corvée, conjugal duties, unlimited production of children, etc.), a relation which lesbians escape by refusing to become or stay heterosexual.[123]

In Winterson's tale, Jordan and the Dog-Woman, do disrupt those categories and live; through times of war, plague and fire these two refuse to be abject and their twentieth-century counterparts continue to resist apathy, hypocrisy and arbitrary confinement. The young woman protesting against mercury pollution in rivers and the vested interests of the World Bank, the Pentagon and the leaders of nations 'want to build dams, clear the rain forests, finance huge Coca-Cola plants and exploit the rubber potential' finds a consolation in the 'hallucination' that she is a 'giant', 'huge' and 'raw', able to enact righteous retaliation: 'I had an *alter ego* who was huge and powerful, a woman whose only morality was her own and whose loyalties were fierce and few'. Like the Dog-Woman in another century, she waits 'outside' society, campaigning for and imagining a different one:

> [...] all the men line up for compulsory training in feminism and ecology. Then they start on the food surpluses, packing it with their own hands, distributing it in a great human chain of what used to be power and is now co-operation. We change the world and on the seventh day we have a party at the wine lake and make pancakes with the butter mountain

121 Ibid., p. 140.

122 M. Wittig, 'One Is Not Born A Woman', *The Straight Mind and Other Essays* (Hemel Hempstead: Harvester Wheatsheaf, 1992), cited in Saguaro, op. cit., p. 284.

123 Ibid., p. 288.

and the peoples of the earth keep coming in waves and being fed and being clean and being well. And when the rivers sparkle, it's not with mercury ... (p. 123)

In 1981, the French feminist, Hélène Cixous, published in English an essay entitled 'Castration or Decapitation?', which challenged the manner in which masculine castration anxiety worked to decapitate and thus silence women, the 'already castrated' Other, whose power and difference were both feared and maligned. Cixous's writing is lyrical and fanciful and yet it is also polemical and politically charged. One passage in particular is strikingly evocative of the Dog-Woman – and of her contemporary alter-ego, too:

> And so they want to keep woman in the place of mystery. [...] as they say 'keep her in her place', keep her at a distance; she's always not quite there ... but no one knows exactly where she is. She is kept in place [...] the place of the sphinx ... she's kept in the place of what we might call the 'watch-bitch' (*chienne chanteuse*). That is to say, she is outside the city, at the edge of the city – the city is man, ruled by masculine law –and there she is. [...] 'Watch-bitch', the sphinx was called; she's an animal and she sings out [...] it's this mystery that leads man to keep overcoming, dominating, subduing, putting his manhood to the test, against the mystery he has to keep forcing back.[124]

This is how the Dog-Woman (whose name Dog is the reverse of God), living in the grounds of the garden designed by the Frenchman Mollet, explains her place as 'the Watch-bitch'; it correlates well with Cixous's version:

> For myself I prefer the running stream that leads from the bank planted with cherry and makes a basin in the grotto with the statue of the hermit. The stream is shallow [...] There is a rock near to its source and I very often hide behind it at evening, singing songs of love and death and waiting for the sun to set. (p. 42)

It could be said that Winterson is positing a counter-myth to that of the Garden of Eden, its fateful apple and its male and female couple, always in opposition. However, that would seem in itself to be too static and too prescriptive. What she recommends instead is the liberation from consolatory fictions that limit the very possibility of asking new questions, experimenting with new forms, and discovering to be real the hitherto unimaginable or fantastic. In this she is in accord with another French theorist so influential in postmodern and New-Historical critical approaches; in *The Order of Things: An Archaeology of the Human Sciences*, first published in France in 1966 and available in English in 1973, Michel Foucault offers a distinction between Utopias and heterotopias which is germane to *Sexing the Cherry*:

> *Utopias* afford consolation: although they have no real locality there is nevertheless a fantastic, untroubled region in which they are able to unfold; they open up cities with vast avenues, superbly planted gardens, countries where life is easy, even though the road to them is chimerical. *Heterotopias* are disturbing, probably because they secretly undermine language, because they make it impossible to name this *and* that, because they

---

124 H. Cixous, 'Castration or Decapitation?', in Saguaro, op. cit., p. 238.

shatter or tangle common names, because they destroy 'syntax' in advance, and not only the syntax with which we construct sentences but also that less apparent syntax which causes words and things (next to and also opposite one another) to 'hold together'. This is why utopias permit fables and discourse; they run with the very grain of language and are part of the fundamental dimension of the *fabula*; heterotopias [...] desiccate speech, stop words in their tracks, contest the very possibility of grammar at its source; they dissolve our myths [...][125]

Winterson concludes her fiction with Jordan's musings on the future, which lies ahead 'like a glittering city', but, chimerical 'like cities of the desert', 'disappears when approached'. Jordan, who has imagined many fabulous cities – like the city of words – realises that there are no hard borders between things: past or present, this country or that, one gender or another. The Utopian world invariably turns into a village like Newton where time's arrow – and too many other things – are 'straight', whereas Jordan's vision is of a quantum universe: 'And even the most solid of things and the most real, the best-loved and well-known, are only handshadows on the wall. Empty space and points of light' (p. 144).

Carol Shields: Space

Larry's Party, published in 1997 by Carol Shields, records twenty years (1977 to 1997) in the life of the eponymous Larry Weller, from the age of twenty-six, when he is about to graduate from a diploma course in Floral Arts, to the age of forty-six when he has become an established and successful maze designer. In this period, Larry experiences two marriages and their respective failures, the birth of a son, the death of his parents, hospitalisation and coma, and the change and development of a career which moves from florist to maze *aficionado* and international designer. The changes in name of the florist businesses – from 'Flower Folks' – 'a small chain with a reputation for friendly service and a quality product' – to 'Flowercity' – 'the California-based multinational' – and then, to 'Flower Village' – 'taken over by a Japanese conglomerate' – emblematises the various cultural shifts taking place in the 1980s, while the passion for maze designs and installations is 'very 9Os': 'since 1992, a remarkable renaissance of mazes and labyrinths has blossomed in a fashion no-one could have imagined [...] an intriguing phenomenon of the late 20th

---

125 Michel Foucault, 'Preface', *The Order of Things: An Archaeology of the Human Sciences*, (New York: Vintage, 1973 [1966]), p. xviii.

century'.[126] The novel culminates in a party, Larry's party, where the guests include his two ex-wives, Dorrie and Beth, and his girlfriend of the moment, Charlotte. It is this party that heralds the reunion of Larry and Dorrie, his first wife, who still lives in the house she originally shared with him, with its remnants of the maze she once half-destroyed. Thus, after many twists and turns in Larry's fortunes, it is with Dorrie that he finds himself both returning and yet beginning again. The theme and form of the novel, with its attention to combinations of accident and design (in life, in mazes, in narratives), is brought to a fitting 'exit' at a place where – after the intervening experience of 'treading the maze' (in this case, taking twenty years) – an earlier entrance had been: to begin a life together with Dorrie. The fragment of a nineteenth-century poem that Beth cites, and which completes the novel, reinforces the correlation:

> A maze of path, of old designed
> To tire the feet, perplex the mind,
> Yet pleasure heart and head;
> 'Tis not unlike this life we spend,
> And where you start from, there you end.[127]

At this stage, Dorrie could also be construed as the hidden goal, suddenly revealed at the maze's centre: 'the prize, the final destination, what the branching path is all about' (p. 149). Or, rather, they are each other's goal: 'here they are, suddenly [...] The journey they appear to have taken separately has really been made together' (p. 328).

The novel sustains its dual attention throughout: it is about both Larry Weller (this fictional character's life and times), and mazes (their history, design and cultural meaning). Some of the mazes referred to in the book are verifiably real, like Hampton Court's, whereas others, such as Larry's own creations, are not. As with so many postmodern novels, there are also playful visual accoutrements to complement the narrative. In relation to Larry's life these include a photograph of an infant sitting in a high chair: Larry. He refers to this near the novel's end – 'a photo someone had taken of him [...] propped up in an elaborate highchair'– (though the photo is a 'real' one, its referent is a fiction). Other 'evidence' of Larry's existence include a copy of Larry's own-company business card for A/Mazing Space Inc. and a seating plan, map and party menu penned by Larry's girlfriend. Further, each of the fifteen chapters in the novel, dated chronologically and with titles such as 'Larry's Work, 1981' or 'Larry's Living Tissues, 1996', has a maze design on its frontispiece. These designs, however, are readily identifiable in sourcebooks and would have contributed to Larry's – and Shields's – research into mazes. For instance, the second chapter, which recounts Larry's first honeymoon in England and his life-

---

126   Jeff Saward, *Magical Paths: Labyrinths and Mazes in the 21st Century* (London: Octopus, 2002), p. 7.

127   'Bradfield, Sentan's Wells, 1854', *Larry's Party* (London: Fourth Estate, 1998), p. 39.

transforming experience 'getting lost' in Hampton Court, unsurprisingly presents the Hampton Court Maze design at its outset. Other design-diagrams are often less obviously or straightforwardly linked to the chapters' content and themes,[128] but each can be traced and identified by reference to one or other of two sources: *Mazes and Labyrinths: Their History and Development* by W.H. Matthews or Aidan Meehan's *Celtic Design: Maze Patterns*.[129] (The title of the Matthews text is accurately cited as a reading resource for Larry but the Meehan is referred to as *Celtic Mazes and Labyrinths*). When Larry visits Europe and Britain again, this time with Beth, his second wife, his tour provides a reliable compendium of maze and labyrinth sites. Other references, however, especially those 'back home' in North America, are not reliable and no image is available, although Larry's own commissioned projects are very reminiscent of 'real' ones completed in the 1990s by 'garden maestros' of the time. But other references, such as the eminent Eric Eisner 'the granddaddy of America's great landscape artists', appear to be as fictive as Larry himself. The researcher who looks for ready correlations or reliable information, and trusts Shields's method to unfailingly provide them, may find instead that, as Dee Goetz puts it 'what seems like a clue is really a red herring'.[130] Like many writers of postmodern narratives, Shields deliberately plays with the concepts of fact and fiction – and the factitiousness of either term; the reader who trusts too readily to the path laid out will find some unexpected twists and turns.

Larry becomes passionate about mazes, voraciously learns about them, and eventually, from small beginnings, designs them and is commissioned by wealthy private and public patrons. Although Larry, at the height of his career as a designer and installer of garden mazes, is described as 'a member of a rarefied and eccentric profession', 'a rare breed' of 'fewer than a dozen maze makers in the world', his success reflects a cultural phenomenon of the 1980s and 1990s in North America and Europe, in particular, in which mazes became increasingly popular:

> Within the past twenty-five years or so, the popularity of mazes and labyrinths in a diverse range of settings around the world has increased to an extraordinary degree. This dramatic revival started slowly at first, with a few people experimenting with new design concepts and materials. This had happened before when, at different places and points in time, maze crazes had flourished and faded, only to spring back to life in a different culture with a slightly different take on the original concept. However, since 1992 a remarkable

---

128 As Dee Goertz notes: Hampton Court 'is the only maze design that actually figures significantly in the plot. The value of the other designs as illustrations of the text is dubious.' 'Treading the Maze of *Larry's Party*', in *Carol Shields, Narrative Hunger, and the Possibilities of Fiction*, eds Edward Eden and Dee Goertz (University of Toronto Press, 2003), p. 237.

129 W. H. Matthews, *Mazes and Labyrinths: Their History and Development* (New York: Dover 1970 [1922]) and Aidan Meehan, *Celtic Design: Maze Patterns* (London: Thames and Hudson, 1996). See also D. Goertz, 'Appendix: Identification of Maze Designs in *Larry's Party*', Eden and Goertz, op. cit., pp. 250-51.

130 Ibid., p. 237.

renaissance of mazes and labyrinths has blossomed in a fashion no-one could have imagined.

Barely a summer now goes by without our hearing about another record-breaking maize maze that is featured in the media, another stately home or entertainment park that has installed a splendid new hedge maze, or a television gardening program that creates a small floral labyrinth to enhance a suburban garden or back yard. [...] consider, for instance, the number of computer games that revolve around solving a maze [...] Watch for them as metaphors for confusing matters in legal and financial advertising. Mazes and labyrinths became an intriguing phenomenon of the late 20th century, and now, in the early 21st century, they continue to capture the imagination in ever more surprising ways.[131]

With his distinguished and groundbreaking career, Larry is reminiscent of designers such as Adrian Fisher who, since the 1980s, has constructed over three hundred mazes worldwide, in seventeen countries, across five continents[132] and who, in 1993, designed the world's first cornfield Maize Maze in Pennsylvania.[133] (Interestingly, in a chapter bearing the date 1988, Larry designs a maize maze constructed from hay-bales, his 'Saskatchewan maze':

> [...] constructed entirely from bales of hay stacked one on one to a height of seven feet and forming a meandering hay-fragrant tunnel that drew over one-hundred and fifty thousand tourists toward its center, which was a wheel of earth tilted slightly forward and planted with prairie wild flowers [...] (p. 150)

Although, as the fictional precursor to Fisher and others with their projects of standing maize crops, Larry laments the lack of 'vital plant tissue'). Adrian Fisher, who runs his own company, Adrian Fisher Mazes Ltd., also publishes popular books on mazes including the 1997 bestseller, *Secrets of the Maze*. Another maze designer of note at this time is Randall Coate, whose first creation, a vast yew-hedged footprint entitled 'The Imprint of Man', was installed in a private garden in Gloucestershire, England in 1975[134] and who collaborated with Fisher and Graham Burgess on a variety of public projects in the 1980s, including hedge mazes in England at Blenheim Palace, Leeds Castle and Newquay Zoo.[135] In America, California-based Alex Champion pioneered contemporary labyrinthine earthwork installations inspired by neolithic embankments and other ancient earthworks. Typically, and just like the fictional Larry Weller, these designers began in their own gardens and progressed to extensive

---

131 Jeff Saward, op. cit., p. 7.

132 Ibid., p. 50.

133 'Adrian Fisher Maze Design', http://www.mazemaker.com/company_profile.htm; Adrian Fisher and Howard Loxton, *Secrets of the Maze: An Interactive Guide to the World's Most Amazing Mazes* (London: Thames & Hudson, 1997), p. 79; 'The first maize maze was made in 1993 by Adrian Fisher and Don Frantz at Annville, Pennsylvania, in the shape of a giant stegosaurus, for a Red Cross fund-raising event', Jeff Saward, op. cit., p. 58.

134 J. Saward, op. cit., p. 89.

135 Ibid., p. 91.

commissions in public and private spaces. Larry's commissioned work ranges from a hedge maze in the grounds of the Milwaukee Memorial Children's Hospital to a Manhattaner dweller's *faux* meadow roof-garden to the Great Snow Maze in Ulan Ude in Siberia.

Mazes and labyrinths may have undergone a popular resurgence in the 1980s and 1990s but they have an extremely long history and, as a world-wide phenomenon, a complex significance:

> From the Bronze Age settlements on the Atlantic coastline and the shores of the Mediterranean Sea, through the Roman Empire and the medieval Christian Church to modern usage in both secular and spiritual contexts, labyrinths are everywhere. The archetypal labyrinth symbol occurs from Iceland, Scandinavia, Arctic Russia, throughout Europe, north Africa and the Middle East down into the Indian subcontinent and Indonesia. It is also found in a historical context in the American Southwest, Mexico and Brazil.[136]

In Europe, spirals, chevrons and other intricate patterns are evidently pre-historic, the figurative and religious art of Cromagnon Man, for example, or according to Aidan Meehan, the signs of a goddess culture: 'the form of the maze is directly linked to the art of that ancient female-centred epoch', where the fertility of the earth was emblematised in designs depicting the female figure.[137] The Bronze Age Labyrinth of Egypt, a monument built circa 2000 BC, and said by Herododotus, amongst others, to rival and even surpass the Pyramids, is the earliest example of a structure known as a labyrinth.[138] Pliny was to report on its sublimity:

> To describe the whole of it in detail would be quite impossible, as it is divided up into regions and prefectures, called *nomes*, thirty in number, with a great palace to each; in addition it must contain temples of all the gods of Egypt and forty statues of Nemesis in the same number of sacred shrines, as well as numerous pyramids [...] Some of the palaces are so made that the opening of a door makes a terrifying sound as of thunder. Most of the buildings are in total darkness.[139]

In Classical history and myth, the Cretan Labyrinth at Knossos is perhaps the most renowned. It was constructed by Daedalus, the inventive father of the doomed Icarus. (One critic notes that Shield's subtle allusions to the myth – Larry's failures, particularly in his relationships, represent 'an old irony, handed down from the Daedelus myth' – and that his son's nickname 'Flyin' Ryan', later re-named 'Lyin' Ryan' after his disgrace, alludes to the fall of Icarus).[140] The dreadful and ferocious Minotaur, half bull, half man, that dwelt in the labyrinth was eventually slain by Theseus. He had the help of a maiden, Ariadne, who provided him with a thread which, secured at the entrance and unravelled as he proceeded, could be rewound, assuring him of the

---

136 J. Saward, op. cit., p. 8.
137 A. Meehan, op. cit., p. 58.
138 W. H. Matthews, op. cit., pp. 6ff.
139 Ibid., p. 10.
140 D. Goertz, op. cit., p. 246.

way as he retraced his steps. (The chapter called 'Larry's Threads', ostensibly about his sartorial history, is a playful reminder of this myth.) The pagan myth, which has the heroic conquest of the terrible monster as the heart and goal of the labyrinth, was later transposed to a Christianised allegory, the first example of which appeared in Roman Algeria on the floor of the basilica at Al-Asnam in AD 324.[141] Here, the earlier convention of the depiction of the Minotaur at the labyrinth's centre was replaced by a word-square spelling out 'Sancta Eclesia' (Holy Church).[142] Church labyrinths, increasingly popular throughout the twelfth and thirteenth centuries in France and Italy (a notable example is Chartres Cathedral), represented the pre-ordained path of Christian believers, 'full of twists and turns but with no choices and ultimately leading to only one goal.'[143] This double heritage of the pagan and the Christian has provided a wide-reaching secularised legitimacy for the modern fascination with the coded 'energy' of mazes. C. G. Jung's archetypal psychology incorporated the maze-like mandala symbol, traditionally a Chinese Taoist diagram used in meditation, to represent the unconscious processes connected with the individuation of the Self. In literary representation, Jorge Luis Borges's influential *Labyrinths*, a collection of short fictions, essays and 'parables' written in the late 1950s, used the trope of the maze (as in 'The Garden of the Forking Paths', for example) to represent the relative perspectives of a post-Einsteinian vision of time and space: 'an infinite series of times [...] a growing, dizzying net of divergent, convergent and parallel times'.[144] Mazes are also seen as mystical, magical, therapeutic. Walking a maze can now also take on meaning in terms of healing and reconnection with the earth and its energies, a kind of mantra in motion: 'The seven concentric paths of the classical labyrinth have become associated with the seven colours of the rainbow and the seven chakras, the "energy centers" of the human body, in popular literature within the field.'[145] Mazes are also mathematically exacting puzzles, where computers, lasers and a range of media and materials, tangible or virtual, resilient or ephemeral, bring to the designs a technological exuberance and experimentation.

A wide range of views on the 'how' and 'why' of mazes are expressed by various characters throughout *Larry's Party*. Eric Eisner, for instance, refutes the 'awful cute theory' that 'the medieval garden maze constituted a holy pilgrimage in microcosm, a place where a pilgrim might wend his way to the maze's secret heart and thereby find sanctuary and salvation' (pp. 138-9). His post-Freudian view is that 'the underlying rationale of the maze is sexual', that it 'twists through the mystery of desire and frustration [...] It's aroused by its own withholding structure. In the center, hidden – but finally, with a burst, revealed – lies sexual fulfillment, heaven' (p. 139). Another view, from one of Larry's clients who is dying of cancer, is that: 'I've felt all my life

---

141 J. Saward, op. cit., p. 21.

142 Ibid.

143 Ibid., p. 22

144 Jorge Luis Borges, 'The Garden of Forking Paths', *Labyrinths* (Harmonsdworth: Penguin, 1964).

145 Saward, op. cit., p. 165

that I was a kind of maze myself, my body, I mean. There was something hidden in the middle of me, but no one could find it, it was so deeply concealed' (p. 175). There are also less explicit analogies such as when Larry muses on History: 'whimsical notions, curious turnings, a surprising number of dead ends' (p. 27) or on Language: 'words were everywhere; you couldn't escape them'. The discussion at the party near the end of the novel includes many snippets *about* mazes, but the reader experiences the rendition of the overlay and intermittence of dinner-party conversations as a maze in itself. The maze is an emblem and a metaphor but it can also be an event. As Larry notes: 'A maze [...] is a kind of machine with people as its moving parts [...] A maze is designed so that we get to be part of the art' (pp. 218-19). The walk can be solitary, with the effects and symbolism of the experience intensely individual, or taken with others, to enact harmony, solidarity and community.

Larry's Party is about mazes but it also *is* a maze. Quite deliberately, Shields has not only included a popular phenomenon as a topic and theme in her novel, but has chosen a form that is maze-like, with its deliberate design, its peritextual signposts (epigraphs, photo, maze designs), and its circling, compartmentalised narrative progression. Although the narrative is presented chronologically, from 1977 to 1997 (fifteen chapters cover twenty years), the storytelling is not strictly sequential. Chapters are dominated by themes or issues rather than driven solely by 'what happened next', as in 'Chapter 7: Larry's Penis', for instance, a chapter sub-headed '1986' – not the only year Larry had one. Each chapter returns to, expands upon or glimpses information that has been encountered by the reader before. Each return presents the information as if it were being apprehended for the first time. For example, the all-important event at Hampton Court Maze on Larry's honeymoon, which is first and thoroughly reported in a chronological mode in Chapter 2 (subtitled '1978'), is returned to in Chapter 4 ('1981') as if this information is newly encountered:

> Larry's maze craze (as Dorrie calls it) started three and a half years ago when they got married and went to England for their honeymoon. The highlight of the trip was a tour through the famous Hampton Court maze outside London, and ever since then Larry's been reading library books about mazes. (p. 71)

In Chapter 8: (1988), the details are delivered again as if it were the first time:

> The 'bug' first bit when Larry and Dorrie visited Hampton Court during their 1978 English honeymoon. There the combination of arch formality and plotted chaos hummed to his young heart, and so did the notion that seedlings could be teased into dense, leafy, living walls so thick they baffled those who entered their midst. It caught him by surprise; it still does. (p. 151)

Information about Larry's life is parcelled out, and in the narrative's new context, is reflected upon differently but the narrator makes no reference to the earlier telling. In this sense, the fabric of the novel itself is like the fabric of the maze described above: 'arch formality and plotted chaos'. This is writing acutely aware of its own artifice (constructed in the way a maze is plotted and designed) – and at the same time aware of its own contingency and accident (like the maze itself, and like every experience of the maze).

'Accident' is a key term in the text. It opens with 'By mistake' in a chapter that goes on to reiterate a series of mistakes and accidents that sets Larry on the path of his marriage(s) and career: 'It was sort of a mistake the way they got together' and 'It was an accident how Larry got into floral design'. On occasion, the narrative voice introduces information that is proleptic (again, maze-like in its implications, for this is the future glimpsed), such as: 'Departures and arrivals: he didn't know it then but these two forces would form the twin bolts of his existence – as would the brief moments of clarity that rose up in between', or: 'The day will arrive in his life when work – devotion to work – will be all that stands between himself and the bankruptcy of his soul.' One of these – 'Larry Weller of Chicago, soon to pull up stakes and relocate to Toronto' – introduces a future which will, by 'accident', bring Dorrie and Larry together again, whereby Larry – (and the reader, of course), will see that this was the goal at the centre of the maze of Larry's life. Now the 'maze' of the narrative can be viewed from above, as it were, and the full design revealed: 'The whole thing about mazes [...] is that they make perfect sense only when you look down on them from above' (p. 219). As with most postmodern narratives, *Larry's Party* provides its own reflections on the artifice and acts of writing and reading. For instance, the explanation of the manner in which Larry comes to apprehend the 'history of Dot Weller, and how she killed her mother-in-law', provides a model for the way Larry's story will be told and should be apprehended: 'in small pieces, by installments [...] he's not sure, in fact, if he's ever been presented with a full account, start to finish, all at once' (p. 47). The correlation between maze-makers/'aficionados' and the postmodern writer/reader is also similarly in evidence:

> Maze aficionados tend to possess an off-key imagination, a sense of history (be it warped or precise), a love for teasing mysteries or else a desperate drive toward the ultimata of conspicuous affectation. (p. 146)

One of Larry's mazes is reviewed in a manner that would be appropriately applied to the novel: 'classical in its suggestions and contemporary in its small postmodern gestures' (p. 153). This 'intertextuality' – that is the incorporation and transposition of the classical, the precursor, a range of cultural sign-systems including the visual[146] is a feature common to the contemporary novel and the modern maze. This means that the signifying aspect of the maze has been changed from a metaphor (life is like a maze, the body is like a maze, language is like a maze) – although its metaphorical power remains – to a mutual metonymy: the maze stands for text, text stands for maze. Thus the poststructuralist tag taken from or attributed to the French philosopher Jacques Derrida, 'there is nothing outside the text,' could be read as 'there is nothing outside the maze', a profoundly sceptical view, perhaps, that is not entirely borne out

---

146 See Julia Kristeva, 'Revolution in Poetic Language', *The Kristeva Reader* (Oxford: Blackwell, 1986), p. 111.

in the novel. However, Shields gestures to this just enough for us to see her use of the maze as more complex and profound than is sometimes suggested by her critics.

Some critics have viewed Shields's use of the maze in this novel less than entirely favourably.[147] For some, the symbolism is too intrusive and cumbersome. The happy ending, too, can be viewed as too neat, too complete. And yet, if the text *is* maze, such 'completion' is simply part of the design and its artifice, aesthetic more than 'authentic'. The meaning one ascribes to it is another matter. While Larry finds in his maze-making 'spiritual optics' and spiritual excitement, part of his 'Search for the Wonderful and the Good', Shields's writing attends to 'those [...] transcendental moments when you suddenly feel everything makes sense and you perceive patterns in the universe'.[148] The 'real' story is not like this – and is bigger than can be told. Larry's maze-treading ends here only for the purposes of the fiction. Each maze-completion as a lived experience is a maze within a larger maze; Shields's own acknowledgment of this is demonstrated by her chapters, which, she said, would each be 'a little maze in itself'.[149] There would be more mazes to come in Larry's life if it were to continue beyond the text. However, although Larry and Dorrie have returned to an acknowledgment of their love for one another, the ending of the novel is otherwise entirely open, and any conventional 'happy ever after' conclusion is undercut by the fragmentation at the novel's close – a series of disparate messages via voice mail, email and fax. Ending the novel with the fragment of the nineteenth-century poem, sent by Beth and part of her fax, should not lead us to think of that this is the 'real' ending. Moreover, it was seen as compulsory in the nineteenth century for the novel to end with a marriage and happy conclusion, and this can be seen as Shields's playful parody of that compulsion – and the postmodern reader's anachronistic readiness to 'go there'. Once again, however, there is another clue to reading available to us. At the party, a maze of disembodied voices is represented, discussing mazes amongst a range of other topics, and someone says:

> 'We've always needed the idea that history moves forward, toward improvement of some kind, at the very least renewal. But this maze of Larry's hints at the circular journey which is really, when you stop to think about it –' (p. 313)

It is this that needs to be extended to a reading of the novel's ending, revealing this text, at least, in Shields's work, to be more thoroughly postmodern, parodic and sceptical than has sometimes been claimed.

---

147 Reviewers tend either to love or hate the mazes. Maggie O'Farrell ('Lost in a Maze,' *New Statesman* (12 September 1997), p. 46) and Candice Rodd (review of *Larry's Party, Times Literary Supplement* (22 August 1997), p. 22) are particularly scornful, while Michiko Kakutani finds the maze symbolism "an artful strategy" (Br'er Rabbit, Ordinary in Nearly Every Way, *New York Times* (26 August 1997), p. 13); D. Goertz, op. cit., note 3, pp. 251-2.

148 Cited in Goertz, op. cit., p. 233.

149 Shields in a radio interview, *Bookclub*, BBC Radio 4, 5 March 2000, cited in Goertz, op. cit., p. 253.

Larry the maze-maker and Shields the fiction-writer are Canadian – although Shields began her life in Illinois before moving to Canada in 1957 and living there until her death in 2003. Larry, in reverse, goes from his native Canada to work in the United States (Illinois) before moving back to Canada again. Larry was born and brought up in the prairie province of Manitoba in the city of Winnipeg (where Shields lived for most of her adult life). Throughout the novel there are references to Canada: Larry's parents arriving in the 1940s as immigrants, the extremes of weather, the conservativism, the parochialism. In gardening terms, there is reference to the terrible irony of Larry's mother's homesteading skills; the myth of North American self-reliance (or, in specifically Canadian terms, as Margaret Atwood explained – 'survival'), is undercut when dutifully growing and preserving her own beans, Mrs Weller kills her mother-in-law with botulism: 'She would have preferred a patch of fine lawn and a bed of flowers [...] but an anxious, learned frugality kept her concentration on what she and Stu and baby Midge could consume' (p. 49). Back from his honeymoon and inspired both by the complex network of England's hedgerows and Hampton Court Maze, Larry constructs a maze in his own Canadian suburban yard: 'there's nothing else like it in the city of Winnipeg, and probably not even in the province of Manitoba. [...] The last thing he wants is to move to Linden Woods, where [...] the by-laws probably prohibit eccentric gardening' (p. 71). Other references refer to familiar aspects: Canada's periodic below zero temperatures, 'frozen lakes and woodlands', snow, wilderness, 'bald prairie', proximity to and yet difference from the United States. Interestingly, Larry's first materials as a maze-maker are ones that are particularly Canadian: maple, maize, snow.

Canada itself, however, is now something of a maze. Originally seen as a blank slate (the name is believed to derive from the Spanish *aca nada* – nothing here),[150] Canada continued to bear a reputation, culturally, of having 'nothing there,' although it also has a history of being open to immigrants and to various cultural inscriptions. Margaret Atwood summarised this Canadian situation in a foreword to the aptly named *Ambivalence*:

> Two official languages, and many more unofficial ones; many cultures; several distinct regions, extremes of climate; East-West tensions, North-South ones; it's no wonder that any attempt to sum the place up will always be subject to qualification.[151]

Canada's literary 'coming of age'[152] occurred in the 1970s (precisely the time that *Larry's Party* opens): 'What the rest of the world was starting to call postmodernism had arrived in Canada – but the form it took was a distinctly Canadian one'.[153] In her

---

150 Om P. Juneja and Chandra Mohan, eds, *Ambivalence: Studies in Canadian Literature*, (Allied Publishers: New Delhi, 1990), p. xv.

151 Ibid., p. v.

152 Linda Hutcheon cites, in *The Canadian Postmodern*, Earle Birney's description of Canada as a 'highschool land/deadset in adolescence', but notes 'something new began to appear in the seventies and eighties', p. 1.

153 Ibid.

book dedicated to the subject of Canadian postmodern fiction and its writers (foremost among them Margaret Atwood, but including others now well known, such as Alice Munro and Michael Ondaatje), Linda Hutcheon explained the circumstances that finally bestowed distinctiveness on Canadian arts:

> [...] Canada's own particular moment of cultural history does seem to make it ripe for the paradoxes of postmodernism, by which I mean those contradictory acts of establishing and then undercutting prevailing values and conventions in order to provoke a questioning, a challenging of 'what goes without saying' in our culture. [...] taking pot-shots at the culture of which they know they are unavoidably part but that they still wish to criticize. This almost inevitably puts the postmodern writer into a marginal or 'ex-centric' position with regard to the central or dominant culture [...] Since the periphery or the margin might also describe Canada's perceived position in international terms, perhaps the postmodern ex-centric is very much part of the identity of the nation.[154]

In terms of a Canadian 'tradition' of classics and precursors, it took the parodic postmodern to bring even these to light. For instance, it was Margaret Atwood's volume of poetry, *The Journals of Susanna Moodie*, published in 1970, that re-visioned the out-of-print 'Canadian classic' of 1852, *Roughing It in the Bush* by Susanna Moodie, and heralded a new literary consciousness. Six years later, Shields's first published novel, *Small Ceremonies* (1976), also used Susanna Moodie as its subject, where the project of biographer Judith Gill is to piece together the 'real story' of Susanna Moodie from traces, published and unpublished.[155] Although this is in itself reminiscent of the method by which Shields assembles Larry's 'biography', it is the story of 'the bush', and its relation to Canadian identity, that is also being traced in *Larry's Party*. *Roughing It in the Bush* and *Larry's Party* seem at first to be at some remove from one another; whereas Susanna Moodie had 'sublime natural goings on in the misty distance – sunsets, mountains, spectacular views – only to be brought up short by disagreeable things in her immediate foreground, such as bugs, swamps, tree roots and other immigrants',[156] Larry has a much more sanitised, secure and suburban existence although he fills the small blank space of his yard with the mock-wilderness of a hedge-maze, combining the 'curved lines' of Nature ('Nature is labyrinthine, complex, curved')[157] with the 'squares' and 'straight lines' that belong to 'the order of Western European man'.[158] As Rosemary Sullivan notes: 'Until it is civilised, the wilderness is the enemy, but by the early twentieth century,

154 Ibid., p. 3.

155 M. Atwood, *The Journals of Susanna Moodie* (Toronto: Oxford University Press, 1970); Susanna Moodie, *Roughing It in the Bush* (London: Virago,1986 [1852]); C. Shields, *Small Ceremonies* (Harmondsworth: Penguin, 1996 [1976]).

156 M. Atwood, *Survival: A Thematic Guide to Canadian Literature* (Toronto: Anansi, 1972), p. 51.

157 Ibid., p. 120.

158 Ibid.

the terror of the wilderness has already turned into a nostalgia for the same wilderness as technology makes its inroads'.[159]

Two years after the publication of *The Journals of Susanna Moodie*, Atwood published *Survival: A Thematic Guide to Canadian Literature* (1972), which was groundbreaking not least in the notion that there was such a thing as 'Canadian literature'. The first chapter is entitled: 'What, Why and Where is Here?' and the chapter comes to a close with:

> Canada is an unknown territory for the people who live in it [...] I'm talking about Canada as a state of mind, as the space you inhabit not just with your body but with your head [...] What a lost person needs is a map of the territory; with his own position marked on it so he can see where he is in relation to everything else.[160]

This is the experience that Shields dramatises in *Larry's Party* and for which the maze so aptly stands. To situate the novel in this specific Canadian context is to understand its intricacy and the full range of its engagement and scholarship, from Classical myth to a contemporary crisis of national identity, from the sixteenth century of Sebastiano Serlio to the cultural polemic of twentieth-century Canada. One representative of the latter was the critic Northrop Frye, to whom Atwood dedicated *Survival* and whom she cited in its opening pages (one of the other dedicatees is Eli Mandel who wrote a poetry sequence in the 1950s called *The Minotaur Poems*). The passage she cites is from Frye's collection of Essays on 'the Canadian Imagination', *The Bush Garden* – a title taken in turn from Atwood's cycle of poems, *The Journals of Susanna Moodie*, and an oxymoronic play in itself on Moodie's earlier *Roughing it in the Bush*:

> It seems to me that Canadian sensibility has been profoundly disturbed, not so much by our famous problem of identity, important as that is, as by a series of paradoxes in what confronts that identity. It is less perplexed by the question 'Who am I' than by some such riddle as 'Where is here?'[161]

To use the symbol of the maze is thus ubiquitous and over-determined but in ways that are not always obvious. For instance, is there not an echo of this very passage in Larry's own musings on his mazes and their materials, and do not shrubs allegorise the twentieth-century Canadian experience?

> There's a paradox – that useful word again – built into the shrubs he's chosen. [...] Shrubs, he feels, are shy exiles in the plant kingdom. They're not quite trees, not quite anything, really, but they have, nevertheless, been awarded by the experts out there, your professors, your writers of gardening books, full botanical classification. (pp. 92-3)

---

159 R. Sullivan, 'The Forest and the Trees', in *Ambivalence*, op. cit., pp. 43 and 44.
160 M. Atwood, op. cit., *Survival*, p. 18.
161 Northrop Frye, *The Bush Garden* , cited in Atwood, *Survival*, op. cit., p. 10.

These shrubs, with their full classification but their ambiguous position as 'shy exiles' and 'not quite anything really', are thus emblematic of Canadians, citizens of a country that has gone from 'a pre-national phase to a post-national phase without ever having become a nation',[162] despite the confident optimism proclaimed in 1965 with its scarlet maple-leaf flag.

In 2001, another Canadian writer, Naomi Klein, published her book of startling polemic on the colonisation and congestion of space by branding: *No Logo*. Looking back to her own high-school days, she presents analogies and images that are now familiar:

> In our final year of high school, my best friend, Lan Ying, and I passed time with morbid discussions about the meaninglessness of life when everything had already been done. The world stretched out before us not as a slate of possibility, but as a maze of well-worn grooves like the ridges burrowed by insects in hardwood. Step off the straight and narrow career-and-materialism groove and you just end up in another one – the groove for people who step off the main groove [...] everywhere we imagined ourselves standing turned into a cliché beneath our feet [...] Crowded by the ideas and styles of the past, we felt there was no open space anywhere.[...] What haunts me is not exactly the absence of literal space so much as a deep craving for metaphorical space: release, escape, some kind of open-ended freedom.[163]

One of the preoccupations of *Larry's Party* – and of Canadians more generally, perhaps, but of Canadian writers certainly – is the near impossibility of dispensing with clichés and finding uncharted terrain, in a globally inscribed world, itself 'a maze of well-worn grooves'. The postmodern view that 'there is nothing new' is manifest in double meaning: ('everything had been done'; 'no open space anywhere'). In *Larry's Party*, Carol Shields utilises this trope of the maze to explore the Canadian specificity of a generally paradoxical postmodernism, from 'bush' to 'shrub'.

* * * *

The gardens in this chapter are not well-defined or obvious spaces, easy to identify as such. Nothing is very settled or certain in these postmodern garden-oriented texts: rather, plants are in transit, experiments are afoot and people themselves are in transition. The texts call into question the contexts and contributing factors that have given rise to Western-dominated notions of nomenclature, classification, order, rights, progress, knowledge, sex, religion art and nature. These texts have presented what their authors already knew: there is much that is *not* natural about Natural History. Thus, the botanical aspects in these four fictions are more about process than product, the cultural processes that determined or still determine Western ideas of nature in the pursuit of scientific knowledge. That nature did not always

---

162 Frye cited in L. Hutcheon's introduction, 'The Field Notes of a Public Critic', in N. Frye, *The Bush Garden* (Toronto: Anansi Press) 1995 [1971], p. xvi.

163 Naomi Klein, *No Logo* (London: Flamingo, 2001 [2000]), pp. 63-4.

correspond with 'natural' human social models called many ideological premises into question. 'Historiographic metafiction' questions the critical 'moments' when Western optimism and confidence encountered disjunctions between what was expected and what was observed.

Europe believed that the world was a garden – a field, more simply – to which it had the right to unlimited access; it was all in the name of what was now the highest calling: knowledge (for which, ironically, Adam and Eve were cast out of Eden). As the next chapter, 'Postcolonial Landscapes', will consider, one culture's higher calling was another's (the Other's) disaster. Natural History, like the postcolonial landscape that was its result, is deeply implicated in theories such as 'the white man's burden' or 'Manifest Destiny'. It is not just a question of what gardens might signify – status, wealth, taste, public, private – but rather that ideologies and analogies by which nature (plants, insects, animals and humans) were described and named were those which commanded narratives of singular and straightforward development. Postmodernism delights in exposing the bias and self-interest of the 'enlightenment certainties' that so often gave the West a dispensation to interpret the world through its own progressive lens. That is precisely why these postmodern narratives undercut, in content and in narrative form, the consolidated, confident view and instead attend to: rumour, gossip and legend, evolution and natural selection, multiple temporalities and various perspectives, the deconstruction of binary opposition and duality, contingency, accident, pastiche. The gardens in the postmodern fictions are there to show how their meaningfulness in one time or place can be re-visioned from another, to startling – and playful – effect. All of the texts look at the impact of science upon former religious (Biblical) certainties (which find their genesis in the Garden of Eden). This garden is never the singular trope for postcolonial writers, for their cultural consciousness is almost always 'double' (at least) and furthermore, many of the gardens that were established in the colonies by Christian colonisers were anything but Eden-like. Postcolonial writers may share many of the concerns and stylistic features with postmodern writing but the political analysis is, perhaps must be, at variance. It is one thing to interrogate one's own culture, as these postmodern writers have done, having the luxury and freedom to posit theories about split subjectivities, grand narratives and the vested interests of historiography. It is quite another to have been the disenfranchised Other, colonised and made subject to Western cultural hegemony, to be not-at-home wherever one finds oneself, rootless and displaced. For that colonising culture self-reflexively to deconstruct its former ideological premises, and to find new alignments with previously denigrated colonial cultures, does little to appease the damage done. Some of the features in the writing may be similar to postmodern texts but the impetus – and the botanical correlations – will be very different.

Chapter 3

Postcolonial Landscapes

I was reading a book and that book [...] happened to be about
the conquest of Mexico, or New Spain, as it was then called,
and I came upon the flower called marigold and the flower
called dahlia and the flower called zinnia, and after that the
garden was more to me than the garden as I used to think of
it. After that the garden was also something else [...] When
it dawned on me that the garden I was making (and am still
making and will always be making) resembled a map of the
Caribbean and the sea that surrounds it [...] I only marveled
at the way the garden is for me an exercise in memory, a way
of remembering my own immediate past, a way of getting to
a past that is my own (the Caribbean Sea) and the past as it
is indirectly related to me (the conquest of Mexico and its
surroundings).

Jamaica Kincaid
My Garden (Book) (2000)

We cannot deny the reality: cultures derived from plantations;
insular civilization [...]; social pyramids with an African
or East Indian base and a European peak; languages of
compromise; general cultural phenomenon of creolization;
pattern of encounter and synthesis; persistence of the African
presence; cultivation of sugarcane, corn and pepper; site
where rhythms are combined; peoples formed by orality.

Edouard Glissant
Caribbean Discourse: Selected Essays (1989)

Essential to the development of the biotechnology industry
have been legislative and judicial acts enabling private firms to
secure proprietary rights to plant genes, previously undescribed
species, and novel breeding programs. An individual can now
go to a remote farming tribe, collect a previously undescribed
crop variety, and take out a patent or trademark on it. Such
commercialization and rights usurpations have already
become contentious issues with regard to blue corn, squashes,
chile peppers, colored cotton, and amaranths.

Gary Paul Nabhan
Cultures of Habitat: On Nature, Culture and Story (1998)

The gardens collected in this chapter are represented as real and tangible from places across the globe: the Cape in South Africa; various locations in North America – including the arid Southwest, mid-western Oklahoma, California and Long Island; England; Italy; Trinidad. The writers who so deliberately include gardens in their texts are, respectively: a white South African of English and Afrikaner lineage (J. M. Coetzee), a West Indian of Indian peasant Hindu descent (V. S. Naipaul), an African American whose great-grandmother was Native American (Toni Morrison) and a Native American of Native, Mexican and European ancestry (Leslie Marmon Silko). The gardens are various but over all of them there hangs the shadow of centuries of conquest: the wide installation of the plantation system, the prohibition of indigenous 'heathen' practices; the insistence on monocultures (crops and people); and the enforced displacement of people. Such displacements occur either in terms of the systematic removal from land desirable in the interests of 'progress' (as with the Native Americans) or the transportation of people from homelands to work in another location in the interests of 'efficiency', (as with slavery and indentured servitude).

These policies and the discourses used to promote and normalise them (render them hegemonic) has made a difference to each of these diverse authors, to their protagonists, and to the gardens they represent. The 'Other' gardens that are posited in contrast to those of the dominant culture are, not surprisingly, smaller, diverse, include more food crops (which of course, also flower), are, literally, 'closer to the ground', products to eat or sell or exchange. This is true of Michael K's pumpkins in the veld, Consolata's wild black peppers in the Convent, Jack's allotment vegetables and Indigo's gladiolus tubers. These gardens should not be romanticised, however; for many of the protagonists they are not a viable place of return. For many of the protagonists and their creators these gardens represent the vestigial remnants of a past that is no longer realisable. Instead, as V. S. Naipaul puts it in relation to globalised suburbia, 'we had come out of the nightmare; and there was nowhere else to go,'[1] and certainly not back. For example, Native Americans presently have one of the highest incidence of diabetes in the world now that so many of their favoured food-plant species, methods of growing them and communal ceremonies have been lost.[2] Jamaica Kincaid cites a similar instance in the Caribbean where any positive association with the land and its tillage has been devastated:

---

1   V. S. Naipaul, *The Enigma of Arrival* (London: Picador 1987), p. 385.

2   See Gary Paul Nabhan, 'Diabetes, Diet and Native American Foraging Traditions', in *Cultures of Habitat: On Nature, Culture and Story* (Washington, D.C.: Counterpoint, 1998), p. 197ff., or 'Rooting Out the cause of Disease: Why Diabetes is So Common Among Desert Dwellers' in *Why Some Like It Hot: Food, Genes, and Cultural Diversity* (Washington, D.C.: Island Press, 2004), pp. 163ff. The American Diabetes Association confirms that diabetes has reached 'epidemic proportions' in Native American populations: 'One tribe in Arizona has the highest rate of diabetes in the world. About 50% of these adults between the ages of 30 and 64 has diabetes', http://www.diabetes.org/diabetes-statistics/native-americans.jsp.

Apparently, if you look at the surface, Antigua is very prosperous. But it has the highest incidence of malnutrition in the eastern Caribbean, 35 per cent. Antigua used to grow enough food to support itself. Do you know the French painter Millet? There is a great tradition of painting agricultural workers, people enjoying the cutting of the weed, the way the golden sunlight falls on them they're in touch with God. In the West Indies, this cannot happen, because agricultural work is associated with enforced labor, with slavery. You cannot see any heroic cane-cuttiing, or any heroic cotton-picking. It's associated with conquest, it's associated with hell.[3]

Thus, while each of the texts in this chapter has gardens to the fore, each of them challenges the naïve notion of a neutral space, a natural sanctuary or a politics-free zone. Empire and colonisation have always included agriculture and horticulture as an integral part of their own economic growth, and much damage (and some good, of course – this is not unacknowledged) has been done in the imperial expansions of the nineteenth century, in particular. The effects of decolonisation, however, can also be drastic for those areas originally identified by colonisers as lush paradises. These texts explore what it means to be a gardener in a location associated with one person's paradise and another's hell, and which may or may not be 'home'. These explorations are in themselves a prime illustration of what could stand as a postcolonial motto: 'never again will a single story be told as though it were the only one'.[4]

Of the several literary categories needing to be defined in the course of this book, postcolonial is at once the most frequently used (postcolonial world; postcolonial writer; postcolonial theory and criticism) and the most thoroughly debated. What is certain is that 'postcolonial' does not strictly mean that colonisation is a thing of the past (although one particular kind of manifestation has diminished another is on the ascendant – more on this later) or that decolonisation has been fully accomplished. The term 'postcolonial' refers rather to a set of concepts – and experiences – that were engendered after large parts of the world formerly held by European imperial powers sought independence and when a marked increase in cross-cultural migrations ensued (rather than the hitherto more common one-way traffic from the colonising country to a colony). Postcolonialism is also now a companion to terms such as 'multiculturalism' and 'globalisation'. This is a study of writing in English and so the British Empire is the colonial power held to the fore, although through the seventeenth, eighteenth and nineteenth centuries Spain, Portugal and France joined Britain in the contest of conquest, for a range of strategic, economic and ideological purposes, as previous chapters here have shown. As a *facet* of imperialism, colonialism is 'the settlement of territory, the exploitation or development of resources, and the attempt to govern

3   Jamaica Kincaid with Gerhard Dilger, in *Writing across Worlds: Contemporary Writers Talk*, ed. Shusheila Nasta (London & New York: Routledge, 2004), p. 91.
4   Michael Ondaatje citing John Berger, ibid., p. 9.

the indigenous inhabitants of occupied lands'.[5] By the end of the nineteenth century, Britain's colonies were extensive and included parts of Africa, Asia, Australasia, Canada, the Caribbean and Ireland. America, once a British colony, was an early instigator of decolonisation with its Declaration of Independence.

However, America constitutes a prime example of the complexity of the issue: America declared independence from a colonial power, Britain, in the eighteenth century, but it is itself (by virtue of its European settlers) a coloniser of the indigenous people, the native 'Indians', whose territories it settled, whose resources it exploited, and whose diverse peoples it aimed to govern and assimilate – in line with the definition of colonialism given above. America always did treat the Native Americans as 'sovereign nations', hence the proliferation of, albeit broken, treaties. Further, America's involvement in the slave trade is categorically another act complicit with economic imperialism and included the enforced immigration of people from other places, in particular, Africa.

> Most post-colonial theorists who have engaged with the issue have seen the study of black cultures in the Americas as, in part, the study of one of the world's major diasporas. In this respect, the history of African Americans has some features in common with other movements of oppressed diasporic peoples […] Comparative studies of these movements are a productive development in recent post-colonial theory, not least in the consideration of the different effects of these large-scale events on individual groups that such studies reveal […] Beyond the prime fact of oppression and violence, however, the relationships between the newly independent American societies, the wider diasporic black movement, and the modern independence movements in Africa itself, remain complex.[6]

Nevertheless, America is itself a 'postcolonial' nation in the eighteenth century at the same time as it is establishing itself as a colonial power. The abolition of slavery in the mid-nineteenth century was another manifestation of the 'postcolonial', but at precisely this time, America was also ruthlessly curtailing the individual rights and cultural independence of native peoples to the point of genocide. However, American writers are not always included in anthologies or critical overviews as 'postcolonial writers' perhaps because the United States is, and has been for some time, the most powerful nation in the world.

The present chapter 'Postcolonial Landscapes' will thus include novels by an African American and a Native American (they will be discussed first in this introduction, although they appear second and last respectively in the chapter) in the conviction that these texts have both been informed by postcolonial studies in the 1980s and 1990s and that they have a contribution to make to furthering its insights. Quite apart from the folly of bracketing off selective pockets of the 'legitimately postcolonial', Toni Morrison's text, *Paradise*, for instance, nonetheless includes in

---

5   Elleke Boehmer, *Colonial and Postcolonial Literature* (Oxford University Press, 1995), p. 2.

6   Bill Ashccroft, Gareth Griffiths, and Helen Tiffin, *Key Concepts in Post-colonial Studies* (London & New York: Routledge, 1998), pp. 6-7.

its reference the cultural complexity of Brazil, the religious syncretism of African, Indian and Catholic ritual, the encounter between black Catholic nuns and Native American boarders and Marcus Garvey's 'back to Africa' movement. Above all, Morrison's text is an interrogation of that ubiquitous and colonial notion of finding or establishing Paradise by the exclusion of undesirable others. As Morrison is at pains to point out, the garden-locus of Paradise always casts or keeps someone *out*. Shortly after the publication of *Paradise*, Morrison was asked by an interviewer, Elizabeth Farnsworth, 'is there something in African-American history that makes you especially interested in this separate place?' Morrison's reply situates her writing firmly in the context of world-wide diasporas (from the Greek word for 'to disperse'), willing and voluntary or unwilling and enforced, and where the terms home, heaven and hell become interchangeable depending on one's place, position and perspective:

> Yes, because only [...] African-Americans were not immigrants in this rush to find a heaven. They had left a home. So they're seeking for another home, while other people are doing the same thing, except the other people were leaving a home they didn't want to be in any longer, or couldn't be in any longer. Native Americans were being moved around in their home. African-Americans were looking for a second one and hopefully one that would be simply up to them, their own people, their own habits, their own culture, and to contain themselves in that. So it makes the motive for paradise a little bit different.[7]

Morrison, who grew up in the relatively neutral and inclusive town of Lorain, ('Lorain could not maintain strict segregation because the town attracted so many kinds of immigrants seeking work')[8] in the mid-western state of Ohio, a place she describes as 'neither plantation or ghetto',[9] posits a more inclusive view of what paradise should be. Although Morrison has also noted that segregation can help ethnic communities maintain their culturally specific traditions in ways that are vital and sustaining, she is keen to get away from racial markers as 'the first thing you know' and the thing that matters most, particularly in terms of inclusion or exclusion:

> There are racial differences among us. Exaggerated and exploited for political and economic purposes. And we have a great deal of baggage, personal feelings about other races because the society has been constructed along racial division. But in fact, when we meet another person one on one, and we know or recognize their race, we pull from that large suitcase of stereotypical information, of learned responses, of habitual reaction, which is the easiest and the laziest way to evaluate other people. The difficult thing and the important thing is to know people as individuals. So knowing that an individual is Asian or white or black is knowing next to nothing. It's knowing some cultural information which one can assume, but one must be wrong. But one must know much more than

7 *Conversation: Toni Morrison* (with Elizabeth Farnsworth) (9 March 1998), http://www.pbs.org/newshour/bb/entertainment/jan-june98/morrison_3-9.html.

8 Jill Matus, *Toni Morrison* (Manchester & New York: Manchester University Press, 1998), p. 6.

9 Cited ibid.

simply a racial marker. Knowing another person's race is like knowing their height or some other almost irrelevant piece of biological information. [...] Forcing people to react racially to another person is to miss the whole point of humanity.[10]

Morrison's notion of paradise is not a place that keeps out or casts out – or keeps racial markers to the fore – but one that welcomes diversity.

Fellow American, Leslie Marmon Silko, on the other hand, is also a justified inclusion under the heading 'postcolonial' – if such a justification were needed – not only on the basis of 'the history and continuing effects of race-based discrimination within US society',[11] but also because Silko believes herself to be writing, in *Gardens in the Dunes*, a novel about the effects of the history of European colonisation of the Americas by the Spanish and the British. Her attention to Native gardens in the Southwestern desert and combined with the tour of European gardens in a nineteenth-century setting, is a postcolonial reflection on the politics of colonisation and its related religious, racial and gender aspects. Further, Silko also writes in the context of recent postcolonial-inflected endeavours which explore the Western preoccupation with monocultures (horticultural and human) and the world-wide relevance of biodiversity. In the interests of the wide-ranging issues of sustainability, studies such as 'ethno-biology', 'biogeography' and 'archaeobotany' now acknowledge, for instance, that Native peoples have far more of a history of gardening than the settlers – and many since – have hitherto been able or willing to acknowledge. The traditional European interpretation of cross-cultural exchange represented in the national holiday, Thanksgiving, for example, is that Indians 'provided' corn and wild turkey (passively, by virtue of it simply being there, like the Indians) and the Europeans (actively) taught them methods of cultivation in return. As Silko – and contemporary researchers – show, the fault of such misapprehension lay in the confident European models of interpretation rather than Native ignorance of methods of cultivation. However, Silko is also at pains to express the ways in which 'purity' or isolated traditionalism is not now, nor ever was, a Native American aspiration. Exchange was always valued.

Hybridity, at least in the sense of a horticultural analogy which Silko extends in *Gardens in the Dunes* is a 'postcolonial theory' she is happy to claim, despite it being a controversial term in postcolonial studies:

One of the most widely employed and most disputed terms in post-colonial theory, hybridity commonly refers to the creation of new transcultural forms within the contact zone produced by colonization. As used in horticulture, the term refers to the cross-breeding of two species by grafting or cross-pollination to form a third,' hybrid' species. Hybridization takes many forms: linguistic, cultural, political, racial, etc. [...] The term 'hybridity' has been most recently associated with the work of Homi. K. Bhabha, whose analysis of colonizer/colonized relations stresses their interdependence and mutual

---

10   *Time* interview (21 January 1998), http://www.time.com/time/community/transcripts/chattr012198.html

11   J. Matus, op. cit.., p. 7.

construction of their subjectivities [...] Hybridity has frequently been used in post-colonial discourse to mean simply cross-cultural exchange. This use of the term has been widely criticized, since it usually implies negating and neglecting the imbalance and inequality of the power relations it references.[12]

Leslie Marmon Silko's own ancestry, however, is a mixture of Laguna, Mexican and white; born in Albuquerque, New Mexico in 1948, she grew up on the Laguna Pueblo reservation. She comments frequently on what it means to be a 'Native American writer', a category that came into its own in the 1970s. In Silko's view, it is 'the community' and 'what you know' that counts more than any racial 'pedigree':

> You can talk all day long about identity, census numbers, etc. You can be a full blood and grow up in Cincinnati and lose touch. Their experience is different from the person who is in the community where there is constant concern for language. The community is tremendously important. That's where a person's identity has to come from, not from racial blood quantum levels.[13]

While Silko resists over-simplifications which try to identify a 'legitimate' or 'authentic "Native American"' perspective, she doubts that white writers can ever successfully represent Native American experience, consciousness, or culture and that 'sooner or later in one's imagery and one's handling of that consciousness this non-Indian writer is going to get [...] into trouble'.[14] She has referred to some of those who have attempted this, and she comments on the distortions and false expectations that have ensued, both for writers, and then, readers, of 'Native American' literature:

> it seems that the writers are bowing to expectations, that is, they feel that they are expected, because they are Native Americans, to write in a special way [...] I think it is probably the white writers more than any who have actually dictated what they think 'Indian writing' should be. People like Rothenberg and of course Gary Snyder perfected the 'white shamanism' movement. The attitude of the white shaman is that he knows more about Indians than the Indians know. It has happened with Indian graphic art and painting. The people who buy the paintings tell the Indian artist, 'Don't do that, that's abstract – Indians ought to only do realistic sorts of paintings', and 'Oh, don't paint that, that's a picture of a drunken man passed out on the street of Gallup. That won't sell in our gallery, you know'.[15]

---

12   Ibid., p. 118-19.

13   Per Seyersted, *Leslie Marmon Silko* (Boise, ID: Boise State University Press, 1980), p. 15.

14   Per Seyersted, 'Two Interviews with Leslie Marmon Silko', *American Studies in Scandinavia*, Vol. 13 (1981), p. 20.

15   Ibid., p. 25

In this respect she is rather like V. S. Naipaul who objects to the tag 'West Indian writer' as 'patronizing and limiting, like saying someone is a Yorkshire writer'.[16] Silko is a proponent, as are all the writers here, of diversity and, as each, has a keen sense of paradox and complexity – as befits a postcolonial world:

> As far as perspective goes, there's mine [...] the perspective I have involves very definitely Laguna and Laguna people and Laguna culture [...] but I don't think one should oversimplify and say this is a Laguna point of view. It's my point of view, coming from a certain kind of background and place.[17]

The other two authors considered here are respectively – and ostensibly, due to complex origins and destinations – West Indian and South African, writing from countries which sit more easily under the umbrella term 'postcolonial', including: Canada, South Africa, Australia and New Zealand on the one hand; India, Pakistan, Ceylon (Sri Lanka), Jamaica, Trinidad and Tobago on the other. By the early 1960s, independence had been granted by Britain to most of its former colonies and dominions but, of course, the space or place denoted 'postcolonial' is a highly ambiguous one. Colonised peoples do not and cannot (if, indeed, it is their wish) return to a 'precolonial' existence or location and notions of belonging become thoroughly perplexed. It is the complex consequences of colonialism that the postcolonial writer and critic considers.

V. S. Naipaul is an example of a writer from – and of – many places, a not unusual postcolonial position. In Naipaul's case, his family came from India to Trinidad as indentured servants after slavery had been abolished there. The complex upheavals that colonisation and decolonisation create in its wake were experienced by Naipaul as a boy growing up in Trinidad and compelled him to leave as a young man, as one literary-critical biographer outlines:

> He hated the narrow, circumscribed, brutal life which surrounded him in colonial Trinidad with its limited possibilities, small range of professions, notorious political corruption and racial and religious conflicts. He felt that traditional Indian culture was decaying, its rituals incongruous in Trinidad, and bound for extinction. The Indians among whom he lived had a social world of their own uninvolved with the other races. The Trinidadians of African descent appeared to have no traditional culture of their own and modeled themselves on the English, their centuries of humiliation resulting in resentment, a brotherhood of skin colour, and fantasies of deliverance. The local whites had produced nothing of lasting value, were often drunkards, uneducated and privileged. They had the best jobs. There was, however, a bond between the descendents of former slaves and slave owners from

---

16   Bruce King, *V. S. Naipaul* (Basingstoke & New York: Palgrave Macmillan, 2003), p. 4.

17   Silko in Dexter Fisher, 'Stories and Their Tellers: A Conversation with Leslie Marmon Silko', *The Third Woman: Minority Women Writers in the United* States (Boston; Houghton Mifflin, 1980), p. 21.

which the Indians were excluded and which resulted in the blacks replacing the whites as the dominant group as Trinidad moved towards self-government.[18]

One of the consequences of the hegemony of Empires is that their colonised peoples *know* the metropolitan 'mother country' through its language and literature. Colonisation also has an effect on how one views one's own country; authoritative colonial discourses have informed the self-estimation of diverse cultures. The process of decolonisation, which promises to be liberating, can be devastating when all one's perspectives have to be adjusted. Britain, once visited, is also a surprise: it is not what Wordsworth's daffodils or Dickens's London, made familiar in a tropical classroom, has led one to expect. V. S. Naipaul's *The Enigma of Arrival* charts the process of traversing the world with the aim of seeing things rightly. Naipaul also left Trinidad with the express aim of being a writer of English fiction in England. Many others who, like Naipaul, left their homes in former colonies, extended the histories of forced diasporas to more 'willing' dispersals and migrations but only to complicate further the sense of 'home': a citizen of which nation or country? Thus, Naiplaul's first journey was not to the India of his forbears but to Oxford. Similarly, Jamaica Kincaid did not leave Antigua to seek Africa ('the great traditions of village life in Africa just absolutely escaped me')[19] in the first instance, but former slave-trafficking America. Kincaid explains:

I left at the time, in 1965, because I wanted to. People left, they went to England – I happened to go to America – they left for economic reasons. I left for the same reasons people tend to leave places they live in, because they feel they will find happiness of some kind somewhere else, they feel that they'll feel better about themselves. They hope to be prosperous [...] I wanted to go to America and I would make sense of myself to myself.[20]

As already indicated, one of the predominant features of postcolonial texts is the paradox of postcolonial politics and the ways in which individual lives – and texts – are perplexed by these. Every writer examined here is from time to time seen as 'difficult', which most often means 'difficult to pin down and pigeon-hole'. Bruce King explains this in relation to Naipaul and the controversies he tends to generate:

His views often have the effect of paradox and surprise forcing a re-examination of received opinions. He has said that replacing traditional farm life with industrialization can be liberating to a peasant [...] A severe critic of India and the shortcomings of newly independent nations, he feels humiliated by the weakness and exploitation of the colonized; he blames European imperialism for the horrors of slavery and for the problems it left its former colonies, while praising it for bringing peace and modern thought to areas of the

---

18 B. King, op. cit., p. 8.
19 Jamaica Kincaid with Gerhard Dilger, *Writing across Worlds*, op. cit., p. 82.
20 Ibid., p. 81.

world that remained medieval and debilitated by continual local wars and destructive non-Western invasions.[21]

Finally, J. M. Coetzee's experience (and writing) is similarly fraught with paradox and complexity. As a South African who was a white English-speaking Afrikaner, Coetzee was in a position of contesting hierarchies and various illegitimacies in a 'new, neo-colonial period of South Africa's history':

> By the end of World War II the economy of the Union of South Africa had shifted definitively from a rural to an urban base. In 1948 a party of Afrikaner nationalists came to power and began to sever political and cultural ties with Europe; as apartheid began to be implemented, moral ties were severed too; and from being the dubious colonial children of a far-off motherland, white South Africans graduated to uneasy possession of their own, less and less transigent internal colony.[22]

Coetzee began writing at a time of prevailing and ruthless apartheid laws which included, 'from the early 1960s until about 1980', 'one of the most comprehensive censorship systems in the world [...] in official parlance [...] "publication control"'.[23] Who speaks and for whom, who is silent and why, are among Coetzee's most pressing concerns. While he does represent black characters in his fictions as he portrays the complexities of power and disempowerment, he is careful, too, to depict their 'dis-articulation', as in Friday's tongueless condition in *Foe* or here, in Michael K's hare lip. Coetzee never supposes to be able to escape 'the skin you are born with', as he puts it, but he does propose relentlessly to scrutinise what it *means* when the skin one is in is the most significant marker in a particular time and place, and to interrogate who wields the power to name and who suffers the impotence of being the named. In 1987, Coetzee was awarded The Jerusalem Prize for Literature, and in his acceptance speech he noted:

> In a society of masters and slaves, no one is free. The slave is not free, because he is not his own master; the master is not free, because he cannot do without the slave. For centuries South Africa was a society of masters and serfs; now it is a land where the serfs are in open rebellion and the masters are in disarray.
> The masters, in South Africa, form a closed hereditary caste. Everyone born with a white skin is born into the caste. Since there is no way of escaping the skin you are born with [...], you cannot resign from the caste. You can imagine resigning, you can perform a symbolic resignation, but, short of shaking the dust of the country off your feet, there is no way of actually *doing* it. [...][24]

---

21 B. King, op. cit., p. 4.

22 J. M. Coetzee, *White Writing: On the Culture of Letters in South Africa* (New Haven, CT & London: Yale University Press, 1988), p. 11.

23 J. M. Coetzee, *Giving Offence: Essays on Censorship* (Chicago & London: University of Chicago Press, 1996), p. 34.

24 J. M. Coetzee , 'Jerusalem Prize Acceptance Speech', *Doubling the Point: Essays and Interviews* (Cambridge, MA & London: Harvard University Press, 1992), p. 96-7.

Coetzee is also attentive to the myths built up around 'the land', the inherent 'garden-ness' of South Africa; love of the land in South Africa appears over-determined in a country often otherwise bereft of love.

It is not insignificant, nor an accident, that each of the novels selected for this chapter has a journey at its core; this might indeed be called the postcolonial condition. Here is Coetzee's Michael K, travelling from a civil-war-torn Cape Town to the veld of, not just his mother's domestic service on an Afrikaner's farm, but his own Hottentot forbears. Or, there is Morrison's 'Eight Rock' pure-blood families traveling north and west hopefully to greater freedom than a former slave-holding American South could ever afford. Naipaul's first-person (and largely autobiographical) narrator travelling from Trinidad to England and back again – to return again – and Silko's Sand Lizard runaway, escaping boarding school and going instead on a Grand Tour of eastern America, England and Italy reflect the peripatetic experience of not just the postcolonial protagonist, but the postcolonial writer as well who has come to be familiar as a:

> cultural traveler, moving words/worlds across cultures and transporting the imagination beyond the maps of narrowly defined borders [...] writing has always been a form of cultural travelling, a means of transporting words into other worlds, of making crossings and forging connections between apparently conflicting worlds. Such literary crossings are not new, though perhaps in the context of the mass migrations of the late twentieth century – whether enforced or voluntary – the nature and perspective of the voyages are.[25]

Postcolonial writing used to be synonymous with 'writing from the margins', as opposed to writing from the metropolitan centre, but now the margins have become central. The literary 'canon' being dominated by WASP (White Anglo Saxon Protestant) writers has been thoroughly displaced on school and university syllabi by writing previously known as 'Other'. Toni Morrison's *Beloved*, for instance, published in 1988, with its combination of history, spiritual and supernatural aspects, and sheer narrative innovation, became a multi-prize winner and was adopted widely for study programmes. It is worth noting here that each of the authors in this chapter has won numerous literary prizes and that three of the four have won the highly prestigious Noble Prize for Literature: Morrison in 1993 (for 'novels characterised by visionary force'), Naipaul in 2001 ('for having united perceptive narrative with incorruptible scrutiny [...] to compel us to see the presence of suppressed histories') and Coetzee ('who in innumerable guises portrays the surprising involvement of the outsider') in 2003. Thus writers and writings from 'the margins' have become mainstream, a move, some cynics would say, that is just another marketing gambit. However, this returns us to the representative difference between postmodern writing and postcolonial writing. Although the two genres share many textual features, their agendas are quite different. For the writer of the postcolonial text, the political and historical issues still matter, human agency and the power to protest against inequity

---

25 S. Nasta, *Writing across Worlds*, op. cit., pp. 5-6.

or poverty or persecution are still held to the fore, and the dissemination of the details of suppressed histories and oppressed peoples must continue. That the questions postcolonial writing posits remain unanswered is not a failing or a sell-out to market forces, but, rather, integral to a duty to express and keep these realities visible:

> although in the past few years a popular interest in literary prizes combined with the globalization of the publishing industry have drawn the diversity of contemporary writing to the attention of a much wider international readership, many unanswered questions still linger, questions that remain indissolubly linked to the perpetuation of stark global inequalities, old and new imperial histories, as well as the ever-present realities of race and class.[26]

As in the other chapters, each of the sections that focuses on a particular text has a sub-title that is relevant to the specific work and illustrative of an aspect of 'postcolonial writing'. Here, unusually, the sub-titles will each have two terms combined: the first is a positive, more hopeful one (for each of these writers does express hope), but the second acknowledges difficulty and a continuing process. Thus, there is: 'Belonging /Marginalisation'; 'Reconciliation/War'; 'Migration/Rootlessness'; 'Hybridity/ Homogeneity'.

J. M. Coetzee: Belonging/Marginalisation

J. M. Coetzee is best known as a novelist although he has also written an extensive range of essays and reviews, many of them reflecting his interests in linguistics and literary theory. Coetzee began publishing his fiction in the 1970s, first with *Dusklands* in 1974, followed by *In the Heart of the Country*, in 1977, which was also later made

---

26 Ibid., p. 7.

into a film: *Dust.*[27] Winning major literary prizes at home in South Africa and abroad (he has the rare distinction of having won the Booker Prize on two occasions),[28] his international reputation as a writer was established in the 1980s with the novels *Waiting for the Barbarians* (1980), *Life and Times of Michael K* (1983) and *Foe* (1986). In 1988 he published a collection of essays entitled *White Writing: On the Culture of Letters in South Africa*. From the outset, these essays focus on the impact of the South African landscape on its white colonisers and their representations of it. As his first paragraph attests, the European colonisation of the southern tip of the African continent, the Cape of Good Hope, began as, simply, a garden: 'In 1652 [...] it was set there for a specific and limited purpose: to provide fresh produce to East Indiamen trading between the Netherlands and Asia.'[29] In 2002, this time within the explicit and autobiographical context of young white South African abroad in Britain in the 1960s, Coetzee notes again the issue of the garden-outpost that became a contested colony:

> What had seemed perfectly natural while he still called that continent his home seems more and more preposterous from the perspective of Europe: that a handful of Hollanders should have waded ashore at Woodstock beach and claimed ownership of foreign territory they had never laid eyes on before; that their descendents should now regard that territory as theirs by birthright. Doubly absurd, given that the first landing-party misunderstood its orders, or chose to misunderstand them. Its orders were to dig a garden and grow spinach and onions for the East India fleet. Two acres, three acres, five acres at most: that was all that was needed. It was never intended that they should steal the best part of Africa.[30]

This is, of course, the accident that would ultimately give rise to South Africa's systematised apartheid of some three hundred years later, which in turn gave rise to civil and racial unrest and a series of international crises not formally appeased until the mid-1990s. While the Dutch East India Company ran the original seventeenth-century settlement, it limited any interest in further establishment reporting that 'the hinterland of the Cape [...] was barren, inhospitable, and sparsely populated by primitive Hottentots and Bushmen',[31] although the Company's merchants brought botanical specimens back to the Netherlands, to be collected in the Amsterdam Physic Garden, for instance, as its catalogue of 1697-1701 reveals.[32] In 1772 and 1773, the Cape was a destination for plant-hunting expeditions from Kew. Led by Francis Masson, these expeditions highlighted both the ruggedness and the richness of the region. The garden historian, Jane Fearnley-Whittingstall, explains its challenges and its bounty:

---

27 *Dust* (1985), written and directed by Marion Hänsel, starring Trevor Howard and Jane Birkin.

28 In 1983 for *Waiting for the Barbarians* and in 2000 for *Disgrace* – both set in South Africa, both focusing on rural life in the Karoo – or South African veld.

29 J. M. Coetzee, *White Writing*, op. cit., p. 1.

30 J. M. Coetzee, *Youth* (London; Vintage, 2003 [2002]), p. 121.

31 J. M. Coetzee, *White Writing*, op. cit., p. 1.

32 P. Hobhouse, *Plants in Garden History*, op. cit., p. 125.

It would be difficult to exaggerate the romance, excitement and danger of early plant-hunting expeditions. Masson travelled 650km (400 miles) by ox-drawn trekking wagon through rugged, almost impassable territory. He found much to interest him, and returned a year later with the Swedish botanist Thunberg. They had to fend off attacks by hyenas, leopards and lions, they nearly ran out of food and water, their wagon almost fell apart and their oxen fell sick. Nevertheless Masson was able to add more than 400 species to Kew's collection. They included ixias, gladioli, gazanias, chincherinchees, irises, stapelias, and Cape jasmine (*Gardenia stellata*).[33]

Despite such inhospitable conditions and hardships the British were to cede power on the Cape to the Dutch only after years of conflict between the dual colonisers of the area. The struggles of the nineteenth century between white Europeans, the Afrikaners and the British, became eclipsed (though not entirely obscured) in the twentieth by the most rigid system of racial apartheid.

In the introduction to *White Writing*, Coetzee claimed that the book would reflect two main concerns. His preoccupations would be: 'with certain of the ideas, the great intellectual schemas, through which South Africa has been thought by Europe; and with the land itself, South Africa as landscape and landed property'.[34] In the endeavour, he focuses on 'white writing' in both Afrikaans and English. Coetzee also writes with an acute awareness of his own position, acknowledged elsewhere as being himself 'written [...] as a white South African into the latter half of the twentieth century, disabled, disqualified – a man-who-writes reacts to the situation he finds himself in of being without authority', writing without authority.[35] Coetzee's white South African position has a further complexity, a 'double-consciousness' that includes a linguistic duality as well as another set of contesting allegiances:

> A sense of being alien goes back far in his memories. [...] as a child from an Afrikaans background attending English-medium classes, at a time of raging Afrikaner nationalism, a time when laws were being concocted to prevent people of Afrikaans descent from bringing up their children to speak English, provoke in him uneasy dreams of being hunted down and accused; by the age of twelve he has a well-developed sense of social marginality. (People of his parents' kind are thundered at from the pulpit as <u>volksverraaiers</u>, traitors to the people. The truth is, his parents aren't traitors, [...] they are merely, to their eternal credit, indifferent to the <u>volk</u> and its fate.)
>
> His years in Worcester are followed by adolescence in Cape Town, as a Protestant enrolled in a Catholic high school, with Jewish and Greek friends. For a variety of reasons he ceases visiting the family farm, the place on earth he has defined, imagined, constructed, as his place of origin. All of this confirms his (quite accurate) sense of being outside a culture that at this moment in history is confidently setting about enforcing itself as the core culture of the land.[36]

---

33 J. Fearnley-Whittingstall, *The Garden*, op. cit., p. 200.
34 J. M. Coetzee, *White Writing*, op. cit., p. 10.
35 J. M. Coetzee, *Doubling the Point*, op. cit., p. 392.
36 J. M. Coetzee, Ibid., p. 393-4.

At the same time, he also experiences a real facility with the Afrikaans language ('when he speaks Afrikaans, all the complications of life seem suddenly to fall away'[37]), defending its pronunciation in the face of English-speakers' distortions ('superciliously'), although continuing to reject (and feeling rejection by) Afrikaners and their own use of the language: 'they wield their language like a club against their enemies […] yet […] he finds himself unwilling to yield up the Afrikaans language to them.'[38] And so, in his analysis of the 'white writing' of South Africa he explores writing informed by – and writing back to – the Netherlands on the one hand and Britain on the other. He explores the predominant South African genres of landscape poetry, of the Afrikaner *Plaasroman*: ('for two decades of this century, 1920-40, the Afrikaans novel concerned itself almost exclusively with the farm and *platteland* (rural) society, with the Afrikaner's painful transition from farmer to townsman'[39]) alongside the more limited genre of the English farm novel, typified by Olive Schreiner's *The Story of An African Farm* (an 'anti-pastoral'). Coetzee also attends to a range of ethnography, historiography and polemic which he collects under an over-arching term: 'the Discourse of the Cape'. Here, with the support of a range of scientific methodologies, rationales based on morality and advancement and rooted in a northern European Protestant work ethic, South Africa's version of 'manifest destiny' was articulated. *White Writing* analyses the ways in which Europe's 'great intellectual schemas' were projected onto the colony, including the identification of 'natural' rights in relation to a landscape that was considered to have potential for development; it was along these lines that the colonisers could disqualify the idle – and profligate – indigenous inhabitants:

> The first of the European ideas I address is the idea of Man, which the Hottentots in the early years of the Colony in certain respects so puzzlingly and troublesomely failed to live up to [...] The second is the idea of cultural progress, the idea that cultures can be ranged along a scale of evolutionary ascent from 'backward' to 'advanced'. Through this schema the European enabled himself to see in South Africa, layered synchronically one on top of another as in an archaeological site, hunters, pastoralists, early agriculturalists, advanced precapitalists peasant agriculturalists, and even agriculturalists in the process of regressing to nomadic pastoralism, all of whom, belonging to 'simpler' stages of evolution, would be understood as 'simple' people [...] Another is the idea that, mankind being 'naturally' divided into distinct races, sexual unions that cross racial lines are unnatural and yield degenerate offspring [...] A fourth is the idea that, when people are 'at home in' or 'at harmony with' a particular landscape, that landscape speaks to them and is understood by them [...] All of these ideas, deployed with a degree of blind force in proportion as they were held at various times to be self-evident, undeniable, 'natural', constituted part of the repertoire of thinking by which Europe held sway over a far-off, interesting, but finally unimportant part of the world.[40]

37   J. M. Coetzee, *Boyhood: Scenes from Provincial Life* (London; Secker & Warburg, 1997), p. 125.

38   Ibid., p. 124.

39   J. M. Coetzee, *White Writing*, op. cit., p. 63.

40   Ibid., p. 10.

Much of Coetzee's fiction also engages very deliberately with these colonial schemas and their effects, up to the present-day or projected into a near future: *Life & Times of Michael K*, *In the Heart of the Country*, *Dusklands* and *Disgrace* each have a specific and sustained engagement with one or more of these ideas – and their consequences.

Although a place of vast expanse, striking and varied landscape, rich resources and largely clement weather, the Cape colony, unlike the Americas, was not mythologised or projected according to that most familiar Western trope: Eden. At the outset of *White Writing*, Coetzee considers the reasons for this:

> Why did the garden myth, the myth of a return to Eden and innocence, fail to take root in the garden colony of the Cape? For while the promise of a fresh start on a fresh continent deeply affected the shape of history n Europe's New World colonies, in South Africa, in many respects a *lui-lekker land* (land of ease and plenty), the only myth that ever came to exert a comparable animating force was the story of the wanderings of the Israelites in search of a Promised Land, a story of tribal salvation appropriated as their own by the wandering Afrikaner tribes.[41]

Africa 'could never, in the European imagination, be the home of the earthly paradise because Africa was not a "new world"'.[42] Whereas the 'discovery' and colonisation of the Americas did give rise to speculations of an Eden, with its indigenous peoples reported, at least initially, in the seventeenth century, as being 'in a state of innocence', 'the Cape, by contrast, belonged not to the New World but to the farthest extremity of the Old [...] peopled by natives whose way of life occasioned curiosity or disgust but never admiration'.[43]

> Yet the topos of the garden, the enclosed world entire to itself, is more extensive than the Judeo-Christian myth of Eden. In its isolation from the great world, walled in by oceans and an unexplored northern wilderness, the colony of the Cape of Good Hope was indeed a kind of garden. But the future promised by the Cape seemed to be less of the perfection of man in a recovered original innocence than of the degeneration of man into brute. Again and again visitors to the colony warned that, from lack of any spurt to activity in the economically stagnant hinterland, colonists were declining into the idle and brutish state of the Hottentots. Like Joseph Conrad after them, they were apprehensive that Africa might turn out to be not a Garden but an anti-Garden, a garden ruled over by the serpent, where the wilderness takes root once again in men's hearts. The remedy they prescribed against Africa's insidious corruptions was cheerful toil.[44][...]
>
> To understand why the Hottnetot way of life, characterized by (and stigmatized for) its idleness, was in no way held up to Europe as a model of life in Eden, we must be aware of attitudes towards idleness prevailing in Europe at the time when Europe, particularly Protestant Europe, was colonizing the Cape[45] [...] The consensus is that the

41   Ibid., p. 2.
42   Ibid.
43   Ibid.
44   Ibid., p. 3.
45   Ibid., p. 19.

Hottentot way of life, characterized by low-level subsistence maintained by the minimal resort to wage-labour ('laziness'), wandering in search of greener pastures ('vagrancy') and a sometimes casual attitude toward private property ('thieving'), will have to be reformed by *discipline* (a key word of the age) if the Hottentot is to have any stake ('pull his weight') in the Colony.[46]

White Writing was published in 1988 but most of its chapters, separately and in versions, had appeared prior to this date. Many of the critical formulations Coetzee makes in *White Writing* are incorporated into his novel of 1983, *Life & Times of Michael K.*

Set in the context of a civil war, taking place at an unspecified time – in the 'near future' in the words of one critic writing in 1992 – the main character, Michael K, is a figure variously disenfranchised. Again, Coetzee dramatises by way of Michael K's various evasions, arrests, and incarcerations, another point made in *White Writing*:

> By the middle of the seventeenth century what Michel Foucault calls 'the great confinement' had got under way. The culmination of a series of measures designed to put an end to vagrancy and begging as a way of life, it began with the confinement of the beggar class and went on later to sweep up the insane and the criminal. During crises of unemployment the houses of confinement became in effect prisons for the workless; during economic upswings they acted as hostels cum factories. As productive organizations these were a failure, but that did not matter: their purpose was not to turn a profit but to proclaim the ethical value of work.[47]

Of course, this ideological shift in Europe was transported to and imposed upon its colonies. The tale of Michael K's life and times also involves a very specific late-twentieth-century context of the South African state under apartheid laws, about which Coetzee has been outspoken. The following estimation of the South African context, published in 1986, links directly with the critical formulations found in *White Writing* and the 'fictional' portrayals of *Life & Times of Michael K*:

> The response of South Africa's legislators to what disturbs their white electorate is usually to order it out of sight. If people are starving, let them starve far away in the bush, where their thin bodies will not be a reproach. If they have no work, if they migrate to the cities, let there be roadblocks, let there be curfews, let there be laws against vagrancy, begging and squatting, and let offenders be locked away so that no-one has to hear or see them.[48]

Although Michael K's race or colour is never explicit, it is to be inferred that he is black, or, in the nomenclature of apartheid South Africa, either 'native', 'black African' or 'mixed-race Coloured'.[49] It is, however, Coetzee's discussion of the

---

46 Ibid., p. 26.

47 J. M. Coetzee, *White Writing*, op. cit., p. 20.

48 J. M. Coetzee, 'Into the Dark Chamber: The Writer and the South African State' (1986), *Doubling the Point*, op. cit., p. 361.

49 Coetzee discusses the categories in 'Apartheid Thinking' in *Giving Offense*, op. cit., pp. 163-84.

Discourse of the Cape in *White Writing* that gives us the clues to place Michael as an 'idle' Hottentot, at least in some near aspect of his lineage. As Michael journeys from the war-torn city of Cape Town back to his rural beginnings on a Afrikaner farm in the Karoo, where his mother was once a servant, he learns strategies for surviving, literally, *outside*, making and living in a burrow in the earth while waiting for his secret crops of pumpkin and melon to grow. As he moves further away from the city, shedding its various impositions, Michael is forced to adopt – or re-adapt to – a mode of being which, while distressing (especially to onlookers) in its consequences, is increasingly acceptable, even familiar, to Michael. A passage such as: 'but most of all, as summer slanted to an end, he was learning to love idleness [...] He was neither pleased nor displeased when there was work to do; it was all the same', is most fruitfully read alongside *White Writing*'s chapter 'Idleness in South Africa', helping to identify through this discourse Michael K's Hottentot roots.

At the time of the novel's opening, Michael K is a Gardener, Grade 1 for the Parks and Gardens division of the municipal services of the City of Cape Town. Although the date is unspecified, the city and its environs are identifiable and are, not unfamiliarly, wracked by a state of civil war with its violence, curfews and other regimes for controlling and/or concealing the dispossessed. Michael K has worked for Parks and Gardens since he was fifteen, a period of service interrupted only by a stint (made brief by a violent mugging) as a night attendant at a public lavatory. Before he became a gardener, Michael, who has a hare lip with a disfigured nose and whose mind 'was not quick', was sent to an institution called Huis Norenius 'where at the expense of the state he spent the rest of his childhood in the company of other variously afflicted and unfortunate children'.[50] As the narrative unfolds, Michael is forced to leave his role as a municipal gardener and becomes another kind of gardener, outside the city, outside the law and social order, and, as already noted, more specifically simply outside, for Michael takes up residence in a burrow adjacent to the pumpkins and melons he nurtures on a deserted farm. Michael leaves his job and the city to help his ailing mother find the rural home in the veld, a farm in the district of Prince Albert on which she had been born and that she remembers so positively. However, although Michael has worked for and within 'the system', the system does not work for him, and he and his mother are unable to get the requisite police permits that will enable them to make train reservations. They live together briefly in Anna K's broom-closet room under the stairs, with neither ventilation nor electric light, fearful of being evicted because Anna cannot work and is unable, because of the shortages and disruptions of war, to get basic staples. When Anna's absentee-employers' apartment is ransacked, they in desperation attempt to flee the city, bypassing legitimate channels. Michael constructs a makeshift barrow for his mother, like a gardener's vehicle for transporting materials, and they try to leave the war-torn city by back routes. Their first attempt fails, and on their second, Michael is forced on the way to take his mother to a hospital where she dies. Bearing his

---

50   J. M. Coetzee, *Life & Times of Michael K* (Harmondsworth: Penguin, 1985 [1983]), p. 4.

mother's ashes like seeds, he continues his hazardous journey alone, seeking the farm his mother has described to him. Ravenous, exhausted and filthy, he continues past convoys and checking points, sleeping rough and barely eating, foraging, when he can, vegetables from deserted gardens ('It is God's earth, he thought, I am not a thief') or 'crushed mealies and bonemeal' from livestock feeding-troughs ('At last I am living off the land').

In travelling back to the country, Michael develops, or seems to recall, a credo for relying on the food of the earth, for 'living off the land'. As time goes on, he becomes more and more adamant about what is his 'kind of food', preferring malnutrition and starvation to ingesting food that is not 'of the land'. His relation to the land also takes on new meaning, not least because, finding the now abandoned farm that may or may not have been that of his mother's memories, he finds a home for her ashes. He makes several attempts to bury these, digging deep into stony and inhospitable earth, but the ceremony is not successfully completed until he broadcasts them as if they were seed: 'bending low so that they would not be carried away by the wind, he distributed the fine grey flakes over the earth, afterwards turning the earth over spadeful by spadeful'. This is the act that consitutes 'the beginning of his life as a cultivator' (p. 59)

His life as a cultivator is further consolidated when he salvages some seeds in the outbuildings of the neglected farm and begins to garden in the new mode that the country instils, so unlike his Parks and Gardens work:

> On a shelf in the shed he had found a packet of pumpkin seeds, some of which he had already idly roasted and eaten; he still had the mealie kernels; and on the pantry floor he had picked up a solitary bean. In the space of a week he cleared the land near the dam and restored the system of furrows that irrigated it. Then he planted a small patch of pumpkins and a small patch of mealies; and some distance away on the river bank, where he would have to carry water to it, he planted his bean, so that if it grew it could climb into the thorntrees [...] His deepest pleasure came at sunset when he turned open the cock at the dam wall and watched the stream of water run down its channels to soak the earth, turning it from fawn to deep brown. It is because I am a gardener, he thought, because that is my nature. He sharpened the blade of his spade on a stone, the better to savour the instant when it clove the earth. The impulse to plant had reawoken in him; now, in a matter of weeks, he found his waking life bound tightly to the patch of earth he had begun to cultivate and the seeds he had planted there. (p. 59)

Gardening at the farm constitutes several ceremonies of cultivation, growing food plants from salvaged seeds on soil that bears his mother's ashes, and confirms his own sense of vocation as a gardener. However, the food plants that could save him can also betray him, revealing the secret of his invalid and unlawful existence. Michael is forced, through a variety of eventualities and entrapments, to retreat further and further from the established order of things, hiding in his burrow, camouflaging his plants, barely subsisting – learning to leave no trace.

As a gardener dwelling in and cultivating the veld, Michael reflects on his preference for the dry, ostensibly barren, dusty open landscape to the densely rich humus of the city park where he had worked, and on the changes within himself that this represents. For the postcolonial writer and reader, the two models represent more subtle, cultural differences, too:

> His thoughts went to Wynberg Park, one of the places where he had worked in the old days. [...] But he was no longer sure that he would choose green lawns and oak-trees to live among. When he thought of Wynberg Park he though of an earth more vegetal than mineral, composed of last year's rotted leaves and the year before's and so on back to the beginning of time, an earth so soft that one could dig and never come to the end of the softness [...] I have lost my love for that kind of earth, he thought, I no longer care to feel that kind of earth between my fingers. It is no longer the green and the brown that I want but the yellow and the red; not the wet but the dry, not the dark but the light; not the soft but the hard. I am becoming a different kind of man, he thought, if there are two kinds of man. If I were cut, he thought [...] the blood would no longer gush from me but seep, and after a little seeping, dry and heal. I am becoming smaller and harder and drier every day [...] I would be dried out by the wind in a day [...]. (p. 67)

Describing his new self in terms of his own desiccation – and he is dehydrated and starving much of the time – is also identification with the landscape of the veld. Not only this, but by 'becoming something smaller and harder and drier everyday', he is himself growing more analogous to a seed, 'dried out by the wind' and prepared to be disseminated by it. For Michael, this should be a light, traceless dissemination akin more to the interred ashes of his mother than anything individual or singularly identifiable:

> Every grain of this earth will be washed clean by the rain, he told himself, and dried by the sun and scoured by the wind, before the season turns again. There will be not a grain left bearing my marks, just as my mother has now, after her season in the earth, been washed clean, blown about, and drawn up into the leaves of grass. (p. 124)

Michael seems to be thinking of himself as both cultivator and cultivated, a caster of seeds and, ultimately, like his mother, a seed to be cast. However, his views about fertility in terms of fatherhood, or sustaining his line through his own seed, are negations: 'How fortunate that I have no children, he thought: how fortunate that I have no desire to father. I would not know what to do with a child out here in the heart of the country' (p. 164). At the opening of the novel the reader is informed that Michael has no woman friends 'because of his face'. Once, in one of the camps in which he is detained, he expresses a short-lived uncertainty over, rather than infatuation for, a newly bereaved eighteen-year-old mother, otherwise there is no reference to Michael's own sexual desires (although having returned to Cape Town and near death, a woman vagrant performs oral sex on him – one of a number of unwelcome and compromising acts of charity). When Michael does muse on his role as a father, and his experience of fathering, he reveals an interesting double heritage of his own:

it is not hard to live a life that consists merely of passing time [...] He thought of the camp at Jakkalsdrif, of parents bringing up children [...] and the children of cousins and second cousins [...], on earth stamped so tight by the passage of their footsteps day after day, baked so hard by the sun, that nothing would ever grow there again. My mother was the one whose ashes I brought back, he thought, and my father was Huis Norenius. My father was the list of rules on the door of the dormitory, the twenty-one rules of which the first was 'There will be silence in dormitories at all times,' and the woodwork teacher with the missing fingers who twisted my ear when the line was not straight, and the Sunday mornings when we put on our khaki shirts and our khaki shorts and our black socks and our black shoes and marched two abreast to the church on Papegaai Street to be forgiven. They were my father, and my mother is buried and not yet risen. That is why it is a good thing that I, who have nothing to pass on, should be spending my time here where I am out of the way. (pp. 104-05)

It is as if his role as a gardener in the Cape Town parks – as with his time in the orphanage – were in the 'land of the father', the father being the colonial enterprise, the city, the places of order and confinement, and of apartheid. Of Michael's blood father nothing is revealed, and it may be that he was white. This would bring Michael under the apartheid category 'Coloured'. It is clear that his real connection is through a matrilineal line; although he has been, in most respects, abandoned by his mother while living in Cape Town where she worked as a domestic servant, when he returns with her (that is, her ashes) to the Karoo, he begins to reflect on his connection to the place: 'I want to live here, he thought: I want to live here forever, where my mother and my grandmother lived, it is as simple as that'(p. 99). The relation of his mother and grandmother to the farm and to the land on which the farm was situated is a complex one; they are servants on an Afrikaner Farm, removing, as so many Afrikaners and their servants were forced to do, to towns and cities.

Anna K had been born on a farm in the district of Prince Albert. Her father was not steady; there was a problem with drinking; and in her early years they had moved from one farm to another. Her mother had done laundry and worked in various kitchens; Anna had helped her. Later they moved to the town of Oudtshoorn, where for a while Anna went to school. After the birth of her own first child she had come to Cape Town. There was a second child, from another father, then a third one who died, then Michael. In Anna's memories the years before Oudtshoorn remained the happiest of her life, a time of warmth and plenty. (p. 8)

Of these siblings, or their fathers, there is no sign. In the passage where Michael identifies his father as Huis Norenius and all it stands for, the identification of his mother is much more provisional. She is not identified in oppositional terms but rather as something more ephemeral and protean; she represents something in process: 'my mother was the one whose ashes I brought back' and 'my mother is buried and not yet risen'. The burying of his mother's ashes is a route back to something that is *prior to* and *outside* the farm. Although Michael does not articulate this particular return as explicitly as this, he does, throughout the book, demonstrate his resistance to the systems which, despite some of their remonstrances, he is able to see will circumscribe and constrain him. For instance, when the deserter, grandson of the departed Afrikaner landowner, 'boss Visagie's grandson', returns to the farm needing a hide-away and negotiates with Michael 'his cooperation' ('otherwise there is no future for either of us'), Michael silently leaves the farm but, instead of running errands as instructed, he goes to live in caves in the mountains. Dressed in his mother's coat, he curls up in a foetal position in the cave having escaped servitude but having had to abandon his newly germinated pumpkins:

> Already it was hard to believe that he had known someone called the Visagie grandson who had tried to turn him into a body-servant. In a day or two, he told himself, he would forget the boy and remember only the farm. He thought of the pumpkin leaves pushing through the earth [...] There was a cord of tenderness that stretched from him to the patch of earth beside the dam and must be cut. It seemed to him that one could cut a cord like that only so many times before it would not grow again. (pp. 65-6)

This natal cord which connects him to the earth is mentioned later in the novel when the farm, to which he has returned at last, is occupied by bivouacking soldiers. Although Michael fantasises revealing himself to them, offering them 'pumpkins, squashes and melons [...] peaches and figs and prickly pears' that he has grown, and imagines himself listening to their stories of adventure, he realises that he must keep his presence secret and himself apart in order to remain true to his vocation:

> [...] enough men had gone off to war saying that the time for gardening was when the war was over; whereas there must be men to stay behind and keep gardening alive, or at least the idea of gardening; because once that cord was broken, the earth would grow hard and forget her children. (p. 109)

However, what immediately follows this moment of illumination and self-understanding, and another step on Michael's recuperation of a vital relation to the land, is something much more awkward and obscure which pertains specifically to the issue of 'story' – and in particular, the story 'when he tried to explain himself to himself': 'there remained a gap, a hole, a darkness [...] into which it was useless to pour words [...] His was always a story with a hole in it: a wrong story, always wrong' (p. 110). As the novel progresses, however, and as Michael develops further his allegiance to gardening, he becomes more resistant to the European notion of story-telling and the compulsion to order and complete narratives. What others (and to an extent and at first, Michael, too) find so perplexing is his resistance to living as if the story mattered more than simply being.

Life & Times of Michael K is a novel in three parts. The first and second parts are narrated in the third person but the repetition of passages or phrases that begin in the first person and finish in the third ('I am just like [...] he thought') give a sense of Michael's own consciousness, although he is not narrating his own story and what he actually says in direct speech in the narrative is limited. The consciousness the reader perceives is not in line with the limitations and disabilities that others who encounter him speak of (idiocy, delirium, drunkenness), and on which grounds they misconstrue or ignore what he does say.

The second part of the novel is narrated in the first person by a doctor in the camp; he and his colleagues get most things wrong in relation to their new patient, referring to him as Michaels (despite Michael's corrections), an old man (despite Michael's own explanation that he is 32), and convinced that he is a dangerous insurrectionist: 'The story is that he was picked up all by himself in the middle of nowhere in the Karoo, running a staging post for guerillas [...] caching arms and growing food, though obviously not eating it' (p. 129). Though well-intentioned, the doctor imposes a seemingly benign meaning on any information he gleans from or about Michael. Of his gardening and the pumpkin seeds Michael is carrying with him, the doctor, who is moved ('quite affected'), responds: 'You must go back to your gardening when the war is over [...] It would be nice to see market gardening carried on in the Penninsula again.' The doctor's attempts to connect Michael with, and understand, 'the full story' are not merely patronising; for all his attempts at sensitivity and liberalism, he cannot begin to think outside his own – or his culture's – story line. Thus, the first question in relation to Michael's gardening, 'Will you go back to the Karoo?' is quickly followed, when Michael is 'cagey', by: 'Of course there is good soil in the Peninsula too, under all those rolling lawns.' 'It would be nice to see market gardening carried on in the Peninsula again' is a gesture toward a new order, the overthrow of white suburbanites by disenfranchised minorities. For all its good intentions, this is still another projection of European models.

Michael is a gardener, but he is not nor would be 'a market gardener'; this is not Michael's logic for growing – or getting – food as he reveals, for instance, when he is interrogated by the camp's director, Noël:

'This garden you had,' said Noël: 'what did you grow there?'
'It was a vegetable garden.'
'Who were these vegetables for? Who did you give them to?'
'They weren't mine. They came from the earth.'
'I asked, who did you give them to?'
'The soldiers took them.'
'Did you mind it that the soldiers took your vegetables?'
He shrugged. 'What grows is for all of us. We are all the children of the earth.' (p. 139)

Both Noël and the doctor want a story to interpret, a story in straight lines, with a temporal progression with which they are familiar. Noël's claim and belief that the war is being fought precisely so 'that minorities will have a say in their destinies' requires, in his terms, a translatable or straightforward narrative. Again, for all their good intentions, these two men are unable to think outside their own cultural norms. The doctor's 'letter to Michaels' and, later, his imaginary-delivered discourse to Michael on his 'meaning', are composed for the benefit of himself in his frustration at not being able to break Michael's silence or persuade him to eat hospital food. And so he resorts to a series of interpretations and recommendations which are familiar colonial impositions: 'We ought to value you and celebrate you, we ought to put your clothes on a maquette in a museum, your clothes and your packet of pumpkin seeds too, with a label; there ought to be a plaque [...] commemorating your stay here', or 'Your stay in the camp was merely an allegory, if you know that word. It was an allegory [...] of how scandalously, how outrageously a meaning can take up residence in a system without becoming a term in it. Did you not notice how, whenever I tried to pin you down, you slipped away?' (p. 166). The only way that the doctor can 'translate' Michael is to valorise his 'Otherness' but this reduces him to an anthropological item, a museum-piece predicated on being outmoded, anachronistic, rare, and bound to vanish. As with so many Western ethnographic enterprises which sought to categorise 'the primitives', the view is that assimilation into a colonising culture and the inherent unviability of an underdeveloped group means that the primitives will vanish, with traces only to be found in ethnographic reports and museum displays. The truths, however, that are recorded by Western colonisers, are unable to accommodate the incomprehensible elements of another culture. The doctor's musings always slide into finding meaning and equivalence – a lesson and a message – for although the Other is vanquished and vanishing, the Westerner tends to project some soulful lesson of their own onto the inscrutable primitive, like the doctor's 'I was the only one who saw that you were more than you seemed to be'. The doctor's own awareness of this propensity, and his denial of it in the case of 'Michaels' ('Michaels means something and the meaning is not private to me. If it were, the origin of this meaning were no more than a lack in myself'), does little to contradict the view that what the doctor is trying to 'read into' Michael, by requiring from him a story which is 'sensible', will supplement his own search for a meaningful story in which he and Michael both occupy a stable place. Interestingly, of his own experience and reticence with interviewers, Coetzee has an apposite observation: '[...] interviewers want speech, a flow of speech. That speech they record, take away, edit, censor, cutting out all waywardness, till what is left conforms to a monologic ideal'.[51]

Michael's gardening, too, has meaning imposed on it by the doctor in a way that is familiar but which misses the mark. In an interpretation of what Michael has said – and even more so, of what he has not – the doctor imagines himself confronting Michael in this regard:

> And now, last topic, your garden [...] Let me tell you the meaning of the sacred and alluring garden that blooms in the heart of the desert and produces the food of life. The garden for which you are presently heading is nowhere and everywhere except in the camps. It is another name for the only place where you belong, Michaels, the only place where you do not feel homeless. It is off every map, no road leads to it that is merely a road, and only you know the way. (p. 166)

As persuasive as this sounds, it is a view that continues to impose meaning from outside and it continues to romanticise Michael – and all without due attention to what Michael himself has said. The persistent use of the wrong name, despite Michael's

---

    51   'Interview', *Doubling the Point*, op. cit., p. 65.

corrections, is one indication of this; at other times, if what Michael says does not fit with what is expected from him, then it is illness or idiocy or perversity that is seen as the reason. The doctor is far more comfortable with the discourse he is able to compose in relation to Michael than to deal with the matters on which Michael's does speak, such as his mother's treatment once she became ill: 'My mother worked all her lifelong [...] But when she was old and sick they forgot her. They put her away out of sight' (p. 136). The doctor uses metaphor after metaphor (like a stone, squirrel, ant, bee, mouse, grain of sand, or a primitive artifact, ill-formed, sexless and rudimentary) in an apparent search to deal with the complexity of Michael, when in fact Michael's own utterances are simple and straightforward and attest to the inhumane treatment of 'a multitude in the second class'.

As Michael later acknowledges, it suits a system to be able to treat its victims as objects of charity rather than as fully human, exercising an agency at odds with the prevailing discourses of that system. He realises, too, that what charitable people want from him is for him 'to open [his] heart and tell them the story of a life lived in cages', a contiguous narrative 'of a life passed in prisons where I stood day after day, year after year', affecting the listeners more than the lived experience of the subject. But Michael's story is simpler, and the simplicity is not by virtue of his affliction but a matter choice and inclination:

> Whereas the truth is that I have been a gardener, first for the Council, later for myself, and gardeners spend their time with their noses to the ground. K tossed restlessly on the cardboard. It excited him, he found, to say recklessly, '*the truth, the truth about me*'. '*I am a gardener,*' he said again, aloud. On the other hand, was it not strange for a gardener to be sleeping in a closet within sound of the beating of the waves of the sea? I am more like an earthworm, he thought. Which is also a kind of gardener. Or a mole, also a gardener, that does not tell stories because it lives in silence [...] At least, he thought, at least I have not been clever, and come back to Sea Point full of stories of how they beat me in the camps till I was thin as a rake and simple in the head. I was mute and stupid in the beginning, I will be mute and stupid at the end. There is nothing to be ashamed of in being simple. (pp. 181-2)

Michael's final reveries relate to stories ('the moral of the whole story') and to gardening: there is time enough for everything:

> [...] my mistake was to plant all my seeds together in one patch. I should have planted them one at a time spread out over miles of veld in patches of soil no larger than my hand, and drawn a map and kept it with me at all times so that every night I could make a tour of the sites to water them. Because if there was one thing I discovered out in the country, it was that there is time enough for everything. (pp. 183)

The final passage of the novel reveals Michael's speculation on how he would provide water for his plants now the soldiers have blown up the pump at the Visagie farm's dam: with 'a teaspoon and a long roll of string'. Time, lots of it, and a teaspoon which 'he would lower [...] down the shaft deep into the earth, and when he brought it up there would be water in the bowl of the spoon'. Although much could be said about this image in terms of others that have preceded it – which pertain to storytelling and creativity (the string as narrative thread; the string as umbilical cord; the womb-space of the imagination and of the earth) – the image of the spoon also returns to the opening of the novel, where Michael's mother, Anna K, is attempting to feed her hare-lipped infant son with a teaspoon. The novel concludes: 'and in that way, he would say, one can live'. Another temporal mode, 'time enough for everything', belongs to the primeval, pre-historic aspects of Africa, but it is also the sense of time as fluid and expansive that Michael K adopts when he returns to the Karoo:

> He did not know what month it was, though he guessed it was April. He had kept no tally of the days nor recorded the changes of the moon. He was not a prisoner or a castaway, his life was not a sentence that he had to serve out [...] he was learning to love idleness, idleness [...] as a yielding up of himself to time, to a time flowing slowly like oil from horizon to horizon over the face of the world, washing over his body, circulating his armpits and his groin, stirring his eyelids [...] all that was moving was time, bearing him onward in its flow. Once or twice the other time in which the war had its existence reminded itself to him as the jet fighters whistled high overhead. But for the rest he was living beyond the reach of calendar and clock [...]. (pp. 115-16)

Coetzee's representation and exploration of these two modes of time – what we might in this chapter loosely call the time of the coloniser (European, Protestant, post-Enlightenment, work-ethic) and the time of the pre-colonial (indigenous, pre-industrial) – is further complicated by the specificity of a South African experience. The 'Afrikaner Christian nationalism', which came to power in 1948, had a particular view of time. It was in their interest, Coetzee explains, to have time 'stand still' so that 'it tried to stop dead or turn around a range of developments normal (in the sense of being the norm) in colonial societies. Afrikaner nationalism, with its aim of 'instituting a sluggish no-time in which an already anachronistic order [...] would be frozen in place', combined in the South Africa of Coetzee's own experience with a culture 'looking nostalgically back to Little England' which 'did nothing to quicken time' and which engendered in Coetzee himself 'a horror of chronicity South African style'.[52] Gardening South African style is just as, and similarly complex. The relationship to the land – and to time – of the Hottenot and Bushman, the Afrikaner valorisation of land and volk in the vast countryside of the Karoo and the municipal Gardens in the City Parks and Gardens, are all integral to an understanding of Michael K's journey and his gardening.

This novel thus engages with what Coetzee has identified in *White Writing* as the two dream topographies projected in the South African pastoral:

> One dream topography that the South African pastoral projects is therefore a network of boundaries crisscrossing the surface of the land, marking off thousands of farms, each a separate kingdom ruled over by a benign patriarch with, beneath him, a pyramid of children, grandchildren, and serfs. But there is a rival dream topography as well: of South Africa as a vast, empty, silent space, older than man, older than the dinosaurs whose

---

52   'Interview', *Doubling the Point*, op. cit., p. 209.

bones lie bedded in its rocks, and destined to be vast, empty, and unchanged long after man has passed from its face. Under such a conception of Africa – 'Africa, oldest of the continents' – the task of the human imagination is to conceive not a social order capable of domesticating the landscape, but any kind of relation at all that consciousness can have with it.[53]

The abandoned Visagie farm at Price Albert represents the vision of Afrikaner fiefdoms, which had fallen, post-apartheid and at the time of the novel's imagined setting, into abandonment and neglect. As he returns to the farm where his mother and grandmother have been servants, Michael K does not identify with this system: 'he could not imagine himself spending his life driving stakes into the ground, erecting fences, dividing up the land' (p. 67), and yet, he is not entirely outside it, thoroughly Other, or free to be so. The fences of the master-class remind Michael 'that he is a trespasser as well as a runaway' but what he is not in a position to do, is to know or develop a way of being that does not have reference to the fences of a landowner class or the strictures of, say, the orphanage Huis Norenius – nor is Coetzee in a position to give him the power to do it. As a white South African with an Afrikaner background, Coetzee would be presumptuous to give too much rein to Michael's voice; as he noted in his Jerusalem Prize acceptance speech, one can imagine oneself 'escaping the skin you're born with', and perhaps imagine oneself in another coloured skin, but this can only be speculative and in symbolic terms.

Coetzee did, of course, shake the dust of the country from his feet, leaving South Africa, first to England and then to America, before returning to South Africa. However, in his first volume of autobiography-told-in-the-third-person, *Boyhood: Scenes from Provincial Life*, published in 1997, there are some striking similarities to certain features of *Life & Times of Michael K*. Most obvious, perhaps, are the details of a farm in Prince Albert, owned by the narrator's paternal grandfather; in the description of the grandparents' farm are the highlighted features that were so significant in the Visagie farm in *Life & Times of Michael K*:

> In a corner of the stoep, in the shade of the bouganvillea, hangs a canvas water-bottle. The hotter the day, the cooler the water – a miracle, like the miracle of the meat that hangs in the dark of the storeroom and does not rot, like the miracle of the pumpkins that lie on the roof in the blazing sun and stay fresh. On the farm, it seems, there is no decay.
>
> The water from the water-bottle is magically cool, but he pours no more than a mouthful at a time. He is proud of how little he drinks. It will stand him in good stead, he hopes, if he is ever lost in the veld. He wants to be a creature of the desert, this desert, like a lizard.
>
> Just above the farmhouse is a stone-walled dam, twelve feet square, filled by a wind pump, which provides water for the house and garden. (pp. 82-3)

That Coetzee should have called upon his recollection of his family's farm is unsurprising, particularly when, in *Boyhood*, he records the impact that visits to this farm (which were in other ways complicated) had on him:

---

53 J. M. Coetzee, *White Writing*, op. cit., pp. 6-7.

there is no place on earth he loves more or can imagine loving more [...] The farm is called Voëlfontein, Bird-fountain; he loves every stone of it, every bush, every blade of grass, loves the birds that give it its name, birds that as dusk falls gather in their thousands in the trees around the fountain [...] It is not conceivable that that another person could love the farm as he does. (pp. 79-80)

What does surprise are passages in *Boyhood* which appear as echoes of those in *Life &Times of Michael K*, but most surprising are the passages which render Michael K as yet another of Coetzee's 'autobiographical' voices: ('all writing is autobiography' just as 'all autobiography is storytelling').[54] Of course, it seems audacious even to suggest – for Coetzee or his readers – that the experience of a white South African and a Coloured subject could ever be conflated. And they are not – or not entirely. A distance is maintained as, for instance, when Ros and Freek, the 'Coloured help' on the farm are discussed. Of Freek, the narrator explains:

Freek is a hired man. He is paid a wage, he can be given notice and sent packing. Nevertheless, seeing Freek sitting on his haunches, his pipe in his mouth, staring out over the veld, it seems to him that Freek belongs here more securely than the Coetzees do – if not to Voëlfontein, then to the Karoo. The Karoo is Freek's country, his home; the Coetzees, drinking tea and gossiping on the farmhouse stoep, are like swallows, seasonal, here today, gone tomorrow, or even like sparrows, chirping, lightfooted, short-lived. (p. 87)

There are similarities, certainly, between the remembered Freek and the fictional Michael K but there are also similarities between this narrator's view and those given in the novel to Michael himself. Yet another passage in the memoir reveals such a connection; in *Boyhood* we find Coetzee speaking of his young self, as usual, in the third person: 'He has two mothers. Twice-born: born from woman and born from the farm. Two mothers and no father' (pp. 95-6). (As Michael was twice-born, once from his mother and once from the natal earth on which her ashes were scattered, and fatherless in the ways that Michael has no father.) The memoir, however, in its exploration of *belonging*, one of the most ubiquitous and, indeed, most problematic preoccupations of postcoloniality, addresses the particular distortions for a young white South African whose experience is *also* at odds, albeit to a different degree, with the dominant white culture:

The secret and sacred word that binds the boy of the memoir him to the farm is *belong*. Out in the veld by himself he can breathe the word aloud: *I belong on the farm*. What he really believes but does not utter, what he keeps to himself for fear that the spell will end, is a different form of the word: *I belong to the farm*.
   He tells no one because the word is misunderstood so easily into its inverse: *the farm belongs to me*. The farm will never belong to him, he will never be more than a visitor: he accepts that. [...] *I belong to the farm*: that is the furthest he is prepared to go, even in his most secret heart. But in his secret heart he knows what the farm in its way knows too:

54   Ibid., p. 17.

that Voëlfontein belongs to no one. The farm is greater than any of them. The farm exists from eternity to eternity. When they are all dead, when even the farmhouse has fallen into ruin like the kraals on the hillside, the farm will still be here.[55]

Again this is not to say that a figure like Michael – or Freek – could ever 'be in the same place' ontologically (as Coetzee says, 'you cannot change your skin') or disavow all that accrues to the body's signs in a cultural system that insists on such markers of difference. The difficulty of who can speak for whom, who has the right to presume to give voice – in fiction and art – to the silenced and dispossessed is one of which Coetzee is profoundly aware. His fictions have been criticised for doing what is inescapable: writing through one's own lens no matter how thoroughly one aims to look through another's. Self scrutiny is also deeply problematic in this regard. Of course, in the postcolonial world there is no 'pure' otherness, for in the process of colonial assimilation no subject is untouched. Indeed, at the opening of the novel Michael K is more thoroughly the indoctrinated child of the colonisers' 'ideas', as represented by the orphanage (his 'father') and by the City Parks and Gardens, than of any other, for nothing else was available to him. And yet, a life that involves systematised terror and torture is not to be represented lightly, nor, on the other hand, can it be ignored – and about this, Coetzee has written at length.[56] The purpose of this present book, however, is to explore the place of gardens in such complex representational terrain.

As discussed previously, in *White Writing* Coetzee outlined the various ways in which familiar Western Garden tropes such as Eden, pastoral and other garden or agrarian ideals have never 'taken root' in South Africa. Nevertheless, a complex discourse of land and volk arose in the service of Afrikaaner nationalism, a discourse of exclusion, hatred, property, slavery and hardship that, in itself, mocked any graceful garden idyll. Indeed, Coetzee sees the failures and unfreedom of South Africa to be bound up in the 'hereditary masters' rhetoric of love for the land:

> At the heart of the unfreedom of the hereditary masters of South Africa is a failure to love. To be blunt: their love is not enough today and has not been enough since they landed on the continent; furthermore, their talk, their excessive talk, about how they love South Africa has consistently been directed toward *the land*, that is, toward what is least likely to respond to love: mountains and deserts, birds and animals and flowers [...] The vain and essentially sentimental yearning that expresses itself in the reform movement of South Africa today is a yearning to have fraternity without paying for it [...] The very lowest price is the destruction of the unnatural structures of power that define the South African state.[57]

If Coetzee can be seen as expressing fraternity with someone like Michael K, then it is in the attempt, perhaps, to pay his own dues – with no sentimentality – with

---

55 *Boyhood*, op. cit, pp. 95-6.

56 In 'Into the Dark Chamber' (*Doubling the Point*, op. cit.), for instance, and in *Giving Offence*, op. cit..

57 J. M. Coetzee, *Doubling the Point*, op. cit., p. 97.

a thorough-going exposure of some of the grotesque distortions created by the unnatural social structures that have been installed in a place of such great natural beauty.

Toni Morrison: Reconciliation/War

Toni Morrison's 1998 novel has its focus on 'the Garden' evident in the title: *Paradise*. The novel questions the criteria for paradise: what must it include? what need it exclude? according to whom? for whom? Can the criteria ever be consensual? Originally, the title chosen for the novel was *War*, but Morrison's publishers were not pleased with it and encouraged her to change it to something more appealing. The conventional opposite of War is Peace, synonymous with, it is to be presumed, and integral to Paradise ('and the Lion shall lie down with the Lamb' as the Bible puts it), and yet more wars are fought and continue to be fought in the establishment of Paradise according to different visions and versions of it. As Morrison has, on various occasions, explained:

> I was interested in the kind of violent conflict that could happen as a result of efforts to establish a Paradise. Our view of Paradise is so limited: it requires you to think of yourself as the chosen people – chosen by God, that is. Which means that your job is to isolate yourself from other people. That's the nature of Paradise: it's really defined by who is *not* there as well as who is. So I agreed with my publishers that *Paradise* was perhaps a good conceptual title. I was very hesitant at first, but then I realized that since the book was an interrogation about the very idea of Paradise, the title made sense. It has a sort of question mark implied behind it.[58]

Furthermore, the energy and anxiety bound up in sustaining a paradise, according to one or other particular precept, means that it is invariably a place set apart, gated, monitored, frozen in time, and static in its precepts. 'The isolation, the separateness, is always part of any utopia' noted Morrison in one interview, but isolation 'carries the seeds of its own destruction because as times change, other things seep in'.[59] In this novel, what seeps into one 'paradise' is another: two paradises with different priorities, and hence, a 'war' ensues in which nine 'pure' and vigilant protectors

---

58 'This Side of Paradise', James Marcus with Toni Morrison, Amazon.com interview http://www.amazon.com/exec/obidos/ts/feature/7651/103-2684994-59999054.

59 *Conversation: Toni Morrison*, op. cit.

of one paradise, 'the New Fathers' take reprisal on the other, entering it and murdering five 'harmless' women. The New Fathers, from the all-black town of Ruby, Oklahoma, are known as '8-Rs' or 'eight-rocks', descended from nine 'intact' and pure-blooded families who had originally established Ruby's mother town, Haven, and who were 'coal black' in colour and thus named after a 'deep, deep level in the coal mines'. Of the women at the community they invade, known as the Convent, four are black, ' bodacious black Eves unredeemed by Mary' (p. 18) and one is white. The novel 's opening line is: 'They shoot the white girl first', but the reader never knows which of the women is the white one. With 'God at their side, the men take aim. For Ruby' – and yet the paradisiacal town of Ruby is not sustained but rather tainted by such action. Although through the course of the novel we understand there to be 'a story that explained why neither the founders of Haven or their descendents could tolerate anybody but themselves' (p. 13), the reader is also aware of the hypocrisy and criminality attendant on this vengeful vigilance. The founders of Ruby and their forebears have been enslaved, persecuted, made homeless and migratory, 'disallowed' variously, excluded by other black communities – either with lighter skins or restrictive 'self supporting clauses' – and have otherwise struggled to survive on a long journey to self-determination. Purity becomes their covenant with God, but by shooting the women at the Convent the irony is apparent: 'How could so clean and blessed a mission devour itself and become the world they had escaped?'(p. 292) Such separatist vigilantism against the forces of 'Out There', 'where your children were sport, your women quarry, and where any person could be annulled; where congregations carried arms to church and ropes coiled in every saddle [...] where every cluster of whitemen looked like a posse' (p. 16), has now rendered their actions to be just like the white men that were their opposite: against women, black and white. As Reverend Misner notes: 'How exquisitely human was the wish for permanent happiness, and how thin human imagination became trying to achieve it' (p. 306).

Toni Morrison, who was awarded, amongst other prestigious prizes too numerous to mention here, the Nobel Prize for literature in 1993, began publishing novels in the 1970s with *The Bluest Eye* in 1970. Perhaps her best known work to date is *Beloved* (1987) for which she won the Pulitzer in 1988. The main story-line in that novel was of a woman who, rather than let her children be captured and taken back into slavery, tries to kill them herself, cutting the throat of one of them. The fiction was based on a newspaper report of the 1856 case of Margaret Garner who fled in winter with her husband and four children from her Kentucky owner. Morrison encountered it when, as a senior editor at Random House, she was involved in compiling *The Black Book*, a compendium of black history in anecdotes, folklore, newspaper clippings and other testimonies and artefacts. The novel is devoted to the 'rememory' of the story and histories of black American slaves, 'how to rip that veil drawn over proceedings "too terrible to relate"',[60] and is dedicated, as its epigraph attests, to the 'sixty million and

---

60   Toni Morrison, 'The Site of Memory', in *Inventing the Truth: the Art and Craft of the Memoir*, W. Zinsser ed., cited in J. Matus, op. cit., p. 16.

more' who suffered or perished under the regime of slavery and its violent racism. As Morrsion later explained:

> There is no place you or I can go, to think about or not think about, to summon the
> presences of, or recollect the absences of slaves, nothing that reminds us of the ones who
> made the journey and of those who did not make it. There is no suitable memorial or
> plaque or wreath or wall or park or skyscraper lobby. There's no 300-foot tower. There's
> no small bench by the road. There is not even a tree scored, an initial I can visit, or you can
> visit in Charleston or Savannah or New York or Providence, or better still, on the banks
> of the Mississippi. And because such a place doesn't exist (that I know of), the book had
> to.[61]

In *Paradise*, she memorialises another aspect of black America history: all-black communities and towns established after 'emancipation' during the period known as Reconstruction. Morrison used the invented town of Ruby, Oklahoma ('it's my invention of the all-black town that might have lasted until now, until at least the [19]80s. It's based on towns that did exist and some that still are there')[62] – towns such as 'Boley, Langston City, Rentiesville, Taft, Clearview, Mount Bayou, Nicodemus' (p. 108) in order to explore

> that whole period when ex-slaves, freed men, left plantations, sometimes under duress,
> because Southerners frequently wanted them to stay but managed to take advantage of the
> land that was offered in places like Oklahoma and build whole towns, churches, stores,
> banks, many houses.[63]

These towns, however, while exclusively black, were at the same time, selective. A newspaper column promoting Langston City in the early 1890s stated: 'Come Prepared or Not at All' (noted in *Paradise*), warning ex-slaves planning to join the community that they would have to meet minimum requirements for their own resources.[64] Morrison was affected by 'an account describing how two hundred freedmen and their families were turned away from an all-black town by other ex-slaves'[65] because they could not contribute as required. That the solidarity of black ex-slaves could be jeopardised by resources or by the lightness or darkness of their black skin was inexplicable unless it was seen in the light of the extreme precariousness – and severe necessity – of the struggle to survive and thrive. There was another germ for this novel, too:

---

61 T. Morrison, cited in J. Matus, op. cit., p. 30.

62 T. Morrison, http://www.pbs.org/newshour/bb/entertainment/jan-june98/morrison_3-9.html.

63 Ibid.

64 J. Brooks Bouson, *Quiet As It's Kept: Shame, Trauma and Race in the Novels of Toni Morrison* (Albany: State University of New York Press, 2000), p. 192.

65 Ibid.

On a trip to Brazil in the 1980s, Ms. Morrison heard about a convent of black nuns who took in abandoned children and practiced candomblé, an Afro-Brazilian religion; the local populace considered them an outrage, and they were murdered by a posse of men. 'I've since learned it never happened,' Ms. Morrison said. 'But for me it was irrelevant. And it said much about institutional religion and uninstitutional religion, how close they are'.[66]

These two facets, for all the complexity of each, form the dual focus of the novel emblematised here by the all-black, very controlled and controlling, patriarchal community of Ruby, established in 1950, and 'the Convent', which, by the time of the story's main setting in the mid-1970s, is the open-door and unofficial refuge of an intermittent and fluid population of hurting and confused women who repeatedly return to it: 'in no time at all they came to see that they could not leave the one place they were free to leave' (p. 262).

The Convent is no longer the Catholic community it was. Established in the mid-1920s by an Order known as 'Sisters Devoted to Indians and Colored People' (based on the Sisters of the Blessed Sacrament for Indian and Colored People, the wealthy founder of which, Katherine Drexel, 1858-1955, was canonised as America's first saint in 2000), it functioned as an 'asylum/boarding school for Indian girls in some desolate part of the American West'. The site chosen was an opulent mansion, formerly 'an 'embezzler's folly' (but dreamt of as a paradise, no doubt), and incongruous, 'like a castle, full of a beauty [...] to be eliminated at once'. By the mid-1950s, the Convent, largely redundant and depleted of resources, has only 'three feckless students' and three adult inmates remaining: Sister Roberta, Mother Mary Magna, the elderly white nun, and the mixed-race Brazilian, Consolata, whom Mary Magna 'kidnapped' from the 'shit-strewn streets' of a city in Brazil when Consolata was an street orphan of just nine years old. Together they begin to take 'steps to keep up the property and not incur debt the foundation could not meet' (p. 241), leasing enough land to grow 'rough corn and alfalfa' and selling other garden and kitchen produce: 'Garden things. Things I cook up. Things [people] don't want to grow themselves':

> They made sauces and jellies and European bread. Sold eggs, peppers, hot relish and angry barbecue sauce [...] Most of their customers in 1955 drove trucks between Arkansas and Texas. Ruby citizens seldom stopped to buy anything other than peppers, since they were supreme cooks themselves and made or grew what they wanted. Only in the sixties, when times were fat, did they join the truckers and look upon what they called Convent-bred chickens as superior enough to their own to be worth a journey. Then they would also try a little jalapeño jelly, or a corn relish. Pecan saplings planted in the forties were strong in 1960. The Convent sold the nuts, and when pies from the harvest were made, they went as soon as posted. They made rhubarb pie so delicious it made customers babble, and the barbecue sauce got a heavenly reputation based on the hellfire peppers. (pp. 241-2)

---

66 Dinitia Smith, 'Toni Morrison's Mix of Tragedy, Domesticity and Folklore', *The New York Times* (8 January 1998), http://www.nytimes.com/library/books/010898toni-morrison-interviw.html.

The renowned 'black-as-eight-rock peppers the convent grew' had been Consolata's discovery, a 'wild bush heavy with stinging-hot peppers', and it is she who cultivates them and sells strings 'of purply black peppers or a relish made from them. Either took the cake for pure burning power' (p. 11). Though customers try to propagate the seeds, 'the peppers grew nowhere outside the Convent garden' (p. 11). Other produce grown in the Convent garden includes: 'Flowers mixed in with or parallel to rows of vegetables […] plants grow in a circle, not a line, in high mounds of soil […] a patch of melons [untidy and looking as if 'gone to weed'.] An empire of corn beyond' (pp. 40-41).

Ruby's gardens are quite different. At about the time that the Convent had to 'diversify' and its market garden was being established in its ad hoc way, the town of Ruby was being laid out and ordered: 'a wide street, past enormous lawns cut to dazzle in front of churches and pastel-colored houses' (p. 45), but later, 'when there was time', 'the garden battles' staged by the women residents of Ruby ensue, with the consequence that extravagant flower borders or other 'non-essentials', grown according to 'desire not necessity', take precedence over the hitherto more necessary and practical vegetables:

> The garden battles – won, lost, still at bay – were mostly over. They had raged for ten years, having begun suddenly in 1963, when there was time. The women who were in their twenties when Ruby was founded, in 1950, watched for thirteen years an increase in bounty that had never entered their dreams […] In every Ruby household appliances pumped, hummed, sucked, purred, whispered and flowed. […] The humming, throbbing and softly purring gave the women time.
>
> The dirt yards, carefully swept and sprinkled in Haven, became lawns in Ruby until, finally, front yards were given over completely to flowers for no good reason except there was time in which to do it. The habit, the interest in cultivating plants that could not be eaten, spread, and so did the ground surrendered to it. Exchanging, sharing a cutting here, a root there, a bulb or two became so frenetic a land grab, husbands complained of neglect and the disappointingly small harvest of radishes, or the too short rows of collards, beets. The women kept on with their vegetable gardens in back, but little by little its produce became like the flowers – driven by desire, not necessity. Iris, phlox, rose and peonies took up more and more time, quiet boasting and so much space new butterflies journeyed miles to brood in Ruby. (pp. 89-90)

The 'new Mothers' of Ruby are the daughters – as their husbands are the sons – of the mothers memorialised by Alice Walker in her well-known essay 'In Search of Our Mothers' Gardens'. Walker remembered the black women of the 1920s, when time was definitely not on their hands, but these women have much more in common with the women at the Convent than with the notion of womanhood that is now allowed to prevail in Ruby. This is a disavowal of their own people, perpetrated by themselves. Walker discusses 'the mothers and grandmothers' who, 'more often than not anonymously, handed on the creative spark, the seed of the flower they themselves never hoped to see',[67] and who, if history, time, money appliances and men had been on their side, would have been known as Artists, and not just Saints:

> When the poet Jean Toomer walked through the South in the early twenties, he discovered a curious thing: black women whose spirituality was so intense, so deep, so <u>unconscious</u> that they were themselves unaware of the richness they held. They stumbled blindly through their lives: creatures so abused and mutilated in body, so dimmed and confused by pain, that they considered themselves unworthy even of hope. In the selfless abstractions their bodies became to the men who used them, they became more than 'sexual objects', even more than mere women: they became 'Saints'. Instead of being perceived as whole persons, their bodies became shrines: what was thought to be their minds became temples suitable for worship. These crazy Saints stared out at the world, wildly, like lunatics – or quietly, like suicides; and the 'God' that was in their gaze was as mute as a great stone.
>
> Who were these Saints? These crazy, loony, pitiful women? Some of them, without a doubt, were our mothers and grandmothers.
>
> In the still heat of the post-Reconstruction south, this is how they seemed to Jean Toomer: exquisite butterflies trapped in an evil honey, toiling away their lives in an era, a century, that did not acknowledge them, except as 'the <u>mule</u> of the world'. They dreamed dreams that no one knew – not even themselves, in any coherent fashion – and saw visions no one could understand. They wandered or sat about the countryside crooning lullabies to ghosts, and drawing the mother of Christ in charcoal on courthouse walls.[68]

The passage is resonant in relation to *Paradise* for it not only renders Consolata (and some of the damaged women of Ruby who seek her help) similar to these female forebears (in the sexual abuse she suffers on the streets of Brazil and in her creativity), but it also further renders the homicidal actions of the men of Ruby to be something akin to matricide.

Seventeen miles separate the two communities, which are in themselves isolated; the closest other town to Ruby is ninety miles away. The exchanges between the residents of Ruby and the Convent have been limited, apart from the customers seeking Convent relish or spicy barbecue sauce. It is as a customer that one of the town's '8-rock' pedigree New Fathers, Deek (Deacon) Morgan, meets Consolata and begins a torrid affair with her in 1954. 'All he wanted was some black peppers' (p. 228). Married, and ultimately, frightened by Consolata's passion onto which he displaces a range of emotions to make her distasteful and 'disallowed' and himself self-righteous, he is one of the men who hunts down the Convent women in 1975. Despite Deacon's restraining hand at the last minute, it is his twin, Steward, who shoots Consolata – Steward who, together with Deacon has behaved as if 'God were their silent business partner' in the interests of preserving Ruby, the town named after their dead sister, who had died because 'no colored people were allowed in the [hospital] wards' (p. 113).

---

67 Alice Walker, 'In Search of our Mothers' Gardens', *In Search of our Mothers' Gardens: Womanist Prose* (London: The Women's Press, 1984), p. 240.

68 Ibid, pp. 231-2.

Consolata, on the other hand, experiences a kindred feeling with the 'eight-rocks' when she first sees the residents of Ruby. Consolata herself is described as having 'green eyes', 'tea-colored hair' and 'smoky sundown skin' but she recognises in them scenes from her childhood in Rio, and perhaps, ancestors beyond them; they conjure up 'a memory of just such skin and just such men, dancing with women in the streets to music beating like an infuriated heart […] and although they were living here in a hamlet, not in a loud city full of glittering black people, Consolata knew she knew them' (p. 226) In time, Deek's wife Soane becomes a friend of Consolata and a visitor at the Convent as, increasingly, are other of Ruby's women – wives, mothers and daughters. The traffic between the two communities begins to increase, but there is a special communion between the women:

> it was women who walked this road. Only women. Never men. […] Back and forth, back and forth: crying women, staring women, scowling, lip-biting women or women just plain lost. Out here in a red and gold land cut through now and then with black rock or a swatch of green; out here under the skies so star-packed it was disgraceful; out here where the wind handled you like a man, women dragged their sorrow up and down the road between Ruby and the Convent. (p. 270)

Set largely in the context of the racial strife and civil rights movement of the 1950s and 1960s, what is perceived as the moral laxity ('fun-obsessed adults were clear signs of already advanced decay') and unwholesome modernity ('toys'; 'raucous music'; 'hollow laughter') of the Convent community becomes a focus for the elders of Ruby. Ruby's three churches have their distinctive and representative core messages: 'Evil Times' hails from New Zion, 'Last Days' from Holy Redeemer and from Calvary, 'Good News'. Two of Ruby's ministers, Reverend Richard Misner from Calvary and Reverend Senior Pulliam form New Zion are particularly at odds. Reverend Pulliam is a stern Methodist, an isolationist for Ruby's sake, afraid of the erosion of values and the purity of the community and its blood-line; his devotion is to a community that is 'unadulterated and unadulteried', 'not only racially untampered with but free of adultery too': controlled men, compliant women and 'duplicates' for children, all within an impenetrable and closed circle. This 'glacial wariness', thinks Reverend Misner, which was once 'confined to strangers', is now increasingly 'directed toward each other' in the effort to ensure 'that nothing inside or out rots the one all-black town worth the pain'. On the other hand, Reverend Pulliam is at ' war' with Misner's 'activities', which he sees as: 'tempting the young to step outside the wall, outside the town limits, shepherding them, forcing them to transgress, to think of themselves as civil warriors' (p. 145). Joining the town in 1970, he comes speaking of history, Africa, civil rights, 'preparedness' and Martin Luther King seven years earlier, 'in whose stead he would happily have taken the sword'. He finds his flock, however, 'believed not only that it had created the pasture it grazed but that grass from any other meadow was toxic' (p. 212). When the town's focal 'shrine', the Oven, is desecrated with the emblem of the Black Power movement, 'the fist, jet black with red fingernails, painted on the black wall of the Oven', the battle to preserve this paradise begins in earnest. The blame, however, for all the ills and unquiet, is attributed to the women at the Convent:

> Before those heifers came into town this was a peaceable kingdom [...] They don't need men and they don't need God. [...] Not women locked safely away from men; but worse, women who chose themselves for company, which is to say not a convent but a coven. (p. 276)

The linguistic interconnectedness between Oven, coven, Convent, covenant is purposeful; meeting at the Oven, the holy symbol of their struggle and survival, passed on from the Old Fathers of Haven to the New ones of Ruby, the men organise their attack on the Convent, or coven, in order to preserve their own holy covenant with God. One paradise wreaks vengeance on another.

The Oven is a complex and interesting monument; it was built in 1890 by the Old fathers of Haven, 'a dreamtown in Oklahoma Territory':

> An Oven. Round as a head, deep as desire [...] The Old Fathers did that first: put most of their strength into constructing the huge, flawlessly designed Oven that both nourished them and monumentalized what they had done. (pp. 6-7) [...]
>
> In 1910 there were two Churches in Haven and the All-Citizens Bank, four rooms in the schoolhouse, five stores selling dry goods, feed and foodstuffs – but the traffic to and from the Oven was greater than to all of those. No family needed more than a simple cookstove as long as the Oven was alive and it always was. (p. 15)

The Oven also bore 'an iron plate five feet by two' at the base of its mouth on which an inscription had been forged: 'Words that seemed at first to bless them; later to confound them; finally to announce what they had lost' (p. 7), words that had been 'given' to Zechariah Morgan: 'something he heard, invented, or something whispered to him while he slept' having discovered on the arduous journey from Mississippi through Louisiana to Oklahoma, 'how narrow the path of righteousness could be'. However, when the Oven is reassembled and the words on the lip reinstated, there is much discussion in Ruby over the actual original words: some are convinced by 'Beware the Furrow of His Brow' whereas others claim that 'Be the Furrow of His Brow' is its message. The Oven, sitting like Ruby's own jewel in its centre, has changed from being an active centre of communal activity, 'the meeting place to report [...] on illness, births, deaths, comings and goings' (p. 111), to a site of contention; a former 'utility had become a shrine (cautioned against not only in scary Deuteronomy but in lovely Corinthians II as well)' (p. 103), but a shrine without sanctity: the lazy young drinking beer, the loud music, the painted fist no one would admit to or help to remove, a meeting place for planning a posse. Whereas the Oven formerly signified life, now, like Ruby itself, it has lost its vital aspect.

Toni Morrison has often emphasised the importance of 'The Ancestor', not just in her own work but in black writing and art generally. In an essay published in 1981, 'City Limits, Village Values: Concepts of Neighbourhood in Black Fiction', she made the observation that the conventional, white American distinctions between country (space, expression of individuality, freedom) and the city (crowded, industrial, enslavement to fads and fashions) were not those seen through black eyes: 'country life through Black eyes produced visions of lynchings, share croppers, slavery and all the fear and facts of Black life in America',[69] whereas many Black writers' pro-urbanism (or perceived pro-urbanism) is due to 'eagerness for acceptance in the city, [...] anxiety to be individually free there, seeking entrance in and associations with the very institutions [...] white brethren deride, [...] a statement against segregation rather than a respect for the intrinsic value of the institution itself'.[70] In the experiences outlined in Black writing, the city's failings are not lack of privacy or freedom or beauty, just as the country is not celebrated for 'nature, serenity or peace'. Crucial, however, is not location as such, but rather, where one locates the ancestor: 'The city is wholesome, loved when such an ancestor is on the scene'; 'the country is beautiful – healing because [...] an ancestor is there'. The ancestor, in the country or the city, brings 'village values' – to the writer and to the writer's protagonists – enabling them to be 'regenerated, balanced and capable of operating on a purely moral axis'.[71] Another well-known essay, first published in 1983: 'Rootedness: The Ancestor as Foundation' expands on the matter. The botanical analogy of rootedness is not to be overlooked – but this, it must be remembered from the 1981 essay, is not 'a pastoral delight in things being right with God' (as it is more often in white American narratives) but, rather, of connectedness in a community and a vital, regenerative relation to 'the ancestor'. The experience of the journeys of the 8-rock families in 1890 and in 1949, a period of lynching and race riots in Oklahoma, as they moved again, two hundred and forty miles further west ('far far from the old Creek Nation which once upon a time a witty government called "unassigned land"' (p. 6), through 'a state shaped like the muzzle of a gun, on through the acres of grass', carrying their Oven 'like the ex-slaves who knew what came first' might be contrasted with the experience of Oklahoma as celebrated in Oscar Hammerstein's famous lyrics. Written in 1953, the musical *Oklahoma!* memorialises 'the brand new state' of the 1890s, and is illustrative of the distinctions between black and white experiences of rurality that Morrison noted in 'City Limits, Village Values':

> Brand new state!
> Brand new state, gonna treat you great!
> Give you barley, carrots and pertaters,
> Pasture fer the cattle,
> Spinach and termayters!
> Flowers on the prairie where the June bugs zoom,
> Plen'y of air and plen'y of room,
> Plen'y of room to swing a rope

---

69   T. Morrison, 'City Limits, Village Values: Concepts of Neighbourhood in Black Fiction' in *Literature and the Urban American Experience*, eds M. C. Jaye and A.C. Watts (Manchester University Press, 1981), p. 39.

70   Ibid., p. 38.

71   Ibid., p. 39.

Plen'y of heart and plen'y of hope.
Oklahoma, where the wind comes sweeping down the plain,
And the wavin' wheat can sure smell sweet
When the wind comes right behind the rain.
Oklahoma,
[…]
We know we belong to the land
And the land we belong to is grand![72]

Such confident exuberance is not available to migrating black homesteaders.

The Oven that the New Fathers of Ruby know instinctively they must haul across the state to a new home has been, in Haven, the dynamic centre of a community still in touch with 'village values' and the symbol of their rootedness and of their relationship with 'the ancestor'. These ancestors, warns Morrison, 'are not just parents' and 'this love of the ancestor should not be confused with some simple minded cant about Black families, broken families, or historylessness'.[73] Rather, 'they are sort of timeless people whose relationship to the characters are benevolent, instructive and protective, and they provide a certain kind of wisdom'.[74] It is this very connection that has been lost in Ruby, and, hence, it is a 'Paradise' carefully controlled but bereft of the rootedness and the regeneration, balance and moral action that comes from it. The arguments and indecision about what the inscription did or should bear is one indication that this community is not listening to the ancestors while the other signs, including the aspiration to control even death (no one should die *in* Ruby), are manifest in the range of symptoms for which the Convent women are blamed. Richard Misner notices, however, that even their stories have stalled, frozen in time. Although they have a 'stock of stories, tales about the old folks, the grands and great-grands; their fathers and mothers', repeat 'testimonies to endurance, wit, skill and strength', and tell 'tales of luck and outrage', 'there were no stories to tell of themselves' (p. 161). 'About their own lives they had shut up. Had nothing to say, pass on. As though past heroism was enough of a future to live by.' Having 'nothing to say', nothing to pass on', is tantamount to the death of rootedness, the annihilation of the ancestor and the 'devastation' of a people. The paradise these New Fathers are protecting is the location of dying.

The Oven is an obviously feminine fertility symbol, but no one remarks on this (only Anna muses to herself that perhaps the Oven's inscription should be: 'Be the Furrow of *Her* Brow'). Rather, it comes to be seen as important because it has been crafted by Zechariah, a leader among the Old Fathers, and its inscription is a patriarchal one: an injunction from He of the Furrowed Brow through the Old Fathers of Haven and thus to the New Fathers of Ruby. Several characters in the

---

72 Oscar Hammerstein and Richard Rodgers, *Oklahoma!* (Winona, MN: Williamson Music, 1981 [1943]), p. 183.

73 Ibid, op. cit., p. 43.

74 Toni Morrison, 'Rootedness: The Ancestor as Foundation', in *Black Women Writers*, ed. Mari Evans (London & Sydney: Pluto Press, 1985 [1983]), p. 343.

novel discern the way in which the men of Ruby feel the need to control the women and to negate their input. Patricia Best, reflecting on her own father's perceived transgression by marrying a light-skinned woman, recalls the ways in which the women tried a more compassionate approach and sought to modify the rigorous censure of the men: 'But they were just women, and what they said was easily ignored by good brave men on their way to Paradise' (pp. 201-02). The obsession with purity, she comes to realise as she compiles and then burns the 8-rock family-trees she has been tracing, doesn't come from God-the Father but from the fears of the human fathers of a rigidly separatist and purist community:

> That was the deal Zechariah had made […] It wasn't God's brow to be feared. It was his own, their own […] Unadulterated and unadulteried 8-rock blood held its magic as long as it resided in Ruby. That was their recipe. That was their deal. For Immortality […] In that case, she thought, everything that worries them must come from women. (p. 217)

Her daughter, Billie Delia, is perceptive enough to realise that the real battles in Ruby are not about specific matters or misdemeanours, 'but about disobedience, which meant, of course, the stallions were fighting about who controlled the mares and their foals'(p. 150). Deek has a reaction to Consolata, which, in many respects, seems more familiarly Freudian than Biblical in its connotations. Of the time when she passionately bit his lip, or when she invited him to join her in her own room at the Convent, set out with exotic salvage from the millionaire's mansion, with Seckel pears and wine, instead of lying with him in the dust under their usual fruitless fig-trees, or when he responded with desire to her golden skin and green eyes, he remembers only:

> the shame and the kind of woman he believed was its source. An uncontrollable, gnawing woman who had bitten his lip just to lap the blood it shed; a beautiful, golden-skinned outside woman with moss-green eyes that tried to trap a man, close him up in a cellar room with liquor to enfeeble him so they could do carnal things, unnatural things in the dark, a Salomé from whom he had escaped just in time or she would have had his head on a dinner plate. That ravenous ground-fucking woman [...] (pp. 279-80)

After the murders at the convent, Richard Misner muses on the tragic ironies of a place that aimed to be Paradise, to be perfect: 'A backward noplace ruled by men whose power to control was out of control and who had the nerve to say who could live and who not and where; who had seen in lively, free, unarmed females the mutiny of the mares and so got rid of them' (p. 308). On the other hand, the community at the Convent is missing something, too. As Consolata takes over, 'like a new and revised Reverend Mother', the broken begin to heal, ceasing to be 'haunted' by tending themselves as if they were flowers in a garden, drawing and colouring in templates of their own outlines on the Convent floor, dancing naked in the rain, listening to Consolata's 'loud dreaming' and lessons on the 'communion' of holy women, fallen and sanctified, mother and daughter, old and new (testament): 'Never break them in two. Never put one over the other. Eve is Mary's mother. Mary is the daughter of Eve' (p. 263). However, another crucial aspect that has been lost in both communities is the integration of male and female.

When Toni Morrison described the Ancestor in 'Rootedness' she noted that Pilate, a character in her earlier novel *The Song of Solomon* (1977), is the 'apogee' of the figure of the ancestor. In contrast to others in the novel, Pilate has 'had a dozen years of close nurturing relationships with two males – her father and her brother' and 'that intimacy and support was in her and made her fierce and loving'.[75] She continues:

> Pilate is the apogee of all of that: of the best of that which is female and the best of that which is male; and that balance is disturbed if it is not nurtured, and if it is not counted on and if it is not reproduced. That is the disability we must guard against for the future – the female who reproduces the female who reproduces the female who reproduces the female [...] there are a lot of people who talk about the position that men hold as of primary importance, but actually it is if we don't keep in touch with the ancestor that we are, in fact, lost.[76]

What Pilate has, Consolata has no access to. Sexually abused as a street child on the streets of Piedade, and her experience with Deek her only other contact with a man, Consolata has not had the benefit of 'balance'. However, her life-long close bond with the nun who 'kidnapped' her, and then the relationship with the broken women who seek refuge or help at the Convent, does at least give her the experience of nurturing and love. Despite her profound love for Mary Magna, it is when she is ailing that Consolata begins to come into her own, opening herself to other ways of thinking than her adoptive faith – or Mary Magna – has permitted. Her voluptuous long dreaming and 'stories of a woman named Piedade who sang but never said a word', her friendship with Lone, who, in her advocacy of magic, tells her 'don't separate God from his elements' and her newly discovered 'gift' of 'stepping in', mean that, in time, Consolata becomes a 'new and revised reverend Mother' who combines 'all the elements'. In line with Morrison's essay, Consolata does begin to reveal her own 'rootedness' in her:

> [...] acceptance of the supernatural and a profound rootedness in the real world at the same time with neither taking precedence over the other. It is indicative of the cosmology, the way in which Black people looked at the world. We are a very practical people, very down-to-earth, even shrewd people. But within that practicality we also accepted what I suppose could be called superstition and magic, which is another way of knowing things. But to blend these two worlds together was enhancing, not limiting. And some of those things were 'discredited knowledge' that Black people had; discredited only because Black people were discredited therefore what they *knew* was 'discredited'. And because the press toward upward social mobility would mean to get as far away from that kind of knowledge as possible. That kind of knowledge has a very strong place in my work.[77]

---

75 Morrison, 'Rootedness', op. cit., p. 344.

76 Ibid.

77 Ibid., p. 342.

Candomblé, the Afro-Brazilian religion which, in the story Morrison heard had been practiced by 'a convent of black nuns' is 'that kind of knowledge'. Candomblé is a religion which brings together tribal beliefs from West Africa with Brazilian Indian spiritual practices. There is also a strong measure of Catholic imagery combined in it, which, when first adopted by the African slaves, was a way of enveloping their practices in the guise of something more acceptable to their Portuguese slave-masters.[78] Perhaps, too, Candomblé's veil of Catholicism afforded a good number of Catholic women more scope than the patriarchal European religion would allow. Candomblé also incorporates religious rituals and medicine involving all aspects of the natural world and, in particular, 'the sacred leaves' of particular species, adapted from knowledge of African to Brazilian flora.[79]

> Plants and herbal medicine are key components to healing in Candomblé. Leaves and bark, seeds and flowers are also essential to rituals of cleansing, initiation, and other ordinary as well as extraordinary rites in the religion. In fact, there is a popular saying in Brazil, 'If there are no plants, there is no Candomblé.'[80]

Many of the ceremonies Consolata intuits or 'knows' are reminiscent of those belonging to Candomblé religious practice. This is the kind of 'discredited knowledge' included by Morrison in the 'Friend' who visits Dovey, for instance, or when, at the end of the novel, the bodies of the slain women have disappeared but are nonetheless described in visitations and reunions. The 'supernatural' encounters are represented using the most vivid palette, a veritable garden of colours: 'viridian', 'umber', 'rose madder', 'a violet so ultra it broke her heart', 'black and yellow'. The very last section of the novel, which finds Consolata by the ocean again, her head cradled in the lap of Piedade, the singer, is equally if not more vivid:

> Ruined fingers troll the tea brown hair. All the colors of seashells – wheat, rose, pearl – fuse in the younger woman's face. Her emerald eyes adore the black face framed in cerulean blue. (p. 318)

Who or what *is* Piedade, this black Madonna? She is perhaps a Catholicised veil over the Canomblé *orixa* figure, Iemanja, the 'ultimate mother figure and the "national" Orixa of Brazil, associated with the sea and with the colours white and blue. But another clue to the figure and to this ending – an added dimension – lies at the novel's beginning.

---

78   Pilot Destination Guide, 'Candomble: A Spiritual Meeting', http://www.pilotguides. com/destination_guide/south_America/brazil/candomble.php.

79   Robert A. Voeks, *Sacred Leaves of Candomblé: African Magic, Medicine and Religion in Brazil* (Austin: University of Texas Press, 1997).

80   Rachel E. Harding, 'Candomblé: A religion of the African Diaspora', http://www. prometra.org/Report_on_Candoble.htm [sic]. See also Rachel E. Harding, *A Refuge In Thunder: Candomblé and Alternative Spaces of Blackness* (Bloomington and Indianapolis, IN: Indiana University Press, 2003 [2000]).

The novel opens with an epigraph taken from the Gnostic texts known as the Nag Hammadi, which were discovered in Egypt in 1945. Morrison also used a short extract from the Nag Hammadi in *Jazz* (1992) and both that and the epigraph to *Paradise* are taken from a section entitled 'Thunder, Perfect Mind'. In conversation,[81] Morrison notes simply that the 'ending of the poem suited the plot, the narrative, of Paradise': 'The notion of sin, redemption and particularly the last line "And you will not die again"'.[82] There is something of a paradox here, however; one of the features of Morrison's *Paradise* is to suggest that paradise must be inclusive of everything; Ruby's terrible flaw was the attempt to keep things out, including death. The last chapter, when the death of Save-Marie is integrated into the community, is a moment of grace: 'there never was a time you were not saved' and the Biblical paradox of 1 Corinthians 15:35-37, cited by Reverend Misner on the occasion of the funeral, reinforces the view that life and death are integral – to each other, to paradise, and to gardens: 'what is sown is not alive until it dies'. Morrison has also asked that the last word in the novel, which is printed in the first edition as Paradise, be changed to its lower-case version to read 'down here in paradise' in order to emphasise that it is not an Other place but here (if 'the disconsolate' will allow it). The image of Consolata and Piedade is set in a paradise of lyrical beauty – and of detritus: 'sea trash; 'discarded bottle tops', 'a broken sandal', 'a small dead radio'. Not to allow death or detritus, it seems to suggest, is not to live fully and not to live fully (which is also to include death) is to let evil – the negative, mirror and anagram of live – prevail. This line is borne out by Morrison's 1993 Nobel speech, too, as she discusses an old woman pondering the conventional view of paradise or heaven:

> The conventional wisdom of the Tower of Babel story is that the collapse was a misfortune [...] That one monolithic language would have expedited the building and heaven would have been reached. Whose heaven, she wondered? And what kind? Perhaps the achievement of Paradise was premature, a little hasty, if no one could take the time to understand other languages, other views, other narratives. Had they, the heaven they imagined might have been found at their feet. Complicated, demanding, yes, but a view of heaven as life; not heaven as postlife.[83]

Further to the last lines of the Gnostic verse, 'Thunder, Perfect Mind', being used as an epigraph to *Paradise* is the fact that the speaker of this entire text is female, a goddess, and black. Paradox is integral to her whole powerful being:

> For I am the first and the last.
> I am the honoured one and the scorned one.
> I am the whore and the holy one.
> I am the wife and the virgin.

---

81 AOLChat with Toni Morrison, 15 Feb, 1998, cited in 'What is "P/paradise" in the novel?', http://www.uni-siegen.de/~fb3amlit/Whatis.htm.

82 Ibid.

83 'Toni Morrison – Nobel Lecture' (7 December, 1993) http://nobelprize.org/literature/laureates/1993/morrison-lecture.html.

I am the mother and the daughter.
I am the members of my mother.
I am the barren one
and many are her sons.
I am she whose wedding is great,
and I have not taken a husband.
I am the midwife and she who does not bear.
I am the solace of my labor pains.
I am the bride and the bridegroom,
the mother of my father
and it is my husband who begot me.
I am the sister of my husband
and he is my offspring.
I am the slave of him who prepared me.
I am the ruler of my offspring.
But he is the one who begot me before the time on a birthday.
And he is my offspring in due time and my power is from him.
 I am the staff of his power in his youth,
And he is the rod of my old age.
And whatever he wills happens to me.
I am the silence that is incomprehensible
And the idea whose remembrance is frequent.
I am the voice whose sound is manifold
And the word whose appearance is multiple.
I am the utterance of my name.[84]

There is a wealth of literature available on Gnosticism and other 'heresies' which incorporate the female into the Godhead, and far too much to be explored in any depth here, except where there are some revealing features in relation to Morrison's *Paradise*. Here, there are traditions that trace the power and prestige of black goddesses or black 'virgins' from Isis, ('I, I am the goddess [...] am the one who is great in Egypt' says the speaker of "Thunder, Perfect Mind"), through Sheba ('I am black, but beautiful, daughters of Jerusalem. Like the black tents of Cedar, like the pavilions of Solomon', Song of Songs 1:5-6) to Mary Magdalene, not only insofar as churches devoted to the Black Madonna are frequently named after her, but as herself black-skinned, as explored in Lynn Picknett's recent *Mary Magdalene: Christianity's Hidden Goddess*.[85] However, these Gnostic texts are not simply revealing 'the influence of archaic pagan traditions of the Mother Goddess', as Elaine Pagels explains, rather:

> for the most part, their language is specifically Christian, unmistakably related to a Jewish heritage. Yet instead of describing a monastic and masculine God, many of these texts

---

84 'The Thunder, Perfect Mind', trans., George W. MacRae, *The Nag Hammadi Library* (Leiden: E. J. Brill, 1977), p. 271.

85 Lynn Picknett, *Mary Magdalene: Christianity's Hidden Goddess* (London: Robinson, 2003).

speak of God as a dyad who embraces both masculine and feminine elements [...] One group of Gnostic sources claims to have received a secret tradition from Jesus through James and through Mary Magdalene. Members of this group prayed to both the divine Mother and Father.[86]

In Gnostic texts, we find Jesus referring to Mary, not as a prostitute or someone formerly possessed by demons, as is conventionally described in the Judeo-Christian tradition, but as 'the Woman who Knows All' and as 'the All';[87] she is one who knows and who speaks with God and as a partner and part of God. Indeed, there is a Gospel of Mary Magdalene, although this is not part of the texts known as the Nag Hammadi. The Nag Hammadi texts were not discovered until 1945 but the 'secret wisdom' is not unfamiliar and is related to the heresies developed by the Knights Templar, the Cathars and Albigensians during the time of the Holy Crusades:

> [...] the Crusaders brought back to Europe many treasures of the East. Among them were exquisite statues of the Black Goddess, Isis. These were enshrined as the Black Virgin. Devotion to her spread from cathedrals to small shrines dotted over the countryside in settings natural to the goddess of fertility. Literally hundreds of shrines to the Black Virgin sprang up throughout Europe in the twelfth and thirteenth centuries.
>
> One reason for the Black Virgin's great popularity during this period was the growing adoration of the chaste Virgin Mary. Courtly love, the legend of the Holy Grail, the veneration of the Virgin, the ascendancy of the idealized woman, were balanced by the compensating adoration of the Black Virgin. She was an underground figure; much of her so-called paganism still adhered to her (fertility, nature. earth). She was revered in an underground way – the blessing of the crops in the field, the blessing of pregnancy and childbirth, the dark excesses of sexuality and delight in the mysteries of the body, and the wisdom that can be experienced in lovemaking [...] In her aloneness she was independent – a liberated image of the feminine.[88]

Indeed, as Elaine Pagels notes, Judaism, Christianity, and Islam are 'in striking contrast to the world's other religious traditions, whether in Egypt, Babylonia, Greece and Rome, or in Africa, India, and North America, which abound in feminine symbolism'.[89] The black Madonna, Piedade, is Morrison's inclusion of and reference to these excluded and negated other traditions. At the close of the novel, Piedade (whose name is the Portuguese word for piety), 'her black face framed in cerulaean blue', sings by the seashore and 'looks to see what has come. Another ship, perhaps [...]'. (Incidentally, Isis, like 'the Magdalene', is 'connected with ships; she rode in her barque or great heavenly boat, ferrying the souls of mankind'[90] just as the name Mary (*maris, mer*) – and her blue robes – also refer to the sea.)

---

86   Elaine Pagels, *The Gnostic Gospels* (New York: Vintage, 1989), p. 49.

87   L. Picknett, op. cit., p. 84.

88   Marion Woodman and Elinor Dickson, 'Dancing in the Flames; The Dark Goddess', in the *Transformation of Consciousness* (Dublin: Gill & Macmillan, 1996), p. 28-9.

89   E. Pagels, op. cit., p. 48.

90   Lynn Picknett, op. cit., p. 127.

It has been noted, by one critic at least,[91] that Piedade is a suburb in Rio de Janeiro and that this must be the setting of Consolata's return home – back to the city that was her home as a street-orphan. However, there is another Piedade on the southern coast of Brazil, approximately equidistant from Rio de Janeiro and Sao Paulo which may be the more likely 'home' of Consolata. Piedade Beach is on an island (one of the three hundred and sixty-five that form the area) known as Gipóia Island. It is frequently advertised as a paradise and the photographs of it do show a tropical sandy crescent. Located at the beach is a beautiful little church, Piedade Church. There is another reason, however, to think that this may be the Piedade Morrison had in mind, for the town of Angra Dos Reis, to which these islands belong, was once the site of sugar plantations and of 'slave-worked sugar refineries' whose economies collapsed after the abolition of slavery.

> From Mangaratiba, the road hugs the coast as it wends its way westwards, rising and falling between towering green-clad mountains and the ocean. Roughly 60km west of Mangaratiba lies the shabby and rather unprepossessing little town of ANGRA DOS REIS . The lands around here were 'discovered' by the navigator André Gonçalves in 1502, though it wasn't until 1556 that a colonial settlement was established. The port first developed as an entrepôt for the exportation of agricultural produce from São Paulo and Minas Gerais in the seventeenth century. Fifteen slave-worked sugar refineries dominated the local economy which, with the abolition of slavery at the end of the nineteenth century, suffered a dramatic collapse. The 1930s saw the economy regenerated, with the construction of a new port, and shipbuilding remains an important local trade – although the latest venture is Brazil's first nuclear power station, located nearby.[92]

My suggestion is that it is on the paradise-island of Gipóia, with its slave-holding and colonial past, its nuclear power plant in close proximity and its tourist detritus, that she finds her 'home' with Piedade – the Black Madonna whose church is there on the edge of a beach that, when it suits them, some people have claimed is Paradise.

The disappearance – or resurrection – of the murdered women's bodies from the Convent garden is a mystery, and yet, we know where they are: Consolata is in the arms of Piedade 'down here in paradise'; Pallas returns to see her mother; Gigi her father; Mavis, her daughter; and Seneca, the mother she never knew. Billie Delia, a friend of the Convent women and someone who had sometimes sought refuge with them 'was perhaps the only one in town who was not puzzled by where the women were or concerned about how they disappeared' (p. 308). Her question is: ' When will they return?' Richard and Anna visiting the Covent garden after the killings – him, holding some of the famous long black pepper pods, and her, having collected five umber eggs – together catch sight of something: 'Or sensed it, rather, for there was nothing to see'. Richard settles for describing it as a window; Anna, a door and together they discuss the meaning of 'the sign rather than the event':

91   J. Matus, op. cit., p. 193.
92   *The Rough Guide to Brazil*, ed. by David Cleary and others (New York, London, Delhi: Rough Guides 2003), p. 141.

Whether through a door needing to be opened or a beckoning window already raised, what would happen if you entered? What would be on the other side? What on earth would it be? What on earth? (p. 305)

Later, officiating at the funeral of Save-Marie, Richard sees the 'window in the garden' again:

when he bowed his head and gazed at the coffin lid he saw the window in the garden, felt it beckon toward another place – neither life nor death – but there, just yonder, shaping thoughts he did not know he had. (p. 307)

This garden with a door or window to another place 'on earth' is a mystery and a paradox but it becomes clearer if set in the context of Gnostic gospels and other unorthodox religious traditions, and of Morrison's conviction that paradise is not viable if thought of as a separate place for a perfect few according to human precepts of 'pomposity, error and callousness', 'unbridled by Scripture, deafened by the roar of [one's] own history'. Together Anna and Richard represent the two most important principles: combination and openness. The aperture in the garden that they both 'see' and 'perceive' is like the mythical navel of the world, the Omphalos in the primal garden:

Omphalos: Greek transliteration of Latin *umbilicus*, the navel or hub of the world, center of the Goddess's body, source of all things. As every ancient nation regarded its own version of the Great Mother as the cosmic spirit, so its capital or chief temple was located at the center of the earth, marked by the stone *omphalos* that concentrated the Mother's essence. [...] Romans placed the world's navel or *omphalos* at the round hearth of the temple of Vesta. Greeks placed it at the *omphalos* of Delphi, 'Temple of the Womb'. Jews placed it at the temple of Zion. Christianity inherited a Jewish cosmogony wherein Jerusalem was regarded as the center of the earth, where Jesus died on the identical spot where the Tree of Life once grew in the primal garden.[93]

Morrison seems to be suggesting that The Oven was first – perhaps more intuitively than methodically – created as the appropriate symbol to represent the Temple of the Womb, the integration of male and female principles and the connection to the Great Mother. However, the dogma and divisions that ensued eclipsed the ancestral wisdom, and by the time Ruby was established, the New Fathers had closed the gates and divorced the principles. Anna and Richard stand at a new garden site, holding their symbolic fruit, in which the principles of male and female will be combined anew under the aegis, not of 'bodacious black Eves unredeemed by Mary', but by 'the Black Goddess':

The Black Goddess is so far hardly more than a word of hope whispered among the few who have served their apprenticeship to the White Goddess. She promises a new pacific bond between men and women ... in which the patriarchal marriage bond will fade away ... the Black Goddess has experienced good and evil, love and hate, truth and falsehood

---

93   Barbara G. Walker *The Woman's Encyclopedia of Myths and Secrets*, op. cit., p. 740.

in the person of her sisters ... she will lead man back to that sure instinct of love which he long ago forfeited by intellectual pride.[94]

Of course, Toni Morrison's novel *Paradise* is not just about principles for paradise; it is also about principles for black fiction: 'It should be beautiful and powerful, but it should also work. It should have something in it that enlightens, something that *opens the door* [my emphasis] and points the way.'[95] Summarising her own work she has noted how much she disliked 'isms' and fixed categories; writing, like life, is not following a 'recipe':

> In order to be as free as I possibly can, in my own imagination, I can't take positions that are closed. Everything I've ever done, in the writing world, has been to expand articulation, rather than to close it, to open doors, sometimes, not even closing the book – leaving the endings open for reinterpretation, revisitation, a little ambiguity. [...] I don't subscribe to patriarchy, and I don't think it should be substituted with matriarchy. I think it's a question of equitable access, and opening doors to all sorts of things.[96]

In Morrison's view, *this* is paradise – and *Paradise*, too.

V. S. Naipaul: Migration/Rootlessness

The Enigma of Arrival is the largely autobiographical account – nonetheless subtitled: *A Novel In Five Sections* – of journeys made between three main points of reference on the world map: Trinidad, England and India. The first-person narrator

---

94 Robert Graves, *Mammon and the Black Goddess*, cited in Ean Begg, *The Cult of the Black Virgin* (London: Penguin, 1996 [1985]), p. 126.

95 T. Morrison, 'Rootedness', op. cit. p. 341.

96 Zia Jaffrey, 'The Salon Interview – Toni Morrison', http://dir.salon.com/books/int/1998/02/cov_si_02int.html

is a man born in Trinidad but whose family has come from India as indentured servants, after the abolition of slavery. Always bent on leaving the island of his birth, the narrator has long-held aspirations to be a writer of English literature, so, at the age of seventeen, he leaves for England on a scholarship to Oxford University. Home, for different reasons, is *and* is not in any of these places. At every juncture in his writing career, and through all his travels, the writer-narrator feels both belated and deluded (arriving too late; arriving in a manner and in places not as imagined). Understanding that his personal world (including the imagination) and the world he travels in have been profoundly affected by European imperialism, slavery, the Indian diaspora and other migrations, he struggles to locate the 'reality' of past and present.

The narrator's biography closely matches that of Naipaul's own life over the period prior to the time of the novel's publication in 1987. The novel uses its five un-chronological sections to describe various journeys, both geographical and intellectual, but the prime location from which to reflect on all these excursions is a rural Wiltshire valley in the 1970s, twenty years after the first journey from Trinidad to England. Discovery is the theme throughout – at 'home' in the valley and abroad, including going 'home' to Trinidad on several occasions – and back again to England. The search is not only for a home, but rather, in the light of complex histories, origins and representations, to arrive at a clear view of the world – as far as possible. Learning to see, and thus understand, the world(s) about him is part of the notion behind the enigmatic arrival of the title. Importantly, landscapes and gardens as culturally determined and historically specific are considered alongside the consideration of something more fundamental, perhaps transcendental – even (cautiously) universal. The narrator's most frequently repeated terms are: history, seeing and sanctity.

The first section of the five is called 'Jack's Garden' and it is Jack and his rural Wiltshire garden that provide the 'unanchored and strange' writer, living as a tenant in a cottage on the grounds of a manor-estate, with new but always shifting and unfolding ways of seeing: 'I saw things slowly; they emerged slowly', or, 'it was Jack's garden that made me notice Jack [...] but it took some time to see the garden' or 'seeing at that time what I wanted to see' are typical statements in this section. The last line of the novel arrives back at the importance of Jack's garden, finishes the very book the writer has been writing about starting, and returns us as readers to that already-encountered first section he is about to begin to write: 'And that was when [...] I laid aside my drafts and hesitations and began to write very fast about Jack and his garden.' There have been, however, a good number of gardens considered on the journeys in between, all of them illuminating to some degree.

Watching Jack and his garden, while instructive, is not, however, the narrator's first lesson in learning to look at land and its 'scapes'. When he first leaves Trinidad, he views the land and sea below from the perspective of being airborne. The 'wrinkled' sea he can immediately relate to and identify; 'the fragment of the poem by Tennyson' is familiar through the literary lens but the landscape of the island itself is a shock, a 'first revelation':

At ground level so poor to me, so messy, so full of huts and gutters and bare front yards and straggly hibiscus hedges and shabby back yards [...] From the air, though, a landscape of logic and larger pattern; the straight lines and regularity and woven, carpet-like texture of sugar-cane fields, so extensive from up there, leaving so little room for people except at the very edges; the large unknown area of swampland [...] the clumps of mangrove and brilliant-green swamp trees casting black shadows on milky-green water; the forested peaks and dips and valleys of the mountain range; a landscape of clear pattern and contours [...] the world in which I had lived all my life so far was a world I had never seen.[97]

The narrator has also long understood the disjunction between the way in which a Caribbean island, 'with all its colonial and holiday motifs', was represented to tourists and the dusty, plantation-impoverished reality: 'the publicized, expected thing [...] the way that as a child I had been taught to draw and colour my island [...] I hadn't believed in that way of seeing' (p. 162). For the most part, however, the 'inability to visualize' and the attempts made to do so, the fantasies (variously informed by literature, film and advertising), are persistent problems for the migrant narrator, arriving, leaving, living, unsettled, unclear. The only clear and focussed vision is the aspiration to be a writer in English; commissions to write travel literature take the writer, 'a colonial travelling among colonials' through landscapes of 'unnaturalness', 'fragments of the past', projections of romance, riddled with memories of pain: the Caribbean, Central America, India, United States, Africa.

The writer (the narrator) comes to live – and to heal – in rural Wiltshire, a tenant in a cottage on the grounds of an Edwardian estate that had once been 'enormous,' 'created in part by the wealth of empire'(p. 56), but now a remnant and shadow of its former vitality. Twenty years after that first trip to England, he has lived in its cities, London, Oxford, Gloucester, but the experience of living in the English countryside is new. Walking daily in rural Wiltshire, near to the cathedral city of Salisbury and to the ancient monument of Stonehenge, he begins to understand that countryside is as 'built' an environment as the cities ('it was new to me to understand that the woods all around had been planted, and all the alternating roses and hawthorns beside the windbreak of beech and pine'), as unnatural, historically fragmented and prone to romantic projections, perhaps, as any other part of Britain's former colonies.

Not only does he begin to see the landscape, including gardens, with new vision, but figures in the landscape, too, are in need of altered perception. This writer from Trinidad is particularly susceptible to illusion because the lens through which he sees both landscape and the figures within it is already inscribed with an expectation of 'Englishness'. Nothing seems to fit the preconceptions that have been informed, for example, by linguistics, ('I knew that both 'walden' and 'shaw' meant wood. One further reason why [...] I thought I saw a forest'), by art (the familiar 'romance of a Constable reproduction' or the drawings for *The Wind in the Willows* by E. H. Shepard), or by literature (especially the English pastoral poets Gray, Goldsmith and Wordsworth). The cows in the fields and farmyards are not in accord with the 'drawing on the label of the condensed-milk tins' in Trinidad, nor, as calf-less milking

---

97   V. S. Naipaul, *The Enigma of Arrival*, op. cit. , p. 113.

'machines' do they fit with the images of an eighteenth-century English pastoral tradition. Further still, they do not fit the Indian peasant notion of cows: 'Among us, the new milk from a cow that had just calved was almost holy'. What 'fits' this English rural scene least of all, and of this he is well aware, coming as he does from peasant India via colonial Trinidad, is his own figure in this landscape: 'The builder of the house and the designer of the garden could not have imagined, with their world view, that at a later time someone like me would have been in the grounds' (p. 55). That he should be there has an irony, too, when his own harsh history, was – and had been ordained by – the very history that created the estate, the landscape and the cultural artefacts that represented it: 'the colonial plantations or estates of Trinidad, to which my impoverished Indian ancestors had been transported in the last century – estates of which this Wiltshire estate, where I now lived – had been the apotheosis' (p. 55). To uproot oneself again, and to consciously and deliberately come to England in order to establish oneself as a writer in English, is the complex position from which the narrator tries to assess his surroundings and get his bearings.

The village, the manor and its gardens and the people who inhabit them or work in them are all revealing of the subtleties of English class and caste. The gardens of the manor have fallen into decay, and at first, the writer claims to enjoy this aspect and finds in it an affinity with the landlord, whom he otherwise rarely sees and who is himself languishing with accidia:

> My meditations in the manor were not of imperial decline. Rather, I wondered at the historical chain that had brought us together – he in his house, I in his cottage, the wild garden his taste [...] and also mine. (p. 56)

In its heyday, forty or fifty years earlier, the estate had sixteen gardeners who 'looked after the grounds and the orchard and the walled garden'. Now, in the 1970s, it is reduced to one, Pitton, until he, too, is released and more ad hoc help is arranged. At first, the writer-tenant is a kind of voyeur of the landscape, manor and gardens; not only does he repeatedly misread what he sees, but what he sees is always 'from a distance'. Although he walks daily in the landscape, becoming increasingly familiar with it, and while he does in due course learn about the seasons, related plants and plant names, he is never 'involved' in gardening as such. Rather, he watches and tries to ascertain what gardens and gardening mean in relation to historical flux and to men's lives (it is always men who are considered thus). He is also interested in the concepts of service – or servitude – and although he never names it 'class' or caste as such, his meditations are on the classification of gardeners, tenants, workers and others he comes into contact with in the local area. Thus, he begins to make distinctions between Jack and his wife, Pitton, Bray, Mr and Mrs Phillips, the farm-worker, Les, and his wife, Brenda, the dairyman, the 'new people' in 'Jack's cottage' conversion – people who, for longer or shorter times, are inserted into the life of the manor and its rural surroundings, just as the narrator himself. He begins to 'read' the various houses and gardens. Bray, who covers the front garden of his 'improved agricultural cottage' with concrete and a range of vehicles, announces 'the idea of proprietorship' – he 'owned his house and wanted that to be known [...] to that he added the idea that he was a free man, a man who worked for himself' (p. 263). Pitton is his neighbour in the adjacent 'experimental "improved" agricultural cottages', which were now 'more genuinely "period"' than the thatched cottages that 'stood for and idea of the rural picturesque'; Pitton's garden, however, is that of a tied tenant and of a particular 'idea' of rural style: tidy, conservative, anonymous. Of the narrator's own cottage 'set right against the beeches', he comes to see that 'this was no country "naturalness"', but that 'the cottage had been designed to create just that effect' (p. 210), and that there is an element of 'play' (more stage-craft than children's games) in the 'ordering' of the manor grounds and estate:

> One day [...] I saw the carved initials of the builder or designer – the last initial proclaimed him a member of my landlord's family – with the year, 1911.
>
> Play, from someone of the family, in that secure, far-off year, the coronation year of the King-Emperor, George the Fifth. With my instinct to accept what I found, it took me time to recognize the element of play, and the extent of it, in the ordering of the manor grounds. (pp. 210-11)

The irony, however, is that while the writer begins to see these elements of contingency and design in the landscape, buildings and gardens and claims to feel an affinity – for reasons of temperament and of history – for flux, decay, 'ruins and superseded things', there is still a sense of regret in having missed the moment. Some eighteen years earlier, as he notes in 'Section Two: The Journey', which chronologically predates the period outlined in Section One, he left London feeling disappointed:

> So I grew to feel that the grandeur belonged to the past; that I had come to England at the wrong time; that I had come too late to find the England, the heart of empire, which (like a provincial, from a far corner of the Empire) I had created in my fantasy. (p. 141)

Although his time in the Wiltshire valley constitutes 'his second life' and 'a second awakening' to the natural world there, there is still a remnant of the feeling that the 'play', for all that it is pretence, has been missed and can never be fully apprehended or understood.

The other distinctions the writer/narrator is at pains to make are: what has sanctity and what is junk (both frequently repeated words throughout the text) and who are the people that are in tune with these distinctions? What is their present relationship to the Victorian-Edwardian estate and how does this compare with those other co-creations of empire, plantation estates: 'I came from a colony, once a plantation society, where servitude was a more separate condition', muses the narrator, ceaselessly observing the English rural workers. The gardener, Pitton, albeit a descendent of one of 'the sixteen' who comprised a team in the manor's heyday, is now deemed to be someone who 'wasn't a true gardener, a man who possessed the mystery', but rather as someone who 'looked more like a visitor, like a man passing through' (p. 255), with a style 'modelled on that of a superior', looking more like a landlord than a gardener. However, the various men who come to tend the manor grounds after Pitton is dismissed, such as Mr Tomm, who arrives with a billhook and nylon sack and announces that he loves gardening ('it's all I want to do') , are seen as 'marauders, vandals':

> the people who came to work in what remained of the garden had become marauders, vandals. The very kind of people who, in the great days of the manor, would have given of their best as carpenters, masons, bricklayers, might have had ideas of beauty and workmanship and looked for acknowledgement of their skill and craft and pains, people of this very sort now, sensing an absence of authority, an organization in decay, seemed to be animated by an opposite instinct: to hasten decay, to loot, to reduce to junk. (p. 355)

In Trinidad, the concepts of gardening and gardeners had their own hierarchies, all of them affected by the country's colonial history. In the Trinidadian past of childhood, before the Second World War, when 'sugar-cane covered the land', the notion of 'a gardener' was difficult to identify. Although watching Jack's gardening stirs memories of his father and 'a garden he tried to get started in a patch of cleared bush', and while the Indian peasantry were supposed to have a special affinity with the fertility of the earth, there was, it seems, no 'tradition' of gardening in Trinidad at that time. Indeed, recollecting an idea of a gardener in Trinidad results in a series of negations and qualifications: 'few gardeners'; 'nothing like gardens'; 'less a gardener, [...] more simply, a worker in a garden'; 'barely above, perhaps merging into, that of yard boy'. In Port of Spain, however, as in most colonial outposts, a large Royal Botanical Garden had been established, but here, curiously, 'the idea of "gardeners" was not contained in the idea of the garden'; in this case, the idea of a 'gardener' had no fixed cosmopolitan or metropolitan currency.

> Flowers were beautiful; everyone loved them. In Port of Spain there were the many acres of the Royal Botanical Gardens, established after the British conquest of the island; and the lily ponds and rockeries of the Rock Gardens. Both places were recognized beauty spots. But the idea of 'gardeners' was not contained in the idea of the garden; in fact, it ran contrary to the idea of the garden. The garden spoke of Port of Spain and comfort and a good office job and Sunday drives around the Queen's Park Savannah. The gardener belonged to the plantation or estate past. The past lay outside Port of Spain, in the Indian countryside, in the fields, the roads, the huts. Literature or the cinema [...] would have given the word different associations. But that knowledge – of swamp and estate and vegetable plot – was the knowledge I took to England. That was the knowledge that lay below my idea of the P.G. Wodehouse gardener and my idea of the gardener in *Richard II* [...] (pp. 247-8)

The narrator, with his own complex heritage – but also, his linguistic precision – is unable to define and identify 'the gardener', both at home and abroad. Instead of the individual 'Jack's Garden', it is, perhaps, the collective 'Union Jack's Garden' that most preoccupies this migrant colonial.

Jack is the gardener-figure to whom, bit by bit and with revisions, he attributes a genuine facility. The chapter on Jack's garden is both eulogy and elegy, for after watching Jack in his garden and feeling to have learnt so much from the process of watching – 'his garden taught me [...] I got to know in a new way [...] it was like learning a second language' – he then watches the garden fall into disarray after, first, Jack's incapacitating illness, and then death:

> His vegetable plot, overrun with weeds, was barely noticeable. His fruit and flower garden grew more wild, the hedge and the rose bushes growing out. His greenhouse at the back (really the front) became empty.
>
> So much that had looked traditional, natural, emanations of the landscape, things that country people did – the planting out of annuals, the feeding of the geese, the clipping of the hedge, the pruning of the fruit trees – now turned out not to have been traditional or instinctive after all, but to have been part of Jack's way. When he wasn't there to do these things, they weren't done; there was only ruin. The new people in the other cottages didn't do what he had done. They seemed to have little regard for their bit of cottage land. Or they saw it differently, or they had another idea of their lives. (p. 49)

What the narrator seems to be struggling to identify is some natural 'rootedness' ('I had seen Jack as solid, rooted in his earth') from which he, the unrooted colonial migrant can learn still further, but what he is forced to see is something fleeting, again, 'something from the past, a remnant, something that would be swept away before my camera would get the pictures'. Wanting to see some inherent, natural sanctity – something 'timeless and unchanging' – he is forced to see 'how tenuous, really, the hold of all these people had been on the land they worked or lived in'(p. 100):

> Jack himself had disregarded the tenuousness of his hold on the land, just as, not seeing what others saw, he had created a garden on the edge of a swamp and a ruined farmyard: had responded to and found glory in the seasons. All around him was ruin; and all around, in a deeper way, was change, and a reminder of the brevity of the cycles of growth and creation. (p. 100)

One of the aspects of Jack's garden in which he is at first most clearly defined as a gardener, is in his 'vegetable allotment, the plot beyond the cottage front gardens, at the beginning of the slope towards the farmer's cultivated fields'(p. 28). Allotments – at home and abroad – begin to take on a particular significance in the novel. Both the English and the Trinidadian landscape have been affected by the relatively new feature of the allotment. In Trinidad, the phenomenon had come about 'after the war,' with 'a new kind of agriculture' and a more secure definition of 'gardeners'. While reminiscent of the similar allotments in England, these had not been 'designed' or imposed as a colonial prototype but rather had happened 'by accident':

> on either side of the highway embankment the Americans had built during the war, former estate workers had leased plots from the estate, a few acres each, and had begun to develop vegetable gardens, slowly redeeming the land from swamp, building it up. The vegetables they grew – aubergines, beans, ochroes – had a shorter cycle than sugar-cane and they were correspondingly more demanding. They required finer attentions [...] the human scale, the many different shades and textures of green gave us a new idea of agriculture and almost a new idea of landscape and natural beauty. The vegetable-growers were Indian, but these

vegetable plots were like nothing in peasant India. The skills, the practices, came from the experimental plots of the Imperial College of Tropical Agriculture – famous throughout the British Empire – [...] Many of the Indian vegetable-growers had worked there as garden labourers. And it was only some years after I had been in England that I saw that the landscape the Indian vegetable-growers had created on either side of the highway [...] – a landscape which had no pattern in Trinidad or India – was like the allotments I saw in England, at the edge of towns, from the railway train. English allotments in a tropical and colonial setting. Created by accident, and not by design; created at the end of the period of empire, out of the decay of the old sugar plantations. (p. 246)

In the former plantation colony, the very concept of 'agriculture' had hitherto been tainted by 'servitude and ugliness' rather than bearing any association with 'magic', the old world of planting and fertility.' In the narrator's eyes, this is what had been identified in Jack – and what is missing in Pitton – as it is the impetus behind the marginal but self-determined allotments:

[...] the idea of fertility, the idea even of the god of the node: the gardener as the man who caused the unremarkable seed to grow into leaves, stalks, buds, flowers, fruit, called this all up from the seed, where it has lain in small, the gardener as magician, herbalist, in touch with the mystery of seed and root and graft, which (with the mystery of cooking) is one of the earliest mysteries that the child discovers [...] It was this childhood sensation, this childhood delight in making things grow, that was touched in England when I saw the vegetable allotments at the edge of towns, beside the railway tracks. (p. 259)

Garden historian, Jane Brown, explains how allotments in England in the 1950s had, in fact, fallen out of favour 'because they were usually so neglected and untidy; there had undoubtedly been some digging fatigue after the great war effort',[98] and notes that throughout the 1960s they were shunned as symbols of 'poverty, charity and wartime needs'.[99] In 1964, Harold Macmillan commissioned an inquiry to assess the feasibility of maintaining these sections of urban land for what might seem to have been an outmoded activity – and an eyesore. However, by the mid-1970s, the time when much of *The Enigma of Arrival* is set, there was a 'green revolution' in England, a resurgence in demand for allotments, with long waiting lists in many towns. For different reasons than in Trinidad, there is a sense of the democratisation of land, of freedom, and certainly, of diversity, afforded by allotments:

One myth is that allotments are somehow free from hierarchies of race or class. This isn't the case, but they do harbour a cross-section of people: at Uplands in Handsworth, Birmingham, where two big sites were joined after the war, making the largest allotment area in Europe, thirty-eight acres, thirteen different ethnic communities garden, competing fiercely at the September flower show and for the autumn pumpkin prize. Families from the West Indies grow squashes, amaranth and sweet corn; Sikh, Indian and Pakistani owners grow methi (fenugreek) for their curry, scented coriander and hot makoo – a black nightshade for extra hot spice – as well as turnips and potatoes [...] a long time allotment

---

98   Jane Brown, *The Pursuit of Paradise*, op. cit., p. 167.
99   Ibid.

owner [...] whose father gardened here fifty years ago, helps the children and raises his own prize dahlias.[100]

The allotment, to which I will return, is also significant, not just to postcolonial politics, but Naipaul's poetics in this novel.

As the narrator's own time in the valley is drawing to a close, much at the manor has also changed. Beeches have been felled and aspens have fallen (the landlord 'liked ivy' and 'did not complain' when the trees collapsed); the gate has been locked and great branches placed in front of it; the children's house has been boarded up and wrapped with barbed wire to prevent any further intrusion from vagrants; the old moss roses have been inexpertly pruned and 'reduced [...] to rampant briar'; the 'hidden garden' has been opened briefly, then closed up ('no-one seemed to know what to do with a hidden garden'). The relatively unkempt manor garden that had suited the writer's temperament formerly has now become unsuitable; too much has fallen into obsolescence, 'unchecked' by and bereft of 'the hand of man' (p. 365). Brown now becomes the overwhelming rather than seasonal feature of the manor garden – and with an attention to colour that might be seen to have self-deprecating racial connotations – it becomes again 'what it had been in Trinidad: not a true colour, the colour of dead vegetation', not a thing one found beauty in, 'trash' (p. 365). The unkempt garden that had earlier revealed so much of interest (such as the surprising peonies, which, after twenty years in England – and without a single reference to Keats – he learns to recognise and name: 'they stood for my new life'), now heralds the time for the narrator to withdraw. However, what he leaves to do is a re-enactment, not of Jack's 'rootedness' or a Trinidadian allotment-holder's 'accident', but rather the overhaul 'by design' of two former cottages, obliterating the fruit and vegetable garden, renovating and re-orientating the house. These are exactly the actions that he had deplored in the conversion of gardens to lawn, of lawns to concrete, or when Jack's cottage was rebuilt as a new house: 'how stripped of sanctity' when 'the quality or attributes of the site changing, the past has been abolished'(p. 99). When an old lady comes to these cottages to see the home she remembers from childhood, he is acutely uncomfortable:

> I was horribly embarrassed. Embarrassed to have done what I had done with the cottages, all the things that had disoriented the old lady [...] the new entrance and drive; the remodelling of what the old lady would have remembered as the back of the cottages into the front of the renovated house; the extension to the house that had done away with half of the building her grandfather had lived in; the landscaped garden that had replaced the fruit-and-vegetable cottage garden the old lady probably remembered [...] I was also embarrassed to be what I was, an intruder, not from another village or county, but from another hemisphere, embarrassed to have destroyed or spoilt the past for the old lady, as the past had been destroyed for me in other places, in my old island, and even here, in the valley of my second life [...] (pp. 346-7)

---

100 Jenny Uglow, *A Little History of British Gardening* (London: Chatto & Windus, 2004), p. 278.

Here is the former visitor to the valley, who daily walked in the landscape, who regularly took the bus into town, who enjoyed the 'human scale' of the manor cottage and who so critically scrutinised the ways of incoming new workers and their remodelled dwellings; they showed that 'the car was more important [...] more important than the house' or revealed a 'more general new attitude to the land, [...] as though they intended to turn all the irregularities of nature into straight lines or graded curves' (p. 60). Now, he settles down and remodels a cottage to have a new entrance and *drive*, an extension and a landscaped garden replacing the very 'symbol' for which Jack was to be remembered: 'the fruit-and-vegetable garden'. The conversion of the cottages – and the narrator's embarrassment in front of the old lady – is related twice in the novel, once in 'Jack's Garden' and again in 'Rooks', and the differences are telling. In 'Jack's Garden', a defensive discomfort prevails: 'I felt ashamed [...] I should have made a clean break but [...] I wanted to stay with what I had found. I wanted to recreate [...] what I had found in the manor cottage'. However, the extent of the details of the 'conversion' as described in 'Rooks', despite the avowed embarrassment, gives the sense that this novel might just as appropriately be entitled: *The Enigma of 'Arriviste'*. Thus, the meaning of the narrator's meditations on Jack is also less easy to identify. He has been inspired by Jack – and his garden – to write, and to write of himself; as the successful writer he has now become after his time in England, he is able to purchase and convert his own rural-English cottages – and to write of it in the context of great historical and cultural complexity. But there remains the question: to what end the meditations on gardens and gardeners and the human-scale of allotments, as opposed to the 'other idea of lives' manifest in estates – plantation and manor and now, peripatetic *nouveau riche*. That what has constituted 'healing' and clarity of vision, afforded by the time in the valley, should lead to the emulation not of those who recognise 'sanctity,' but of those with a propensity to make 'junk', is an enigma indeed.

V. S. Naipaul generates a good deal of critical controversy, sometimes on the basis of what he writes, but at other times, because of things he says. One critical commentator of his work, Bruce King, outlines the ways in which critical opinion has often been predicated on a preconceived notion of the positions that should be adopted by a 'postcolonial' writer:

Here is the essence of what has continued to differentiate Naipaul from his critics over the decades. They desire a literature of cultural affirmation which is part of the struggle for decolonization, Naipaul does not ignore the effects of colonialism or fail to see injustice, but his writing treats such themes in a complex way [...] he has argued that the literature of cultural assertion sometimes selectively ignores the actual horrors of slavery and imperialism. [...] Behind most criticism of Naipaul [...] is the tendency to divide the world into such opposing polarities as centre (England, imperialist, Western civilization) and margins (colonies, Third World, black). Such critics are themselves usually nationalists, on the political Left, and tend to read literature as politics. The authors of the influential *The Empire Writes Back*, although sensitive readers of Naipaul's work, are critical that he is not part of the celebration of new national cultures and societies that followed political decolonization.[101]

As a Caribbean writer, Naipaul is, it appears, expected to take up positions which, with his attention to complexity or his refusal to discuss the 'terrible crimes' of 'slavery and imperialism' as if they were 'uniquely European', he is unwilling to do. His own experience of racism, for instance, was a complex matter in Trinidad, where blacks, the former slave-class, now formed the dominant social group. Inter-racial tension was not simply a matter of black and white, or brown and white, but something more complicated:

> India's weakness led to its people being shipped around the world as indentured labour, to the abandonment of Indians in black-dominated Trinidad and Guyana, the expulsions of Indians from Africa and Fiji. [...] his writings note the humiliation of Indians whether during the Islamic conquests, the British destruction of the former Indian economy, the fear felt by Trinidadian Indians towards black policemen, or the confiscation of businesses in postcolonial Africa. He writes often about the condition of India and the Indian diaspora, of which he is a part. He sees his travels as analogous to those of the diaspora as displaced Indians journey through the modern world attempting to create a home elsewhere and as they revise their history to explain their own predicament.[102]

Fellow-Caribbean writer, the international-award-winning poet and dramatist Derek Walcott, also reviewed *The Enigma of Arrival* unfavourably, but his indictment was on the grounds of having demonstrated an easy seduction by the 'elegiac pastoralism' of English literature ('no other literature is so botanical as English and landscape, so seeded with delight and melancholy in the seasons').[103] Walcott takes the view that Naipaul demonstrates 'a virulent contempt towards the island of his origin'[104] in his complicity with ' the same lovers of gardens [who] enslaved and finally ignored their empire once they had exhausted the soil that produced sugar for afternoon tea'.[105] There may be some justification for noting that the narrator of the novel (who is, of course, not identical to Naipaul) does confuse *seeing* English and *being* English, but it is also valid to dramatise paradox rather than to simply underscore what should not be defeatist but a 'glorious' certainty that 'the provincial, the colonial, can never civilise himself beyond his province, no matter how deeply he immures himself [...] in the leafy lanes of Edwardian England'.[106] For the narrator to install himself in these leafy lanes in his renovated house and landscaped garden does look like 'the other thing that is the final mimicry',[107] but it is an action the inconsistencies

---

101 Bruce King, *V. S. Naipaul*, op. cit., p. 195.

102 Ibid, p. 16.

103 Derek Walcott, 'The Garden Path: V. S. Naipaul' *What the Twilight Says* (London: Faber, 1998), p. 121.

104 Ibid.

105 Ibid.

106 Ibid., p. 131.

107 Ibid.

of which Naipaul, if not the narrator, is well aware. The return to Trinidad for his sister's 'ceremony of farewell' at the end of the novel – before the writer will return to England and start writing the novel that begins with 'Jack's Garden' – gives rise to a reflection on the ubiquity of European suburban life.

This, perhaps, is the real enigma of the book and the one that relates most to the story inspired by the painting by Giorgio de Chirico: the confused traveller in an antique time arrives at a destination, gets lost, panics and eventually with relief finds his way back to the quayside, from which he hopes to depart, as he had arrived. There is, however, no means of doing so: 'The antique ship has gone'. As it is conjectured, the end of the story is: 'The traveller has lived out his life' – a parable, it seems, on destiny and destinations. However, at the end of the novel, the writer makes another link which shows that suburban homes and gardens – or what they represent – constitute the quayside from which there is 'nowhere else to go':

> We had made ourselves anew. The world we had found ourselves in – the suburban houses, with gardens, where my sister's farewell ceremony had taken place – was one we had partly made ourselves, and had longed for, when we had longed for money and the end of distress; we couldn't go back. There was no ship of antique shape now to take us back. We had come out of the nightmare; and there was nowhere else to go. (p. 385)

Observing the landscape of Port of Spain on this occasion, attending his sister's funeral, he finds those 'acres upon acres of vegetable plots' alongside 'highways and clover-shaped exits and direction boards', because 'money, that unexpected bounty, had ravaged and remade the landscape where we had had our beginnings in the New World', 'money had touched us all'. The elegy, at the end of the novel, is the narrator's 'ceremony of farewell' to that 'sanctity' and 'mystery' for which he has been searching: 'Every generation was now to take us further away from those sanctities'. In Trinidad and in England he had been looking for something sacred beneath the legacy of the estate, something of a time when in India his people 'would have felt ourselves to be more whole, more in tune with the land and the spirit of the earth', some allotment for 'earth rites':

> We were immemorially people of the countryside, far from the courts of princes, living according to rituals we didn't always understand and yet were unwilling to dishonour because that would cut us off from the past, the sacred earth, the gods. Those earth rites went back far. They would always have been partly mysterious. But we couldn't surrender to them now. We had become self-aware. Forty years before, we would not have been so self-aware. We would have accepted [...] felt ourselves to be more whole, more in tune with the land and the spirit of the earth. It would have been easier to accept, too, because [...] it would have been all so much poorer, so much closer to the Indian past [...] Now money had touched us all. (p. 384)

The allotment, then, such as Jack's garden or those on the Trinidadian roadside, serves as a corrective motif alongside the 'suburban houses, with gardens', although for this narrator, for the cosmopolitan novelist, it is an unlikely or unfeasible alternative to the globalised seductions enacted by money. Significantly, one report on the allotment movement of the 1970s in England noted:

> Too many people have a wrong impression about allotments. The movement is not wholly dependent for its well-being upon the encouragement given to it by government and local authorities […] Allotments had their origin in self-help (not charity), and even now the concept of self-help remains fundamental.[108]

The allotment will represent for this writer – and perhaps, his readers – the remnant of a ritual relation to the earth and a measure of self-sufficiency and independence, at 'home' and abroad. As such, it is to be incorporated as an 'idea' and a 'theme' into the 'suburban' novel (inevitable dwelling of a modern English 'fiction'), built as it is on the former 'estate' of the nineteenth-century genre. In formal terms, too, this innovative novel in five non-contiguous sections might best be seen as 'allotted' on a human scale rather than plotted on a grander, hegemonic one.

Leslie Marmon Silko: Hybridity/Homogeneity

In an interview conducted in the mid-1990s, the Native American writer, Leslie Marmon Silko, noted that she was presently at work on a novel about gardens but that it was turning out to be very different from what she had originally intended:

> I decided to write a novel about two women and their gardens and flowers. Absolutely no politics. But then I started to study the history of plants and where they came from. Oh my gosh! Right behind the conquistadoras came the plant collectors. So my new novel will focus on gardens and flowers but it turns out gardens are very political.[109]

---

108 From 'The Allotments Movement', *The Recreational Gardener*, Journal of the London Association of Recreational Gardeners, No. 14 (December 1977), cited in David Crouch and Colin Ward, *The Allotment: Its Landscape and Culture* (Nottingham: Five Leaves Publications, 1997 [1988]), p. 12 .

109 Thomas Irmer, 'An Interview with Leslie Marmon Silko', part 2, http://www.altx.com/interviews/silko2.html.

The book in question is *Gardens in the Dunes*, published in 1999. The novel is set in the 1890s, and does indeed, focus on gardens and flowers across America, to England and Italy, and back again. There are more women gardeners in the novel than the original two planned. Grandma Fleet (and her granddaughters, Sister Salt and Indigo, who learn from her), of the Sand Lizard clan, a near extinct people of tribes known collectively as Colorado River Tribes, garden in the arid dune-terraces near the border of what come to be the states California and Arizona. Hattie Palmer, is a young intellectual (or neurasthenic) white woman married to a plant collector and botanist, Edward; they have a large and somewhat disheveled garden, with abundant flowers and a glasshouse for specimens, in Riverside, California. A further woman character with an interest in gardens is Susan James, Edward's sister, who oversees her grand and ever-fashionable gardens in Oyster Bay, Long Island. Aunt Bronwyn, living in England near Bath, has a cloister-and-orchard garden, replete with 'all the plants introduced by the Romans and Normans […] plants from the Americas, Africa and Asia' (p. 246), and a herd of an ancient breed of white cows on a site saturated with traces of the Celts, Romans and early Christians. And there is her friend the *professoressa* Laura, in Lucca, Italy, with her extraordinary gardens devoted to 'old European artifacts', pagan madonnas and the hybridised black gladioli. There is also the Morman woman, Mrs Van Wagnen, a friend to Grandma Fleet, whose garden on the rich flood plains near Needles is full of hollyhocks, roses and marigolds as well as the plants grown on the dunes in very different conditions: apricots and peaches, amaranth, beans and squash – until her home is deliberately burned and destroyed. It is Indigo, the Sand Lizard child, who, having escaped from an Indian boarding school makes the journeys to all these gardens, returning eventually to her beloved gardens in the dunes – with a range of seeds collected throughout her travels. Indigo's 'Grand Tour' of the English and European gardens and sites that she visits, as she accompanies Hattie and Edward in their travels, is part of Silko's exploration of, not just women gardeners *per se*, but of the persistence of pre-Christian traditions in Christian countries and the ways in which these traditions compare with those belonging to Native Americans: 'I am not trying to say it is the same but, perhaps, there are some similarities of what happened' to European people once 'so close to the earth and the trees'.[110] However, the instruction given to Indigo and to the reader on traditional Southwestern Native methods of cultivation and of maintaining an interrelationship with the natural world is the most compelling and original aspect of the book. The late-nineteenth-century, a particularly traumatic time of devastating and long-term consequences for Native tribes and their cultures, is depicted in the novel from a late-twentieth-century perspective which deliberately aims to retrieve those formerly prohibited practices and lost histories of the previous century.

More familiarly, the novel also outlines Edward's expeditions plant-hunting in Honduras, Guatemala and Brazil, joining others 'who came by special request of the Department of Agriculture in cooperation with officials at the Kew Gardens', in an endeavour to corner world markets in rubber and other tropical commodities and

110 Ibid.

specimens. Edward's special interest is in rare species of orchids, the very plants often seen as sacred by the indigenous populations. He has money-making plans to collect – illegally – *Citrus medica* cuttings from Corsica, before going on to plunder a 'diamond-studded' meteor-crater back in Arizona. He is, typically, anxious to collect species previously 'undiscovered' (in the way that America was 'undiscovered' until Europeans claimed and named it) and to give his own name to them as a testament to his 'getting there first'. In terms of environmental and garden politics, Edward typifies the Western nineteenth-century capitalist and colonial attitude of mind where money and individual reputation matter more than any aspect of the natural world, whether human, animal, vegetable or mineral – all of which he is prepared to exploit even to the point of extinction. The natural world and gardens are for him a 'research laboratory'; his personal acquisitiveness is thus given a dispensation, and justified altruistically, as in the interests of the advancement of knowledge and the trophies of national competition.

Edward's sister, Susan – a who is *not* an exemplary woman gardener in this book's terms – is similar to her brother in that everything is deemed to be at the service of her whims, from the latest fashion in garden design to gala parties such as the extravagant Masque of the Blue Garden, in which the only thing that is celebrated is her ability to force the natural world to fit the vision that her wealth allows – or commands. The transplantation of huge copper beeches in the interests of a novel effect on a single night is one of her gardening feats:

> Her gardener had located two great copper beech trees at an old farm on the south shore, and now preparations were completed to move and transplant the beech trees together on the new hills. [...] wrapped in canvas and big chains on the flat wagon was a great tree lying helpless, its leaves shocked limp, followed by its companion; the stain of damp earth like dark blood seeped through the canvas. As the procession inched past, Indigo heard low creaks and groans – not sounds of the wagons but from the trees. (p.185)

Edward and Susan share a similar lack of respect for animals. Indigo's close companions are a monkey and a parrot, both imported from the tropics. The monkey, tellingly named Linnaeus by Edward, had been used by him in the forests of Brazil, trained to locate and fetch rare orchids from otherwise inaccessible treetops and cliffs; the parrot, Rainbow, nameless and neglected until Indigo adopts him, has threatened (by his sole survival) to spoil Susan's idea of a design; two were purchased to be 'handsome in that lovely gilded cage in the conservatory among the orchids', but when one died, the planned look was 'spoiled' (p. 189). Indigo's relationship with the two displaced creatures stands in the book as an exemplar not just of the treatment of animals, but more generally for respect given and responsibility taken.

It is Grandma Fleet who, following her own ancestors, views the entire natural world with reverence, and who instructs her grandchildren accordingly, particularly in relation to the land in which they live:

> Grandma Fleet told them the gardens had always been there. The old-time people found the gardens already growing, planted by the Sand Lizard, a relative of Grandfather Snake,

who invited his niece to settle there and cultivate her seeds. Sand Lizard warned her children to share: Don't be greedy. The first ripe fruit of each harvest belongs to the spirits of our beloved ancestors, who came to us as rain; the second ripe fruit should go to the birds and wild animals, in gratitude for their restraint in sparing the seeds and sprouts earlier in the season. Give the third ripe fruit to the bees, ants, mantises, and others who cared for the plants. A few choice pumpkins, squash and bean plants were simply left on the sand beneath the mother plants to shrivel dry and return to the earth. Next season, after the arrival of the rain, beans, squash, and pumpkins sprouted up between the dry stalks and leaves of the previous year. Old Sand Lizard insisted her garden be reseeded in that way because human beings are undependable; they might forget to plant at the right time, or they might not be alive next year. (pp. 16-17)

Whereas Edward and Susan have exploited animals for their own short-term ends, ultimately seeing them as expendable, the Sand Lizard clan and other peoples view their relationship with animals as interdependent. A clan 'is a social unit that is composed of families who share common ancestors [...] allied with certain, plants, animals or elements',[111] identified at the time of 'the Emergence' (when all life emerged from the four worlds below into this present Fifth World):[112]

The human beings depended upon the aid and charity of the animals. Only through interdependence could human beings survive. Families belonged to clans, and it was by clan that the human being joined with the animal and plant world. Life on the high, arid plateau became viable when the human beings were able to imagine themselves as sisters and brothers to the badger, antelope, clay, yucca, and sun. Not until they could find a viable relationship to the terrain – the physical landscape they found themselves in – could they *emerge*.[113]

Animals are there to be of help in times of hunger and hardship, such as when Indigo, Sister Salt and Grandma Fleet first return to the abandoned gardens following the arrests at the Ghost Dance ceremony, but this should not be taken for granted. Animals can be relied upon for assistance, but only if there is appropriate respect given and care taken in return; there is a measure of self-interest in this, for only if such respect is shown can people expect animals to survive or to remain to provide assistance on human beings' behalf. So, the seeds and fruits collected by a pack rat, for instance, are a 'gift' and must be recognised as such:

[Grandma Fleet] instructed them to be careful whenever they broke into the pack rat's nest to raid the stores of seeds and mesquite beans.
'Old Ratty does all the work for you, so don't harm her!' Grandma Fleet showed them how to close up the rat's nest after they took what they wanted. Years before, when the refugees flocked to the old gardens, hunger drove the people to eat the pack rats; but the

111 Leslie Marmon Silko, *Yellow Woman and a Beauty of the Spirit* (New York: Simon and Schuster, 1996), p. 203.
112 Ibid., p. 204.
113 Ibid., p. 38.

hunger was far worse afterward because there were no pack rats left to gather and store seeds. (p. 49)

Some Native tribes very deliberately used animals to help in tasks of cultivation: the Abenaki, for example, used squirrels to plant nut trees, by putting harvested butternuts or acorns out for the squirrels who would take and hide them: 'The squirrels become tree planters; they gather and bury the nuts in the ground for their food stores, but do not remember where all their seeds are buried'.[114] Respect for animals is also crucial when they are hunted and killed, as Silko explains in the essay, 'Interior and Exterior Landscapes: The Pueblo Migration Stories':

> The antelope merely consents to return home with the hunter. All phases of the hunt are conducted with love: the love the hunter and the people have for the Antelope People, and the love of the antelope who agree to give up their meat and blood so that human beings will not starve. Waste of meat or even the thoughtless handling of bones cooked bare will offend the antelope spirits. Next year the hunters will vainly search the dry plains for antelope. Thus, it is necessary to return carefully the bones and hair and the stalks and leaves to the earth, who first created them. The spirits remain close by. They do not leave us.[115]

Such ceremonies of thanks and giving gifts are also extended to plants, the soil, the rain or a spring, just as reverence is given to stones, rocks and meteor irons.[116] The usual Western apprehension of the Native relation to the natural world is one that is reductive and sentimental. For instance, in 1971, The Crying Indian (who was in fact played by an Italian actor) was widely used in an anti-pollution Public Service Announcement to 'Keep America Beautiful,' happily promoting the view of Indians as inherent environmentalists, taking care of and 'walking softly on the earth' (indeed, in *Gardens*, the Ghost Dancers ensure that they 'drag their feet lightly along the ground to keep themselves in touch with mother Earth' (p. 28)). However, when the West Coast Makah tribe sought to restore their ceremonial rites (and rights) to hunt whales, environmentalists were shocked and thoroughly affronted by native peoples who did not conform to their view of them.[117] They saw the killing of whales as utterly gratuitous and unnecessary in these days when other foods were readily available and survival was not in question. For the Makah Nation, whale-hunting provides something just as necessary as, though less tangible than, food, oil or bone: the spiritual, instructive and inter-relational aspect of a people to their location in the natural world. To those who have appropriated a distorted and romantic stereotype of soft-treading impassive Indians, this is a shock and a terrible sacrilege against the

---

114 Michael. J. Caduto and Joseph Bruchac, *Native American Gardening: Stories, Projects and Recipes for Families* (Golden, CO: Fulcrum, 1996), p. 5.

115 Silko, *Yellow Woman*, op. cit., p. 26-7.

116 See ibid., pp. 187-92.

117 See 'Natural Born Americans', *Secret Histories* (Channel 4, LION Television, 2000).

beautiful whale. The Native view of the natural world is simply not as Europeans have supposed it, whatever the agenda.

To garden in the arid dunes of the Southwest requires specialist knowledge, an intimate familiarity with the subtle diversity of the landscape, and deliberate and selective cultivation. Grandma Fleet remembers years of gardening at the dunes before being displaced by the influx of tribal refugees, themselves displaced from their own homelands by white westward migration. When they return to the gardens, she is able to pass on her own and the collective knowledge of the Sand Lizard ancestors. Terrain that is seen as featureless desert by anyone unfamiliar with it is for Grandma Fleet, with her intimate acquaintance, a rich and complex garden. She teaches her granddaughters to identify:

> differences in the moisture of the sand between the dunes [...] Grandma explained each of the dunes and the little valleys between them had different flows of runoff [...] explained which floodplain terraces were well-drained enough to grow sweet black corn and speckled beans. The squashes and melons were water lovers, so they had to be planted in the bowl-shaped area below the big dune where the runoff soaked deep into the sand. Wild gourds, sunflowers and datura seeded themselves wherever they found moisture. (p. 49)

Grandma is also a keen collector of seeds from wherever they are available – Indigo takes this practice to heart on her travels, remembering her grandmother's advice to collect (and exchange) as many seeds as possible, including those that were 'strange or unknown'. Whereas some tribes would only grow seeds that were food or medicine, 'Sand Lizards planted seeds to see what would come; Sand Lizards ate nearly everything anyway, and Grandma said they never found a plant they couldn't use for some purpose' (p. 86). Indeed, at the end of the novel, Indigo has introduced to the gardens in the dunes the vivid hybridised gladiolus, whose blooms present a beautiful planted pattern and glorious scent, but whose tubers she serves as a new vegetable: 'Those gladiolus weren't only beautiful; they were tasty!'

In the novel, the Sand Lizards are a depleted clan, but the tribe to which they belong is not specifically identified[118] – although a range of Southwestern tribes such as the Paiutes, Walapai, Havasupi Chemeheuvi, Mohave, Apaches and others are mentioned. The novel tells us that the Sand Lizards have been diminished through inter-tribal marriages and removal to reservations, such as the one at Parker. Established in 1865 as the Colorado Indian Reservation, it brought together and included members of such distinctive tribes as the Hopi, Navajo, Chemehuevi and Mohave. We also know from the novel that the gardens in the dunes are south of Needles, itself located on the Colorado River. A Works Progress Administration (WPA) Guide to 1930s Arizona describes the journey across the United States on

---

118 'During a recent reading, Silko revealed that she invented the Sand Lizard tribe to commemorate the hundreds of small tribes that were annihilated at that time', Karenne Wood, 'Review of *Gardens in the Dunes*', *American Indian Quarterly*, Vol. 23, No. 2 (1999) p. 71.

Route 66.[119] Here there is a description of the surviving members of the Hualpai (Walapai) tribe which is reminiscent in a number of respects of the Sand Lizards and the dune gardens as described in the novel. The Guide notes that some of the tribe's members live off the reservation, having as a group 'stubbornly resisted the white man's invasion' until in 1874 they were 'subdued and transported from their desert mountain home [...] to La Paz, in the Colorado Valley south of Parker, where they died by scores'.[120] The location is familiar, but the experience of the westward influx of the whites and the removal of Indians from their homelands in the course of establishing a cross-country railroad, prospecting and mining claims and policies with which to assimilate 'primitive' Natives into 'civilised' Christian culture, was common and widespread. The Battle of Wounded Knee, the Navajo Long Walk or the Cherokee Trail of Tears may be more familiar to the general reader than Wovoka's Ghost Dance (which directly contributed to the events that led to the tragedy at Wounded Knee) but all denote enforced migration and the decimation of many Native peoples. Further, there is a description in the WPA Guide of the wide desert mesas and giant buttes where the Hualpai reside. This passage is also revealing of a Western view of Indian methods of cultivation to which Silko is making a retort in this novel:

> They were never a large tribe [...] Unlike most Indians of the Southwest they developed little agriculture and lived on deer, antelope, mountain sheep, badgers, rabbits, porcupines, birds, many varieties of cacti, both fresh and dried, century plants, yuccas, pine nuts, mesquite beans, acorns and walnuts. [...]They also had wild berries, grapes, and wild tobacco. In their tiny gardens in the depths of canyons corn, beans, squash and melons, and a few peaches were grown.[121]

This may be 'little agriculture' in the sense that the scale is small, but the notion that this is un-cultivated land, unmanaged and simply fortuitous gleaning is all part of the condescension extended to Native cultures more generally. Indeed, at the time that Silko was beginning to draft her book on gardens (in which she hoped at first to escape politics), there was a resurgence of interest in Native plants and methods of cultivating, endorsed and supported by scientists and agro-economists. One of the best-known centres now devoted to the retrieval of both imperilled 'heirloom seeds' and methods of cultivation, Native Seeds/SEARCH, is located in Tucson, Arizona, where Leslie Marmon Silko also presently lives.

In the 'Foreword' to Gary Paul Nabhan's *Enduring Seeds: Native American Agriculture and Wild Plant Conservation*,[122] Wendell Berry remarked that in all the

---

119 'WPA Guide to Arizona, Route 66 Tour', originally published as *Arizona: A State Guide* in 1940, http://members.aol.com/hsauertieg/rt66/wpa_az.htm.
120 Ibid.
121 Ibid.
122 Gary Paul Nabhan, *Enduring Seeds: Native American Agriculture and Wild Plant Conservation* (Tucson: University of Arizona Press, 2002 [1989]).

representations of Indians that prevail, gardeners or cultivators is not often among them:

> Books and movies, radio and television have given us images in abundance of the Indian fighting and hunting and participating in various ceremonies, but few indeed of the Indian farming or gardening.[123]

Gary Nabhan, an ethno-biologist, co-founder of Native Seeds/SEARCH and Director of the Center for Sustainable Environments at Northern Arizona University in Flagstaff, is promoting investment in the conservation and appreciation of Native agriculture. This he and others see as practical and necessary rather than a project of whimsical patronage or a collection of folkloric curios. He refutes any criticism that this work is nostalgic or sentimental. Rather, it is powered on the one hand by 'a sincere and sensible interest in retaining and renovating nutritional, aesthetic, cultural, and ecological values embedded in the native agriculture and culinary traditions',[124] and on the other, by the need to safeguard against the drastic effects that may ensue from the unstinting application worldwide of predominant Western agricultural methods:

> Old grain and bean varieties grown by native farmers are the backup force required to stave off famine should calamity strike the fields where major varieties are grown in monocultures over thousands of contiguous acres […] For any future stability in the global food supply, diversity must be restored to all major food crops. In general, traditional Native American polycultures – several crops mixed in the same field – create greater habitat heterogeneity […] and reduce the probability of a population explosion by any single pest. The majority of indigenous farmers still practice such intercropping […][125]

Nabhan also discusses the various ways in which the West's albeit 'well-intentioned programs to supply hybrid seeds, farm machines, fertilisers, and pesticides to developing nations'[126] are not always appropriate to the recipients' circumstances or cultures. He notes cases where communities have at first welcomed the promise of higher and faster yields, only to return to their native crops, particularly for human consumption and traditional cuisines, on the grounds of lack of flavour or some other missing quality. For Native Americans, who now suffer the high incidence of diabetes and other dietary-related illness, to retain or restore these qualities may indeed afford a profoundly positive effect on health. Further, it has been found that on arid and sandy Southwestern terrain it is the native corn traditionally planted by the Hopi or Navajo 8-12 inches deep (20-30 cm), or the Tohono O'odham variety that grows close to the ground and conserves water by having a small amount of leaf and stalk,[127] that is the corn that *survives* the conditions in that location, regardless of any

---

123 Ibid., p. xiii.
124 Gary Paul Nabhan, *Cultures of Habitat*, op. cit., p. 221.
125 Ibid., p. 222-3.
126 Ibid., p. 217.
127 Michael. J. Caduto and Joseph Bruchac, op. cit., p. 74.

abstractly formulaic application of petro-chemical fertiliser or the latest agricultural technology. It is just such strains, however, that are in danger of being lost forever and just such strains that may be more appropriate for export to developing nations with similar climate or terrain.

The culture that supports mass production and the uniformity of crops, where consistent appearance on the supermarket shelf matters more than subtleties in flavour or other qualities, was also the culture that insisted that America's indigenous people lose their own diversity and distinctiveness. The 'Indian problem' was addressed variously throughout the eighteenth and nineteenth centuries, always with the underlying assumption that these were at any rate people destined to disappear – the 'vanishing Indian' syndrome. In Silko's novel, Edward displays something of this attitude when, upon meeting Indigo, the runaway from the Indian Boarding School to which she has been forcibly removed, he immediately assumes (accurately as it happens) that she must be 'the last remnant of tribe now extinct' (p. 113) but more to the point, he accepts such extinction as a given. The ethnological reports that Edward consults are no doubt those by the Bureau of American Ethnology (James Mooney, for example, was commissioned to write a report on the Ghost Dance movement in 1891). Several years later, Edward S. Curtis's photographic compendium, *The North American Indian*, provided similar extensive and worthy (but nonetheless interpretatively problematic) records of the very customs that were at the same time prohibited by law. The now infamous Dawes Act, also known as the Allotment Act, had devastating consequences for native culture (including agriculture) and was instrumental in ensuring that Indian-ness should vanish through assimilation into white cultural practice:

> Between 1887 and 1934, 60 percent of all tribal trust and treaty lands – some eighty million acres – passed out of Native American hands as a result of the Dawes Act, a bill designed to promote the assimilation of Indians into the dominant society. Between 1920 and 1982 the number of Indians owning, running, or working on farms in the United States dropped from 48,500 to 7,150 despite an overall increase in the Indian population. And as native farmers were forced or lured off the land, centuries-old traditions of planting their families' heirloom seed stocks came to an end.[128]

The Act, described by President Theodore Roosevelt as a 'mighty pulverising engine to break up the tribal mass',[129] promised Indians citizenship and a parcel of land once they had demonstrated their competence in 'civilised' ways. Once the parcels had been allocated to those who were deemed worthy, the remainder of reservation land was brought back into government hands. By 1891, the commissioner of Indian Affairs was able to report that more than twelve million acres – 11.5 percent of all reservation land – had been '"restored to the public domain" in just two years'.[130]

---

128 Ibid., p. 217.
129 James Wilson, *The Earth Shall Weep: A History of Native America* (London: Picador, 1998), p. 303.
130 Ibid., p. 304.

This is the very policy to which Silko refers in the novel, not by naming it as such, but by describing its inconsistencies and consequences:

> Years before the Mojaves and Chemehuevis were given tiny reservations along the river near Needles. The reservation at Parker held all the other Indians who used to live along the Colorado River before the white people came [...] White farmers claimed the best river bottom land. Along this stretch of the river not even the cottonwood trees or willows wanted to grow; the ground was hard-packed clay and old floodplain gravel. Only a small portion of the reservation land was fertile river bottom land, already allotted to regular churchgoers; all the others were left to grow what they could, on land that was too far from the river to irrigate and too parched by the sun to grow much [...] The people were not permitted to farm their traditional fields any longer, and without water nothing grew in the old floodplain gravel. A few old people tried in the beginning by carrying water on their backs uphill to their fields of corn and beans, until they were defeated by the evaporation and the heat. The alluvial plains above the river were only good for sagebrush and rabbits. (p. 206)

The severe depletion of land and the proscription of anything to do with 'Indian ways' has meant that not just heirloom stock but a whole spectrum of cultural practice and understanding has also been severely in danger of being lost. Specific ethnic and spiritual aspects were an integral part of the Native American cultivation of plants, and there is now a commitment from several quarters for this also to be retrieved along with the plants and seed stock. Thus it was that on the five hundredth anniversary of the 'discovery' of America by Christopher Columbus in 1492, a deliberately 'unassimilated' ceremony took place on 'Thanksgiving Day' amongst some of the tribes of the American Southwest:

> On Thanksgiving Day in 1992 – during the five hundredth anniversary of Spanish arrival in the Americas – children from Pima and Maricopa tribal communities in Arizona shared a special feast. They did not eat the foods shared between the Pilgrims and Native Americans. Instead, they ate what their ancestors had eaten before any European ever set his foot on the soil of the North American continent.
> Among the Native foods eaten that day were the drought hardy tepary bean, still a garden crop among the Pima; the flower buds of cholla cactus, a spiny plant grown prehistorically among the Pueblos; and the sweet flour of mesquite pods, from a bean tree that lines nearly every field of Native crops in the Southwest. Some of the foods had been harvested buy the schoolchildren over the previous few weeks. Others had been donated by Pima elders, some of whom still farm the way their grandparents had taught them at the turn of the century. Still others were gifts from Native Seeds/SEARCH, a crop conservation organization now directed by an O'odham man who is a relative of the Pima children. Whatever the immediate source of these foods was, the ultimate sources were the Earth itself, the ancient farming traditions of Native Americans and the circle of Life, which includes all plants and animals.[131]

---

131 Michael J. Caduto and Joseph Bruchac, op. cit., p. xi.

Whereas formerly the distinctiveness and diversity of native Americans themselves were to be homogenised as they were assimilated into the mould of white American standardisation, now theories of biodiversity are being acknowledged by various national institutions as progressive; 'the way forward' is seen to incorporate models that were once deemed so thoroughly backward. These days, when Gary Nabhan recounts a contemporary tale of the ways in which a dominant Western view of selection and standardisation can lead into traps of destructive pre-supposition, he speaks from and to a scientific community that has to admit its myopia and commit resources to addressing some of its oversights:

> On one occasion, I asked a Hopi woman at Moenkopi about seed selection for 'trueness to type'. I had heard that other people discard any unrepresentative seeds in order to maintain a semblance of purity within each seed-stock. I wondered if she regularly selected only the biggest kernels, or ones from one end of the cob, or those consistently of the same hue. The elderly woman listened to my loaded questions, then snapped back at me, 'It is not a good habit to be too picky ...We have been given this corn, small seeds, fat seeds, misshapen seeds, all of them. It would show that we are not thankful for what we have received if we plant certain of our seeds and not others.'
>
> Her acceptance of heterogeneity contrasts markedly with the prevailing assumptions of modern agriculture: uniform seed, for standardized field conditions. Fifteen years ago genetic resource scientist Jack Harlan warned that negative consequences of this obsession were already being manifested:
>
> 'A pure-line mentality, convinced that variation was bad, uniformity was good, and off-types in the field somehow immoral, developed ... Thus it was that we laid ourselves open to epiphytotics [plagues] of serious dimensions.' The pest and disease epidemics that sporadically plague modern farmers are most likely to occur where the environment is so uniform that the same seeds can be sown horizon to horizon.[132]

Native American gardeners certainly do not think of seeds or plants in the way that Westerners do; as Grandma Fleet's lessons explain, plants are beings to be treated with respect and nurtured 'as if they were babies', in the same way that animals, rocks and the earth itself require respect. Native Americans also developed systems of companion planting that were both practical and ceremonial (the two being indistinguishable). Again, without giving it a name as such, Silko describes the tradition of integrated planting – particularly of beans, corn and squash – that was widely known across a number of tribes in Native North America and is frequently referred to as Three Sisters Gardens, although 'the tradition of calling these crops the "Three Sisters" originated with the Haudenosaunee, the " People of the Longhouse," who are also known as the Iroquois'.[133] Traditional stories contain instructions which show that the three plants together aid and support one another (beans fix nitrogen in the soil and climb for support on the corn stalks; large squash leaves provide ground cover and shade) much as is described in *Gardens in the Dunes:* 'The pumpkins and squash sent out bright green runners with huge round leaves to shade the ground,

---

132 Gary Paul Nabhan, *Enduring Seeds*, op. cit., p. 76.
133 Michael J. Caduto and Joseph Bruchac, op. cit., p. 70.

while their wiry green-yellow tendrils attached themselves to nearby weed stalks [...] bush beans sprang up in the shade of the big pumpkin leaves' (p. 16). Native Americans were also skilled at cross-pollinating and hybridising plants. When such crops failed, the Sand Lizards adapted: 'For years of little rain, Sand Lizard gave them amaranth and sunflowers; for times of drought she gave them succulent little roots and stems rowing deep beneath the sand' (p. 17). As Indigo's introduction of the gladiolus shows, new plants were also welcomed. Thus the notion of a static or 'pure' tradition is not accurate nor was it ever desirable or insisted upon by Native communities themselves. In Silko's view, the respect for ethnicity and the necessity to be free to live according to ancient and sacred beliefs should not be misconstrued as a culture wanting to be a museum piece. Rather, it was Europeans that insisted on the 'boxes' and Europeans who asked for categorical distinctions:

> [...] while there may be a concept of the 'traditional Indian' [...] no such being has ever existed. All along there have been changes; for the ancient people any notions of 'tradition' necessarily included the notion of making do with whatever was available, of adaptation for survival. Human beings have lived along the San Jose River for more than twenty thousand years; the people hunted the great mammoths until they disappeared, and gradually as the great herds of elk and bison shifted north, the people took up the dry farming of corn and beans, and they domesticated turkeys. Life continually changes.[134]

What is crucial, however, is that the crisis that ensued for Native peoples 'when the United States government began to forcibly remove [their] children to distant boarding schools in the 1890s' needs to be healed and the people 'reunited with what continues and what has always continued'[135] in their relationship with the 'inviolable' landscape: Mother Earth.

Openness to new ideas and an interest in exchange and change is thus presented in the novel as integral to the Native view of life, one example being Grandma's seed exchanges and her adaptability, whether gardening on the dunes or weaving baskets in a shanty to sell in the railway terminus at Needles. Other instances of openness are the inclusiveness of the Ghost Dance in which Mormans take part, Sister Salt's African-American lover, Big Candy, and Indigo's journeys abroad and back again, carrying her collection of seeds. However, Indigo's visits and conversations with Aunt Bronwyn and Laura exemplify not only the principle of exchange but also a measure of commonality. Both Aunt Bronwyn and Laura incorporate pre-Christian and unorthodox Christian aspects into their gardens, just as Hattie's failed thesis on Gnosticism[136] and her interest in the mysteries of Illuminism, set her apart from the dominant Christian tenets of the time. One of the most obvious garden symbols in this regard is that of the snake or serpent and Silko sustains her attention to this

---

134 Silko, *Yellow Woman and a Beauty of the Spirit*, op. cit., p. 200.

135 Ibid., p. 178-9.

136 Silko acknowledges reading Elaine Pagels' *The Gnostic Gospels* while writing *Gardens in the Dunes* in Robert Cohen, 'An Interview with Leslie Marmon Silko', *Southwest American Literature*, Vol. XXIV, No. 2 (Spring 1999), p. 260.

across significant creature cultures. One of the reasons Hattie's thesis has outraged the theological academic community is its attention to the Gnostic view that the 'Female Spiritual Principle came in the Snake'(p. 102). There is also the carnelian carving from England of the Roman goddess, 'Minerva, seated with a serpent' and Laura's garden full of old European artifacts with statues of archaic snake-goddesses, including 'pictures and statues of the Blessed Virgin Mary standing on a snake. [...] based on a figure from earlier times.' (p. 306) Edward's view on this as they (he, Hattie, Indigo and Laura) tour the garden is that, as 'the child was from a culture of snake worshippers', that is, heathen, 'there was no sense confusing her with the impression the old Europeans were no better than red Indians or black Africans who prayed to snakes'(p. 304). Not surprisingly, in Edward's dualistic terms, the snake represents sin and evil. Similarly, for Edward the colour black is 'symbolic of night and death', whereas for Laura, following the 'Old Europeans, black was the color of fertility and birth, the color of the Great Mother' (p. 298). Back in the gardens in the dunes, a very real rattlesnake is reverenced: 'the spring belonged to him. All desert springs have resident snakes. If people killed the snakes, the precious water disappeared' (p. 38). By the time Indigo returns to the dunes, the snake has been killed by intruders: 'for no reason, they slaughtered the big old rattlesnake who lived there' (p. 478), but at the novel's ending there is another snake residing at the spring, 'Old Snake's beautiful daughter'. In Native Creation stories, female figures are revered as creators. In the Southwestern Pueblo Creation story, Tse'itsi'nako, Thought Woman, together with her sisters, thinks the world into being.[137] Native stories of Mother Earth, Corn Mother or Grandmother Spider all testify to the powerful creativity of the 'feminine principle' that intrigues Hattie, Bronwyn and Laura, coming from a *presently* patriarchal culture.

Leslie Marmon Silko's own ancestry is a mixture of Laguna, Mexican and white; born in Albuquerque, New Mexico in 1948, she grew up on the Laguna Pueblo reservation. About her mixed heritage but also her attachment to the Laguna Pueblo, Silko has written: 'I am of mixed-breed ancestry, but what I know is Laguna. This place I am from is everything I am as a writer and human being.[138] Her mixed background, however, placed her, literally, at the margins. On the reservation, her family was 'put' in a house down by the river and below the village itself. In Silko's own estimation, the enforced medial situation had its effects: 'I always thought there was something symbolic about that, sort of putting us on the fringe of things'.[139] (When tourists came by the Laguna school Silko attended, she was asked to step out of the picture: 'I looked different from my playmates. I was part white and he

137 Silko, *Yellow Woman and a Beauty of the Spirit*, op. cit., p. 27..

138 Silko in K. Rosen, *The Man to Send the Rain Clouds: Contemporary Stories by American Indians* (1974) cited in P. Seyersted, *Leslie Marmon Silko* (Boise, Idaho, Boise State University, 1980), p. 15.

139 Silko in 'A Conversation with Leslie Marmon Silko', *Sun Track: An American Indian Literary Magazine*, 3:1 (Fall 1976) cited in P. Seyersted, ibid., p. 13.

didn't want me to spoil his snapshot of '"Indians".')[140] However, Silko was also in a position to learn intimately and first-hand about two cultures and the nature of their conflicts:

> Because our family was such a mixture of Indian, Mexican and white, I was acutely aware of the inherent conflicts betweens Indian and white, old-time beliefs and Christianity. But from the start, I had no use for Christianity because the Christians made up such terrible lies about Indian people that it was clear to me they would lie about other matters also. My beloved Grandma A'Mooh was a devout Presbyterian, but I can remember, even as a little girl, listening to her reading from the Bible and thinking, 'I love her with all my heart, but I don't believe in the Bible.' I spent time with Aunt Susie and with Grandpa Hank, who was not a Christian. The mesas and hills loved me; the Bible meant punishment. Life at Laguna for me was a daily balancing act of Laguna beliefs and Laguna ways and the ways of the outsiders.[141]

Ideally placed to represent these two ways in her fiction she has found in the garden an apposite venue for their dramatisation. The snake in the garden is at once a creature representative of evil in one culture and sacred in another. Though not impartial, Silko was familiar with both views:

> The gentle giant, Quetzalcoatl, Divine Serpent of Feathers and Flowers, was savagely attacked by the European church and labeled Satan. But in the Americas and in Africa, the people loved and worshipped the gentle giant Damballah, or Quetzalcoatl, or Ma ah shra true ee, Divine Snake of the Beautiful Lake. Maybe the Old Testament garden of Eden story is the first strike by northern tribes against the religion of the Africans to the south and their worship of the great snake, Damballah. Those who loathe snakes have been brainwashed by the Old Testament. Even ordinary snakes are spirit messengers to the spirit beings and Mother earth.[142]

Silko has written powerfully about the great serpent, Ma Ah Shra True Ee, in an essay entitled: 'Fifth World: The Return of Ma Ah Shra True Ee, the Giant Serpent' (where she also describes, and includes a photograph of , the large mural of the snake she painted on a wall in downtown Tucson in the 1980s.) The essay explains the extraordinary way in which a massive stone formation in the figure of a huge snake appeared suddenly one day in ravaged landscape. It was first discovered by two workers on the site of the Jackpile uranium mines:

> The head of the snake was pointed west, its jaws wide open. The stone snake seemed to have always been there. The entire formation was more that thirty feet long and twelve inches high, an eccentric outcrop of yellow sandstone mottled and peppered with darker iron ores, like the stone that had once formed the mesas that had been swallowed up by the open-pit mine.[143]

---

140 Silko, *Yellow Woman and a Beauty of the Spirit*, p. 63.
141 Ibid., p. 17.
142 Ibid., p. 117.
143 Ibid., p. 126.

The manner in which the uranium mines were established on the Pueblo (meaning community or people), and in which they desolated gardens similar to those in the novel, some fifty years after the novel's setting and some fifty years before its publication, reveals the continued persistence of the negation of Native rights:

> Before the days of the mining companies, the people of Paguate village had fields of corn and melon and beans scattered throughout the little flood plains below the yellow sandstone mesas southeast of the village. Apple and apricot orchards flourished there too. It was all dry farming in those days, dependent on prayers and ceremonies to call in the rain clouds [...]. When large uranium deposits were discovered only a few miles southeast of Paguate village in the late 1940s, the Laguna Pueblo elders declared the earth was the sacred mother of all living things, and blasting her open to reach deposits of uranium ore was an act almost beyond imagination. But the advent of the Cold War had made the mining a matter of national security, and the ore deposits at the Jackpile mine were vast and rich. As wards of the federal government, the small Pueblo tribe could not prevent the mining of their land. Now, the orchards and fields of melons are gone. Nearly all the land to the east and south of Paguate village has been swallowed by the mine; its open pit gapes within two hundred yards of the village.
>
> Before the world uranium prices fell, the mining companies had proposed relocating the entire village to a new site a few miles away because the richest ore deposits lay directly under the old village. The Paguate people refused to trade their old houses for new all-electric ones; they were bound to refuse, because there is a small mossy spring that bubbles out of the base of a black lava formation on the west side of Paguate village. This spring is the Emergence Place, the entrance humans and animals used when they first climbed into this, the Fifth World. But the mining companies were not to be stopped; when they couldn't move the people, they simply sank shafts under the village.[144]

For Silko, the sacred snake's emergence is 'magical' but not so surprising since it represents something 'in keeping with Pueblo cosmology': here is 'a sacred messenger' returning from the Earth, 'in spite of everything'.

If the representation of Edward in *Gardens in the Dunes* seems to be rather programmatic and stereotypical, the context must be the persistence of such acts of desecration and highhandedness as at the Jackpile mines. Indeed, one can read how the three mountain peaks now known as the San Francisco Peaks, held sacred by no less than thirteen tribes in the Southwest (known to the Navajo, for example, as Doko'oosliid or Shining on Top), were in the nineteenth century named Humphreys, Agassiz and Fremont respectively in honour of: a surveyor for the railroad to the Pacific and Army commander; a 'geologist and zoologist noted for his classification of marine fossils and theory of the glacial epoch'; the 'governor of Arizona territory (1878-82).'[145] In 2004, these same peaks were the subject of a campaign against US Forest Service plans for a ski-resort expansion on them with recycled wastewater

144 Ibid., pp. 127-8.
145 'WPA Guide to Arizona', op. cit., http://www.members.aol.com/hsauertieg/rt66/wpa_az.htm.

effluent to be used for snowmaking. This is in contradiction of the principles of an earlier proposal by the Department of the Interior to buy out and cease the pumice mining operation on the Peaks 'for reasons including the ongoing desecration of Native American Sacred Lands'.[146] Edward's proclivities to name, own, plunder and lie may seem less stilted in the light of such an ongoing record.

In other respects, the novel can also appear rather programmatic and it has been criticised for its 'agendas' or for being 'awkwardly overplotted.'[147] For gardeners or botanists familiar with England, for instance, there may be some consternation when reading of Hattie's delight in the beauty and floral bounty of the countryside near Bath: 'little clumps of periwinkles, wild pinks, and marshmallows grew above the riverbank. All along the edge of the road foxgloves and primroses stood tall, with wild buttercups and white daisies scattered all around' is by no means an accurate portrayal in terms of the flowering calendar or of botanical detail. (This may in part be the oversight of someone used to the coincidence of all or many flowers blooming together in the desert's short season). One critic, however, remarks tellingly that while the novel 'may frustrate readers accustomed to plots revolving around the inner conflict of a single protagonist', it 'is more in the folk tale tradition'.[148] While Silko's novel can be seen to conform less to the nineteenth-century English novel it at first appears to emulate – and leads the reader to expect – its 'folk tale' quality is more in line with traditional Native modes of storytelling. Paula Gunn Allen, a Native writer (also from Laguna) and academic who has who has written extensively on Native cosmologies and literary theory, discusses the themes integral to 'the old narrative cycle of the Pueblo peoples', which are 'traditionally divided into three sections: creation, emergence and migration'.[149] Using Gunn Allen's description, one can see the way in which Silko's novel conforms to the tradition: the dunes and gardens have been created, the Sand Lizards people emerge forming a profound relationship to the place of their emergence (denoted not least by its sacred spring and snake), and they migrate, with Indigo travelling furthest:

> In the beginning was Thought, and she was Grandmother; the people emerged into the fourth world guided and led by our dear mother, beautiful Corn Woman; under the continued guidance of Thought Grandmother, we migrated from wherever we were to our present homelands [...] and our thought migrated over the globe [...][150]

---

146 Biodiversity Activist: Action Alert, campaign launched 8 April 2004, http://www. actionnetwork.org/BIODIVERSITY/alert-description.tcl?alert_id=2410797.

147 Selected Reviews for *Gardens in the Dunes*, http://www.literati.net/Silko/ SilkoReviews.htm.

148 Tayari Jones, '*Gardens in the Dunes* – Book Review', *The Progressive* (February 2000), http://www.findartices.com/p/articles/mi_m1295/is_2_64/ai_59270836.

149 Paula Gunn Allen, *Off the Reservation: Reflections on Boundary-Busting, Border-Crossing, Loose Canons* (Boston, MA: Beacon Press, 1998), p. 13.

150 Ibid.

Beyond these categories, explains Silko, 'the Pueblo oral tradition knew no boundaries' and 'whatever happened, the ancient people instinctively sorted events and details into a loose narrative structure'.[151] Notably, one reviewer, Karenne Wood, in *American Indian Quarterly* is fulsome in her praise, asserting on behalf of Native readers that:

> Silko leads us back to what we have always known but have perhaps forgotten: that redemption lies within us, within the wisdom that those who preceded us compiled and lovingly left for us. The voice of this wisdom, she affirms, is one that will never be silenced and cannot be taken away.[152]

When Silko explains that 'Pueblo narratives are not mere bedtime stories or light entertainment',[153] and that 'even the most ordinary deer-hunting story is dense with information, from stalking techniques to weather forecasting and the correct rituals to be performed in honor of the dead deer',[154] it is clear that *Gardens in the Dunes* is not what novel readers are accustomed to. This is a novel *story* – rather than a novel as such – with a traditional storytelling framework and ceremonial impetus that may not be recognised by many readers. Speaking from and to both cultural traditions with which she is familiar Silko writes a tribute to the 'geospiritual space of the Southwest'[155] and a testament to its various cross-cultural fertilisations. More importantly, this is storytelling about Native gardens and gardening, 'dense with information' and the 'correct rituals to be performed' in their honour.

* * * *

The gardens presented here are, if not set in postcolonial landscapes, then certainly represented through the lens of a postcolonial world. Each of the protagonists tries to recuperate or discover something of the garden in the pre-colonial landscape and modes of its cultivation. Thus Michael K returns to cultivate and reconnect with the natal earth; the writer in Naipaul's *The Enigma of Arrival* searches to find models of sanctity in relation to gardening and to being in the landscape; Morrrison attends to the rituals and 'discredited knowledge' of the ancestors; and Silko recounts the imperative ceremonies of inter-relationship with the natural world. However, as the epigraph by Gary Nabhan at this chapter's beginning shows, contemporary 'globalisation' and the predominance of technology does not stop for rituals of diversity and the regional or ethnic specificities of cultivation. Colonisation – this time by trademark and branding – has not been halted. Indeed, in the view of Indian

---

151 Silko, *Yellow Woman and a Beauty of the Spirit*, op. cit., p. 31.
152 K. Wood, op. cit., p. 72.
153 Ibid., p. 178.
154 Ibid.
155 P. Gunn Allen, op. cit., p. 231.

writer and activist Arundhati Roy, speaking in 2004, 'New Imperialism is already upon us. It's a remodelled streamlined version of what we once knew.'[156]

In the 1980s, the Slow Food Movement, (with its own logo – a snail), was first established in Italy in protest against yet another McDonald's restaurant in its global empire and its aim to establish 'one world, one taste'. The Slow Food Movement, 'an eco-gastronomic organization, dedicated to preserving food and food traditions from soil all the way to the table'[157] aims to ensure cultural and biological diversity and defends the amount of time – and money – it may take to meet these aims. As Michael Pollan explains:

> This emphasis on celebration and connoisseurship has left Slow Food open to charges of elitism, but the organization has worked hard to reach beyond the affluent foodie crowd. Slow Food USA has launched a garden project for public schools, and a great many of the foods it has championed in the United States are distinctly populist and often cheap [...] 'To me, Slow Food is spending a few quarters on a Spitzenberg apple instead of a Red Delicious,' says Patrick Martins, the energetic young director of Slow Food USA. [...] Sure, fast food is going to be 'cheaper' than slow food, but only because the real costs of the industrial food chain – to the health of the environment, the consumer, and the worker – never get counted.[158]

Which brings us back to the apple: the diversity of apple varieties is diminishing drastically. However, apples, like many other crops, have now become widely available across the world and throughout all seasons. Crops grown on a massive scale and destined for far-flung parts of the globe must be harvested before they are ripe, refrigerated, and treated with ethylene gas at the appropriate time to trigger the ripening process, at the expense of flavour and requiring a good deal of non-biodegradable packaging.

Celebrity branding and selective product branding have also become promotional features in many supermarkets: one apple variety, Pink Lady, has been particularly successful. Pink Lady needs a relatively hot climate, so in Britain, for instance, it must always be imported at the expense of many other locally grown and seasonally-specific varieties. Advertising campaigns for Pink Lady apples have included slogans such as: 'The Apple for Lovers' or 'The Apple of Temptation' and promotions that use 'the Barbie Doll [...] thereby increasing the sale of that variety to young girls by a whopping 300 per cent'.[159] It goes without saying how monoculturally oriented

156 Arundhati Roy, 'The New American Century' (January 2004), http://www.thenation.com/doc.mhtml?i=20040209&s=roy.

157 Rebecca Tuhus-DuBrow, 'Talking about Slow Food: An Interview with Patrick Martins', (1 June 2004), http://www.thenation.com/doc.mhtml?i=20040614&s=tuhusdubro

158 Michael Pollan, 'Cruising on the ark of taste: by pursuing the politics of pleasure, the Slow Food movement hopes to save rare species and delectables – and give the considered life a second chance', *Mother Jones* (May-June 2003), http://www.findarticles.com/p/articles/mi_m1329/is_3_28/ai_100879493.

159 'Beckham banana, anyone?', Food and Drink Europe.com (28 July 2004), http://www.foodanddrinkeurope.com/new/printnews-NG.asp?id=53837.

– from apples to Barbie – these 'pink lady' campaigns are, and how incongruous in relation to the postcolonial texts considered in this chapter.

Biotechnology and genetic modification is also a controversial but ubiquitous aspect of world food production; now trademarked strains of fruit and vegetables can be modified to ensure keeping qualities in transit or on the supermarket shelf. Or, you might find your essential vitamin and enzymes transferred from one organism to another, such as Omega 3 taken from 'smelly' marine sources and transferred innocuously into soya and rape products. Your daily apple might be 'a nutraceutical food system': 'TreeTop Inc. have developed a "low moisture, naturally sweetened apple piece infused with red-wine extract"' to provide in several bites the amount of cancer-fighting flavonoid phenols available in several glasses of wine.[160]

The various debates, some of long-standing and others more recent, about what is 'natural' and 'real' in the garden – as in the wider world – have come to a new pitch. There is, however, no going back to an age of innocence – but are a cellophane-packaged apple named Pink Lady and a Barbie doll the only way forward? Is a cyber garden necessarily fast food or slow – and how many ways does a cyber garden grow?

---

160 'Michael Pollan, 'The Futures of Food', *New York Times Magazine* (4 May 2003), http://www.mindfully,org /Food/2003.Futures-Of-Food4mayo3.htm.

Chapter 4

How Does Your Cyber Garden Grow?

Michael Pollan recently wrote: 'When I was a kid growing up in the early 60s, anybody could have told you exactly what the future of food was going to look like'[1] and the conventional vegetable plot, allotment or mixed farm was not in the picture. Instead, inspired by the 'postwar glamour' of technology, the space programme and cybernetics – 'the branch of science concerned with control systems and comparisons between man-made and biological systems'[2] – Americans, in particular, were fascinated by a 'synthetic food future', a 'meal in a pill', clean, convenient, efficient and abstract from any 'readily identifiable plant and animal species':

> The general consensus seemed to be that 'food' – a word that was beginning to sound old-fashioned – was destined to break its surly bonds to Nature, float free of agriculture and hitch its future to Technology. If not literally served in a pill, the meal of the future would be fabricated 'in the laboratory out of a wide variety of materials' […] including not only algae and soybeans but also petrochemicals.[3]

Although twenty-first-century views on food are more diverse and complicated than those widely-projected in the 1950s and 1960s, what is consistent is that the food most people consume has indeed broken 'its surly bonds to Nature'. Whether bought 'fresh' from the supermarket shelf (a recent food article talked about 'jet-lagged produce') or purchased as pre-prepared or ready-made meals, the 'natural' aspects of food are not evident – although slogans such as 'natural goodness' or 'nature's best' are often called upon. Branded products, genetically modified foods, high-level residues of fungicides, pesticides, preservatives, antibiotics, hormones, flavour enhancers and other additives, presented in non-biodegradable packaging and plastics that are themselves not inert, but contaminate foodstuffs – all have generated a range of responses. These include dramatically increased demand for organically grown produce, calls for explicit labelling, and campaigns such as the international Slow Food Movement, initiated with a demonstration objecting to McDonalds setting up yet another of its 'fast food' outlets under the now globally signifying yellow arches, this time on the ancient Spanish steps in Rome.[4] However, there is also now an exuberant view which sees food-stuffs as the conveying medium

---

1   M. Pollan, 'The Futures of Food', op. cit.

2   *Collins Concise Dictionary* (Glasgow: HarperCollins, 1999), p. 358.

3   Pollan, ' The Futures of Food', op. cit.

4   Carlo Petrini, *Slow Food: The Case for Taste* (New York & Chichester, W. Sussex: Columbia University Press, 2001), p. 8.

of enhanced 'super-foods' or 'nutraceuticals', by which the human body can dose itself with its 'minimum daily requirements' of vitamins, minerals and other extracts, not necessarily normally found in the carrier-host, without having to take the time, or risk an unwanted increase in body weight, eating the vast quantity of diverse food-stuffs otherwise necessary to fulfil recommended daily requirements[5] – thus, the concentrated potency of 'pills-in-a meal' as opposed to the 1960s version, meal-in-a pill.[6] Further, the depletion of the qualities of foodstuffs (through intensive growing conditions, packaging, processing, transportation, the duration between harvest and ingestion) means that either greater quantities will need to be eaten, or supplements will be necessary, for the minimum to be assured. To inject or genetically modify foodstuffs with the desired attributes is seemingly expeditiously to address several dietary issues at once. The Slow Food Movement, on the other hand, recuperates 'the quiet material pleasure' of eating local, fresh and regional cuisines and is dedicated to 'the case for taste' and sensual enjoyment as a defence against the 'contagion' of frenzy which calls itself efficiency and that 'insidious virus: Fast Life'. The Official Slow Food Manifesto, approved at its founding conference in Paris in 1989, contains in its first principles the opposition to a civilisation that 'first invented the machine and then took it as its life model'.[7] The symbol of the Slow Food Movement is a snail, a far cry from the techno and cyberspace dreams of computerised – everything. However, long before globalisation, branding and genetic modification became familiar, writers of science fiction, in particular, were projecting both the tantalising and the dangerous aspects of a brave new world dominated by such technology.

In 1951, the British writer John Wyndham published a book about killer garden plants, which seek to overthrow the hitherto dominating humans that once cultivated them and commodified their valuable by-products. Triffids, as they became well-known to both a reading public and a cinema audience after the film in 1962, constituted a horrific biological inversion: vegetables with intelligence; plants with malice; competitors with the advantage. Once the human population has been rendered sightless, ostensibly by a meteor shower, (although before this, the triffids have been doing their utmost to attack humans' 'unprotected parts', especially the eyes), the communicative, mobile plants are rendered superior. As one of the scientists in the book explains:

> Granted that they do have intelligence; then that would leave us with only one important superiority – sight. We can see, and they can't. Take away our vision and our superiority is gone. Worse than that – our position becomes inferior to theirs because they are adapted to a sightless existence, and we are not.[8]

---

5   Pollan, op. cit.
6   Ibid.
7   Ibid., p. xxiv.
8   John Wyndham, *The Day of the Triffids* (Harmondsworth: Penguin, 1954 [1951]), p. 47.

The film, which has a modified storyline, nonetheless had a poster tag that emphasised the unnaturalness of these plants' behaviour: 'Beware the triffids … they grow … know …walk … talk … stalk … and kill'. Doubly horrific is the fact that the plants have attributes which are both human and inhuman at once. The humans who cultivated the unearthly triffids once they appeared on the Earth, their seeds having been dispersed after a plane crash, treat them at first as plantation material, suitable for large-scale and intensive cultivation in the pursuit of profitable quantities of their oil: 'triffids moved into big business overnight'. Once the triffids reveal themselves to be mobile, they are corralled like cattle in stockades and, later still, tethered and chained like dogs – or like prisoners and slaves. It might be conjectured that it is against this 'inhumanity' that the triffids revolt, but they have been malevolent and violent from the start. The origin of the killer plants, 'vegetables on vacation', 'monsters on the march', is mysterious and unknown, albeit implicated in covert Cold-War-inflected dealings and double-dealings and dubious genetic experimentation. Circling in the earth's atmosphere there are not only 'satellites with atomic heads', but 'others with such things as crop diseases, cattle diseases, radioactive dusts, viruses and infections […] recently thought up in laboratories' (pp. 28-9). The shower of comets which blinds so many of the populace and the ensuing plague are, in the view of the hero, Bill Masen, too-readily attributed to an act of Nature or God. Rather, in his view, it is 'the tightrope' created by science that is to blame – and one or more of the volatile satellites which have caused the world to 'come off it':

> up there, there were – and maybe still are – unknown numbers of satellite weapons circling round and round the Earth. Just a lot of dormant menaces, touring around, waiting for someone, or something, to set them off. What was in them? […] Top secret stuff. All we've heard is guesses – fissile materials, radio-active dusts, bacteria, viruses … Now suppose that one type happened to have been constructed especially to emit radiations that our eyes would not stand – […] all the things up there were diabolical … (p. 247).

The book was written in the context of the height of the Cold War and the development of nuclear weapons and was published in the same year that the Rosenbergs were tried for espionage and treason in America. As science fiction, however, it is a cautionary tale of a world set, not in some far-fetched future, but in a setting and with circumstances largely already realised. Ambulatory carnivorous plants were the stuff of fiction still, but the fear of genetic mutation, ecological imbalance and galactic chaos seemed an all too real and present threat. The most distressing distortion was that what was 'natural' would be rendered horrifically unnatural by the extremes of scientific intervention, competition and experiment.

Another well-known apocalyptic science fiction is Philip K. Dick's novel *Do Androids Dream of Electric Sheep?*, published in 1968 but set in the twenty-first century. It provided the inspiration for the even better-known film, *Blade Runner* (1982). As in *The Day of the Triffids*, the modern sophistications of weaponry and war have wreaked genetic havoc and the extinction of a range of species. World War Terminus has rendered the earth a barren, radioactive-contaminated wasteland. Most people have emigrated to new colonies on Mars in a UN-endorsed colonisation programme exploiting the 'ultimate incentive of emigration: the android servant as a carrot, the radioactive fallout as a stick' (p. 15). What remains on earth, whether human or animal or vegetation, is virtually indistinguishable in terms of being real or artificial. Androids – for the most part 'escaped humanoid robots' who have killed or overthrown their masters – replicate humans in almost every detail; lack of empathy is their only betraying feature and this flaw is to be corrected in future models. Artificial animals are also so 'perfectly working' that mechanical failure becomes indistinguishable from organic disease. Many species, owls first, have been entirely destroyed by the contamination so that any real animal is extremely rare and has the highest value – and some become sanctified. In terms of status, to acquire and display a real animal is the highest achievement. For those who haven't quite made the grade, a mechanical model in a simulated 'natural setting' must suffice. Rick Deckard's sheep is electric, 'tethered on the false covered roof pasture, and a parody of a pastoral idyll':

> Whereon it, sophisticated piece of hardware that it was, chomped away in simulated contentment, bamboozling the older tenants of the building.
>
> Of course, some of their animals undoubtedly consisted of electronic circuitry fakes, too; he had of course never nosed into the matter, any more than they, his neighbours had pried into the real workings of his sheep. Nothing could be more impolite. To say, 'Is your sheep genuine?' would be a worse breach of manners than to enquire whether a citizen's teeth, hair, or internal organs would test out authentic.
>
> The morning air, spilling over with radioactive motes, gray and sun-beclouding, belched about him, haunting his nose. (p. 7)

Rick's extravagant but seemingly well-considered purchase of a real Black Nubian goat ('a goat isn't bothered by contaminated quasi-foodstuffs') ends in disaster when the Nexus-6 android, Rachael, retaliates against Rick, 'the bounty hunter for "andys"', by throwing his real animal off the top of the building on which it has lived, caged. John Isidore, a human 'special' with distorted genes who drives an animal repair truck under the auspices of an animal hospital ambulance, is unable to tell whether the cat he collects is mechanical or living. His assumption is that the cat is so thoroughly real-seeming that it must be a fake – ('the whole thing appeared – not broken – but organically ill') – is wrong. However, 'the fakes are beginning to be darn near real, what with those disease circuits they're building into the new ones' (p. 67). The human replicants that Deckard is employed to 'retire' are also increasingly sophisticated, mass produced models programmed beyond the convincing 'transistorised circuits' of false animals, synthetic 'organic entities,' but as yet without the benefit of biological 'cell replacement'. Rachael Rosen fails the tell-tale empathy test that Deckard routinely administers, but she displays love, jealousy, fear, anger, hope, self-reflexivity and a reluctance to cease being, perhaps with 'an android reason', programmed to emulate, persuade and outwit. Deckard himself looks more like a machine, with his genitals guarded against the radioactive contaminated dust by the 'Mountibank Lead Codpiece' so that he can continue as a 'regular', 'a man who could reproduce within the tolerances set by law' (p. 8), although, sleeping with one of the 'new, extra clever andys' with their 'Nexus-6 brain unit' renders that particular biological concern redundant. Furthermore, the act constitutes 'a violation of a statute', for 'copulation with an android' is 'absolutely against the law', both on earth and in the colonies. Rachael and Deckard celebrate their liaison with extremely rare and expensive bourbon which is 'not synthetic; it's from before the war, made from genuine mash' (p. 159). Post-war, synthetic food stuffs are all that is generally available; 'the garden had perished during the war' (p. 186). The real must be faked, and the fake made to seem real. The real thus becomes extremely valuable on the basis of scarcity, but the sophisticated simulations so convincingly mimic the real that the distinctions become arbitrary and meaningless. The theology of the time, Mercerism, which is based on the simulated communications of Wilbur Mercer through an empathy box, or mood organ, is also implicated in this conundrum. The real and the fake, the self and the other, become indistinguishable and the distinction increasingly irrelevant: they are, like Deckard with Mercer, inextricably 'fused'.

These are the cyborgs of science fiction, and, increasingly, of 'social reality', as Donna Haraway explained in her well-known and frequently anthologised 'A Cyborg Manifesto', first published in 1985:

> A Cyborg is a cybernetic organism, a hybrid of machine and organism, a creature of social reality as well as a creature of fiction. Social reality is lived social relations, our most important critical construction, a world-changing fiction [...] the boundary between science fiction and social reality is an optical illusion. [...] Contemporary science fiction is full of cyborgs – creatures simultaneously animal and machine, who populate worlds ambiguously natural and crafted. Modern medicine is also full of cyborgs [...][9]

The cyborg-focussed science fictions are often cautionary tales, even while being celebratory flights of fantasy. Science fiction conventionally projects its focus into a far-away future, imagining the presently inconceivable. However, the gap between the fictive speculations and already realised or realisable scientific projects has, since the 1950s, been closing. As Hari Kunzru explains, the developments of the space program and its Cold War context introduced cyborgs as both the stuff of entertainment and an embedded facet of 'social reality':

> Cyborg. The word has a whiff of the implausible about it that leads many people to discount it as mere fantasy. Yet cyborgs, real ones, have been among us for almost 50 years. The world's first cyborg was a white lab rat, part of an experimental program at New York's Rockland State Hospital in the late 1950s. The rat had implanted in its body a tiny osmotic pump that injected precisely controlled doses of chemicals, altering various of its physiological parameters. It was part animal, part machine.
>
> The Rockland rat is one of the stars of a paper called 'Cyborgs and Space', written by Manfred Clynes and Nathan Kline in 1960. This engineer/psychiatrist double act invented the term 'cyborg' (short for 'cybernetic organism') to describe the vision of an 'augmented

---

9   Donna J. Haraway, *Simians, Cyborgs and Women: The Reinvention of Nature* (London: Free Association Books, 1991), pp. 149-50.

man', better adapted than ordinary humans to the rigors of space travel. Clynes and Kline imagined a future astronaut whose heart would be controlled by injections of amphetamines and whose lungs would be replaced by a nuclear powered 'inverse fuel cell'.[10]

'Augmented man' is not just the material of fantastic heroes and heroines, supermen and bionic women, but each and every one of us in the westernised world. Heart pacemakers (the first of which was successfully implanted in 1958) are easily seen as 'cyborg' augmentations, but Haraway discusses the ways in which our lived existence is now dependent on computerised systems and technological advancements dedicated to guiding individuals on their 'reconstruction', from exercise regimes with computerised high-tech equipment, the customised gear, specialised footwear, plugged-in headset, high energy, supplement-boosted drink ('the interaction of medicine, diet, training practices, clothing and equipment manufacture, visualisation and timekeeping')[11] to the now increasingly common cosmetic surgery, or something less radical but just as 'scientific': pills, potions, cosmetics, lotions, bleaches, dyes, whiteners, bronzers, silicone, collagen and so on and on. 'By the late twentieth century, our time, a mythic time, we are all chimeras, theorized and fabricated hybrids of machine and organism; in short, we are cyborgs.'[12] For Haraway, however, this prevailing sense of tampering with and improving 'nature' is not to be lamented; she is not someone who longs to recuperate the 'natural' in the ways that, for instance, some eco-feminists do. Citing Susan Griffin, Audre Lorde and Adrienne Rich as examples she explains that their insistence on the natural is stuck in the very binary thinking (man/woman; strong/weak; right/wrong; logic/emotion; culture/nature) to which they in large part object:

> They insist on the organic, opposing it to the technological. But their symbolic systems and the related positions of ecofeminism and feminist paganism, replete with organicisms [...]would simply bewilder anyone not preoccupied with the machines and consciousness of late capitalism.[13]

This is the context for Haraway's oft-cited, controversial claim: 'I'd rather be a cyborg than a goddess'. The goddess, although pagan rather than Judeo-Christian, still works with the paradigms of purity, nature and innocence. However, the cyborg, Haraway claims, 'is not innocent; it was not born in a garden; it does not seek unitary identity and so generate antagonistic dualism without end (or until the world ends).'[14] *This* is the apocalyptic vision, and in Haraway's terms it is with 'technoscience' that

---

10   Hari Kunzru, 'You Are Cyborg' (February 1997), http://www.wired.com/wired/archives/5.02/ffharaway-pr.html.

11   D. J. Haraway cited, ibid.

12   D. J. Haraway, op. cit., p. 150.

13   Ibid., p. 174.

14   Ibid., p. 180.

regeneration lies: 'technoscience is a form of life, a practice, a culture, a generative matrix' with its 'dense nodes of human and non-human actors'.[15]

For Haraway, 'the Garden' is bound up in the Western mythologising which she sees as counterproductive, static and ultimately, unrealistic. With this in mind, she develops a polemical and ultra-democratic view of a 'cyborg world [...] in which people are not afraid of their joint kinship with animals and machines, not afraid of permanently partial identities and contradictory standpoints'.[16] By this, the false consolations of Western myths will be subverted:

> Unlike the hopes of Frankenstein's monster, the cyborg does not expect its father to save it through a restoration of the garden, that is, through the fabrication of a heterosexual mate, through its completion in a finished whole, a city and a cosmos. The cyborg does not dream of community on the model of the organic family, this time without the oedipal project. The cyborg would not recognize the Garden of Eden; it is not made of mud and cannot dream of returning to dust [...] Cyborgs are not reverent; they do not re-member the cosmos. They are wary of holism, but needy for connection [...] The main trouble with cyborgs, of course, is that they are the illegitimate offspring of militarism and patriarchal capitalism, not to mention state socialism.[17]

Haraway is delighted with cyborgs for their potential to deconstruct and reconstruct categories that have hitherto been presented as natural, normal or inevitable. The Garden, as we have seen, has frequently provided the tropes for these categories even though, in many cases, societal models inflected the coding and decoding of the garden rather than the other way round. In truth, the garden has been the place of the most intensive experimentation – and it continues to be so. It is one thing, then, for Haraway to celebrate the cyborg who does not 'long to get back to the garden' and who, in its 'ontology', problematises the myths pertaining to it and another when she welcomes, for instance, the food products of genetic engineering, which will not only represent another chimerical crossed boundary but will constitute the cyborg's cyber-diet. Haraway, for instance, celebrates the transgenic Flavr Savr Tomato with its flounder gene:

> Food crops are perhaps the most lively area of transgenic research worldwide in the 1990s. In late 1991, federal agencies had applications for field testing about twenty transgenic food crops. [...] I find myself especially drawn by such engaging new beings as the tomato with a gene from the cold-sea-bottom-living flounder, which codes for a protein that slows freezing, and the potato with a gene from the giant silk moth, which increases disease resistance. DNA Plant technology, Oakland, California, started testing the tomato-fish antifreeze combination in 1991.[18]

---

15   Donna J. Haraway, *Modest_Witness@Second_Millennium.FemaleMan©_meets_ OncoMouse™: Feminism and Technoscience* (New York & London: Routledge, 1997), p. 50.

16   D. J. Haraway, *Simians, Cyborgs and Women*, op. cit., p. 154.

17   Ibid., p. 151.

18   D. J. Haraway, *Modest_Witness*, op. cit. (1997), p. 88.

In Haraway's view, the objections to such 'transgenic border crossings' are revealing of more concerns than those pertaining to safe, suspect or super-charged consumables entering the chain formerly seen as purely for food. Rather, she finds that these bio-technological interventions are suggestive of other miscegenations, such as those along racial lines or between species in a Western society that has celebrated secure boundaries between self and Other, nature and artificial, 'divine creation and human engineering':

> I cannot help but hear in the biotechnology debates the unintended tones of fear of the alien and suspicion of the mixed. In the appeal to intrinsic natures, I hear mystification of kind and purity akin to the doctrines of white racial hegemony and U.S. national integrity and purpose […][19]

However, what is celebrated in theory (such challenges to those sanctities that have been 'at the heart of the great narratives of salvation history') is less palatable in practice; it is quite another challenge to ingest something whose aspects may have a very personal effect. When Michael Pollan planted in his garden a variety of potato called 'NewLeaf', a Monsanto corporation variety which had been genetically engineered to produce its own insecticide, he did so on the basis of a gardener's interest in experimentation ('the garden has always been a place to experiment, to try out new hybrids and mutations.')[20] When it came to eating a potato with a bacterial toxin permeating its every cell ('every leaf, stem, flower, root, and – this is the unsettling part – every spud'), however, he was less enthusiastic. An interest in new forms is tempered by fearful speculations on unleashed effects, 'unimagined new complexities' and, unwitting but unmanageable monstrosities where, triffid-like, there may be no going back.

While the fictional triffid or the already realised, genetically modified and design-patented plants such as NewLeaf are one model of chimerical, cyber-horticulture, the other model is of plants obliterated and extinct, as in *Do Androids Dream of Electric Sheep*? The radioactive contamination after World War Terminus was drastic and obvious in its consequences. In Don DeLillo's fiction of 1984, *White Noise*, something much more insidious and protracted is engendered by an 'air borne toxic event'. The poisonous cloud which appears in the sky to hover over the suburbs and city is made up of residual toxins, 'packed with chlorides, benzenes, phenols, hydrocarbons, or whatever the precise toxic content', which would 'seep into the genes, show itself in bodies not yet born'.[21]

> Nyodene D. is a whole bunch of things thrown together that are byproducts of the manufacture of insecticide. The original stuff kills roaches, the byproducts kill everything left over. […] no one seems to know exactly what it causes in humans or in the offspring of humans. […] Once it seeps into the soil, it has a life-span of forty years. (p. 131)

---

19   Ibid., p. 61.
20   M. Pollan, *The Botany of Desire*, p. 200.
21   Don DeLillo, *White Noise* (London: Picador, 1986 [1984]), p. 116.

Just as John Wyndham's character, Bill Masen, comes to understand that the common attribution of the comet shower as an 'act of nature' is a false and consoling denial of the real man-made causes of such catastrophic phenomena, so too DeLillo's Jack Gladney ascertains the combination of human hubris and helplessness that both creates and is overwhelmed by these technologically induced environmental effects. Here we have the postmodern Un-Natural Sublime, still 'rich in romantic imagery' with the toxic cloud's 'enormous black mass' and the 'unbearably beautiful sunsets' which have occurred since the 'air borne toxic event':

> Our fear was accompanied by a sense of awe that bordered on the religious. It is surely possible to be awed by the thing that threatens your life, to see it as a cosmic force, so much larger than yourself, more powerful, created by elemental and willful rhythms. This was a death made in the laboratory, defined and measurable, but we thought of it at the time in a simple and primitive way, as some seasonal perversity of the earth like a flood or a tornado, something not subject to control. Our helplessness did not seem compatible with the idea of a man-made event. (pp. 127-8)

Of course, one technologically-induced 'event' has to be countered and contained by others, but in *White Noise* the high-tech containment strategy is described using metaphors of plants and predators: the plan is to 'plant' microorganisms into the toxic cloud's core. These cloud-eating microbes, which were 'genetic recombinations that had a built-in appetite for the particular toxic agents in Nyodene', will disperse the black cloud which at present 'looks rooted to the spot' in the sky above. Jack's colleague Murray sums up the ironic and dual aspect that is 'the whole point about technology'; the technology that renders humans resilient, with their cyborg-augmentations, as Donna Haraway put it, may also be the technology that renders them extinct:

> This is the whole point about technology. It creates an appetite for immortality on the one hand. It threatens universal extinction on the other. Technology is lust removed from nature. [...] It's what we invented to conceal the terrible secret of our decaying bodies. But it's also life, isn't it? It prolongs life, it provides new organs for those that wear out. New devices, new techniques every day. Lasers, masers, ultrasound.[22]

Jack's view of the repercussions of an air borne toxic event is a consumerist mantra: 'everything would be fine, would continue to be fine, would eventually get even better as long as the supermarket did not slip' (p. 170), while not apprehending that concealed behind the simulated perfections of the supermarket shelf, where 'everything seemed to be in season, sprayed, burnished, bright', are contaminations and distortions and toxicities related to the imminent air borne toxic event and other 'events' even more insidious. Similarly, the clinic, Autumn Harvest Farms, that Jack attends for his contamination tests shares the same kind of benign façade as the supermarket:

---

22   D. J. Haraway, 'The Cyborg Manifesto', *Simians, Cyborgs and Women*, op. cit., p. 285.

> Why would such a place be called Autumn Harvest Farms? Was this an attempt to balance the heartlessness of their gleaming precision equipment? Would a quaint name fool us into thinking we live in pre-cancerous times? What kind of condition might we expect to have diagnosed in a facility called Autumn Harvest Farms? (p. 275)

Beyond the organic reference in the name, however, are all the techno-scientific medical accoutrements, computers, scanners, electrodes, monitors and consoles that render patients cyborg. When Jack protests that 'all the gleaming devices' could make a healthy person feel ill by 'just taking all these tests', the doctor responds:

> These are the most accurate test devices anywhere. We have sophisticated computers to anlayze the data. This equipment saves lives [...] We have equipment that works better than the latest X-ray or CAT scanner. We see more deeply, more accurately. (p. 277)

The technology that the doctor believes saves so many lives is the same technology that afflicts those lives with toxins, genetic instability, the 'intelligence and adaptability of the modern virus' and the 'nebulous mass' of cancers. The technology that 'sees more deeply, more accurately' at this sub-atomic level is the technology that cannot fully see or predict the consequences of its experiments. For Autumn Harvest Farms to be the name of this facility is, however, to reveal the deliberate masquerade that technology adopts. Technology does not, it seems, want to abolish the 'natural', the organic or the pastoral touchstones of a now outmoded former age, but rather to simulate them. The originals may be lost but they do not disappear. Species that are 'really' extinct are convincingly reproduced; concepts that are anachronistic, such as 'Autumn Harvest Farms', still have their consoling or inspiring currency. Technology invests in the ability to detect, counter-attack, or belie its own drastic effects rather than to attend to or halt the causes.

In William Gibson's *Virtual Light* (1993), for instance, all the palm trees in the Northern Californian location have been killed by 'the virus'. A company called A-LIFE INSTALLATIONS, NANOTRONIC VEGETATION provides the simulated plastic version of the now eradicated organic species. These are in great demand: 'the replacements were so popular now, people wanted to put them in everywhere' (p. 50). Crews 'plant' the fake trees in their concrete foundations, but the aim is to make every artificial detail as accurate and convincing as the former real ones: 'these new trees were designed so that all kinds of birds and rats and things could nest in them, just like the real ones that had died' (p. 273). Such replications, however, belie any real sense of the loss of originals; nothing is particularly lamented. The killer virus is as much a given as the technological accuracy of the victim's simulated presence. The distinctions between the referent real objects and their simulated representations become irrelevant. It is the simulations that prevail, eclipsing rather than referring to their originals – a condition that Jean Baudrillard, philosopher and theorist of the postmodern, terms the 'hyperreality of simulacra'. As a 'hallucination of the real, the lived, the everyday' this world has been:

reconstituted, sometimes even unto its most disconcertingly unusual details, recreated like an animal park or a botanical garden, presented with transparent precision, but totally lacking substance, having been derealized and hyperrrealized.[23]

The palm trees in *Virtual Light* are thus similar to the artificial replacements in *Do Androids Dream of Electric Sheep?*, although there is a difference in the imagined projections of each novel. In Philip K. Dick's science-fiction tale of the 1960s, the fictional future is still fantastic, still largely alien. William Gibson's new-millennial world set in 2005, imagined in 1993, is already familiar. As Baudrillard says, 'there is no more fiction' in science fiction. In an essay published in 1991, 'Simulacra and Science Fiction', he outlined three orders of simulacra, before considering their relation to science fiction:

1. Natural, naturalistic simulacra: based on image, imitation and counterfeiting. They are harmonious, optimistic, and aim at the reconstitution, or the ideal institution, of a nature in God's image.
2. Productive, productionist simulacra: based on energy and force, materialized by the machine and the entire system of production. Their aim is Promethean: world-wide application, continuous expansion, liberation of indeterminate energy (desire is part of the utopias belonging to this order of simulacra).
3. Simulation simulacra: based on information, the model, cybernetic play. Their aim is maximum operationality, hyperreality, total control.[24]

The first category, he says, projects a utopian, transcendent world where 'the separation from the real world is maximal'. The second category pertains to science fiction 'in the strict sense', where it is 'most often, an extravagant *projection* of, but qualitatively different from, the real world of production'. 'In the limited universe of the pre-Industrial era, utopias counterposed an ideal alternative world', explains Baudrillard, not citing examples although Thomas More's *Utopia* (1516) or Francis Bacon's *New Atlantis* (1626) would perhaps be the exemplars he had in mind. Science fiction, from Mary Shelley to John Wyndham, expands on the 'world's own possibilities' and includes as one of its themes the delicate dividing line between human audacity (and hubris) and promethean or apollonian inventiveness: 'In the potentially limitless universe of the production era, SF *adds* by multiplying the world's own possibilities.' The third category, however, is that of cyber-fiction where, as with the hyperreality it depicts, no gap exists between real and imaginary worlds:

Currently, from one order of simulacra to the next, we are witnessing the reduction and absorption of this distance, of this separation which permits a space for ideal or critical

---

23 Jean Baudrillard, 'Simulacra and Science Fiction', *Science Fiction Studies*, Vol. 18, No. 55, Part 3 (November 1991), http://www.depauw.edu/sfs/backissues/55/baudrillard55art.htm.

24 Ibid.

projection [...] Models no longer constitute an imaginary domain with reference to the real; they are, themselves, an apprehension of the real, and thus leave no room for any fictional extrapolation – they are immanent, and therefore leave no room for any kind of transcendentalism. The stage is now set for simulation, in the cybernetic sense of the word – that is to say, for all kinds of manipulation of these models (hypothetical scenarios, the creation of simulated situations, etc), but now nothing distinguishes this management-manipulation from the real itself: there is no more fiction.[25]

However, despite the 'reduction and absorption' of referential distance, there are in these cyber-fictions the persistent vestiges of the 'natural', organic, or botanical, usually by analogy or metaphor. Often, it is the dislocations and ironies that are most obvious as in 'Autumn Harvest Farms', the high-tech clinic in *White Noise*. In *Virtual Light*, there is a similar misnomer: The stolen virtual-reality sunglasses ('got these little EMP-drivers around the lenses, work your optic nerves direct') contain the secret planning data of a company known as SUNFLOWER, which, while it frequently deploys the verb 'to grow', is nothing like its botanical precursor: 'these towers blooming, there, buildings bigger than anything, a stone regular grid of them [...] each one maybe four blocks at the base, rising straight and featureless' (p. 133); 'these things that kind of grew, but only because they were made up of all these little tiny machines' (p. 273). Even the air above becomes branded space with writing that filled the sky: SUNFLOWER CORPORATION. The CORPORATION has well-defined, albeit secret, plans to cultivate its dominance:

> They're going to rebuild San Francisco. From the ground up, basically. Like they're doing in Tokyo . They'll start by laying a grid of seventeen complexes into the existing infrastructure. Eighty-story office/residential, retail/residence in the base. Completely self-sufficient. Variable-pitch parabolic reflectors, steam generators. New buildings [...] they'll eat their own sewage [...] the buildings. They're going to grow them [...] Like they're doing now in Tokyo. (p. 230) [my emphasis]

In contrast to the corporation-controlled Sunflower towers is the Bridge. Once San Francisco's Golden Gate, it has now, after a desolating earthquake, been reclaimed by a variety of displaced and dispossessed people, an alternative community and a celebratory but adventitious bricolage of cultures: 'none of it done to any plan [...] Not like a mall, where they plug a business into a slot and wait to see whether it works or not' (pp. 162-3):

> The integrity of its span was rigorous as the modern program itself, yet around this had grown another reality, intent upon its own agenda. This had occurred piecemeal, to no set plan, employing every imaginable technique and material. The result was something amorphous, startlingly organic [...] Its steel bones, its stranded tendons, were lost within an accretion of dreams. (p. 58)
>
> This place had just grown, it looked like, one thing patched onto the next, until the whole span was wrapped in this formless mass of stuff, and no two pieces of it matched.

---

25   Ibid.

[...] they looked to be as mixed a bunch as their building materials: all ages, races, colors [...] (p. 163)

The Bridge is a 'patchwork carnival of scavenged surfaces' (including the 'wingless carcass of a 747' which now housed 'the kitchens of nine Thai restaurants') and it possesses a 'queer medieval energy' without having abandoned all the features of a technological modernity. This, however, is a space outside the Corporate plot.

William Gibson is best known for his novel of 1984, *Neuromancer*, a text for which he is often credited with being 'the father of cyperpunk' (although the term itself was not invented by Gibson).[26] *Neuromancer* focuses on a world dominated by computers, world-wide information systems and other information technologies which have been hijacked, hacked into or otherwise deployed by a range of contesting users, from individual 'punk' hackers to mega-corporations. Cyberpunk fiction's relation to information technologies is at once celebratory and subversive; while its depictions are dystopian, it is not technology as such that is being questioned, but rather its control by powerful and corrupt totalitarian interests, like the fictionalised SUNFLOWER CORPORATION in *Virtual Light*. The community on the Bridge anticipates elements of the anti-globalisation protests that became increasingly commonplace throughout the 1990s, with, amongst other agendas, a view to reclaiming the streets and public spaces form corporate colonisation:

> It is one of the ironies of our age that now, when the street has become the hottest commodity in advertising culture, street culture itself is under siege. From New York to Vancouver to London, police crackdowns on graffiti, postering, panhandling, sidewalk art, squeegee kids, community gardening and food vendors are rapidly criminalizing everything that is truly street-level in the life of a city [...] A common theme began to emerge among these struggling countercultures: the right to uncolonized space – for homes, for trees, for gathering, for dancing. What sprang out of these cultural collisions among deejays, anti-corporate activists, political and New Age artists and radical ecologists may well be the most vibrant and fastest-growing political movement since Paris '68: Reclaim the Streets (RTS).[27]

Chevette, the bike-courier in *Virtual Light*, is typical of the person who is both daily aided by technology but also disenfranchised by it because of its domination by corporate interests. Her bike is high-tech, but her own physical efforts and indeterminate choices are also required: in her work, she is the Harawayan cyborg, machine and body combined:

> The bike between her legs she was [...] a sweet and intricate bone-machine, grown Lexan-armored tires, near frictionless bearings, and gas filled shocks. She was entirely part of the city then, one wild-ass dot of energy and matter, and she made her thousand

---

26   Apparently first coined in 1980 by Bruce Bethke who published his short story, 'Cyberpunk' in 1983 in *Amazing Science Fiction Stories*, Vol. 57, No. 4 (November 1983), http://www.en.wikipedia.org/wiki/Cyberpunk.

27   N. Klein, *No Logo*, op. cit., pp. 311-12.

choices, instant to instant, according to how the traffic flowed, how rain glinted […] how
a secretary's mahogany hair fell […] (p. 111).

In a networked world where every site was 'electronically coterminous' with
'distances obliterated by the seamless and instantaneous nature of communication',
Chevette is hired to deliver physical mail by her own physical efforts because of
the electronic system's 'porosity' ('your memo was nowhere, perhaps everywhere,
in that instant of transit'): 'she provided a degree of absolute security in the fluid
universe of data. With your memo in the girl's bag, you knew precisely where it
was' (p. 85). Chevette's job – and her body – has 'reclaimed the street', transforming
the sterility of the controlled space into something more serendipitous and free.
Chevette and the community on the Bridge, of which she has become a part, are
in direct contrast to the corporate planning, whereupon, as one Reclaim the Streets
manifesto explained:

> Everywhere becomes the same as everywhere else. Community becomes commodity
> – a shopping village, sedated and under constant surveillance. The desire for community
> is then fulfilled elsewhere, through spectacle, sold to us in simulated form. A TV soap
> 'street' or 'square' mimicking the area that concrete and capitalism are destroying. The
> real street in this scenario, is sterile. A place to move through not to be in.[28]

Interestingly, metaphors of organicism are applied to both the high-tech corporate
manifestations of a city – SUNFLOWER'S towers or the Autumn Harvest Farms
clinic – and to the counter-cultural agglomerations such as the Bridge. In the fictional
space of *Virtual Light* SUNFLOWER COPORATION aims to 'grow' buildings just
as in the contemporary world of corporate biotechnology, 'the world's crop plants
are being redesigned'. Monsanto, a company reminiscent of the SUNFLOWER
CORPORATION, that has 'only two or three competitors in the world', not only
redesigns plants but also patents and privatises any plant that bears, deliberately or
adventitiously introduced, Monsanto genetic material:

> The marker gene can also serve as a kind of DNA fingerprint, allowing Monsanto to
> identify its plants and their descendents long after they've left the lab. By performing a
> simple test on any potato leaf in my garden, a Monsanto agent can prove whether or not
> the plant is the company's intellectual property.[29]

As Michael Pollan goes on to note: 'whatever else it is, genetic engineering is also a
powerful technique for transforming plants into private property, by giving every one
of them what amounts to its own Universal Product Code'.[30] Plants (and seeds) have
always been seen as one of the most democratising aspects in the world, despite some
of the power plays dramatised in horticultural history; new technologies promised
the same wide enfranchisement. However, with the corporate biotechnology,

---

28 London RTS 'Agitprop' cited in Klein, ibid., p. 323.
29 M. Pollan, *The Botany of Desire*, op. cit., p. 223.
30 Ibid.

the ancient logic of the seed – to freely make more of itself ad infinitum, to serve as both food and the means of making more food in the future – has yielded to the modern logic of capitalism. Now viable seeds will come not from plants but from corporations.[31]

In horticultural terms, the SUNFLOWER CORPORATION would be represented by or representative of a highly systemic monoculture whereas the Bridge would be correlative with bio-diversity. As Michael Pollan notes along these lines, there is a 'whole other meaning of the word monoculture':

> Like the agricultural practice that goes by that name, this one too – the monoculture of global taste – is about uniformity and control. Indeed, the monocultures of the field and the monocultures of our global economy nourish each other in crucial ways. The two are complexly intertwined expressions of the same Apollonian desire, our impulse, I mean, to elevate the universal over the particular or local, the abstract over the concrete, the ideal over the real, the made over the natural. The spirit of Apollo celebrates 'the One,' Plutarch wrote, 'denying the many and abjuring multiplicity.' [...] Apollo is the god, then, of monoculture, whether of plants or of people.[32]

Pollan's reference in 2001 to the sun god of monoculture coincidentally lends further signifying force to the name of the SUNFLOWER CORPORATION in Gibson's novel of 1993.

One of the challenges in a cyber-world is not always being able to tell the difference between, say, a Monsanto NewLeaf and an organically grown species of potato or between an android and a human – a favourite in science fiction, but also now a common place experience; familiarly, in *Virtual Light* a flight reservation is confirmed on the phone by 'someone', 'either a woman or a machine' (p. 4). Donna Haraway celebrates the cyborg and is suspicious of those who resort to notions of purity, nature and categorically separate entities. Michael Pollan, not nearly as sanguine, nonetheless goes so far as to say:

> One way to look at genetic engineering is that it allows a larger portion of human culture and intelligence to be incorporated into the plants themselves. From this perspective my NewLeafs are just plain smarter than the rest of my potatoes. The others will depend on my knowledge and experience when the Colorado beetle strikes. The NewLeafs, already knowing what I know about bugs and Bt, will take care of themselves. So while my genetically engineered plants might at first seem like alien beings, that's not quite right; they're more like us than other plants because there's more of us in them.[33]

'All the more reason not to want to eat them', is also a plausible reply, not because the categories plant/human have been melded, but because the bug-combating toxins imbue every plant-cell; and this, for many, is more than distasteful: it is dangerous – and not just for bugs. Toxins, too, tend not to be respecters of boundaries between

31 Ibid., p. 249.
32 Ibid., pp. 245-6.
33 Ibid.,p. 213.

species and kind; what is toxic for one may be toxic for all. Genetic modifications have unknown consequences, but they may well result in unimagined distortions that include the dark side of species-crossing. However, one of the arrogant assumptions of technological sophistication is that competent 'fixing' is a better approach than cautious prevention. If, like the palm trees eradicated by virus or the species made extinct by radioactivity, humans are made ill or obsolete by disease and contamination, then technology can simply simulate a convincing replica of the original (already far from 'natural'). Rather than invest to preserve, new technology's investment is in extensions with the confident expectation that technology will meet its 'bridges' when it comes to them.

In Brian Aldiss's 'Supertoys Last all Summer Long', first published in 1969 and incorporated into Stephen Spielberg's 2001 film, *AI*, holographic projections provide 'the friendly illusion of gardens set in eternal summer' that belie the desolations of a real world:

> The Swintons lived in one of the ritziest city-blocks. Embedded in other apartments, their apartment had no windows on to the outside; nobody wanted to see the overcrowded external world [...] It was amazing what Whologram could do to create huge mirages in small spaces. Behind its roses and wisteria stood their house; the deception was complete: a Georgian mansion appeared to welcome him.[34]

The loneliness and isolation of over-population is remedied by an intelligent ('in a controlled amount') synthetic life-form serving-man who 'will always answer'. David, the android child who is a surrogate until Monica and Henry win the parenthood lottery (a government policy of population control) and can conceive a 'real' child, loves the mother who cannot be loving to him, knowing what he is. In this and the two related stories, 'Supertoys when Winter Comes' and 'Supertoys in Other Seasons', two related stories from the same collection, it is clear that it is the humans who are most inhuman, controlling their ravaged world – including themselves – to the last florid detail. This includes maintaining a standard of beauty by being implanted with a synthetic, nanobiological control, 'a perfectly safe parasitic worm', the Crosswell Tape, so that it is possible for a human (as long as it is a human who doesn't live where 'three quarters of our overcrowded world are starving') to eat 'up to fifty per cent more food and still keep his or her figure'. The only 'authentic' thing in the stories is the emotion felt by the android child, who, coached by his mechanical Teddy to believe 'nobody knows what "real" really means' nonetheless begins to understand that the root of his rejection by his mother is because he is an android, even though she becomes emotionally attached to the 'serving man'. The roses, whose 'beauty and softness' remind David of Mummy are, in 'Supertoys Last all Summer Long', holographic fakes of perfection. In 'Supertoys When Winter Comes', the entire hologram collapses as the control centre of the house goes down,

---

34 Aldiss, Brian, *Supertoys Last All Summer Long and Other Stories of Future Time* (London: Orbit, 1969), p. 9.

and the 'world is slimy underfoot' and full of acrid smoke, but David plucks a single rosebud from the 'sickly rose growing by a crumbling brick wall': 'Its beauty and softness once more reminded him of Mummy […] Mummy, I love you and I feel sad just like real people' (p. 22). What David the android thinks of as real and what his human parents think of as real, including their 'unnatural,' alienated and dubiously programmed selves, is the irony of the tale. David's humanity lies in his ability to move from the perfect simulacrum to the tattered real, and to identify its value – imperfections notwithstanding. Above all, however, is the message: as long as Apollonian technology can 'fix it' with a new model, another façade, and sustain a simulated hyperreality, then everything in the garden will <u>look</u> perfectly rosy …

Chapter 5

Coevolutionary Histories – the Poetics of a Paradox

The fundamental premise of this book has been that gardens signify, but the diversity of the ways in which they do so, particularly in modern or contemporary narratives, is not always obvious. Rather, ' the garden', a most familiar topic and trope, is so ubiquitous and over-determined that it also becomes overlooked in any detail. It is used – and read – variously as a shorthand term, or metonym, for: Nature, Eden, Paradise, beauty, leisure, pleasure, harmony and health, and is apprehended more generally, simply as consolatory. Others, however, have seen that to depict or to read the garden in this way is both facile, and as this book has shown, often indefensible. As the well-known poem by Rudyard Kipling, with which this volume opened, puts it 'the Glory of the Garden lies in more than meets the eye'. In the poem Kipling outlined the labour required behind the scenes to maintain the beautiful easeful façade of the upper-middle-class Victorian English Garden in its heyday. The Glory of the Garden was also a monument to the glory of Empire, of Englishness, of religious Anglicanism, of a consensual hierarchy where everyone, at home and abroad, knew their place. Despite the implicit work ethic 'Our England is a garden, and such gardens are not made/ By singing: – "Oh, how beautiful! And sitting in the shade"',[1] this is Eden by proxy. The present book, however, investigates how literature engages with 'the Glory of the Garden' once the Victorian certainties have been eroded or replaced. The concept of the 'Glory of the Garden' was political, of course, and, in narrative terms, carefully plotted ideologically. After 'the Fall' of Victorian certainties, and after the 'monumental' narratives of Victorian realist fictions, come the various responses: modernist short fictions; postmodern pastiche and parody; postcolonial 'writing back' to the Metropolis; cyber-cultural simulacra. *All* of these responses share and endorse Kipling's notion that there's more to a garden than at first perceived, but the meaning and emphasis is very different, as has been discussed.

The garden as a trope, as a metaphor or metonym, is difficult to dislocate. Contemporary garden designers also find that the garden is the most conventional of spaces in design terms, as Guy Cooper and Gordon Taylor note: 'Even the most design-conscious people seem to lose their sense of the contemporary in the garden'

---

1   Rudyard Kipling 'The Glory of the Garden', *Kipling's Verse* (London: Hodder and Stoughton, 1948 [1912]), p. 733.

reverting, beyond the garden door, 'to a much more conventional historical solution'.[2] They also cite Topher Delaney, 'a brilliant American designer of leading edge private gardens in California' who says that '75 per cent of her clients would still opt for a traditional layout, as "daring to want a truly contemporary design would be to most clients like cross-dressing in the front yard".'[3] They refer, too, to the creation of a new magazine, in the service of disrupting garden norms. The journal *New Eden*, launched in 1999, albeit with a persistently troped-title which belies the sense of anything radically new, nonetheless stated that it aimed to 'challenge the idea that gardens can only be nostalgic, with billowing borders and acres of lawn. We want to show you that modern gardens suit modern life-styles.'[4] Contemporary Landscape Architect and Harvard Professor of Design, George Hargreaves, goes further:

> I dislike the drive towards everything to do with metaphors and art meanings. Well, you know, a row of trees being simply a row of trees, they don't have to represent the essence of life or some grounding in nineteenth-century or twentieth-century thought, they can simply be a row of trees. [...] They don't have to be skewed into metaphors, they don't have to have a purpose as, or be in something else, they can simply be themselves, a row of trees; it has taken me 20 years to get to that.[5]

Perhaps George Hargreaves is better placed than most to see things for what they are when the site on which they stand is one that constitutes 'his average brief': 'Garbage 60 ft (18 m) deep on landfill or post-industrial sites for eventual public use is where we are most often asked to design, not on idyllic, green-valley sites for corporate villas'.[6] The difficulties of shifting the propensity for re-presenting meaning experienced by the garden designer are, of course, akin to those experienced by the writer – and the reader. Gardens without metaphors, metaphors divorced from gardens, present a fundamental challenge. As Jamaica Kincaid acknowledges, Eden is 'The Garden' to which we all refer, whether we know it or not .'[7] However, the original Eden was the gift of an inscrutable Creator, whereas those who labour to recreate it cannot fill the gap between being (only) and wanting (more). It is this gap that generates the pressure to represent meaning.

However, as 'new Edens' are imagined – or even deconstructed – it is timely to remember that the trouble with Eden is that it did/will not satisfy. Eden was not the place now nostalgically posited as perfectly fulfilled. As Kincaid, a little facetiously, explains: 'The world as we know it, after all, began in a very good

---

2   Cooper, Guy and Taylor, Gordon, *Gardens for the Future: Gestures Against the Wild* (London: Conran Octopus, 2000), p. 13.

3   Ibid., p. 14.

4   Ibid.

5   Ibid., p. 216.

6   Ibid., p. 190. The authors note that this was divulged by Hargreaves: 'In a brilliant and mind-opening lecture on the contemporary landscape given at the Royal Institute of British Architects, London, in November 1993.'

7   J. Kincaid, *Among Flowers: A Walk in the Himalayas* (Washington, D.C.: National Geographic, 2005), p. 189.

garden, a completely satisfying garden – Paradise – but after a while the owner and its occupants wanted more.'[8] Perhaps it is this very aspect of wanting more that really typifies the garden: more knowledge (like Eve), more plants, more colour, more choice, more control, more selection, more seclusion and so on and on. The desire for more is precisely what expelled man and woman from the garden in the first place; wanting more in the pursuit of gardens and landscapes we call 'Edenic' is a fundamental paradox. Desire for more is what drove Eden's original occupants out (<u>the</u> Story); desire for more is what continues to drive history. Humankind will not abandon quests for knowledge (and history) and yet will not abandon the trope of innocent perfection (the Story). Our very gardens – garden design in general – reflects and encompasses precisely this tension, exemplified, for instance, by the almost oxymoronic naming of the journal *New Eden* or, on a different scale, The Eden Project in Cornwall, England. To bring the concept of new knowledge to that of reinstating Eden is itself problematic; this is where the trouble began and yet, it seems, neither concept can be abandoned.

Of late, however, writers on topics botanical and horticultural, and garden designers or directors, such as Tim Smit of *The Eden Project*, have brought to this age-old conundrum a new emphasis. Whereas the quests of the past were more confidently in pursuit of Knowledge, the recent quest is for Understanding and, particularly, of <u>inter-relationship</u>.

> Eden is about plants and people, and visitors will want to know what they are seeing. We are not a botanic garden, with thousands of little plant labels like tombstones all over the place; we are about putting plants into context. We want people to enjoy the atmosphere and sense of place first of all, wherever they are in Eden. I have described the regions of the world we exhibit and some of the themes. We name some individual plants on plant labels, giving basic information about what each one is and what it does. The next grade up is a plant story which offers more of an explanation and maybe an ancestor or two, then there are the big stories which may concern something generic like the description of the Malaysian home garden or a major product such as coffee. For some of our visitors, to understand that rainforests have people living in them, that their livelihoods link with ours, that we use their resources every day, is a revelation. These messages are woven into the fabric of the project, not the signs. In due course we will tackle even bigger issues like biodiversity loss, waste, plants and the future of plants and health. We don't want to bludgeon people into submission with ridiculous amounts of information, nor do we want to tell all the stories at once.[9]

In this description, the categorical notions and comprehensive aspirations that were so prevalent in the eighteenth and nineteenth centuries have been modified ('we are not a botanic garden, with thousands of little plant labels like tombstones') . Here, the key words are: 'context', 'regions of the world', 'link', 'woven', 'stories', with qualifiers such as: 'some', 'maybe', 'in due course'.

---

8   J. Kincaid, *My Garden (Book)*, op. cit., pp. 169-70.
9   Tim Smit, *Eden* (London: Corgi, 2002 [2001]), p. 257.

This change of emphasis has engendered not only a political shift, but, in terms of literary poetics, a generic one. The turn of the twenty-first century saw a plethora of texts, not easily categorised, with titles such as: *The Potato: From the Andes in the Sixteenth Century to Fish and Chips, the story of how a vegetable changed the world* (Larry Zuckerman, 1999); *The Orchid Thief: A True Story of Beauty and Obsession* (Susan Orlean, 1999); *The Tulip: The Story of the Flower that has Made Men Mad* (Anna Pavord, 1999) ; *Tulipomania: The Story of the World's Most Coveted Flower and the Extraordinary Passions It Aroused* (Mike Dash, 2000); *Orchid Fever: A Horticultural Tale of Love, Lust and Lunacy* (Eric Hansen, 2000); *The Botany of Desire: A Plant's-Eye View of the World* (Michael Pollan, 2000). As the titles and subtitles reveal, the narrative terms are familiar: 'true story', 'story', 'tale', 'biography' 'view', but there is a different slant. The central protagonists are not people, as might be expected, but plants, (or fish, or a natural commodity such as salt) .[10] People are present in these tales, but they are not the prime subjects, dealing with and describing from an authoritative (epistemological and ideological) perspective, objects of the natural world, to be discovered, classified, exploited, transported and so forth. Rather, these are stories where the objects take centre-stage and the human subjects are constellated around them, significantly affected by them, and where, as architect and landscape designer Charles Jencks puts it, there is a 'pattern that connects'.[11] With this new alignment, 'the universe, not man (as Protogoras claimed), becomes "the measure of all things".'[12] For Jencks, too, in relation to landscape design, this constitutes 'a new poetics'.[13] In literature, this new poetics is manifest in tales of interaction, adaptation and reciprocal impact. In other words, these are histories of 'coevolution', a term introduced, explained, and demonstrated by Michael Pollan in *The Botany of Desire*:

> The ancient relationship between bees and flowers is a classic example of what is known as 'coevolution'. In a coevolutionary bargain like the one struck by the bee and the apple tree, the two parties act on each other to advance their individual interests but wind up trading favors: food for the bee, transportation for the apple genes. Consciousness needn't enter into it on either side, and the traditional distinction between subject and object is meaningless.
>
> Matters between me and the spud I was planting, I realized, really aren't that much different; we too, are partners in a coevolutionary relationship, as indeed we have been since the birth of agriculture more than ten thousand years ago. [...] All these plants,

---

10   Mark Kurlansky, *Cod: A Biography of the Fish That Changed the World (1999)* (New York: Vintage, 1999) and *Salt: A World History* (New York: Vintage, 2003).

11   Charles Jencks, *The Garden of Cosmic Speculation* (London: Francis Lincoln, 2003), p. 69.

12   Ibid., p. 21.

13   'I wanted to create a new form of landscape design, one based on the waveforms that unite the atom to the galaxy, radio waves to brain waves, ammonites to sunflowers – the pattern that connects, a new poetics', ibid., p. 69.

which I'd always regarded as the objects of my desire, were also, I realized, subjects acting on me, getting me to do things for them they couldn't do for themselves.[14]

In *The Botany of Desire*', Michael Pollan is 'telling the story of four familiar plants – the apple, the tulip, cannabis and the potato – and the human desires that link their destinies to our own',[15] but the shift is evident in 'the unconventional angle' which aims to represent not simply what plants have done for humans to serve their development, but what humans have done for plants, subserviently, in terms of botanical evolution and advancement:

> Many of the activities humans like to think they undertake for their own good purposes – inventing agriculture, outlawing certain plants, writing books in praise of others – are mere contingencies as far as nature is concerned. Our desires are simply more grist for evolution's mill, no different from a change in the weather: a peril for some species, an opportunity for others. Our grammar might teach us to divide the world into active subjects and passive objects, but in a coevolutionary relationship every subject is also an object, every object a subject. That's why it makes just as much sense to think of agriculture as something the grasses did to people as a way to conquer the trees.[16]

This suggests that the title of the present volume might itself need a shift in focus, from *Garden Plots* to *Gardens Plot*, active or interactive subjects rather than passive objects in anthropocentric garden narratives.

The introduction to this volume included an anecdote about Jamaica Kincaid in 1996, challenging a literary festival audience with political and historical perspectives on plants, plant collecting and gardening, views which informed her 1999 volume *My Garden (Book)*. In 2005 she published another volume, commissioned by the National Geographic Society, which chronicled a seed-collecting expedition to Nepal: *Among Flowers: A Walk in the Himalayas*. At first glance, there is something more than a little ironic in Kincaid's undertaking which echoes aspects she has often critiqued. This is the former Antiguan, of African descent, who has spoken and written extensively to indicate the complex repercussions 'in history' of plant hunting abroad or of colonial expansion in the pursuit of paradise ('it would not have been paradise for the people living there'[17]), or who has observed of the English: 'almost as if ashamed of the revulsion and hostility they have for foreign people, [they] make up for it by loving and embracing foreign plants wholesale.'[18] Despite the benign interaction suggested by the preposition 'among' in the title, or the fact that it is only ripe seeds that are collected, there is much that is familiar – and thus, anachronistic. With her companion nursery-proprietors and plant hunters, she partakes of the compelling desire to have more than is indigenous or readily available 'at home':

---

14   M. Pollan, *The Botany of Desire*, op. cit., pp. xii-xiv.

15   M. Pollan, *The Botany of Desire*, op. cit., p. xiv.

16   M. Pollan, *The Botany of Desire*, op. cit., p. xx.

17   J. Kincaid, *My Garden (Book)*, op. cit., p. 116.

18   Ibid., p. 76.

What they wanted was to be in the middle of a forest that had the widest selection of gardenworthy plants. What they wanted was to collect the seeds of plants that would make a gardener like me, someone who wanted to know about and be engaged with the world in the most benign way possible, excited. I have made a garden in a part of the world where the flora is interesting and full of wonder enough [...] But something that never escapes me as I putter about the garden, physically and mentally: desire and curiosity inform the inevitable boundaries of the garden, and boundaries, especially when they are an outgrowth of something as profound as the garden with all its holy restrictions and admonitions, must be violated. The story of the garden, when told by a gardener, is an homage to the gardener's curiosity and explanation of a transgression by a transgressor.[19]

The aspiration ' to know about and be engaged with the world in the most benign way possible' could be seen as many a gardener's creed and the incentive for new Edens. And yet, many of the least benign enterprises in human history have espoused similar aspirations.

Kincaid's own plans to go plant-hunting benignly in Nepal, as described in the book, are first delayed by 'the events of September 2001' and then, when in Nepal, threatened by Maoist guerrillas or inconvenienced by bolshy Sherpas resentful of their subservience to foreigner explorers. These are anecdotes to accompany a present-day tale of travellers, with commercial or personal-propertied interests, from 'comfortable societies', who want more: more flowers, more choice; more adventures; more stories of imagination and wonder; more coevolutionary sagas of the interrelationships between plants and peoples. Kincaid is not unwitting, as she plots to create her present garden in the United States of America in the first decade of the twenty-first century, of the paradoxes with which she deals – and of which she writes, in a genre befitting coevolutionary complexity:

> Eden is never far away from the gardener's mind [...] And it is forever out of reach. As I walked up and down the terrain in the foothills of the Himalayas looking for plants appropriate for growing in the garden I am now (even now, for the garden is ongoing and a stop to it means death) making in Vermont, the strangeness of my situation was not lost to me. Vermont, all by itself should be Eden and garden worthy enough. But apparently I do not find it so. I seem to believe that I will find my idyll more a true ideal, only if I can populate it with plants from the other side of the world.[20]

This goes beyond 'the grass is always greener in someone else's garden'; there are, rather, two distinct 'ideals' or 'idylls' in relation to gardens which constitute a persistent ambiguity. The desire for Eden is a counter-evolutionary mode; despite its implicit organicism it is quiescent, preconceived, unperturbed, stable, amorphous, timeless – without history, development or struggle. However, the mundane toil, the regional, cultural and historical specificities, the trangressive and transglobal desiring ('wanting more'), with its evolutionary dynamism ('the garden is ongoing and a stop to it means death'), is its compelling obverse. Literature about gardens

---

19   J. Kincaid, *Among Flowers*, op. cit., pp. 115-16.
20   Ibid., p. 189.

in the twentieth and early twenty-first century is formulated in the shadow of two modes: the monumental Garden of Myth and the myriad gardens in (coevolutionary) histories.

Select Bibliography

'Adrian Fisher Maze Design', http://www.mazemaker.com/company_profile.htm

Aldiss, Brian, *Supertoys Last All Summer Long and Other Stories of Future Time* (London: Orbit, 1969)

Alfer, A. and Noble, M. J., eds, *Essays on the Fiction of A. S. Byatt* (Westport, CT & London: Greenwood Press, 2001)

Allen, Paula Gunn, *Off the Reservation: Reflections on Boundary-Busting, Border-Crossing, Loose Canons* (Boston, MA: Beacon Press, 1998)

American Diabetes Association, http://www.diabetes.org/diabetes-statistics/native-americans.jsp

Armbruster, K. and Ashcroft, Bill, Griffiths, Gareth and Tiffin, Helen, *Key Concepts in Post-colonial Studies* (London & New York: Routledge, 1998)

Attwell, David, ed., *Doubling the Point: Essays and Interviews* (London and Cambridge, MA.: Harvard University Press, 1992)

Atwood, Margaret, *The Journals of Susanna Moodie* (Toronto: Oxford University Press, 1970)

Atwood, Margaret, *Survival: A Thematic Guide to Canadian Literature* (Toronto: Anansi, 1972)

Atwood, Margaret, 'Wondering What It's like to be a Woman', *New York Times Review of Books* (13 May 1984)

Barker-Benfield, Ben, 'Anne Hutchinson and the Puritan Attitude Towards Women', *Feminist Studies*, Vol. 1, No. 2 (Fall 1972)

Bate, Jonathan, *The Song of the Earth* (London: Picador, 2000)

Baudrillard, Jean, 'Simulacra and Science Fiction', *Science Fiction Studies*, Vol. 18, No. 55, Part 3 (November 1991) http://www.depauw.edu/sfs/backissues/55/baudrillard55art.htm

Beer, Gillian, *Darwin's Plots: Evolutionary Narrative in Darwin, George Eliot and Nineteenth-Century Fiction* (London: Routledge & Kegan Paul, 1983)

Beer, Gillian, *Open Fields: Science in Cultural Encounter* (Oxford University Press, 1996)

Begg, Ean, *The Cult of the Black Virgin* (London: Penguin, 1996)

Bell, Quentin, *Virginia Woolf, 1912-1941* (St Albans: Triad/Paladin, 1971)

Biodiversity Activist: Action Alert, campaign launched 8 April 2004, http://www.actionnetwork.org/BIODIVERSITY/alert-description.tcl?alert_id=2410797

Blackledge, Catherine, *The Story of V: Opening Pandora's Box* (London: Weidenfeld & Nicolson, 2003)

Bloom, Harold, ed., *John Updike: Modern Critical Views* (London: Chelsea House, 1999)

Boehmer, Elleke, *Colonial and Postcolonial Literature* (Oxford University Press, 1995)

Borges, Jorge Luis 'The Garden of Forking Paths', *Labyrinths* (Harmondsworth: Penguin, 1964)

Bowen, Elizabeth, *Bowen's Court and Seven Winters* (London: Vintage, 1999)

Bowen, Elizabeth, *Elizabeth Bowen's Irish Stories* (Dublin: Poolbeg Press, 1978)

Bradbury, M. and McFarlane, J., eds, *Modernism*, (Harmondsworth: Penguin, 1983 [1976])

Brooks Bouson, J., *Quiet As It's Kept: Shame Trauma and Race in the Novels of Toni Morrison* (Albany: State University of New York Press, 2000)

Brown, Jane, *The Pursuit of Paradise: A Social History of Gardens and Gardening* (London: HarperCollins, 1999)

buffcorePhil, 'Guerrilla Gardening' (2004) http://www.kuro5hin.org/story/2004/1/11/31014/1305

Butler, Judith, *Gender Trouble: Feminism and the Subversion of Identity* (London & New York: Routledge, 1990)

Byatt, A.S., *Angels and Insects* (London: Vintage, 1992)

Byatt, A. S. 'True Stories and the Facts in Fiction', *Essays on the Fiction of A. S. Byatt*, eds A. Alfer and M. J. Noble (Westport, CT & London: Greenwood Press, 2001), pp. 193-4

Caduto, Michael. J. and Joseph Bruchac, *Native American Gardening: Stories, Projects and Recipes for Families* (Golden, CO: Fulcrum, 1996)

Cash, W. J., *The Mind of the South* (Harmondsworth: Penguin, 1973)

Casid, Jill H., *Sowing Empire: Landscape and Colonization* (Minneapolis & London: University of Minnesota Press, 2005)

Childs, Peter, *Modernism* (London and New York: Routledge, 2000)

Chinery, Michael, *Butterflies and Moths* (London: Collins, 1981)

Cixous, Hélène, 'Castration or Decapitation?', *Psychoanalysis and Woman*, ed. S. Saguaro (London: Macmillan, 2000)

Cleary, David and others, eds, *The Rough Guide to Brazil* (New York, London, Delhi: Rough Guides, 2003)

Coetzee, J. M., *Boyhood: Scenes from Provincial Life* (London; Secker & Warburg, 1997)

Coetzee, J. M., *Disgrace* (London: Secker & Warburg, 1999)

Coetzee, J. M., *Doubling the Point: Essays and Interviews* (London & Cambridge, MA: Harvard University Press, 1992)

Coetzee, J. M., *Giving Offence: Essays on Censorship* (Chicago & London: University of Chicago Press, 1996)

Coetzee, J. M., *Life & Times of Michael K* (Harmonsdworth: Penguin, 1985)

Coetzee, J. M., *Stranger Shores: Essays 1986-1999* (London: Vintage, 2002)

Coetzee, J. M., *White Writing: On the Culture of Letters in South Africa* (New Haven, CT & London: Yale University Press, 1988)

Coetzee, J. M., *Youth* (London: Vintage, 2003)

Cohen, Robert, 'An Interview with Leslie Marmon Silko', *Southwest American Literature*, Vol. XXIV, No. 2 (Spring 1999)

Collins Concise Dictionary (Glasgow: HarperCollins, 1999)

Cooper, Guy and Taylor, Gordon, *Gardens for the Future: Gestures Against the Wild* (London: Conran Octopus, 2000)

Coupe, L. ed., *The Green Studies Reader: From Romanticism to Ecocriticism* (London & New York: Routledge, 2000)

Craig, Patricia, *Elizabeth Bowen* (Harmondsworth: Penguin, 1986)

Crouch, David and Colin Ward, *The Allotment: Its Landscape and Culture* (Nottingham: Five Leaves, 1999)

Cunningham, Gail, 'The Riddle of Suburbia: Suburban Fictions at the Victorian *Fin de Siècle*', in *Expanding Suburbia*, ed. Roger Webster (New York & Oxford: Berghahn Books, 2000)

DeLillo, Don, *White Noise* (London: Picador, 1985)

Dick, Philip K. *Do Androids Dream of Electric Sheep?* (London: Millennium, 2000)

Drayton, Richard, *Nature's Government: Science, Imperial Britain, and the Improvement of the World* (New Haven, CT & London: Yale University Press, 2000)

Duffy, Carol Ann, *The World's Wife* (London: Picador, 1999)

Eden , Edward and Goertz, Dee, eds, *Carol Shields, Narrative Hunger, and the Possibilities of Fiction* (University of Toronto Press, 2003)

Escott, Paul D. and others, eds, *Major Problems in the History of the American South*, Volume II (Boston, MA: Houghton Mifflin 1999)

Evans, Elizabeth, *Eudora Welty* (New York: Frederick Ungar, 1981)

Fara, Patricia, *Sex, Botany & Empire: The Story of Carl Linnaeus and Joseph Banks* (Cambridge: Icon, 2003)

Fearnley-Whittingstall, Jane, *The Garden: An English Love Affair* (London: Weidenfeld & Nicolson, 2002)

Fisher, Adrian and Loxton, Howard, *Secrets of the Maze: An Interactive Guide to the World's Most Amazing Mazes* (London: Thames and Hudson, 1997)

Fisher, Dexter, 'Stories and Their Tellers – A Conversation with Leslie Marmon Silko', *The Third Woman: Minority Women Writers of the U.S.* (Boston, MA: Houghton Mifflin, 1980)

Forster, E. M., *A Room With a View* (Harmondsworth: Penguin, 1983)

Foster, Hal, ed., *Postmodern Culture* (London & Sydney: Pluto Press, 1985)

Foucault, M., *The Order of Things: An Archaeology of the Human Sciences* (New York: Vintage, 1973)

Freud, Sigmund, *On Psychopathology*, Pelican Freud Library, Vol. 10 (Harmonsdworth: Penguin, 1987)

Fry, Roger, *Vision and Design* (London & New York: Oxford University Press, 1990)

Frye, Northrop, *The Bush Garden* (Toronto: Anansi, 1971)

Garmey, Jane, ed., *The Writer in the Garden* (London: Pavilion, 2000)

Gibson , William, *Virtual Light* (Harmondsworth: Penguin, 1994)

Glendinning, Victoria, *Elizabeth Bowen: Portrait of a Writer* (London: Weidenfeld & Nicolson, 1977)

Glissant, Edouard, *Caribbean Discourse: Selected Essays* , ed. & trans. J. Michael Dash, Charlottesville: University Press of Virginia, 1989)

Goertz, Dee, 'Treading the Maze of *Larry's Party*', in *Carol Shields, Narrative Hunger and the Possibilities of Fiction*, eds E. Eden and D. Goertz (Toronto, Buffalo & London: University of Toronto Press, 2003)

Gribbin, John, *Science: A History (1543-2001)* (London: Penguin, 2003)

Hammerstein, Oscar and Rodgers, Richard, *Oklahoma!* (Winona, MN: Williamson Music, 1981 [1943]), p. 183

Hanscombe, Gillian, 'Katherine Mansfield's Pear Tree', *What Lesbians Do In Texts*, eds E. Hibby and C. White (London: The Women's Press, 1991)

Haraway, Donna , J., *Modest_Witness@Second_Millennium.FemaleMan©_meets_OncoMouse™: Feminism and Technoscience* (New York & London: Routledge, 1997)

Simians, Cyborgs and Women: The Reinvention of Nature (London: Free Association Books, 1991)

Harding, Rachel E., *A Refuge in Thunder: Candomblé and Alternative Spaces of Blackness* (Bloomington & Indianapolis, IN: Indiana University Press, 2003)

Harding, Rachel E., 'Candomblé: A religion of the African Diaspora', http://www.prometra.org/Report_on_Candoble.htm [sic]

Hawking, Stephen, http://www.pbs.org/wnet/hawking/universehtml/univ/html

Hawking, Stephen, http://www.pbs.org/wnet/hawking/mysteries/html/uns_kaku1-2html

Hawthorne, Nathaniel, *The Scarlet Letter* (Harmondsworth: Penguin, 1986)

Hawthorne, Nathaniel, *Selected Tales and Sketches* (Harmondsworth: Penguin, 1987)

Head, D. *J. M. Coetzee* (Oxford University Press, 1997)

Hobhouse, Penelope, *Plants in Garden History: An Illustrated History of Plants and their Influence on Garden Styles – from Ancient Egypt to the Present Day* (London: Pavilion, 1997), http://www.50states.com/bio/nickname4.htm

Holy Bible: New International Version (Grand Rapids, MI: Zondervan Bible Publishers, 1978)

Hunt, Kristin, 'Paradise Lost: The Destructive Forces of Double Consciousness and Boundaries in Toni Morrison's *Paradise*', *Reading Under the Signs of Nature: New Essays in Ecocriticism*, ed. John Tallmadge and Henry Harrington (Salt Lake City: University of Utah Press, 2000)

Hutcheon, Linda, *The Canadian Postmodern: A Study of Contemporary English-Canadian Fiction* (Oxford, Toronto & New York: Oxford University Press, 1988)

Hutcheon, Linda, *The Politics of Postmodernism* (London: Routledge, 1989)

Irmer, Thomas, 'An Interview with Leslie Marmon Silko', http://www.altx.com/interviews/silko2.html

Jaffrey, Zia, 'The Salon Interview – Toni Morrison', http://dir.salon.com/books/int/1998/02/cov_si_02int.html

Jencks, Charles, *The Garden of Cosmic Speculation* (London: Frances Lincoln, 2003)

Jones, Tayari , '*Gardens in the Dunes* – Book Review', *The Progessive* (February 2000) http://www.findartices.com/p/articles/mi_m1295/is_2_64/ai_59270836

Juneja, Om P. and Mohan, Chandra, eds, *Ambivalence: Studies in Canadian Literature* (Allied Publishers: New Delhi, 1990)

Kakutani, Michiko 'Br'er Rabbit, Ordinary in Nearly Every Way,' *New York Times* (26 August 1992)

Kellaway, D., *The Virago Book of Women Gardeners* (London: Virago, 1995)

Kerridge, R. and Sammells, N., eds, *Writing the Environment: Ecocriticism and Literature* (London and New York: Zed Books, 1998)

Kincaid, J., *Among Flowers: A Walk in the Himalayas* (Washington, D.C.: National Geographic, 2005)

Kincaid, J., ed., *My Favourite Plant: Writers and Gardeners on the Plants They Love* (London: Vintage, 1999)

Kincaid, J., *My Garden (Book)* (London: Vintage, 2000)

Kincaid, J., *A Small Place* (London: Virago, 1988)

King, Bruce, *V. S. Naipaul* (Basingstoke & New York: Palgrave Macmillan, 2003)

Kipling, Rudyard, *Kipling's Verse* (London: Hodder and Stoughton, 1948)

Klein, Naomi, *No Logo* (London: Flamingo, 2001)

Kristeva, Julia, *The Kristeva Reader* (Oxford: Blackwell, 1986)

Kunzru, Hari, 'You Are Cyborg' (February 1997), http://www.wired.com/wired/archives/5.02/ffharaway-pr.html

Kurlansky, M., *Cod: A Biography of the Fish that Changed the World* (New York: Vintage, 1999)

Kurlansky, M., *Salt: A World History* (New York: Vintage, 2003)

Laplanche, J. and J. B. Pontalis, *The Language of Psychoanalysis* (London: Karnac, 1988)

Lawrence, D. H., *Stories, Essays and Poems* (London: Dent & Sons, 1939)

Lee, Hermione, *Virginia Woolf; A Biography* (London: Chatto & Windus, 1996)

Lodge, David, 'Post-Pill Paradise Lost: John Updike's *Couples*', in *John Updike*, ed. Harold Bloom (New York; New Haven, CT; Philadelphia, PA: Chelsea House, 1987)

Lowndes Sevely, J., *Eve's Secrets: A New Perspective on Human Sexuality* (London: Bloomsbury, 1987)

Lykke, Nina ,'Between Monsters, Goddesses and Cyborgs: Feminist Confrontations with Science', in *The Gendered Cyborg: A Reader*, eds G. Kirkup, L. Janes, K. Woodward, F. Havenden (London: Routledge, 2000)

MacRae, George, W., trans., *The Nag Hammadi Library* (Leiden: E. J. Brill, 1977)

Mansfield, Katherine, *The Aloe*, ed. V. O'Sullivan (London: Virago, 1985)

Mansfield, Katherine, *Collected Stories of Katherine Mansfield* (London: Constable & Co., 1953)

Mansfield, Katherine, *Letters and Journals*, ed. C. K. Stead (Harmondsworth: Penguin, 1977)

Mansfield, Katherine, *The Letters of Katherine Mansfield*, ed. John Middleton Murray (Hamburg: Albatross, 1934)

Marcus, James, 'This Side of Paradise', James Marcus with Toni Morrison, Amazon. com interview, http://www.amazon.com/exec/obidos/ts/feature/7651/103-2684994-59999054

Margolick, David, *Strange Fruit: Billie Holliday, Café Society and an Early Cry for Civil Rights* (Edinburgh: Canongate, 2002)

Marvell, Andrew, *The Complete English Poems* (London: Allen Lane, 1974)

Matthews, W. H., *Mazes and Labyrinths: Their History and Development* (New York: Dover, 1970)

Matus, Jill, *Toni Morrison* (Manchester & New York: Manchester University Press, 1998)

McNeil, H. *The Ponder Heart* (London: Virago, 1980)

Meehan, Aidan, *Celtic Design: Maze Patterns* (London: Thames and Hudson, 1996)

Milton, John, *Poetical Works* (Oxford University Press, 1979)

Mitchell, Joni, *The Complete Poems and Lyrics* (London: Chatto & Windus, 1997)

Mitchell, Juliet 'The Question of Femininity and the Theory of Psychoanalysis', in *Psychoanalysis and Woman: A Reader*, ed. S. Saguaro (London: Macmillan, 2000)

Moodie, Susanna, *Roughing It in the Bush* (London: Virago, 1986)

Morrison, Toni, Amazon.com interview, http://www.amazon.com/exec/obidos/ts/feature/7651/103-2684994-59999054

Morrison, Toni, AOLChat with Toni Morrison (15 February 1998), cited in 'What is "P/paradise" in the novel?', http://www.uni-siegen.de/~fb3amlit/Whatis.htm

Morrison, Toni, *Beloved* (London: Picador, 1988)

Morrison, Toni, 'City Limits, Village Values: Concepts of Neighborhood in Black Fiction', in *Literature and the Urban American Experience*, eds M. C. Jaye and A. C. Watts (Manchester University Press, 1981)

Morrison, Toni, *Conversation: Toni Morrison* (with Elizabeth Farnsworth) (9 March 1998), http://www.pbs.org/newshour/bb/entertainment/jan-june98/morrison_3-9.html

Morrison, Toni, *Paradise* (London: Chatto & Windus, 1998)

Morrison, Toni, 'Rootedness: The Ancestor as Foundation', in *Black Women Writers*, ed. Mari Evans (London & Sydney: Pluto Press, 1985)

Morrison, Toni, 'This Side of Paradise', James Marcus with Toni Morrison,

Morrison, Toni, *Time* interview (21 January 1998), http://www.time.com/time/community/transcripts/chattr012198.htm

Morrison, Toni, 'Toni Morrison – Nobel Lecture' (7 December, 1993) http://nobelprize.org/literature/laureates/1993/morrison-lecture.html

Musgrave, Toby and Musgrave, Will, *An Empire of Plants: People and Plants that Changed the World* (London: Cassell, 2000)

Nabhan, Gary Paul, *Cultures of Habitat: On Nature, Culture, and Story* (Washington, D.C.: Counterpoint, 1998)

Nabhan, Gary Paul, *Enduring Seeds: Native American Agriculture and Wild Plant Conservation* (Tucson: University of Arizona Press, 2002)

Nabhan, Gary Paul, *Why Some Like It Hot: Food, Genes, and Cultural Diversity* (Washington, D.C.: Island Press, 2004)

Naipaul, V. S., *The Enigma of Arrival* (London: Picador, 1987)

Nasta, Susheila, ed., *Writing across Worlds: Contemporary Writers Talk* (London & New York: Routledge, 2004)

'Natural Born Americans', *Secret Histories* (Channel 4, LION Television, 2000)

O'Faolin, Nula, *My Dream of You* (Harmonsdworth: Penguin, 2001)

O'Farrell, Maggie, 'Lost in a Maze', *New Statesman* (12 September 1997)

Ostler, Mirabel, *A Gentle Plea for Chaos* (London: Bloomsbury, 1989)

Overy, Angela, *Sex in Your Garden* (Golden, CO: Fulcrum, 1997)

Ovid, *Metamorphoses*, trans. Mary Innes (Harmondsworth: Penguin, 1955)

Pagels, Elaine, *The Gnostic Gospels* (New York: Vintage, 1989)

Petrini, Carlo, *Slow Food: The Case for Taste* (New York & Chichester, W. Sussex: Columbia University Press, 2001)

Phillips, Adam, *Darwin's Worms* (London: Faber & Faber, 1999)

Picknett, Lynn, *Mary Magdalene: Christianity's Hidden Goddess* (London: Robinson, 2003)

Pilot Destination Guide, 'Candomble: A Spiritual Meeting', http://www.pilotguides. com/destination_guide/south_America/brazil/candomble.php

Plath, James, ed., *Conversations with John Updike* (Jackson: University of Mississippi Press, 1994)

Plath, James, 'Giving the Devil His Due: Leeching and Edification of Spirit in *The Scarlet Letter* and *The Witches of Eastwick*', in *John Updike and Religion: The Sense of the Sacred and Motions of Grace*, ed. James Yerkes (Grand Rapids, MI & Cambridge, UK: Wm. B. Eerdmans, 1999)

Pollan, Michael, *The Botany of Desire: A Plant's-Eye View of the World* (London: Bloomsbury, 2002)

Pollan, Michael, 'Cruising on the ark of taste: by pursuing the politics of pleasure, the Slow Food movement hopes to save rare species and delectables – and give the considered life a second chance', *Mother Jones* (May-June, 2003), http://www. findarticles.com/p/articles/mi_m1329/is_3_28/ai_100879493

Pollan, Michael, 'The Futures of Food', *New York Times Magazine* (4 May 2003), http://www.mindfully.org/Food/2003.Futures-Of-Food4may03.htm

Pollan, Michael, *Second Nature: A Gardener's Education* (London: Bloomsbury, 2002)

Porter, Katherine Anne, 'Introduction', Eudora Welty, *A Curtain of Green and Other Stories* (1941), in *The Selected Stories of Eudora Welty* (New York: Random House, 1943)

Purkiss, Diane, *The Witch in History: Early Modern and Twentieth-century Representation* (London & New York: Routledge, 1996)

Quest-Ritson, C., *The English Garden: A Social History* (London: Penguin, 2003)

Reames, K., *Toni Morrison's 'Paradise': A Reader's Guide* (New York & London: Continuum, 2001)

Rich, Adrienne, *Blood, Bread and Poetry* (London: Virago, 1987)

Rich, Adrienne, *Of Woman Born: Motherhood as Experience and Institution* (London: Virago, 1984)

Robinson, James M., ed., *The Nag Hammadi Library* (Leiden: E. J. Brill, 1977)

Rodd, Candice, 'Review of *Larry's Party*', *Times Literary Supplement* (22 August 1997)

Rough Guide to Travel, http://www.eztrip.com/dg_viewLocation_formId-64625.html

Roy, Arundhati, 'The New American Century' (January 2004) http://www.thenation.com/doc.mhtml?I=20040209&s=roy

Saguaro, Shelley, *Psychoanalysis and Woman* (London: Macmillan, 2000)

Saward, Jeff, *Magical Paths: Labyrinths and Mazes in the 21st Century* (London: Octopus, 2002)

Seyersted, Per, *Leslie Marmon Silko* (Boise, ID: Boise State University, 1980)

Seyersted, Per, 'Two Interviews with Leslie Marmon Silko', *American Studies in Scandinavia*, Vol. 13 (1981)

Shields, Carol, *Larry's Party* (London: Fourth Estate, 1998)

Shields, Carol, *Small Ceremonies* (Harmondsworth: Penguin, 1996)

Shuttleworth, Sally 'Writing Natural History: "Morpho Eugenia"', in *Essays on the Fiction of A. S. Byatt*, eds A. Alfer, and M. J. Noble (Westport, CT & London: Greenwood Press, 2001)

Silko, Leslie Marmon, 'A Conversation with Leslie Marmon Silko', *Sun Track: An American Indian Literary Magazine*, Vol. 3, No. 1 (Fall 1976)

Silko, Leslie Marmon, *Gardens in the Dunes* (New York: Simon & Schuster, 1999)

Silko, Leslie Marmon, *Yellow Woman and a Beauty of the Spirit* (New York: Simon & Schuster, 1996)

Silver, B. R., ed., '"Anon" and "The Reader": Virginia Woolf's Last Essays', *Twentieth Century Literature*, Vol. 25, No. 3/4 (1979)

Smit, Tim, *Eden* (London: Corgi, 2003)

Smith, Angela, *Katherine Mansfield: A Literary Life* (Basingstoke: Palgrave, 2000)

Smith, Angela, *Katherine Mansfield and Virginia Woolf: A Public of Two* (Oxford: Clarendon Press, 1999)

Smith, Dinitia, 'Toni Morrison's Mix of Tragedy, Domesticity and Folklore', *The New York Times* (8 January 1998), http://www.nytimes.com/library/books/010898toni-morrison-interviw.html

Sontag, Susan *Illness as a Metaphor/Aids and its Metaphors* (Harmondsworth: Penguin, 1991)

Spalding, Frances, *Roger Fry: Art and Life* (London: Granada, 1980)

Spretnak, Charlene, ed. *The Politics of Women's Spirituality: Essays on the Rise of Spiritual Power within the Feminist Movement* (New York: Doubleday, 1982)

Sullivan, R., 'The Forest and the Trees', in *Ambivalence: Studies in Canadian Literature*, eds Juneja, Om P. and Mohan, Chandra (Allied Publishers: New Delhi, 1990)

Tanner, Tony, *City of Words: A Study of American Fiction in the Mid-Twentieth Century* (London; Jonathan Cape, 1976)

The Tradescant Garden, Museum of Garden History, http://www.cix.co.uk/~museumgh/garden.htm

Tomalin, Claire, *Katherine Mansfield: A Secret Life* (London: Viking, 1987)

Tradescant's Orchard, Ashmolean Museum, http://www.bodley.ox.ac.uk/dept/scwmss/wmss/1500-1900/mss/ashmole/1461a.htm (MS. Ashmole1461, fol. 25r)

Tuhus-DuBrow, Rebecca, 'Talking about Slow Food: An Interview with Patrick Martins' (1 June 2004), http://www/thenation.com/doc.mhtml?I=20040614&s=tuhusdubrow

Turner, Tom, *Garden History: Philosophy and Design, 2000 BC-2000 AD* (Abingdon, Oxfordshire & New York: Spoon Press, 2005)

Uglow, Jenny, *A Little History of British Gardening* (London: Chatto & Windus, 2004)

Uglow, Jenny, *The Lunar Men: The Friends Who Made the Future, 1730-1810* (London: Faber & Faber, 2003)

Updike, John, *Assorted Prose* (New York: Alfred A. Knopf, 1965)

Updike, John, *Audio Interview with John Updike*, interview with Don Swaim (1984), http://wiredforbooks.org/johnupdike/

Updike, John, *Facing Nature: Poems* (New York: Alfred K. Knopf, 1985)

Updike, John, *Front Row*, in conversation with Mark Lawson, BBC Radio 4 (18 March 2002)

Updike, John, *Hugging the Shore: Essays and Criticism* (Harmonsdworth: Penguin, 1985)

Updike, John, *Self-Consciousness: Memoirs* (Harmondsworth: Penguin, 1990)

Updike, John, 'Remarks upon Receiving the Campion Medal', in *John Updike and Religion: The Sense of the Sacred and Motions of Grace*, ed. James Yerkes (Grand Rapids, MI & Cambridge, UK: Wm. B. Eerdmans, 1999)

van Zuylan, G., *The Garden: Visions of Paradise* (London: Thames & Hudson, 1995)

Voeks, Robert A., *Sacred Leaves of Candomblé: African Magic, Medicine and Religion in Brazil* (Austin: University of Texas Press, 1997)

Waid, Candace, 'Eudora Welty', in *Modern American Women Writers: Profiles of Their Lives and Works – from the 1870s to the Present*, eds E. Showalter, L. Beacher and A. Walton Litz (New York: Collier, 1993)

Walcott, Derek, *What the Twilight Says* (London: Faber, 1998)

Walker, Alice, *In Search of our Mothers' Gardens*: *Womanist Prose* (London: The Women's Press, 1984)

Walker, Barbara, *The Woman's Encyclopedia of Myths and Secrets* (San Francisco, CA: Harper & Row, 1983)

Watt, Ian, *The Rise of the Novel* (London: Hogarth Press, 1987).

Webster, Roger (ed.), *Expanding Suburbia: Reviewing Suburban Narratives* (New York and Oxford: Berghahn Books, 2000)

Welty, Eudora, *Conversations with Eudora Welty*, ed. Peggy Whitman Prenshaw (Jackson: University Press of Mississippi, 1977)

Welty, Eudora, *A Curtain of Green and Other Stories* (New York: Random House, 1943)

Welty, Eudora, *The Eye of the Story: Selected Essays and Reviews* (London: Virgao, 1987)

Welty, Eudora, *One Time, One Place* (Jackson: University Pressof Mississippi, 1996)

Welty, Eudora, *One Writer's Beginnings* (London: Faber & Faber, 1985)

Welty, Eudora, *A Writer's Eye: Collected Book Reviews* (Jackson: University of Mississippi Press, 1994)

Westling, Louise, *Eudora Welty* (Basingstoke: Macmillan, 1989)

Westling, Louise, *Sacred Groves And Ravaged Gardens: The Fiction of Eudora Welty, Carson McCullers and Flannery O'Connor* (Athens, GA: University of Georgia Press, 1985)

Westling, Louise, *The Green Breast of the New World: Landscape, Gender and American Fiction* (Athens, GA: University of Georgia Press, 1996)

White, Katharine S., *Onward and Upward in the Garden* (New York: Farrar, Straus & Giroux, 1997)

Williams, Raymond, *The Country and the City* (London: Hogarth Press, 1993)

Wilson, James, *The Earth Shall Weep: A History of* Native *America* (London: Picador, 1998)

Winterson, J., *Art Objects: Essays on Ecstasy and Effrontery* (London: Vintage, 1996)

Winterson, J., *Oranges Are Not the Only Fruit* (London: Vintage, 2001)

Winterson, J., *Sexing the Cherry* (London: Vintage, 1989)

Winterson, J., *The World and Other Places* (London: Vintage, 1999)

Wittig, M. 'One Is Not Born A Woman', *The Straight Mind and Other Essays* (Hemel Hempstead: Harvester Wheatsheaf, 1992)

Wood, Denis, ed., Poets in the Garden: An Anthology of Garden Verse (London: John Murray, 1978)

Wood, Karenne, 'Review of *Gardens in the Dunes*', *American Indian Quarterly*, Vol. 23, No. 2 (1999)

Woodman, Marion and Elinor Dickson, *Dancing in the Flames; The Dark Goddess in the Transformation of Consciousness* (Dublin: Gill & Macmillan, 1996)

Woods, Tim, *Beginning Postmodernism* (Manchester & New York: Manchester University Press, 1999)

Woolf, Virginia, 'Anon', ed. B. R. Silver, *Twentieth Century Literature*, Vol. 25, No. 3/4 (1979)

Woolf, Virginia, *Between the Acts* (St Albans & London: Granada, 1978)

Woolf, Virginia, *Collected Essays: Volume 1* (London: Hogarth, 1966)

Woolf, Virginia, *The Complete Shorter Fiction*, ed. Susan Dick (London: Triad Grafton Books, 1991)

Woolf, Virginia, *The Essays of Virginia Woolf, Volume 3, 1919-1924* (London: Hogarth, 1988)

Woolf, Virginia, *A Haunted House and Other Stories* (London: Granada, 1982)

Woolf, Virginia, *Moments of Being: Unpublished Autobiographical Writings* (London: Triad/Granada, 1982)

Woolf, Virginia, *Mrs Dalloway* (St Albans: Granada, 1981)

Woolf, Virginia, *Orlando* (London: Grafton, 1977)

Woolf, Virginia, 'Professions for Women', *Women and Writing*, ed. Michèle Barrett (London: Women's Press, 1979)

Woolf, Virginia, *A Room of One's Own* (St Albans & London, Grafton, 1983)

Woolf, Virginia, *To the Lighthouse* (Harmondsworth: Penguin, 1974)

Woolf, Virginia, *A Writer's Diary* (London: Triad/Granada, 1978)

'WPA Guide to Arizona, Route 66 Tour', originally published as *Arizona: A State Guide* in 1940, http://members.aol.com/hsauertieg/rt66/wpa_az.htm

Wyndham, John, *The Day of the Triffids* (Harmondsworth: Penguin, 1954)

Yerkes, James, ed., *John Updike and Religion: The Sense of the Sacred and Motions of Grace* (Grand Rapids, MI & Cambridge, UK: Wm. B. Eerdmans, 1999)

Index

Adam xii, 96
additives 205–6
Africa 131, 135, 141, 142, 153, 162, 168,
    184
    Afrikaner 140–41, 152–3
    Hottentot 137, 142, 144, 152
    South Africa xi, 128, 134, 136, 139–44
African-Americans 130, 131, 164
    agriculture 129, 177, 181, 187, 192, 194,
        196, 226
AIDS 70, 78, 80
Aldiss, Brian
    Supertoys Last all Summer Long 220–21
allotment 128, 180–81, 185–8
Allotment Act 194
Amazon 73, 85–6, 88, 92–3
    Explorers 86, 95–7
America
    Louisiana 163
    Mississippi 44–6, 48
    Oklahoma 158, 163–5
    Rhode Island 69, 70, 71
    The South 48, 50, 51, 52, 161
    The Southwest 191, 192, 195, 200
American Indian Quarterly 202
ancestor 163–5, 167, 191, 195
androids 208, 219, 220, 221
Angels 85, 87, 89
    'Angel in the House' 11, 12, 89
animals 188–90, 208
apartheid 143, 147, 149
Apollonian 219, 221
apple xii, 41, 68, 101, 104, 108, 111, 203–4,
    226
    Pink Lady 203–4
Art 6, 15, 17–18, 21, 33, 34, 64, 65, 83, 99,
    176, 185
    Impressionist 17, 18
    Post-Impressionist 15–16, 18–19
Ashcroft, Bill 130
Atwood, Margaret 70–71, 76, 121, 122

Survival: A Thematic Guide to
    Canadian Literature 122, 123
The Journals of Susanna Moodie 122,
    123

banana 98–9
Bates, Henry Walter 86
Baudrillard, Jean 214–16
Beer, Gillian 67, 88–9, 96
Bell, Quentin 15, 19
Bell, Vanessa 6, 15, 17
Belonging 134, 138, 139–56
Bergson, Henri 17, 33
Berry, Wendell 192–3
Bethke, Bruce 217
Bible ix, 51, 169–70
biodiversity 196
biography 16
bio-technology xi,127, 203–4, 212, 218–19
Birney, Earle 121
Black Madonna 168, 170–72
Blackledge, Catherine 106, 107, 109
    The Story of V: Opening Pandora's Box
        106, 107, 109
Blade Runner 207
Blomfield, Sir Reginald 17
Bloomsbury Group 15
Boehmer, Elleke 130
bois dormant 40
Borges, Jorge Luis 117
Botanical Gardens xii, 3, 11, 12, 18, 25,
    179, 225
Bouson, J. Brooks
Bowen, Elizabeth 1, 2, 23, 35–44
    Bowen's Court 37, 39–40
    Look at all Those Roses 35
    Pictures and Conversations 43
    'Summer Night' 35, 38–43
    The Last September 39
Brazil 159, 168, 172, 187
Brett, Dorothy 24, 27
Brown, Jane 58, 100, 181

Bruchac, Joseph 190, 193–4, 195, 196
buffcorePhil 61
    Guerrilla Gardening 61
Bureau of American Ethnology 194
Butler, Judith 109–10
butterflies 6, 11, 81, 82, 85, 86, 95, 97, 160,
    161
Byatt, A. S. 62, 63, 66, 85–98
    Angels and Insects 63, 66
    'Morpho Eugenia' 62, 63, 66, 85–9,
        92–8
    'The Conjugial Angel' 85

Caduto Michael J. 190, 193–4, 195, 196
Canada 68, 69, 121–4, 130
    the Canadian postmodern 68–9,122, 124
cancer 70, 73
Candomblé 168
Caribbean xii, 127, 128, 129, 130,176, 184
Carson, Rachel 70, 71
    Silent Spring 70, 71
Cash, W. J. 48–51
Champion, Alex 115
cherry 100, 106
childbirth 75, 77, 78, 105, 198
Childs, Peter 29–30, 59
Chirico, Giorgio de 185
Civil Rights Movement 55, 57, 162
Cixous, Hélène 111
clitoris 106–7
Coate, Randall 115
Coetzee, J. M. xi, 66, 128, 136–7, 138–56
    Boyhood: Scenes from Provincial Life
        153
    Disgrace 142
    Doubling the Point 136, 150, 152, 155
    Dusklands 138, 142
    Foe 139
    Giving Offence 136, 155
    In the Heart of the Country 138, 142
    Life and Times of Michael K. xi, 139,
        142, 143–56
    Waiting for the Barbarians 139
    White Writing 136, 139, 140, 141, 142,
        143, 144, 152, 153, 155
    Youth 139
coevolutionary histories xii, 223–9
Cohen, Robert 197
Cold War 65, 200, 207, 209

colonialism xii, 11, 21–4, 129–30,134,
    155,188, 202
companion planting 196
Conrad, Joseph 12, 142
Cooper, Guy 224
corn 127, 160, 196
cotton 196
Craig, Patricia 36, 40, 43
Crouch, David 186
Curtis, Edward S. 194
    The North American Indian 194
cyber-fiction 216
cyber garden 204, 205–21
cyberpunk xi, 217
cyborg xii, 209–11, 217, 219

Darwin, Charles 66, 69, 85, 88–90, 92, 95–7
Darwin, Erasmus 90
Dawes Act (Allotment Act) 194
decolonisation 129, 135
Delaney, Topher 224
DeLillo, Don 212–14
    White Noise 212–14
designers 82, 115, 218, 223–4,
desire 30, 225, 227, 228
devil 70, 74, 76, 77, 82, 83
diabetes 128, 193
Dick, Philip K. 207–9, 212, 215
    Do Androids Dream of Electric Sheep?
        207–9, 212, 215
Dickson, Elinor 171
Drayton, Richard 12–15
Drexel, Katherine 159
Duffy, Carol Ann 61
Dust 139
Dionysian 83

earthworms 95, 97, 151
economic individualism 4
Eden ix, xii, 3, 5, 10, 30, 48, 51–2,81, 104,
    111, 142, 155, 211, 223, 224, 225,
    228
    Project (Cornwall) 69, 225
Eden, Edward 114, 116, 120
Ehrenreich, Barbara 77
Einstein, Albert 69, 104
Empire xiii, 3, 11, 13, 14, 18, 30,129, 135,
    175, 183–4, 202, 223
English, Deidre 77

entropy 66, 69-85
environmentalism 70, 73–4, 77, 84,190, 203
estate 37–9, 127, 175, 176, 179, 183, 185
    Plantation 48–9, 177, 178, 179, 183
    Victorian-Edwardian 86, 88, 178
ethnography 150, 194
Evans, Elizabeth 44, 54
Eve xii, 68, 159, 166, 225
evolution 66–7, 69, 85–98, 227, 228

Famine, The Great 37–8
Fara, Patricia 89–90, 91
Fearnley-Whittingstall, Jane 100, 139–40
feminism 70, 77, 79–80
    eco-feminism 77, 79, 110
fertility 20, 27, 47, 53, 75, 54, 84, 116, 165,
    171, 181, 198
fig 166
Fisher, Adrian 115
Fisher, Dexter 134
food 211–12, 215, 219
    genetic engineering 206, 212, 218
    organic 206, 219
    synthetic 205–6
forbidden fruit ix, 30, 52, 68, 98, 101, 104
Forster, E. M. 4
Foucault, Michel 111–12
Fox-Genovese, Elisabeth 55
Frazer, James 47, 53, 55
    The Golden Bough: A Study in Magic
      and Religion 47, 53, 55
Freud 27, 28, 30, 33, 34–5
    'Childhood Memories and Screen
      Memories' 34–5
    The Interpretation of Dreams 34
    The Psychopathology of Everyday Life
      34
fruit *see* apple, banana, cherry, pineapple,
    and pomegranate
Fry, Roger 6–7, 15–16, 18–19
Frye, Northrup 123, 124
fungicides 205

gardens
    allotment 128, 180–81, 185–6
    botanic xi, xii, 14–16, 20, 25
    cyber xi, 204, 205–21
    desert 132, 150, 188–9, 191–3 195–7
    design 115, 223–5

flower 22, 160, 179, 180, 191
    hortus conclusis 48
    market 149, 160
    plantation ix, 48–9, 51, 177, 178, 183
    public 3, 9, 14, 144, 146
    suburban 1, 4
    vegetable 149, 150, 159, 160, 179, 180
    Victorian **x,** 86, 88, 128, 178
gardener 144, 145, 157, 178–9, 181
Garsington Manor 22
genetic modification xi, 206, 212, 218
Ghost Dance 189, 190, 192, 194, 197
Gibson, William 214, 215, 216–19
    Neuromancer 217
    Virtual Light 214, 215, 216–19
gladiolus 128, 191, 197
Glendinning, Victoria 44
Glissant, Edouard 127
    Caribbean Discourse 127
globalisation 129, 138, 206
gnosticism 169–71, 197, 228
Goddess 76, 78, 116, 169, 170, 173–4, 210
    Black 169, 170, 173–4
Goertz, Dee 114, 116, 120
grafting 102–3
Graves, Robert 174
gravity 69, 98–112
Gribbin, John 104
Griffiths, Gareth 130
Gunn Allen, Paula 201, 202

Hammerstein, Oscar
    Oklahoma! 164–5
Hampton Court Maze 114, 118
Hanscombe, Gillian 30
Haraway, Donna xii, 209, 210, 211, 213
    'A Cyborg Manifesto' 209, 210, 211,
      213
    *Modest_Witness@Second_Millennium_*
      FemaleMan© _meets_OncoMouse™
      211
    Simians, Cyborgs and Women 209, 210,
      211, 213
Harding, Rachel E. 168
Hargreaves, George 224
Hawking, Stephen 104
Hawthorne, Nathaniel 69, 76
    'Mrs Hutchinson' 69
    The Scarlet Letter 76

healing 75, 76, 77, 167–8
hegemony 125, 212
heterosexuality 103, 105, 108–10
historiographic metafiction 64, 124–5
history xii, 6. 15, 16, 35–44, 63, 92, 118,
		225, 227
	historiography 63
	natural 61–125
Hobhouse, Penelope 1, 51, 100, 139
Hogarth Press 6, 22, 23, 33
Holliday, Billie 52
Hooker, Joseph Dalton 13
Hooker, William Jackson 13
horticulture 13, 100, 129, 218–19
Howard, Ebenezer
	Garden Cities of Tomorrow 58
Human Genome Project 67
Hutcheon, Linda 62, 64, 68, 121, 124
Hutchinson, Anne 69, 76, 77, 78
hybrid 197, 212
hybridity 132–3, 186–202
hyperreality 65, 214–15

idleness 142, 144
Imperialism xiii, 3, 11, 13, 14, 129, 135,
		175, 183–4, 203, 223
Impressionist 17, 18
incest 87, 88, 89
India 174, 176, 177, 184
insects 87, 89
	ants 87, 93, 96
	butterflies 86, 96, 97
intertextuality 119
Ireland 60–73
Irmer, Thomas 186
Isis 170–71

Jekyll, Gertrude 17–18
Jencks, Charles
	The Garden of Cosmic Speculation 226
Jung, C. G. 117
jungle 48, 70, 86, 89, 92, 94, 97, 188

Kew Gardens xi, 9, 11–15, 25, 139, 187
Kincaid, Jamaica xii–xiii, 127, 129, 135,
		224, 225, 227, 228
	*Among Flowers: A Walk in the
		Himalayas* 224, 228
	My Garden (book) 127, 225, 227

King, Bruce 135, 136, 184
Kipling, Rudyard
	The Glory of the Garden ix, 223
Klein, Naomi
	No Logo 124, 217, 218
Kunzru, Hari 209–10
Kurlansky, Mark 226

labyrinth 114, 116, 117, 122
	church 117
	Knossos 116
	of Egypt 116
landscape 17, 44, 72, 141, 142, 145, 155,
		175, 176, 189, 190, 191, 199, 202,
		226
Lawrence, D. H. 1, 3, 4
Lee, Hermione
	Virginia Woolf 7, 10, 20, 23
legend 50, 65
lesbianism 30, 108, 110
Linnaeus, Carl 90–91, 94, 96
literary prizes 44, 136, 137, 157
Lowndes Sevely, Josephine 106, 107
Lutyens, Edwin 18
lynching 53, 164

Makah tribe 190
Mandel, Eli 123
Mansfield, Katherine 1, 23–35
	'At the Bay' 26, 27
	'Bliss' 23, 27, 28–30, 52
	Collected Stories 26
	'In the Botanical Gardens' 25–6
	Letters and Journals 22, 24, 27
	The Aloe (Prelude) 22, 24, 25, 27, 28, 30
Manuka tree 27
Marcus, James 156
marginalization 137, 138, 156, 198
Marvell, Andrew
	'The Mower Against Gardens' 102
Mary Magdalene 170–71
Matthews, W. H. 114, 116
Matus, Jill 131, 132, 158, 172
maze 112–24
	Celtic 114
	designers 112, 115
	Hampton Court 114, 118
	labyrinth 114, 116, 117
	maize 115, 121

McDonald's 203, 205
Meehan, Aidan 114, 116
Meeropol, Abel
   Strange Fruit 52–3
memory 5, 21–35
Michelet, Jules 77
migration 174–86, 190, 191
Milton, John 51–2, 66, 96–7
Mitchell, Joni 81
Mitchell, Juliet 97
modernism xi, 2, 18, 29, 32, 57–9
modernist xi, 2, 3, 4, 20, 57–9
monoculture x, 128, 203–4, 219
Monsanto 212, 218, 219
Moodie, Susanna
   Roughing It In the Bush 122–3
Mooney, James 194
Morrison, Toni 128, 130–32, 137, 156–74,
   202
   Beloved 157
   'City Limits, Village Values' 163–4
   Jazz 169
   Paradise 130–31, 156–74
   'Rootedness: The Ancestor as
      Foundation' 164, 165, 167, 174
   The Black Book 157
   The Bluest Eye 157
multiculturalism 129
Murray, Margaret 77
Musgrave, T. & W. 13
myth ix, 6, 20, 39, 47, 44–57, 66, 76, 94, 95,
   96, 104, 108, 116, 181, 229

Nabhan, Gary Paul 127, 128, 192, 193, 196,
   202
   *Cultures of Habitat: On Nature, Culture
      and Story* 127, 128, 193
   *Enduring Seeds: Native American
      Agriculture and Wild Plant
      Conservation* 192, 196
   *Why Some Like It Hot: Food, Genes and
      Cultural Diversity* 128
Nag Hammadi 169–70
Naipaul, V. S. 128, 134–6, 174–86
   *The Enigma of Arrival: A Novel in Five
      Sections* 128, 135, 174–86
Nasta, Susheila 129, 137, 138
Native American 128, 130, 131, 132, 133,
   137, 186–202

agriculture 187, 188–9, 191, 192, 195–7
boarding school 137, 187, 197
ceremonies 189–90
Pueblo 198, 200
reservation 191, 198
storytelling 201–2
'The Crying Indian' 79, 190
Native Seeds/SEARCH 193, 195
natural history xi, 62, 64, 92
nature 62, 69, 70, 73, 74, 75, 79, 82, 84,
   122, 205, 207, 210, 223
New Eden 225
Newton, Isaac 104–5

O'Faolain, Nuala 38
Oklahoma! 164–5
Omega Workshops 6
Omphalos 173
Ondaatje, Michael 122, 129
Overy, Angela
   Sex in Your Garden 61
Ovid
   Metamorphoses 47, 55, 96

paganism 79, 83, 171
Pagels, Elaine 171, 187
Paradise ix, 79, 80, 96, 98, 129, 131, 156,
   165, 166, 169, 172, 174, 223, 225
peaches 98, 148, 192
pear tree 28–30, 51, 52, 74
penis 106, 118
peppers 127, 128, 159–60, 172
performativity 109–10
pesticides 205, 212
Petrini, Carlo 205
phallic 30, 32, 76, 78, 99, 103, 106
   mother 103
Phillips, Adam 92, 95, 97
Picknett, Lynn 170–71
Piedade 167, 168, 171–2
pineapple 98–100, 103, 108
plant hunting 51, 67, 85–6, 88, 96, 139–41,
   187–8
plantation ix, 48-49, 51–2, 177, 178, 183
plot xiii, 3, 7, 186, 201
Pollan, Michael 73, 75, 84, 203, 204, 205,
   206, 212, 218–19, 227
   Second Nature 73, 74

The Botany of Desire 84, 212, 218–19, 227
pomegranate 101
Porter, Katherine Anne 46–7
postcolonial xi, xiii, 127–204, 223
Post-Impressionist 15–16, 18
postmodern xi, 61–125
pumpkins 127, 128, 148, 181
Purkiss, Dianne 75

Quest-Ritson, Charles 99, 100, 101

race 47, 48, 53, 141, 154–5, 164, 184
racism 53, 55, 56, 57, 136, 139, 140, 142–3, 152–3, 157, 158, 161–3, 184
reconciliation 156–74
religion 74, 83, 85, 92, 100–101, 159, 168–71, 205
Rich, Adrianne 77, 105
Robinson, William 17
rootedness 164, 165, 167, 174
rot 84–5
Roy, Arundhati 203

Sackville West, Vita x
Saward, Jeff 113, 115, 116, 117
Schreiner, Olive 141
science 67, 69, 73, 74, 83, 85, 86, 89, 91, 95, 97, 104, 111, 112
science fiction xi, 205–21
seeds 145, 146, 151, 160, 181, 189–91, 195, 218
serpent 42, 197–8, 199
    The Giant Serpent 199
sex 32, 42, 61, 65, 69, 70, 76, 80, 83, 85, 87, 88, 89, 90–92, 102, 103, 105–10, 117
Seyersted, Per 133, 198
Shields, Carol 63, 68, 112–24
    Larry's Party 63, 68, 112–24
    Small Ceremonies 122
Shuttleworth, Sally 66
Silko, Leslie Marmon x, 132–4, 186–202
    Gardens in the Dunes 186–202
    Yellow Woman and a Beauty of the Spirit 189–90, 197, 199–200, 202
simulacra 214–15
slavery 50, 70, 72, 88, 136, 150, 168, 184
Slow Food Movement 203, 205, 206

Smit, Tim 225
Smith, Angela 23, 24, 25, 26, 33, 34, 35
Smith, Dinitia 159
snake 42, 197–8, 199
Sontag, Susan 78
South Africa 128, 134, 136, 139–44
space 112–24
Spielberg, Stephen
    AI 220
story 3, 4, 5, 59, 112, 148–50, 157, 165, 226
suburbs 1, 4, 47, 57, 128, 185–6
sugar cane 127, 181, 184
Sullivan, Rosemary 122–3
supermarket 203–4, 213–14

Tanner, Tony 73
Taylor, Gordon 204
technology 205–21
Thanksgiving 132, 195
Thompson, F. M. L.
    The Rise of Suburbia 4
Three Sisters Gardens 196
'Thunder, Perfect Mind' 169–70
Tiffin, Helen 130
time 16–17, 152
Tomalin, Clare 23, 26, 33
Tomatoes 69, 75
    Flavr Savr 211
Toomer, Jean 161
toxins 69–70
Tradescants, John
    Elder 100, 101
    Younger 63, 67, 99, 100, 101, 102
tree ix, 27, 28–30, 32, 47, 50–53, 66, 74, 182, 188, 214
Trinidad 134, 135, 137, 174–86

Uglow, Jenny 90, 100
Updike, John 63, 73, 69–85
    Facing Nature:Poems 84–5
    Hugging the Shore 80
    Self-Consciousness 73, 80
    The Witches of Eastwick 63, 65, 69–85
Utopia 58, 111, 215
    heterotopia 111

Vietnam War 70, 72, 80, 81–2
virtual reality 216, 219, 220
vision 5, 6–21

Voeks, Robert A. 168

Walcott, Derek 184
Walker, Alice 56, 161
   In Search of our Mother's Gardens 161
   The Color Purple 56
Walker, Barbara 94, 101
Wallace, Alfred 85, 86, 96
   Narratives of Travels in the Amazon and
     Rio Negro 85
War 40, 144, 156–74
   American Civil War 48, 53, 97, 100, 101
   Cold War 65, 200, 207, 209
   English Civil War 67
   First World War xi, 11, 16, 24, 59
   Napoleonic War 20
   Second World War xi, 35, 36, 59
   Vietnam War 70, 72, 80, 81–2
Ward, Colin 186
Watt, Ian 3
Welty, Eudora 1, 2–3, 44–57
   'A Curtain of Green' 47–55
   A Curtain of Green and Other Stories 47
   'A Worn Path' 46
   'Death of a Travelling Salesman' 46
   One Time, One Place 45–6, 57
   One Writer's Beginnings 45–6, 55
   'Some Notes on River Country' 48
   The Eye of the Story 48, 55
   The Golden Apples 47
   The Robber Bridegroom 47
Westling, Louise 53, 54
Wilde, Oscar 26
Wilderness 70, 75
Williams, Raymond 1, 5
Wilson, James 194
Winterson, Jeanette 63, 64, 67, 98–112
   'Art and Life' 104

'Newton' 105
Oranges are not the Only Fruit 68, 98,
   105, 108, 109
Sexing the Cherry 67, 68, 98–112
'The Poetics of Sex' 108
'The Semiotics of Sex' 108
The World and Other Places 105
Written on the Body 108
WITCH (Women's International Conspiracy
   from Hell) 78
witchcraft 74–8
Wittig, Monique 110
Wood, Karenne 191
Woodman, Marion 171
'Woodstock' 80–81
Woodstock Music and Art Fair 80–81
Woolf, Virginia xi, 1, 2, 3, 6–21, 22, 23, 24,
   25, 43
   'Anon' 10, 11
   A Haunted House 6
   A Room of One's Own 12, 19
   'A Sketch of The Past' 7, 10
   A Writer's Diary 6, 9, 20
   Between the Acts 8, 10, 20
   'Kew Gardens' xi, 6–21
   'Modern Fiction' 9
   'Modern Novels' 9
   'Mr Bennett and Mrs Brown' 15
   Mrs Dalloway 20
   Orlando 17
   'Professions for Women' 11–12
   'The Ancestors' 10
   'The Reader' 11
   The Waves 9
   To the Lighthouse 9
Works Progress Administration (WPA) 45–6
Wyndham, John 215
   The Day of the Triffids 206, 207